CRISIS
MANAGEMENT

SECOND EDITION

CRISIS
MANAGEMENT

LEADING IN THE NEW STRATEGY LANDSCAPE

SECOND EDITION

WILLIAM RICK CRANDALL
University of North Carolina, Pembroke

JOHN A. PARNELL
University of North Carolina, Pembroke

JOHN E. SPILLAN
University of North Carolina, Pembroke

Los Angeles | London | New Delhi
Singapore | Washington DC

Los Angeles | London | New Delhi
Singapore | Washington DC

FOR INFORMATION:

SAGE Publications, Inc.
2455 Teller Road
Thousand Oaks, California 91320
E-mail: order@sagepub.com

SAGE Publications Ltd.
1 Oliver's Yard
55 City Road
London EC1Y 1SP
United Kingdom

SAGE Publications India Pvt. Ltd.
B 1/I 1 Mohan Cooperative Industrial Area
Mathura Road, New Delhi 110 044
India

SAGE Publications Asia-Pacific Pte. Ltd.
3 Church Street
#10-04 Samsung Hub
Singapore 049483

Acquisitions Editor: Patricia Quinlin
Editorial Assistant: Katie Guarino
Production Editor: Laura Barrett
Copy Editor: Pam Suwinsky
Typesetter: Hurix Systems Pvt. Ltd.
Proofreader: Stefanie Storholt
Indexer: Judy Hunt
Cover Designer: Janet Kiesel
Marketing Manager: Liz Thornton
Permissions Editor: Adele Hutchinson

Printed in the United States of America

*A catalog record of this book is available from the
Library of Congress.*

ISBN 978-1-4129-9168-1

This book is printed on acid-free paper.

SUSTAINABLE FORESTRY INITIATIVE
Certified Chain of Custody
Promoting Sustainable Forestry
www.sfiprogram.org
SFI-01268
SFI label applies to text stock

15 16 17 10 9 8 7 6 5 4 3 2

Brief Contents

Preface   xvii

  1. A Framework for Crisis Management   1
  2. The Crisis Management Landscape   25
  3. Sources of Organizational Crises   51
  4. A Strategic Approach to Crisis Management   81
  5. Forming the Crisis Management Team and
     Writing the Plan   107
  6. Organizational Strategy and Crises   137
  7. Crisis Management: Taking Action When
     Disaster Hits   167
  8. Crisis Communication   195
  9. The Importance of Organizational Learning   223
 10. The Underlying Role of Ethics in Crisis Management   255
 11. Emerging Trends in Crisis Management   287

Appendix. Crisis Management Plan Template   311
Index   325
About the Authors   355

Detailed Contents

Preface   **xvii**

1. A Framework for Crisis Management   1

    Visualizing Crisis Management   1

    Setting the Context   2

    Developing a Framework for Studying Crisis Management   3

        Definition of *Crisis*   3

        The Life Cycle of a Crisis   5

        Strategic Orientation   6

        Previous Crisis Management Frameworks:
        Classifications of Crises   7

        Previous Crisis Management Frameworks: Stages of Crises   8

    A Framework for Crisis Management   11

        Landscape Survey   12

        Strategic Planning   13

        Crisis Management   13

        Organizational Learning   14

    Development of the Book   15

        Chapter 1: A Framework for Crisis Management   15

        Chapter 2: The Crisis Management Landscape   15

        Chapter 3: Sources of Organizational Crises   15

        Chapter 4: A Strategic Approach to Crisis Management   16

        Chapter 5: Forming the Crisis Management Team
        and Writing the Plan   16

        Chapter 6: Organizational Strategy and Crises   16

        Chapter 7: Crisis Management: Taking Action
        When Disaster Hits   16

Chapter 8: Crisis Communication   16

Chapter 9: The Importance of Organizational Learning   17

Chapter 10: The Underlying Role of Ethics in
            Crisis Management   17

Chapter 11: Emerging Trends in Crisis Management   17

Summary   17

Questions for Discussion   17

Chapter Exercise   18

Mini-Case: Scandal at Penn State   18

References   22

2. The Crisis Management Landscape   25

Opening Case, Part 1: How a Distance of 10 Feet
can be Fatal   25

Introduction   28

The Crisis Management Landscape   28

Crises Have Become More Transboundary in Nature   29

Terrorism Remains an Ongoing Threat   32

Social Media and the Internet Intensify the
Effects of a Crisis   33

Human-Induced Missteps Are at the Core of
the Majority of Crises   34

Environmental Damage and Sustainability of
Resources Cause Crises to Have a Global Impact   38

Globalization Increases the Risk of Organizational
and Societal Crises   40

Summary   44

Questions for Discussion   45

Chapter Exercise   45

Opening Case, Part 2: How a Distance of
10 Feet Can be Fatal   46

References   47

3. Sources of Organizational Crises   51

Opening Case: Kleen Energy Gets Into a Dirty Explosion   51

Introduction   53

Crises and the External Environment   54

Political–Legal Forces   54

Economic Forces   57

Social Forces   59

Technological Forces   63

Crises and the Industry Life Cycle   66

Introduction Stage   66

Growth Stage   67

Shakeout Stage   68

Maturity Stage   68

Decline Stage   68

Crises and the Organizational Life Cycle   69

Stage 1: Existence   69

Stage 2: Survival   70

Stage 3: Success   71

Stage 4: Renewal   71

Stage 5: Decline   72

Summary   73

Questions for Discussion   74

Chapter Exercise   74

Mini-Case: Sony Gets Hacked   75

References   76

4. A Strategic Approach to Crisis Management   81

Opening Case, Part 1: The Professor, "Arrogant Amy"   81

Introduction   83

A Strategic Approach to Crisis Management   84

Understanding Environmental Uncertainty   87

Environmental Scanning   90

Identifying Potential Crises Using the SWOT Analysis   92

Organizational Culture and Crisis Planning   99

Summary   100

Questions for Discussion   101

Chapter Exercise   101

Opening Case, Part 2: The Professor, "Angry Amy"   101

References   104

5. Forming the Crisis Management Team and Writing the Plan 107

Opening Case: Roof Party at Local College
Goes Terribly Wrong 107

Introduction 108

Forming the Crisis Management Team 109

    Goals of the CMT 109

    Team Member Characteristics 110

    Team Composition 112

    Virtual Crisis Management Teams 113

    Potential Problems Within CMTs 115

The Crisis Management Plan 117

    Basic Components of the Plan 118

    Distribution of the CMP 121

Crisis Management Training 121

    Regular CMT Meetings 122

    Disaster Drills 123

    The Mock Disaster 124

Summary 129

Questions for Discussion 130

Chapter Exercise 130

Mini-Case: Industrial Accident 131

References 133

6. Organizational Strategy and Crises 137

Opening Case, Part 1: The BP Gulf of Mexico Oil Spill 137

Introduction 141

Strategy and Crises 141

    The Multiple Levels of Strategy 142

Corporate-Level Strategies 142

    Industry Dimension 142

    Growth Dimension 145

Business-Level Strategies 149

    Low-Cost Strategies 149

    Differentiation Strategies 151

    Focus–Low-Cost Strategies 152

Focus-Differentiation Strategy	153
Combining Low-Cost and Differentiation Strategies	155
Strategic Control	155
Overview	156
The Strategic Control Process	156
Summary	160
Questions for Discussion	161
Chapter Exercise	161
Opening Case, Part 2: The BP Gulf of Mexico Oil Spill	162
References	164

7. Crisis Management: Taking Action When Disaster Hits — **167**

Opening Case, Part 3: The BP Gulf of Mexico Oil Spill	167
Introduction	170
Strategies at the Beginning of a Crisis	171
Leadership of the CMT	171
Situational Assessment	173
Mitigation Strategies	176
Initial Communications	177
Information Needs	178
Strategies During the Crisis: Response and Mitigation	179
Damage Containment	180
Communicating With Internal and External Stakeholders	181
Evaluating What Is Going Right and What Is Not	182
The End of the Crisis: Getting the Organization Back on its Feet	184
Business Continuity	184
Employee Needs After the Crisis	185
Summary	186
Questions for Discussion	187
Chapter Exercise	187
Opening Case, Part 4: The BP Gulf of Mexico Oil Spill	188
Notes	191
References	191

8. Crisis Communication   195

   Opening Case: The Domino's Boogergate Incident   195

   Introduction   197

   Crisis Communication Basics   198

      Initiating the Communication Process   198

      Crisis Communication with Internal Stakeholders   199

      Crisis Communication with External Stakeholders   201

      Communicating With the News Media   204

      Communicating With Customers   206

   Crisis Communications and Social Media   207

      The Impact of Blogging   207

      Living in a YouTube World   209

      Impact on Crisis Communications   210

   Evaluating the Success of the Crisis Communication Process   213

      Debriefing and Postcrisis Analysis   213

   Crisis Communication Training   215

      Media Training   215

   Summary   216

   Questions for Discussion   217

   Chapter Exercise   217

   Mini-Case: Taco Bell Thanks You for Suing Them   218

   References   219

9. The Importance of Organizational Learning   223

   Opening Case: "Passing the Trash" by the
Michigan Board of Education   223

   Introduction   225

   What Is Organizational Learning?   225

      Single-Loop Learning   225

      Double-Loop Learning   226

   Building a Learning Organization   230

      Systems Thinking   230

      Personal Mastery   230

      Mental Models   231

      Building Shared Vision   231

      Team Learning   232

Learning From a Crisis 232

    Landscape Survey 233

    Strategic Planning 235

    Crisis Management 236

    Organizational Learning 239

Degrees of Success in Crisis Learning 241

Barriers to Organizational Learning 242

    Operational Considerations 243

    Organizational Cultural Considerations 245

Summary 247

Questions for Discussion 247

Chapter Exercise 248

Mini-Case: Stage Collapse at the Indiana State Fair ... 248

References 251

10. The Underlying Role of Ethics in
Crisis Management 255

Opening Case: Hawks Nest 255

Introduction 257

What Is Business Ethics? 258

    Business Ethics and the Crisis Management Framework ... 260

Landscape Survey: Uncovering the Ethical Boulders ... 262

    The Company Founder, CEO, and the Board of Directors ... 262

    The Safety Policies of the Organization 264

    The Economic Motives Among Top Executives
and Management 265

    The Disconnect Between Organizational
Mission and Existence 267

    The Degree of Industry Vulnerability 268

    The Vulnerability of the Organization in the
Global Environment 268

Strategic Planning: Confronting the Ethical Boulders ... 270

    The Enthusiasm for Crisis Management and Training ... 270

    The Ethical Culture of the Organization 271

    The Existence of Government Regulations 271

    The Existence of Industry Standards 273

Crisis Management: Further Considerations
During an Ethical Crisis   274

    The Management of Internal Stakeholders   274

    The Management of External Stakeholders   275

Organizational Learning: Lessons From the Ethical Crisis   275

    The Evaluation of the Ethical Management Process   275

    The Commitment to Organizational Learning   276

    The Benefits of Industry Renewal   277

    The Inevitability of New Government Regulations   277

    The Anticipation of New Stakeholder Outlooks   279

Summary   280

Questions for Discussion   281

Chapter Exercise   281

Mini-Case: The Melamine Milk Crisis in China   282

References   284

11. Emerging Trends in Crisis Management   287

    Opening Case: The Problem of Hanging
    Out with the Crowd   287

The Landscape Survey   290

The Landscape Survey   290

    The Internal Landscape   290

    The External Landscape   292

Strategic Planning   294

    The Internal Landscape   294

    The External Landscape   295

Crisis Management   298

    The Internal Landscape   298

    The External Landscape   299

Organizational Learning   300

    The Internal Landscape   300

    The External Landscape   301

Summary   304

Questions for Discussion   304

Chapter Exercise   304

Closing Book Case: The Great Boston Molasses Flood   305

References   308

Appendix. Crisis Management Plan Template   **311**

Index   **325**

About the Authors   **355**

Preface

Ever since my graduate school years, I have been fascinated with the area of crisis management. In the late 1980s, the field was just emerging, and we had witnessed a trio of great calamities: the 1984 Bhopal, India, gas leak that killed thousands; the 1986 radiation accident at Chernobyl that killed thousands more; and in the same year, the tragic loss of the Space Shuttle *Challenger*, an unmistakable fireball in the sky that took the lives of seven American astronauts. Then, in 1989, while we were catching our breath, Exxon's supertanker, the *Exxon Valdez*, hit a reef off the coast of Alaska. The result was one of the most geographically dispersed oil spills ever and a front-page example of crisis management gone astray. There were containment booms in the dock that could not be mobilized because that particular boat was under repair. There was the chief executive officer, Lawrence Rawl, who, although meaning well, did not travel to the disaster site to address the situation directly. Oil spilled everywhere, creating a monstrous slick that sucked life out of the environment. The ship's captain had consumed too many drinks and had illegally put the tanker under the leadership of a junior officer. The rest is history; the importance of crisis management was clear.

While developing this fascination in the field of crisis management, I met John Parnell. John was a prolific writer with a passion for strategic management. Our discussions prompted the idea for a book that would address the field of crisis management within a strategic context. Our other colleague, Jack Spillan, shared our growing interest in the field of crisis management and was a logical choice for collaborating on this book.

Our diverse research backgrounds—human resources management, strategy, and marketing—influenced our growing interest in the field and our eventual decision to write the book. Collectively, we have lectured in a number of countries, including China, the United Kingdom, Egypt, Mexico, Peru, Guatemala, Chile, Bolivia, and Poland. We learned that crisis management approaches differed markedly across borders, and we began to consider the pros and cons of myriad perspectives on the field.

We were convinced that crisis management should not be just a response to an unfortunate event; it needed to be a management mind-set practiced within a proactive strategic framework. After a number of long discussions, the framework for the book emerged. Crisis management is a process, not a reactive event that comes up only occasionally. The four stages we propose should be incorporated into the strategic management process of the organization.

There are many others whose research influenced this project. You will find their names in the reference sections of this book. We are indebted to them for documenting their interest in crisis management and making this much-needed field a growing discipline. I remember reading Larry Barton's first book on crisis management, *Crisis in Organizations*, and thinking, *I want to make this my research field too*. As I read more on the topic, a number of other writers seemed to be major contributors to this growing area of management. Ian Mitroff was an early contributor to the field and is still writing today. Others were frequent contributors to the growth of this field, including Stephen Fink, Thierry Pauchant, Christopher Roux-Dufort, Paul Shrivastava, Denis Smith, and Karl Weick. Robert Hartley's manner of writing case studies of catastrophic events is the best I have ever seen. He concludes each case with practical lessons learned, an obvious need for students and practitioners as well as impatient researchers like the three of us. "Reframing Crisis Management," by Christine Pearson and Judith Clair, appeared in a 1998 issue of *Academy of Management Review*. This article not only influenced the prevailing perspectives on crisis management but also helped advance the field as a legitimate academic discipline.

In recent years, there have been a number of additional contributors to the field. Timothy Coombs has written extensively on the communication aspects of crisis management. He has also advocated crisis management as a necessary component for all organizations, referring to it as the DNA of the organization. Other names continue to surface in the literature on a regular basis, including Dominic Elliott, Christopher Lajtha, Timothy Sellnow, Matthew Seeger, Robert Ulmer, and again Ian Mitroff. You will find many more mentioned in the reference section at the end of each chapter. To these authors, we are grateful for what you have done to advance this growing field.

On behalf of John Parnell and John Spillan, I take this moment to thank Deya Saoud, associate editor at SAGE Publications, for her excellent guidance and patience with us while we produced this manuscript. For your hard work and dedication to this craft we call writing, we are indeed very grateful. I also thank the following reviewers for their valuable critiques of earlier versions of the manuscript: Lucy A. Arendt, University of Wisconsin-Green Bay; Stephen C. Betts, William Paterson University; Dana Moore Gray, Ph.D., APR; Eyun-Jung Ki, The University of Alabama; Dr. Marcia J. Kurzynski, Lock Haven University of Pennsylvania; Karen M. Leonard, Ph.D., Indiana University-Purdue University Fort Wayne; Alicia M. Mason, Pittsburgh State University; Tami Moser, Ph.D., Southwestern Oklahoma State University; David X. Swenson, PhD, LP Management, The School of Business and Technology, The College of St. Scholastica; Andrew P. Yap, Florida International University, Miami; Julie A. Davis, College of Charleston; Linda M. Dunn-Jensen, Indiana University; Gary Ford, Webster University; Barbara S. Gainey, Kennesaw State University; Naim Kapucu, University of Central Florida; Simon Moore, Bentley College; Anne H. Reilly, Loyola University Chicago; Irv Schenkler, New York University; Stephen Sloan, University of Central Florida.

We would be remiss if we did not thank our wives, Susan, Denise, and Martha, who patiently put up with our obsession for researching and writing, which, translated, meant many hours in front of our laptop computers. To you three we are most grateful, and appreciate your love and patience with us.

—*William "Rick" Crandall,* Ph.D.

CHAPTER 1

A Framework for Crisis Management

Visualizing Crisis Management

Visualize the term *crisis management,* and a number of images may pop into your head. Consider these possibilities:

- Maybe you thought of a recent YouTube video of two Domino's Pizza employees, one of whom put cheese up his nose and then placed it on a sandwich. The video received nearly one million views on YouTube before it was removed (Beaubien, 2009).
- Perhaps you remembered stories about numerous outbreaks of violent weather, particularly tornadoes that have hit the Midwest and southern portions of the United States in recent years. These weather patterns were not only sudden, but were catastrophic the physical and human damage they inflicted.
- On a broader level, you might have envisioned a team of managers trying to deal with a fire that has destroyed part of the production facilities at their manufacturing plant. Indeed, fires remain one of the most prominent types of crises that managers must address.
- You might have thought of the tsunami that hit Japan in 2011, causing widespread death, destruction, and the interruption of global supply chains. This event was further complicated by the spread of nuclear fallout in the air and water.

Indeed, the term *crisis management* invokes a number of images in the mind of the reader. However, crisis management is not just a one-time response to an unfortunate event. It is much broader than that. We view it as a strategic process that must occur far before the first crisis ever takes place in the life of the organization. It is a process that must be planned both before and after the crisis occurs.

When we view crisis management as a holistic process, a conceptual framework must be developed to understand how this process should be organized. A framework functions as a map that helps us see how the different parts of a process are interrelated. This book offers a framework to help you understand the field of crisis management and how you can better prepare for crisis events that may occur in your organization.

The onset of crises in organizations is a common occurrence in our contemporary environment. And yet many people associate a crisis with a highly dramatic event that produces mass destruction and even causalities. Most organizational crises are far less dramatic but can still have a substantial negative impact on the firm. The problem with associating only catastrophic events with a crisis is that they sound so dramatic that most organizational leaders may assume an "It can't happen to us" mentality. But then, consider these crises that are still damaging, yet less prominent:

- In January 2012, Coca-Cola Company encountered a problem with its orange juice products, Simply Orange and Minute Maid. Some of the products sold in the United States contained small amounts of carbendazim, an unapproved fungicide used with oranges from Brazil. Although the fungicide is approved in that country, it is not in the United States, prompting Coca-Cola to move into crisis management mode (Kiernan & McKay, 2012).
- General Motors (GM) faced a setback in late 2011 when its electricity-propelled Chevy Volt performed poorly in three crash tests that resulted in fires or sparks from the vehicle's battery pack. GM, realizing it was facing a crisis, offered loaner cars to any of the 6,000 Chevy Volt owners while engineers worked to fix the problem (Terlep, 2011).
- In 2008, a now-infamous online advertisement by Johnson & Johnson (J&J) promoting its pain reliever, Motrin, met resistance from young mothers. The ad stated that mothers who carry their babies in a sling are making a "fashion statement," something that many of the moms found offensive (Wheaton, 2008). Johnson & Johnson quickly pulled the ad from the Internet.

As these examples illustrate, not every organizational crisis is dramatic, but each one can have a far-reaching impact if it is not managed properly.

Setting the Context

Unfortunate events will occur in the life of most organizations. We refer to these events as *crises*. There are two broad approaches to the managing of these events: (1) Try to keep them from occurring in the first place, and (2) mitigate or soften the impact of the crisis when it does occur. Crisis management is the discipline that addresses these two approaches.

Crisis management is a field of growing interest because many managers now realize that their firms are not immune to those sudden, unexpected events that can put an organization into a tailspin, and sometimes even out of business. This book is written for managers and students of crisis management. As present or future leaders in your organizations, the key issue you will face is not whether a crisis will occur, but when, and what type. As a result, an understanding of crisis management is an essential part of your toolkit for organizational and professional success.

Developing a Framework for Studying Crisis Management

A starting point for understanding crisis management is to view it in terms of a framework. Frameworks group or organize what we experience in organizational life. In this book, we develop a framework that looks at crisis management in four distinct phases. In addition, each phase is divided into its internal and external dimensions, a distinction we call *landscapes*. Our framework begins with a definition of the term, presented in the next section.

Definition of *Crisis*

The word *crisis* has been used interchangeably with a number of other terms, including *disaster, business interruption, catastrophe, emergency,* or *contingency* (Herbane, 2010). Hence, the definition of a crisis must be established before a suitable framework can be developed. Numerous definitions have been offered, and most synthesize previous definitions to some extent. Pearson and Clair (1998) have offered the most widely used definition of an organizational crisis:

> An organizational crisis is a low-probability, high-impact event that threatens the viability of the organization and is characterized by ambiguity of cause, effect, and means of resolution, as well as by a belief that decisions must be made swiftly. (p. 60)

The following implications of this definition should be highlighted:

- A crisis is a "low-probability" event. This characteristic makes the planning for a crisis even more troublesome. Events that are not perceived to be imminent are hard to plan for. In addition, it is often difficult for management to find the motivation to plan for such an event. The notion is, "Why plan for something bad if it may not occur?" (Spillan & Crandall, 2002). Many managers have asked that same question until they were confronted with a major crisis.

- A crisis can have a high-damage impact. A crisis can devastate an organization, even kill it, or at best, leave it badly wounded.

- The reference to "ambiguity of cause" means that the origins and effects of the crisis might not be known initially. As humans, we instinctively like to point to simple causes. We especially seek to look for human stakeholders such as management or company owners who might have contributed to negligence, ultimately causing a crisis. However, as we will see throughout this book, multiple interrelated factors can lead to a certain trigger event that can initiate a crisis.

- The ambiguity in this definition also implies that the means of resolving the crisis are often debatable. In other words, several viable options may be available for the crisis management team to use in its goal of mitigating the crisis.
- Certain aspects of managing a crisis may require swift decision making. The failure to act decisively during the acute stage of the crisis can often intensify the ordeal.

All of these definitions provide a starting point for understanding crisis management. As more understanding of crisis management has emerged, more contemporary ideas and interpretations of crisis and crisis management have been developed.

Timothy Coombs's (2007) has developed one of the most recent conceptualizations of a crisis:

> A crisis is the perception of an unpredictable event that threatens important expectancies of stakeholders and can seriously impact an organization's performance and generate negative outcomes. (pp. 2–3)

This definition emphasizes perception. A crisis is generally perceived to be a threat by the organization's stakeholders, various groups that have an interest in the organization. Employees, customers, and the community in which the organization resides are considered stakeholders. Coombs infers that not all stakeholders will perceive that a crisis is occurring. A product defect that is detected by consumers, but not individuals inside the company, is an example of the incongruity that can take place. Nonetheless, a crisis has occurred, because the perceptions of at least one group of stakeholders have been affected in a negative manner by the event. Recognizing this distinction is important because there are occasions when management has gone into denial, proclaiming that no crisis has occurred (or could ever occur, for that matter), when in fact one has transpired (Sheaffer & Mano-Negrin, 2003). Textbooks are full of examples of this type of denial, such as General Motors' denial that anything was wrong with its Corvair automobile (Nader, 1965). In this early 1960s example of a corporate crisis, consumers and the media claimed that the Corvair automobile was subject to instability when going into a turn. Indeed, several accidents involving fatalities had occurred as a result of this structural problem. GM maintained that the problem of instability was caused by driver error, not a defect in the car. This denial by GM that a crisis existed resulted in a huge public image problem for the company.

This book follows these crisis definition guidelines. We build on the definition offered by Pearson and Clair in 1998 (which is the most frequently cited in the crisis management literature), but we also include the perspective offered by Coombs. To paraphrase Pearson, Clair, and Coombs, we offer the following definition to serve as our reference point throughout the book:

A crisis is an event that has a low probability of occurring, but should it occur, can have a vastly negative impact on the organization. The causes of the crisis, as well as the means to resolve it, may not be readily clear; nonetheless, its resolution should be approached as quickly as possible. Finally, the crisis impact may not be initially obvious to all of the relevant stakeholders of the organization.

One characteristic of a crisis that should be mentioned is this: they rarely occur without warning. Instead, a number of preconditions usually exist that breed a crisis. Put differently, crises have life cycles, and understanding what occurs before a crisis commences is important to helping prevent it.

The Life Cycle of a Crisis

Researchers usually examine a crisis in a sequential manner to better understand its evolution. One approach is to look at a crisis in four stages: preconditions, the trigger event, the crisis itself, and the postcrisis.

1. *Preconditions.* Smith (1990) was one of the first to point out that a set of smaller events typically interact before a crisis occurs. This combination of events eventually leads to a significant occurrence, commonly called the "trigger event" (Roux-Dufort, 2009; Smith, 1990), which causes the crisis to commence. For example, the trigger event at Union Carbide's Bhopal India plant in 1984 was the entry of water into a gas storage tank that subsequently caused the unit's temperature to rise. The resulting pressure increase forced the dangerous gas methyl isocyanate (MIC) to escape, resulting in the deaths of thousands of innocent civilians. However, responsibility for the crisis cannot be attributed solely to those involved with that step in the crisis because numerous preconditions contributed to the origin of the accident. These included shutting down a refrigeration system, failing to reset the tank temperature alarm, the nonfunctioning gas scrubber, and an inoperative flame tower designed to burn off toxic gases (Hartley, 1993).

2. *Trigger event.* The trigger event is the point at which the crisis escalates and upsets the normal equilibrium of the organization. The firm has been functioning normally up to this point, but preconditions brewing "beneath the surface" have been leading up to the trigger event, ultimately setting the crisis in motion and making it noticeable to the key stakeholders of the organization. Some might equate it to the point "where all hell breaks loose" or "the straw that broke the camel's back" (Crandall, 2007).

3. *Crisis.* The escalation of the crisis produces the greatest damage to the organization and its stakeholders. Potential stakeholders include employees, management, owners or stockholders, customers, those who use social media outlets, suppliers, the local community, and government regulators. Damage can be extensive during this acute stage of the crisis and can have a major effect on the business or organization's continuity.

4. *Postcrisis.* When the acute phase of the crisis is over, management should reflect on the event and glean lessons on what changes need to be made to prevent future crisis events (Kovoor-Misra and Nathan, 2000; Smith & Elliott, 2007). For example, after the first cyanide poisoning in 1982 of extra-strength Tylenol, Johnson & Johnson switched to a tamper-proof container. After the second poisoning in 1986, J&J made additional changes and manufactured the product as a caplet, a nonpenetrable material that cannot be adulterated by cyanide.

Strategic Orientation

In many instances, crisis events in organizations are addressed with a short-term, reactive perspective. When a crisis occurs, select individuals in an organization—perhaps those on an established crisis management team—convene to minimize the damage and present a positive image to the public. Any preparations for dealing with such crises often focus on effective communications and public relations. In contrast, organizations continually face strategic challenges. They must adapt to their changing business environments and modify their strategies to survive and remain competitive. In doing so, their managers tend to adopt a long-term perspective on strategic planning.

Between the extremes of an organizational crisis and a strategic challenge are obstacles to organizational success that are not always easy to classify. Indeed, distinguishing between a crisis and a strategic challenge may be difficult. Consider these potential scenarios, all of which are based on a number of events that have occurred over the past several years:

■ A supplier in another country produces a product that turns out to be defective and the product is assembled as a component into a domestically manufactured product. The final product fails, and in the process, kills three people. Is this a crisis or a strategic challenge? The answer is both. It is a crisis because there has been a loss of life because of a defective product. It is a strategic challenge because the supplier might have been selected solely for its ability to manufacture the component product at a low cost.

■ A labor union stages a mass boycott of certain products that are sold by domestic companies but manufactured overseas. The message from the protest is that these products have caused the loss of domestic jobs. The boycott causes some revenue loss for the companies that manufacture and retail these products. In a few cases, vandalism occurs on retail store properties that offer the products. Is this a crisis or a strategic challenge? Again, it is both. It is a crisis because of the sudden and unexpected loss of revenue for the companies involved. Furthermore, the damage and public apathy is of concern because it requires swift and effective decision making to ease the problem. It is a strategic challenge because the products are made overseas for cost reasons.

■ A major pharmaceutical company begins a program for the expansion of products that involves addressing health needs for baby boomers, a market that is seen as a major revenue source in the years to come. Several new drugs are approved and introduced to the market. After a few years, however, one of the drugs is linked to a deadly heart disease. Pressure to withdraw the drug is put firmly on the pharmaceutical company. Is this a crisis or a strategic challenge? Once again, it is both. It is a crisis because stakeholder attention is questioning the credibility of the drug and, indirectly, the credibility of the company. A major repercussion could result from this event, and swift decisions are required. And it is a strategic challenge because the drug was in the firm's long-term arsenal of products that would be popular and viable over the next 20 years.

■ A major corporation establishes a compensation plan for its management staff that rewards them on the basis of performance. As hoped, performance indicators begin to look good in certain areas of the company, despite the fact that the local economy has been faltering. For seven quarters, two managers receive bonuses based on meeting the performance indices established under the compensation plan. Unfortunately, it is discovered later that both managers have been "cooking the books." They are eventually fired, and the company is fined. During the ordeal, the company receives negative press because of the "unethical acts of its managers." Is this a crisis or a strategic challenge? Of course, this answer is both. The crisis aspect was manifested by the reputational and financial damage the company suffered. This dilemma also has roots as a strategic challenge. The decision to set up a bonus plan based on performance was, in itself, not a poor decision. Indeed, most managers in both service and manufacturing industries are compensated in part on the basis of performance. However, some plans are set up in such a way that they can invite unethical decisions on the part of management.

Because of crises' link with strategic challenges, planning for them should be a part of the strategic management process. While traditional crisis management approaches view this function as a separate planning process, crisis planning should not exist in a vacuum but should intertwine with strategic planning. This theme is developed throughout the book.

Previous Crisis Management Frameworks: Classifications of Crises

Some of the earlier frameworks looked at types of crises. In their work on presenting corporate policy during a crisis, Marcus and Goodman (1991) identified three types of crises: accidents, product safety and health incidents, and scandals. Pearson and Mitroff's (1993) framework identified seven crisis families: economic attacks, environmental accidents, occupational health diseases, psycho events (e.g., terrorism, sabotage, product tampering), damage to reputation, informational attacks, and breaks (e.g., recalls, product defects, computer breakdowns). In a similar crisis family arrangement, Myers (1993) offered a framework of crises consisting of natural disasters (floods, hurricanes, etc.), environmental events (aircraft accidents, contamination events, explosions), and incited incidents (arson, sabotage, vandalism). Crandall, McCartney, and Ziemnowicz (1999) used a five-family crises framework in their study of internal auditors. Specifically, they identified crises in terms of operational problems, negative publicity events, fraudulent crises, natural disasters, and legal issues.

Coombs (2006) has offered this more recent framework and classified crises as follows:

- *When an organization is attacked:* Computer hacking or tampering, rumors, product tampering, workplace violence, and terrorism. The common theme is that the attacks originate from outside the organization. However, that is not to say that all attacks are externally generated. Certainly a disgruntled employee can cause an attack as well, particularly in relation to a workplace violence episode.
- *When things go bad:* Defective products caused by company error, loss of key personnel, industrial accidents, transportation problems, and stakeholder challenges (when an outside group accuses the company of wrongdoing). Often these types of crises arise because of operational problems in the company.
- *When the organization misbehaves:* Not addressing known risks, improper job performance that leads to an accident, legal and regulatory violations. The common theme is that an ethical breach has occurred.

Another framework is worth mentioning, especially in light of the 2007 Virginia Tech massacre incident when a student, Seung-Hui Cho, went on a shooting rampage and killed 32 people. Prior to this incident, Mitroff, Diamond, and Alpaslan (2006) had completed their own assessment of crises categories that could occur on an American college or university campus. Their framework consisted of criminal activities, informational crises (identity theft, fraud, confidentiality problems), building safety issues, athletic scandals, public health problems (such as a disease outbreak or food safety problem), unethical behavior or misconduct (plagiarism, record tampering, or fraud), financial crises, natural disasters, legal or labor disputes, and reputation problems. While such a framework may seem like just a list, it is important to note that crises tend to reside in common families or categories.

Using a framework for classifying crisis events into families is a useful way to organize what we experience. Mitroff (1989) was one of the first crisis management researchers to note that while it is impossible to prepare for every type of crisis that might happen to an organization, preparing for a few families of crises is feasible. In this book, we present a framework of crisis families that takes into account the internal and external landscapes of the organization's environment. But first we need to acknowledge that crisis events occur in stages.

Previous Crisis Management Frameworks: Stages of Crises

Frameworks have also been developed that account for the various stages of a crisis. The more familiar frameworks emerged in the 1990s and generally followed a three- or four-stage approach to analyzing the life of a crisis. Crisis researchers realized that analyzing the stages of a crisis led to a more thorough understanding of the crisis phenomenon. A crisis was more than just an event. It was a life cycle phenomenon that had a birth, an acute stage—the crisis—and an aftermath, a time of learning and reflection. Table 1.1 provides an overview of the various frameworks that are discussed next.

Table 1.1 Frameworks for Crisis Management

Three-Stage Framework: General	Three-Stage Framework: Smith (1990)	Three-Stage Framework: Richardson (1994)	Four-Stage Framework: Myers (1993)	Four-Stage Framework: Fink (1996)	Five-Stage Framework: Pearson and Mitroff (1993)	This Book: Crandall, Parnell, and Spillan (2010, 2013)
Before the Crisis	Crisis of management	Precrisis/disaster phase	Normal operations	Prodromal crisis stage	Signal detection	Landscape survey
↑					Preparation/prevention	Strategic planning
During the Crisis	Operational crisis	Crisis impact/rescue phase	Emergency response	Acute crisis stage	Containment/damage limitation	Crisis management
↑			Interim Processing	Chronic crisis stage		
After the Crisis	Crisis of legitimation	Recovery/demise phase	Restoration	Crisis resolution stage	Recovery	Organizational learning
↑					Learning	

Three-Stage Frameworks

The most basic framework is the simple three-stage approach that follows a precrisis, crisis, and postcrisis format. Smith (1990) offered a three-stage format consisting of a precrisis period, the crisis of management; a crisis period, the operational crisis; and a postcrisis stage, the crisis of legitimation. The crisis of management stage held that the actions of organizational leaders—plus a culture that does not put a premium on preparedness—can lead to a climate in which all that is needed is a trigger event to start the crisis. Once the crisis is under way, the organization manages the crisis as best it can during the operational crisis stage. This stage is characterized by building a supportive climate among the key players involved in the crisis. Unfortunately, the crisis of legitimation stage may be characterized by scapegoating on the part of a number of parties, including the organization itself as well as the government and the media. The scapegoating process involves apportioning blame for the crisis to various stakeholders.

Richardson (1994) offered a three-step framework similar to the one proposed by Smith. The precrisis/disaster phase focuses on prevention by addressing the threats that can cause a crisis. The crisis impact/rescue stage is the occurrence of the crisis. During this period, management should seek to mitigate the crisis and offer support to those affected by it. The recovery/demise stage involves restoring stakeholder confidence in the organization.

Four-Stage Frameworks

By adding an additional stage, the four-stage frameworks offer a more precise approach. Myers (1993) offered a four-stage approach that begins with the normal operations stage, a time when prevention practices are established. In this stage, operations are normal, but preparations are made to address a crisis event should one occur. The second stage, emergency response, encompasses the activities during the first hours following the onset of the crisis. Interim processing, the third stage, represents an intermediate phase when temporary procedures are set up until normal operations can resume. Restoration, the final stage, focuses on the organization's transition back to normal operations.

Fink (1996) also offered a four-stage framework beginning with the prodromal stage. This stage occurs before the full-blown crisis and contains warning signs that signal a crisis may be imminent. In this stage, it is possible to prevent the crisis if the warning signs are heeded. The acute crisis stage follows next and is evidenced by the sudden onset of the event. The crisis is most noticeable by outsiders at this stage. The chronic crisis stage is less dramatic in appearance but is still significant because the organization is attempting to address the lingering damages from the episode. The final stage is the resolution stage, when the organization is returning to its precrisis existence.

Five-Stage Framework

Unlike the four-stage frameworks, Pearson and Mitroff's (1993) five-stage framework provides an even more comprehensive approach to understanding the stages of a crisis. These stages include:

1. *Signal detection.* The occurrence of a crisis always begins with some forms of warning. Signal detection is the stage that advances those warnings. Becoming adept at signal detection is a mind-set, as well as a skill, that organizations need to embrace.

2. *Preparation/prevention.* This stage involves the formation of a crisis management team and a plan for addressing those crises that may occur. Crisis management is approached in a systematic and ongoing manner to the point at which it is almost a science. The goal is to prevent as many crises as possible and effectively manage those that do occur.

3. *Containment/damage limitation.* This stage is where the management of the crisis occurs. The intent is to contain the crisis to the greatest extent possible and to mitigate the event so that organizational and stakeholder damage is kept to a minimum.

4. *Recovery.* In this stage, attempts are made to resume activities as much as feasible. The recovery will often proceed in stages as well. Short-term recovery aims to get the system back on line so a minimal acceptable level of service is achieved. Long-term recovery follows as operational activities are restored to their precrisis level. In some cases, improvements are made in the recovery process that bring the level of operations up to a higher level than before the crisis. An example would be a company that experiences a fire in its production facilities. After the fire, the rebuilt facility is usually better equipped with more modern machinery and technology than what existed in the old facility.

5. *Learning.* This stage involves reflecting on what can be learned from the crisis. The emphasis is not on searching for scapegoats and displacing the blame onto other parties, a response often encouraged in a litigious society. Instead, maximum attention is focused on improving current operational problems and preventing future ones.

A Framework for Crisis Management

Figure 1.1 presents another framework for crisis management—the one adopted in this book—in the form of a two-by-four matrix. With this framework, we draw from the work of previous crisis management researchers and add another dimension to the analysis, the existence of the internal and external landscapes that engulf the organization. The internal landscape exists within the organization. It consists of the employees as well as the organizational culture of the organization. It is the human side of the company that exhibits the strengths and weaknesses of the organization.

The external landscape resides outside of the organization. It consists of all stakeholders who have some vested interest in the organization but are not directly part of it. These include government regulatory agencies, consumer groups, industry associations, and the media. It also consists of groups that are not necessarily stakeholders but can still have a huge impact on the operations of the company.

	Landscape Survey	Strategic Planning	Crisis Management	Organizational Learning
The Internal Landscape	What crisis threats exist INSIDE of our organization?	How can our organization plan for potential crisis events?	How should we manage our INTERNAL stakeholders during a crisis?	What can our organization learn from this crisis?
The External Landscape	What crisis threats exist OUTSIDE of our organization?	What planning has been done outside of our organization to help us prepare for potential crisis events?	How should we manage our EXTERNAL stakeholders during a crisis?	What learning is taking place outside of our organization in relation to the type of crisis we just experienced?

Figure 1.1 A Framework for Crisis Management

These may include terrorist groups or even a jealous spouse of an employee who works in the organization. The external environment can also include forces such as the weather and other natural disasters as well as a downturn in the economy.

The progression of stages in the crisis management process follows a four-phase sequence. There is the landscape survey, followed by strategic planning, then crisis management, and finally the organizational learning stage. Of course, these stages can overlap to some degree. Each stage is discussed next.

Landscape Survey

The framework begins with the landscape survey, shown on the far left side of Figure 1.1. The top half of the landscape survey looks at processes that management needs to evaluate (i.e., inside the internal landscape). Identifying the strengths and weaknesses that exist within the organization is one such process. Such weaknesses indicate points at which the company may be vulnerable to a crisis attack. Enthusiasm for crisis management planning is another key element to gauge. Some organizations are highly prepared for crisis events, whereas others are more complacent (Pearson & Mitroff, 1993). The degree of enthusiasm for crisis management is also a function of the organization's culture (Stead & Smallman, 1999), its ethical environment, and the diligence with which the company enforces its safety policies.

The bottom half of the landscape survey (the external landscape) focuses on events occurring outside of the organization. The industry vulnerability is at the forefront of the types of crises a specific organization encounters. For example, companies in the chemical industry are concerned about chemical leaks. Food manufacturers focus on crises pertaining to disease problems such as an *E. coli* outbreak. Within the hotel and lodging industry, the physical safety of guests is a major concern. The location of a hotel, for example, on coastal areas, can open up to vulnerabilities of flooding, earthquakes, and potential tsunamis (Henderson, 2005).

For companies operating across international borders, the degree of political stability of the host country is important to consider. Another key factor is the general attitude of the host country toward the home country of the multinational corporation (MNC). Any heightened tensions that may exist between these two groups can lay the groundwork for a potential crisis. Globalization implications must also be evaluated. Much globalization seems to progress at the expense of a major stakeholder, the home country's manufacturing employees. For example, manufacturing operations that leave the home country for cheaper labor in another country usually leave a wake of unemployed workers back in the home country. Such moves do not sit well with local stakeholders such as labor unions.

The technological advancements within an industry must also be considered part of the external landscape. For some industries, technology can lay the groundwork for a crisis. In the commercial airlines industry, the smooth functioning of all technological systems is essential for the safety of those on the flight. In other industries, technology is important but not necessarily life threatening—yet it can still be the source of a major crisis. Retail chains rely on information technology to communicate and manage their field units. A malfunction in such a system will create a crisis, but not one that is physically harmful to employees or customers.

Strategic Planning

Within the internal landscape of the organization, the strategic planning phase focuses on preventing crises when possible and planning how to mitigate their effects when prevention is not possible. Within the internal landscape of the organization, crisis planning begins with forming the crisis management team. The team acts as the management unit that prevents or directs the organization through the crisis. One of the tasks of the team is to periodically assess potential crises that may occur to the organization. For example, school districts for all grade levels, as well as colleges and universities, should plan regularly for a dysfunctional student who may become violent on school property. Another potential crisis involves the quick evacuation of a building, such as in the event of a fire.

Crisis management teams also formulate plans that provide general guidelines for managing a crisis (Coombs, 2006). Such guidelines include who should address the media as well as specific procedures for managing specific crises that are unique to the organization. In other words, these guidelines address the organization's potential crises. During the strategic planning stage, some teams conduct mock disasters in order to test the organization's crisis management response.

Within the external landscape, activities focus on what is occurring in the industry to prevent and manage crisis events. Existing government regulations in many industries are designed to prevent a crisis from occurring. Examples of these types of agencies abound. The Federal Aviation Administration (FAA) and the Transportation Security Administration (TSA) work to ensure safety in the air travel industries. Nearly all industries impose additional standards through associations that exist for the industry.

Crisis Management

We define *crisis management* as the stage at which the organization is encountering some type of crisis that has occurred. During this stage, efforts are focused on addressing the crisis and resuming operations as quickly as possible. This process involves managing the various primary and secondary stakeholders. Primary stakeholders typically include the owners, employees, customers, local communities, and suppliers (Wheeler & Sillanpää, 1997). Secondary stakeholders include any other groups that have some type of interest in the organization. For example, People for the Ethical Treatment of Animals (PETA) has an interest in companies that use animals for laboratory research. A crisis can result when such a group takes an activist stand against a company that uses animals for this purpose.

Stakeholders can also be divided into internal and external groups. Internal stakeholders include the owners and the employees. External stakeholders include customers, suppliers, the local community, various government entities, and special interest groups. Within the internal landscape, the crisis management process focuses on addressing the needs of the owners and the employees during the crisis. The external landscape looks at how the organization manages the remaining stakeholders that exist outside of the firm.

Organizational Learning

Within the internal landscape, the key question that management must ask is, What can be learned from the crisis? One of the keys to learning from a crisis is not to wait too long after the event has occurred, lest management reach a stage termed "forgetfulness" (Kovoor-Misra & Nathan, 2000). In this stage, the organization has returned to normal operations, and the motivation to evaluate and learn from the crisis wanes.

The focus of learning should center around two themes: (1) what can be done to prevent the crisis from recurring, and (2) if a similar crisis does occur, what can be done to soften its impact? It is possible that management will discover that it handled some processes well during the crisis, while not performing as well on other aspects. Pearson and Clair (1998) suggested that such an evaluation be examined in terms of degrees of success and failure. For example, an organization may succeed in resuming operations in a timely manner but fail at protecting its reputation. Learning to examine failures on the part of management is a necessary ingredient in being more proactive in the future (Carmeli & Schaubroeck, 2008). Instead of learning from a crisis, some organizations do not seem to heed the lessons from the event, and as a result, repeat the same mistakes when similar incidents occur in the future. Yet an organization that is successful at learning will change its policies and procedures when necessary and apply that new knowledge to future crisis events.

In the external landscape, government regulators often reevaluate and renew their directives after a crisis. Certainly the airline industry has changed dramatically in terms of safety regulations after America's worst terrorist incident on September 11, 2001. Government regulations are often implemented or upgraded after a crisis, usually to increase the safety of stakeholders in the affected industry. Stakeholders external to the organization may also change their outlooks after a crisis. At a minimum, such stakeholders will be more aware and compassionate toward an organization that has experienced a crisis. After the Virginia Tech massacre in April 2007, a wave of sympathy and solidarity spread among many citizens throughout the country, and even worldwide. At the same time, some parties were critical of the university, questioning whether certain measures could have been taken to prevent or mitigate the crisis. Indeed, in 2012, a jury found the university negligent for not warning students in a timely manner of the threat of an active shooter on campus (Lipka, 2012).

Development of the Book

Chapter 1: A Framework for Crisis Management

This chapter outlines the framework that is presented in the book. Figure 1.2 overviews the progression of the remaining chapters.

Chapter 2: The Crisis Management Landscape

This chapter begins our survey of the strategic landscape that serves as a breeding ground for many of the crises organizations face. The focus is on six of the broader trends that are common across most cultures and business environments.

Chapter 3: Sources of Organizational Crises

In this chapter, we explore the sources of crises from several perspectives. First, an analysis of the external environment is presented from the political–legal, economic, social, and technological perspectives. The external environment is important to analyze because many crisis events emerge from the volatility of these four sectors of the environment. Crises are also viewed from the industry and organizational life cycle perspectives because different stages of the life cycle have their own unique vulnerabilities to a crisis.

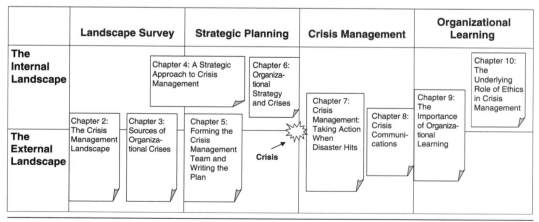

Figure 1.2 Overview of the Book

Chapter 4: A Strategic Approach to Crisis Management

In this chapter, we outline the strategic planning process and its link to crisis anticipation and prevention. One of the key themes of the chapter is the need to incorporate crisis management into the strategic management process of the organization. As such, some of the traditional tools used in strategic planning, such as the SWOT (strengths, weaknesses, opportunities, and threats) analysis, should also be used in assessing crisis vulnerability.

Chapter 5: Forming the Crisis Management Team and Writing the Plan

The essence of crisis planning is forming the crisis management team (CMT) and then writing the crisis management plan (CMP). Guidelines are provided for both tasks in this chapter. The composition of the CMT is discussed, including the qualities team members should have. Components of the CMP are overviewed and a template is included as the Appendix at the end of this book. The chapter concludes by offering guidelines for crisis management training efforts.

Chapter 6: Organizational Strategy and Crises

This chapter links the organization's strategy to its crisis vulnerability at the corporate and business levels. Corporate strategies determine the type of industries in which the organization operates while business strategies focus on how the company competes in its chosen industry. The choice of strategies at both levels influences the types of crises the organization may face in the future.

Chapter 7: Crisis Management: Taking Action When Disaster Hits

In this chapter, the tactical responses to a crisis are explored. The response strategy is divided into three phases: when the crisis first hits, during the crisis, and when the crisis winds down. Each phase has unique decision points that need to be addressed. An emphasis on effective decision making and evaluation is stressed throughout each phase.

Chapter 8: Crisis Communication

One of the most important challenges of crisis management is effective communication with both internal and external stakeholders. This chapter presents guidelines for maneuvering in this area of communication. In addition, one of the new challenges of crisis communication is learning how to manage the complicated world of social media. Examples of social media crises are presented and guidelines on how to use this new method of communication are offered.

Chapter 9: The Importance of Organizational Learning

This chapter focuses on the need to learn from the crisis event. Organizational learning does not come naturally, however, because the push to get the organization back to normal operations often supersedes the need to reflect on preventing future crises. This chapter examines the potential learning areas in each of the four stages of the crisis management framework. Barriers that can impede learning are discussed, as well as approaches to build a learning organization.

Chapter 10: The Underlying Role of Ethics in Crisis Management

This chapter examines how executive misbehavior is a key force behind many crises that occur in organizations today. The reasons why ethical blunders take place are examined. Changing the organizational culture is needed to improve the ethical climate of the company. The ways in which this change can be accomplished are presented.

Chapter 11: Emerging Trends in Crisis Management

This chapter examines the future of crisis management. Emerging trends are identified in each of the four stages of the framework: landscape survey, strategic planning, crisis management, and organizational learning.

Summary

The field of crisis management is growing in scope and sophistication. This book acknowledges these changes by recognizing that crisis management should be a part of the organization's strategic management process. Drawing on the work of others in the field, we employ a crisis management framework that utilizes a two-by-four matrix that recognizes four phases of the crisis management process. In addition, we add the importance of acknowledging the internal and external landscapes that exist within each phase.

Questions for Discussion

1. Why is it important to understand a crisis in terms of its different stages?

2. Identify a recent crisis event that occurred where you work. Discuss the different stages of the crisis in terms of:

- Landscape survey

  - Were there any events occurring in your organization that might have contributed to the formation of this crisis?
  - What events outside of your organization contributed to the crisis?

- Strategic management

  - Did your organization have any plans in place to address this type of crisis?
  - What industry controls or government regulations were designed to prevent this type of crisis?

- Crisis management

  - How well did your organization respond to the crisis?
  - Were any outside agencies or stakeholders involved in helping your organization manage the crisis?

- Organizational learning

  - What lessons did your organization learn from experiencing this crisis?
  - Were there any changes in your industry or within government regulations that took place after this crisis occurred?

Chapter Exercise

As a class, determine the following:

1. What events could happen to the class that would constitute a crisis? Write these on the board and then seek a consensus as a class on the top five crisis events. Focus on these as you proceed to the next step.

2. What crisis plans are available that could address each of these five potential crises? Distinguish between resources that are available inside the classroom and those that exist outside of the classroom.

Mini-Case: Scandal at Penn State

For years, assistant Penn State football coach Jerry Sandusky had appeared to be a model citizen in the community. He was a respected football coach under the legendary Joe Paterno and was the founder of The Second Mile, a charitable organization to help disadvantaged youth. He was also a serial child rapist.

Of course, many people would think that it was unfortunate that no one was aware of this his dark behavior. Perhaps if someone knew and contacted the authorities, Sandusky could have been caught and stopped. In fact, people knew about Jerry Sandusky, and some of them were in high places at Penn State University. An internal investigation of the incident summarizes the findings:

Four of the most powerful people at The Pennsylvania State University—
President Graham B. Spanier, Senior Vice President-Finance and Business
Gary C. Schultz, Athletic Director Timothy M. Curley and Head Football
Coach Joseph V. Paterno—failed to protect against a child sexual predator
harming children for decades. Those men concealed Sandusky's activities
from the Board of Trustees, the University community and authorities. They
exhibited a striking lack of empathy for Sandusky's victims by failing to
inquire as to their safety and well-being, especially by not attempting to determine the identity of the child who Sandusky assaulted in the Lasch Building
in 2001. (Freeh, Sporkin, & Sullivan, 2012, p. 14)

An examination of meeting notes and e-mails reveals that Spanier, Schultz,
Curley, and Paterno had met and discussed the problem with various authorities,
not including the board of trustees. However, the criticism and what led to the scandal was that they did not do enough to prevent further reoccurrences of Sandusky's
predatory behavior. Was it an attempt to cover up an incident so as not to embarrass
the university and its stakeholders? Or was it a strategy on their part of the leadership to be discreet concerning a university employee with nearly 30 years of service?
Or was the event so bizarre and uncomfortable that they just did not know how to
manage it properly?

What is known is that these four university officials went into crisis management mode and attempted to manage the scandal. They held numerous meetings,
devised various strategies, and contacted various authorities, including the university police and legal office. Specifically, two areas in their crisis management efforts
were not sufficient: (1) the board of trustees was not kept in the information loop,
and (2) the victims of the assaults were not properly identified and protected. Crisis
management is a huge task and must be taken seriously. For these four men, it
cost them their jobs; it put the university through an agonizing trial; and perhaps
most important, it changed the lives of a number of young men forever because of
repeated assaults from a child predator.

The Scandal

Jerry Sandusky joined the coaching staff of Penn State in 1969 where he
remained until his retirement in 1999. After his retirement, he continued to have
access to the Penn State campus athletic facilities because of his status as an emeri-
tus professor. The scandal that involves Sandusky became the worst ever in the history of college sports and led to harsh penalties by the National Collegiate Athletic
Association (NCAA) against the university (Wolff & Gagne, 2012).

The crisis commenced with two events that occurred more than a decade ago. In
May 1998, a mother reported to the University Police Department that Sandusky
had showered with her 11-year-old son in the Lasch Building on the Penn State
campus (Freeh et al., 2012). The police investigation does not reveal evidence of
a crime, but it did bring a reprimand from a police detective not to shower with
any other children. A caseworker from the Department of Public Welfare was present at this meeting. Police Chief Thomas Harmon closed the case: "Sandusky was

advised that there was no criminal behavior established and that the matter was closed as an investigation" (Freeh et al., 2012, p. 20). At this point, all four Penn State officials—Spanier, Schultz, Curley, and Paterno—were informed of the police report and proceeded as if the event were now behind them.

That was to change on February 9, 2001, when Mike McQueary, a Penn State football assistant, witnessed a sexual encounter involving Jerry Sandusky and a 10-year-old boy in the showers of the Lasch Building. McQueary reported the incident to Coach Paterno the following day. Paterno met with Curley and Schultz on Sunday, February 11. University president Spanier joined them to discuss a strategy for addressing the incident in late February. They agree to confront Sandusky. On March 5, Curley met with Sandusky and informed him that he was uncomfortable with his behavior with young boys. Curley advised Sandusky not to bring any more boys to the athletic facilities. On March 19, Curley met with the executive director of the Second Mile charitable organization, of which Sandusky is the founder, and informed him of the incident that was observed by Mike McQueary. The Second Mile leadership did not take action and concluded that it was a "non-incident" (Freeh et al., 2012). Meanwhile, President Spanier made no mention of the Sandusky incident at the board of trustees meeting on March 16, 2001.

Eight and a half years later, on January 7, 2010, the university received subpoenas from the Pennsylvania attorney general for personnel records on Sandusky. During 2010–2011, investigations were launched concerning Jerry Sandusky, and the crisis rapidly escalated, resulting in charges of child sex abuse that occurred both on and off the Penn State campus. The resulting trial occurred in 2012, and on July 23, Sandusky was found guilty of 45 counts of child sex abuse.

The Response

The viewpoints of the stakeholders associated with this case varied. Some think the university should be vilified for its lack of empathy for the victims and its inability to keep a child predator out of its midst, resulting in harsh sanctions by the NCAA. Others feel that the scandal was a "witch hunt" with authorities looking for scapegoats to blame. The crisis has become an emotional hot point in State College, Pennsylvania, where those loyal to the university and the late coach Paterno have been pitted against others who believe the university was irresponsible (Fitzpatrick, 2012).

The Board of Trustees Response

The board of trustees removed legendary football coach Joe Paterno and President Graham Spanier from their positions. The two other officials, Senior Vice President for Finance and Business Gary C. Schultz and Athletic Director Timothy M. Curley both stepped down (Tsikoudakis, 2011).

In a dramatic move, interim Penn State president Rodney Erickson, who took over after Graham Spanier was ousted, ordered the removal of a statue of Coach Paterno from outside Beaver Stadium. Although the decision was controversial, particularly from alumni, he felt the icon was a "lightning rod of controversy" and needed to be removed so that healing could occur. Erickson commented, "Were it to remain, the statue will be a recurring wound to the multitude of individuals across the nation and beyond who have been the victims of child abuse" (Brown, 2012).

The NCAA Response

The sanctions handed down by the NCAA were especially harsh, so much so that it even surprised some sports journalists, who felt the association was more accustomed to dealing with athletes who receive illegal gifts such as free tattoos or athletic shoes (Wolff & Gagne, 2012). The penalties to Penn State were meant to punish, and in doing so, many innocent stakeholders also suffered. The sanctions included:

- The football program is barred from any postseason games for four years, starting with the 2012 season.
- Scholarships were cut back beginning in 2013.
- Coach Paterno's wins for the past 14 years will be taken off the books, a total of 111 from his once-record 409 victories.

The sanctions have come under considerable criticism because of the far-reaching extent of the punishments. Indeed, the intent of the NCAA was to rebuild "a culture that went terribly awry" (Maher Bachman, & Miller, 2012). However, the sanctions rely heavily on a single report issued by former FBI Director Louis Freeh and two associates at his law firm, also known as the Freeh Report (Maher et al., 2012).

Mini-Case Questions

1. Review the definition of a crisis given in this chapter. How does this event illustrate a crisis?

2. Given that the initial events occurred as far back as 1998, why do you think this case took so long to become public knowledge?

3. Were the sanctions by the NCAA too harsh, too lenient, or appropriate? Why?

Mini-Case References

Brown, E. (2012, July 23). NCAA set to act as Penn State removes statue. *Wall Street Journal,* p. A3.

Fitzpatrick, F. (2012, June 4). Fury returns to Penn State. *Newsweek,* 14–16.

Freeh, L., Sporkin, S., & Sullivan, E. (2012, July 12). *Report of the Special Investigative Counsel regarding the actions of The Pennsylvania State University related to the child sexual abuse committed by Gerald A. Sandusky.* Retrieved August 2, 2012, from http://www.thefreehreportonpsu.com/REPORT_FINAL_071212.pdf.

Maher, K., Bachman, R., & Miller, J. (2012, July 24). NCAA slams Penn State—Top college football program is hobbled for years; Paterno wins record negated. *Wall Street Journal,* p. A3.

Tsikoudakis, M. (2011). Penn State abuse scandal sharpens focus on risks. *Business Insurance,* *45*(45), 1, 21.

Wolff, A., & Gagne, M. (2012, July 2). Is this the end for Penn State? *Sports Illustrated,* 38–41.

References

Beaubien, G. (2009). Domino's YouTube flap: "A landmark event in crisis management." *Public Relations Tactics, 16*(5), 4.

Carmeli, A., & Schaubroeck, J. (2008). Organizational crisis-preparedness: The importance of learning from failures. *Long Range Planning, 41,* 177–196.

Coombs, W. (2006). *Code red in the boardroom: Crisis management as organizational DNA.* Westport, CT: Praeger.

Coombs, W. (2007). *Ongoing crisis communication: Planning, managing, and responding* (2nd ed.). Thousand Oaks, CA: Sage.

Crandall, W. R. (2007). Crisis, chaos, and creative destruction: Getting better from bad. In E. G. Carayannis & C. Ziemnowicz (Eds.), *Re-discovering Schumpeter four score years later: Creative destruction evolving into "Mode 3"* (pp. 432–455). Basingstoke, UK: MacMillan Palgrave.

Crandall, W. R., McCartney, M., & Ziemnowicz, C. (1999). Internal auditors and their perceptions of crisis events. *Internal Auditor, 14*(1), 11–17.

Fink, S. (1996). *Crisis management: Planning for the inevitable.* New York: American Management Association.

Hartley, R. (1993). *Business ethics: Violations of the public trust.* New York: Wiley.

Henderson, J. (2005). Responding to natural disasters: Managing a hotel in the aftermath of the Indian Ocean tsunami. *Tourism and Hospitality Research, 6*(1), 89–96.

Herbane, B. (2010). Small business research—time for a crisis-based view. *International Small Business Journal, 28*(1), 43–64.

Kiernan, P., & McKay, B. (2012, January 13). Coke, Pepsi Attempt to Ease O.J. Fears. *Wall Street Journal,* p. B1.

Kovoor-Misra, S., & Nathan, M. (2000, Fall). Timing is everything: The optimal time to learn from crises. *Review of Business,* 31–36.

Lipka, S. (2012, March 23). Jury's verdict against Virginia Tech sends strong messages to colleges. *Chronicle of Higher Education, 58*(29), p. A32.

Marcus, A., & Goodman, R. (1991). Victims and shareholders: The dilemmas of presenting corporate policy during a crisis. *Academy of Management Journal, 34*(2), 281–305.

Mitroff, I. (1989, October). Programming for crisis control. *Security Management,* 75–79.

Mitroff, I., Diamond, M., & Alpaslan, C. (2006). How prepared are America's colleges and universities for major crises? *Change, 38*(1), 60–67.

Myers, K. (1993). *Total contingency planning for disasters: Managing risk . . . minimizing loss . . . ensuring business continuity.* New York: Wiley.

Nader, R. (1965). *Unsafe at any speed.* New York: Grossman.

Pearson, C., & Clair, J. (1998). Reframing crisis management. *Academy of Management Review, 23*(1), 59–76.

Pearson, C., & Mitroff, I. (1993). From crisis prone to crisis prepared: A framework for crisis management. *Academy of Management Executive, 7*(1), 48–59.

Richardson, B. (1994). Socio-technical disasters: Profile and prevalence. *Disaster Prevention and Management, 3*(4), 41–69.

Roux-Dufort, C. (2009). The devil lies in details! How crises build up within organizations. *Journal of Contingencies and Crisis Management, 17*(1), 4–11.

Sheaffer, Z., & Mano-Negrin, R. (2003). Executives' orientations as indicators of crisis management policies and practices. *Journal of Management Studies, 40*(2), 573–606.

Smith, D. (1990). Beyond contingency planning: Towards a model of crisis management. *Industrial Crisis Quarterly, 4*(4), 263–275.

Smith, D., & Elliott, D. (2007). Exploring the barriers to learning from crisis: Organizational learning and crisis. *Management Learning, 38*(5), 519–538.

Spillan, J., & Crandall, W. R. (2002). Crisis planning in the nonprofit sector: Should we plan for something bad if it may not occur? *Southern Business Review, 27*(2), 18–29.

Stead, E., & Smallman, C. (1999). Understanding business failure: Learning and un-learning lessons from industrial crises. *Journal of Contingencies and Crisis Management, 7*(1), 1–18.

Terlep, S. (2011, November 29). GM scrambles to defend Volt. *Wall Street Journal*, p. B1.

Wheaton, K. (2008, December 1). Middle road in Motrin-gate was right choice. *Advertising Age, 79*(44), 12.

Wheeler, D., & Sillanpää, M. (1997). *The stakeholder corporation: A blueprint for maximizing stakeholder value.* London: Pittman.

The Crisis Management Landscape

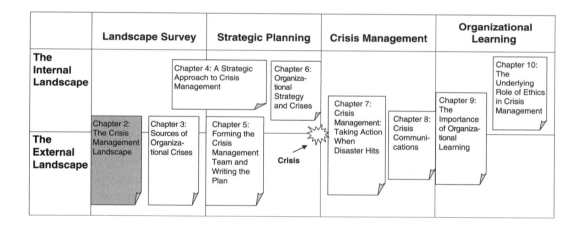

	Landscape Survey	Strategic Planning	Crisis Management	Organizational Learning
The Internal Landscape		Chapter 4: A Strategic Approach to Crisis Management	Chapter 6: Organizational Strategy and Crises		Chapter 10: The Underlying Role of Ethics in Crisis Management
				Chapter 7: Crisis Management: Taking Action When Disaster Hits	Chapter 8: Crisis Communications	Chapter 9: The Importance of Organizational Learning	
The External Landscape	Chapter 2: The Crisis Management Landscape	Chapter 3: Sources of Organizational Crises	Chapter 5: Forming the Crisis Management Team and Writing the Plan	**Crisis**		

Opening Case, Part 1: How a Distance of 10 Feet Can Be Fatal

Ghent, West Virginia, is a small community near the Winterplace Ski Resort on Flat Top Mountain. The Little General Store is located about a mile away from the resort on U.S. 19, a two-lane highway that connects Ghent to nearby Beckley, West Virginia. For years, the Little General Store was the hub of the community. It was a typical convenience store with gas pumps, a small grocery store, and a pizza shop. Locals and skiers frequented the Little General for gas, coffee, some friendly conversation, and quick groceries. That all changed at 10:53 A.M. on January 30, 2007, when a propane tank exploded behind the store, killing four people and injuring five others (Busick, 2012). The store was leveled in the blast. Today, the area is vacant, save for the memorials that have been placed to honor those who died. The Little General Store never reopened in that location.

The Little General Store had a fatal design flaw that existed for years before it was finally uncovered. The flaw was not with the building or the gas pumps, but with the location of a 500-gallon propane tank used to heat the ovens to bake the pizza in the store. The propane tank was located adjacent to the back of the store, only inches from the outer wall of the building. However, the West Virginia Fire Commission and the Occupational Safety and Health Administration (OSHA) required a tank of 500 gallons or more to be located at least 10 feet from the building (U.S. Chemical Safety Board [CSB], 2008).

The Explosion

What was supposed to occur that morning was a simple propane transfer between tanks. Two technicians from the Appalachian Heating Company were performing the liquid transfer from a 500-gallon tank located next to the building to another tank located 10 feet away from the structure. The tank adjacent to the building was owned and operated by the Ferrellgas Company and had been in that location since 1994. The new tank was operated by Appalachian Heating, which was taking over the contract to supply propane to the store (CSB, 2008).

At some point in the morning, the lead technician (who had one and a half years of experience with propane) left to service another call, leaving the junior technician (who had about six weeks of experience on the job) to work alone. At 10:25 A.M., the junior technician attempted to extract the plug from the old tank, and propane began to spew out uncontrollably. The technician was not able to stop the flow. The U.S. Chemical Safety and Hazard Investigation Report describes what happened next:

Liquid propane sprayed upward, against the roof overhang, and dense propane gas accumulated at ground levels around the tank and the foundation of the building. Over the next 25 minutes, the escaping propane entered the Little General store through openings in the roof overhang. (CSB, 2008, p. 5)

The dissipation of propane inside and around the store was creating a deadly situation. If the propane encountered an open flame in a pizza oven, or an electrical spark, certain detonation would occur. At 10:40 A.M., the junior technician called 911 and alerted the lead technician of the problem by phone. The Ghent Volunteer Fire Department responded with a captain and two emergency medical technicians (EMTs). The lead technician for Appalachian Heating also returned to the store. Meanwhile, there were still four employees inside the store, which was now accumulating a dangerous quantity of propane.

At approximately 10:53 A.M., the worst-case scenario occurred, an explosion that leveled the store. The two technicians, a former captain of the Ghent Fire Department and an EMT were killed. All were standing outside near the leaking propane tank. The four store employees, a firefighter, and another EMT were injured (Busick, 2010). The blast was so forceful that it registered on seismographs at Virginia Tech, some 50 miles away (Heyman, 2007). Ben Monast, the manager at the nearby ski shop, was seated at his desk and felt the concussion from the blast in his chest. "I thought we'd been hit by lightning. . . . The whole place shook pretty violently" (Urbina, 2007, p. 12).

The Grieving

For the small community of 800 residents, the event was devastating. This is an area where everybody knows everybody else, and many in the community are lifelong residents. "For us, it's just like 9/11," commented Roy Coalson, a volunteer firefighter for 25 years for the Ghent Fire Department (Heyman, 2007, p. 19). William Manning, a bartender at the nearby Bear Den, remarked, "I don't cry over things easily. . . . They're my best friends. I've known these people most of my life. You can't replace them" (Urbina, 2007, p. 12). For Governor Joe Manchin III, the explosion was yet another event that had made his tenure in office a difficult one. Only a year earlier, 12 coal miners had died in an accident at the Sago Coal Mine in Sago, West Virginia. That accident too, was caused by a dangerous gas, methane, a sinister vapor that is a continual threat to coal miner safety (Madsen, 2009).

Opening Case Part 1 Discussion Question

One of the problems with an accident like this one is that regulations already exist that—if followed—could have prevented it. Public outcries for "more government regulation" are often misplaced, when better enforcement is what is really needed. For the case involving the Little General Store, regulations were in place to govern the use of propane.

However, there are certainly other instances where additional regulation of a work activity may be necessary. When an industry attempts to regulate itself, without existing laws, it is referred to as "self-policing." As a class, discuss the effectiveness of self-policing. Does it always work? What industries might benefit from additional regulations? Are some industries over-regulated?

Opening Case Part 1 References

Busick, J. (2010, October 1). Propane: This common fuel can be uncommonly deadly. *Safety Compliance Letter,* Issue 2518, 5–6.

U.S. Chemical Safety Board (CSB). (2008, September). *Investigation Report: Little General Store—Propane Explosion.* U.S. Chemical Safety and Hazard Investigation Board. Retrieved July 29, 2012, from http://www.csb.gov/assets/document/CSBFinalReportLittleGeneral.pdf.

Heyman, D. (2007, February 1). Propane blast hits a small town hard. *New York Times,* p. 19.

Madsen, P. (2009). These lives will not be lost in vain: Organizational learning from disaster in U.S. coal mining. *Organization Science, 20*(5), 861–875.

Urbina, I. (2007, January 31). Four killed in gas explosion near West Virginia resort. *New York Times,* p. 12.

Introduction

Crises are the ultimate result of many actions and inactions. Some are acts of God, but human decision making and action or inaction are usually responsible for most of the crises we encounter. All of these are unexpected events that can produce serious negative repercussions. Any organization can be confronted with and should be prepared for a "what-if scenario," what we commonly call a crisis. As stated in Chapter 1, a crisis is an event that has a low probability of occurring, but, should it occur, can have a vastly negative effect on the organization.

One of the most prominent examples of a crisis in recent history is the terrorist attacks on September 11, 2001, on New York City's World Trade Center buildings and the Pentagon in Washington, D.C. However, terrorism represents only a small component of the potential crisis events that can hit an organization. Other types of crises include fires, natural disasters, industrial accidents, workplace violence, extortion attempts, product or company boycotts, and negative publicity due to outsourcing jobs to other countries. Crises related to "information age" activities, including computer system sabotage, copyright infringement, and identity theft and counterfeiting, are common. In addition, the popularity of social media can turn almost any negative event into an organizational crisis under the right circumstances.

This chapter begins our study of crisis events by examining what we call the *crisis management landscape.* Important trends are identified that are occurring on a widespread basis throughout the global environment. In our discussion, we overview and link these trends to crisis management.

The Crisis Management Landscape

Six trends in the crisis management landscape, ranging from less to more controllable, are identified in Figure 2.1. Trends on the left side of the figure are less subject to strategic planning, while those on the right side of the figure can often be managed with effective strategic planning. They also shift upward as they move from left to right, indicating that the internal environment becomes an increasingly stronger factor in the origin of these crises events. Our discussion begins with the transboundary nature of crises and then proceeds to the right of the figure, ending with a discussion on the movement toward globalization and outsourcing.

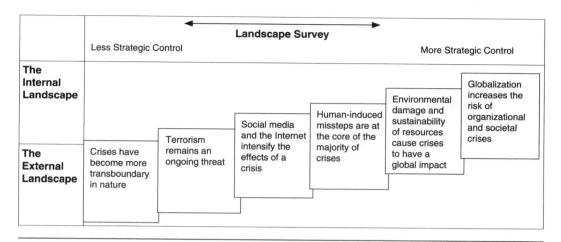

Figure 2.1 Trends in the Crisis Management Landscape

Crises Have Become More Transboundary in Nature

Typically, we think of an organizational crisis as having distinct geographical boundaries. An industrial accident, a fire, or an unexpected loss of production capability can render a company useless meeting the needs of its customers. But today's fragile supply chains that focus on lean management and global suppliers mean an organizational crisis can be transboundary in nature. For example, the 2011 tsunami that hit Japan interrupted supply chains all over the world, particularly in the automotive industry. Disruptions were most acute among Japanese firms like Toyota, Nissan, and Honda, but the effects were even felt at carmakers based in the United States and other parts of the world (Shappell, 2012). A crisis that affects stakeholders in multiple countries is called a *transboundary crisis.* These are especially challenging to manage because of their complexity.

Crisis scholar Arjen Boin (2009) maintains that transboundary crises have four characteristics: (1) they cross geographical boundaries, (2) they cross functional boundaries, (3) they cross traditional time barriers, and (4) they involve a tightly woven web of critical infrastructures.

1. A Transboundary Crisis Crosses Geographical Boundaries

Transboundary crises transcend geographical barriers that extend far outside the confines of a single organization. For example, in August 2003, a seemingly insignificant power utility malfunction was mishandled by authorities in Ohio, culminating into a major blackout affecting millions of citizens in the northeastern United States as well as the Canadian province of Ontario (Lagadec, 2009). Severe weather and natural disasters can occur in one part of the world and wreak havoc in another part because of the impact on supply chains. A pandemic such as the SARS (severe acute respiratory syndrome) epidemic can interrupt international travel, as it did in late 2002 and 2003. Indeed, this affected the authors of this book, who were preparing to take crisis management students to China, only to have their plans cancelled due to a crisis: the threat of a widespread flu outbreak.

The occurrence of natural disasters is also a function of geography. Earthquakes, for example, occur near fault zones. In the United States, active fault zones exist in California and along the New Madrid seismic zone, an area that encompasses southeastern Missouri, northeastern Arkansas, and western Tennessee. Unusual weather patterns such as typhoons and cyclones can be especially devastating in developing countries. In these areas, fatalities can be especially high. A tsunami is another natural phenomenon that can have widespread impact. On December 26, 2004, an earthquake off the coast of Sumatra (Indonesia) triggered a tsunami that killed nearly 250,000 people in South Asia (Cheung & Law, 2006).

A transboundary crisis can affect important resources over a more localized geographic area. In the United States, consider the impact of Hurricane Ike on the highly automated refinery industry in the Gulf of Mexico, a region responsible for about 20 percent of the nation's oil-producing capacity (Lee & Thurman, 2008). When the storm hit in August 2008, refineries "shut in" operations to minimize damage to oil-producing facilities. After the storm passed, production slowly resumed, but not fast enough to offset gas shortages in major cities such as Nashville, Tennessee; Atlanta, Georgia; and Charlotte, North Carolina. The effects of the shortages were intensified by panic buying and high prices.

2. A Transboundary Crisis Crosses Functional Boundaries

Transboundary crises can cross functional boundaries and threaten multiple life-sustaining systems and infrastructures (Ansell, Boin, & Keller, 2010). Put another way, the responsibility for managing the crisis may rest with multiple organizations, some of which may not be closely related. For example, both British Petroleum (BP) and various U.S. government agencies managed the BP oil spill in the Gulf of Mexico. Likewise, the response to Hurricane Katrina was managed by multiple stakeholders in both the private sector—those businesses that sustained damage—as well as government agencies at the local, state, and federal levels. What makes the crisis response difficult is that stakeholder response is often loosely coupled with other stakeholders (Ansell et al., 2010), making coordination more complex.

Transboundary crises can also consist of a "package of disasters" (Green, 2004, p. 61), such as the combination of a severe weather event and a natural disaster. What is commonly referred to as the 2011 tsunami strike in Japan was actually a trio of disasters consisting of an earthquake, a tsunami, and a nuclear calamity. Developing countries are especially vulnerable to these types of crises, with the result usually involving a large number of fatalities (Spillan, Parnell, & Mayoro, 2011). For example, a civil war may be followed by a famine, or a natural disaster may instigate a flood of refugees as people are forced to leave their ravished homes. The wars in Mozambique illustrate how an already damaged country fared very poorly when hit with heavy rains and flooding in 2000 (Green, 2004). Developed countries such as the United States have not seen such high rates of casualties from these multiple disasters, although Hurricane Katrina was an example of a package of crises with many fatalities. In this example, the hurricane was followed by the breakdown of law and order and by general government incompetence across a number of functional boundaries.

3. A Transboundary Crisis Crosses Time Boundaries

Transboundary crises do not have definite beginning or ending points. Instead, they can have deep roots in their origins and linger for many years in their effects. Global climate change, oil spills, and the 9/11 attacks on the World Trade Center are examples of how time is blurred in a transboundary crisis (Ansell et al., 2010).

One of the themes of this book is the extensive impact social media can have on a crisis. Indeed, many crises may have origins in a rather obscure, unknown event that becomes public via an outlet such as YouTube. Long after the crisis appears to have ended, remnants can still be played and viewed by the public on YouTube or other websites. Such is the case with singer Dave Carroll's now-famous *United Breaks Guitars* video. Carroll and his band were flying from Canada to the United States in March 2008 when they observed United Airlines baggage handlers throwing their guitars while waiting for their connecting flight in Chicago. Carroll's guitar was damaged and he sought compensation from United Airlines. The airline refused, prompting him to write a song about his dilemma and post it on YouTube. The incident proved to be a huge public embarrassment for the airline (Grégoire, Tripp, & Legoux, 2011). This example is indeed a transboundary crisis, because the YouTube video can still be viewed worldwide years after the original event occurred.

4. A Transboundary Crisis Involves a Tightly Woven Web of Critical Infrastructures

Much of contemporary society consists of interlinking critical infrastructures. For example, the power grid that provides electricity for parts of the United States and Canada is tightly networked (Wachtendorf, 2009). As previously noted, a malfunction in Ohio can affect the power supply in Ontario. Perhaps the most notable example of a potential crisis that illustrated this web of critical infrastructures is the now-famous Y2K computer bug. In the early days of computer technology, programmers would save valuable space by using only two digits for the year. For example, instead of using four digits for 1999, the code would simply read 99. The Y2K bug concern occurred because a computer that rolled over to 2000 (which would read 00) might inadvertently read the date as 1900 (which would also read 00). A wide variety of speculation existed as to how the computer might function in such an instance, and many people believed that computers might produce strange and inaccurate results (Stallard, 1999).

During the years leading up to 2000, a vast amount of work was completed to correct this potential problem. In many instances, companies used the Y2K crisis as a chance to completely upgrade their operating systems. The Y2K bug proved to be a nonevent, however, thanks in part to the effort invested in preparing for the worst. However, the cultural phenomenon that was occurring concurrently, particularly in the United States (Schaefer, 2004), was anything but a nonevent. Speculation was brewing in the late 1990s that the 2000 rollover would produce worldwide catastrophes. Although they did not materialize, this example illustrates how computer systems have created a tightly woven global web of critical infrastructures.

Terrorism Remains an Ongoing Threat

Terrorism has always been a threat to entities throughout the world. Historically, terrorist acts were motivated by political ideals rather than religious ones (Pedahzur, Eubank, & Weinberg, 2002). Since the early 1990s, however, terrorism has changed on at least three fronts. First, the number of victims per attack has increased, because suicide bombers in particular are able to move into crowded areas before detonating their explosives, thus increasing the number of casualties exponentially. Second, religious extremists are behind the majority of the assaults (Perliger, Pedahzur, & Zalmanovitch, 2005). Finally, the targets of terrorist attacks are extending around the globe, not just in traditionally troubled areas such as the Middle East. In the United States, for example, the 1993 bombing of the World Trade Center signaled that terrorism with Middle Eastern ties had struck close to home. Because the perpetrator was a U.S. citizen, the 1995 bombing of the Alfred P. Murrah Federal Building in Oklahoma City destroyed Americans' long-held notion that terrorism originates only from abroad. The innocence of the United States had been violated. The events of September 11, 2001, reinforced the continued threat of terrorism from abroad.

The Geographic Factor in Terrorism

Modern terrorists often strike in urban areas because they represent the financial, political, and cultural centers of the state (Perliger et al., 2005). Striking an urban target inflicts a psychological as well as a physical blow to the local area and can maximize the number of casualties that can be inflicted with a single blow. Given the high concentration of businesses and government offices in urban areas, crisis management plans should include terrorist contingencies. Industries like destination tourism are most vulnerable.

Destination tourism is affected when an event occurs in a region of the world that causes the number of travelers to visit that region decline. A number of events, such as wars, localized diseases, and terrorist attacks, can affect tourism in a certain area (Glaesser, 2005). Terrorism puts geographic restrictions on a region, even if the region is relatively otherwise peaceful. For example, the country of Jordan is relatively safe, but because of its Middle East location it is subject to variations in tourism revenue (Ali & Ali, 2010).

Managers and employees who were not previously convinced of the serious nature of terrorism changed their views after the attacks of September 11, 2001. In one day, the need for organizations to anticipate, prepare for, and respond to these potential events was made clear (Greenberg, Clair, & Maclean, 2002). For some businesses, the attack resulted not only in the tragic loss of a substantial number of employees but also a loss of key facilities and data (Greenberg, 2002). Many organizations decimated by this attack never reopened. While the companies that were located in the World Trade Center's Twin Towers were affected directly, thousands of other businesses were affected indirectly. Supply chains were interrupted, key information networks were destroyed, clients were lost, and business travel—at least in the short run—was seriously curtailed. In fact, the events of September 11 caused the worst disruption of worldwide tourism since World War II and triggered a temporary slowdown in the world's economy (Ali & Ali, 2010). Clearly, terrorism strikes at a region physically in fatalities and property destruction and indirectly in disruptions to the commerce.

Preparing for Terrorism

Preparing for terrorist attacks is not an easy task for either the small business owner or the large corporate management team. Indeed, most organizations in developed nations depend on government entities to protect them from terrorist attacks. Following the September 11 terrorist attack on the World Trade Center, the U.S. government created the first Department of Homeland Security. Scholarly research on the effectiveness of combating terrorism followed, including three key journals. An online journal, the *Journal of Homeland Security and Emergency Management,* was launched in 2003 (Nickerson, 2011). In 2008, *Critical Studies on Terrorism* was begun, and one year later, *Behavioral Sciences of Terrorism and Political Aggression* commenced. Because terrorism is unlikely to disappear, crisis management teams should prepare for this threat, understanding that it could intensify in the years to come.

Social Media and the Internet Intensify the Effects of a Crisis

The Internet is closely related to organizational crises in two ways: it can facilitate or it can even trigger one (González-Herrero & Smith, 2008). The Internet can facilitate a crisis by permitting individuals to spread negative information about an organization rapidly and over a broad geographical region at little or no expense. Consumers can discuss their negative experiences with products and services on discussion forums, in YouTube videos, and on blogs, all forms of social media. Private individuals and groups have established websites dedicated to disseminating negative information about major firms, including such sites as www.allstateinsurancesucks .com, www.walmartwatch.com, and www.ihatestarbucks.com.

One example that illustrates the power of social media concerned Procter & Gamble (P&G) and its diaper product Dry Max Pampers. The product was introduced in March 2010 as "driest and thinnest" nappy ever. A number of parents complained about the product via blogs, claiming it was causing their babies to develop a rash. A Facebook page with 6,000 followers appeared and claimed children were developing "chemical burns" from the product (Birchall, 2010). P&G was quickly thrown into crisis management mode and was soon inviting mothers to their corporate headquarters in Cincinnati, Ohio, to discuss their concerns. The extent to which the product caused harm is not the only issue. From a crisis perspective, if one consumer believes the product caused the problem and communicates it via social media, others may agree, even without consulting a medical opinion (Birchall, 2010).

One aspect of the Internet that enhances its ability to facilitate a crisis is the lack of oversight on of what is presented online. This occurs because editorial filters that are traditionally associated with print journalism do not exist in cyberspace (Bernstein, 2006). Put differently, the gatekeeper function that exists in traditional mass media does not exist in the online world (González-Herrero & Smith, 2010). Magazines, journals, and newspapers have some degree of oversight over the material that is printed in their venues. Opinions, whims, and downright anger can be expressed on some Internet sites, however, and in real time. As a result, organizations are urged to monitor the Web regularly to stay abreast of public sentiment (Ziemnowicz, Harrison, & Crandall, 2011). Some companies such as Southwest Airlines and Dell have specialists who monitor bloggers and social networks and respond as needed (Conlin, 2007).

The Internet can also be the trigger point for a crisis, one example of which is the existence of a highly motivated hacker community (González-Herrero & Smith, 2008; Kovoor-Misra & Misra, 2007). Several types of hacking can occur. A denial-of-service attack causes the organization's website either to slow down or to stop functioning altogether. Such an attack can lead to a sizable loss of revenue, similar to shutting down the store for the duration of the attack. Hacking can also occur in the form of security breaches in which customer database information is stolen, and ultimately to identity theft, a crisis that can create monumental problems for both the company and its customers. Another malicious attack occurs when a copycat website emerges that mimics a legitimate organization's website (González-Herrero & Smith, 2010). Such websites can cause unsuspecting customers to send money and private credit card information to scammers who keep the cash but do not deliver the goods.

An alternate trigger point caused by the Internet occurs when a website malfunctions for a technical reason. When service is not available, customers cannot place their orders and the company's revenue stream is interrupted. The impact can be significant for brick-and-mortar businesses, but can even be devastating for organizations that rely solely on Internet revenue.

Human-Induced Missteps Are at the Core of the Majority of Crises

Since 1994, the Institute for Crisis Management has been tracking the types of crises that strike organizations. The consulting firm's 2010 annual report noted that 50 percent of all reported crises originated with management and 32 percent were initiated by employees (Institute for Crisis Management, 2011). Corporate scandals, mismanagement, and other forms of white-collar crime contribute to the high percentage of management-induced crises. What is disturbing about these findings is that the majority of these crises need not occur in the first place. Unlike externally induced crises such as hurricanes or natural disasters, human-induced crises often emanate from poor examples set by top management (Carroll & Buchholtz, 2003; Hartley, 1993). When lower-level employees are not sure how to react in a certain situation, they look to their leaders for guidance. Hence, problems can arise when ethics is lacking at the top, leading to the spread of crises throughout the organization. Because this area of crisis management is complex, Chapter 10 of this book is devoted to the ethical implications of organizational crises. The remainder of this section examines human-induced crises in terms of workplace violence, human error and normal accident theory, and sloppy management.

Workplace Violence

Human-induced crises include various forms of workplace misbehavior. Griffin and Lopez (2005, p. 988) coined the term "bad behavior" to refer to those actions that are potentially injurious to the organization and/or its members. They further classified bad behavior into four categories: deviance, aggression, antisocial behavior, and violence. *Workplace deviance* includes behavior that violates the accepted norms of the organization. Organizational deviance is composed of actions taken against the company and includes leaving early, wasting resources, stealing, and sabotaging equipment. Interpersonal deviance is directed toward another individual in the workplace and can include verbal abuse, gossiping, and sexual harassment (Diefendorff & Mehta, 2007). *Workplace aggression* is assertive and threatening behavior that is directed toward a person or an object but is non-physical in nature. Consider a terminated worker who verbally threatens his supervisor. Management should always be concerned about verbal threats because they can signal a potential physical assault. *Antisocial behavior* is a set of behaviors that can produce physical, economic, psychological, or emotional harm (Robinson & O'Leary, 1998). This behavior is manifested when an employee is not sociable with others and/or is hostile and disruptive to organizational norms (Griffin & Lopez, 2005). Once the behavior becomes physical, it is considered *workplace violence* (O'Leary-Kelly, Griffin, & Glew, 1996).

Of the behaviors described by Griffin and Lopez, workplace violence generates the most attention in the field of crisis management. In recent years, there has been an abundance of research on workplace violence. A personality profile of a potential killer in the workplace has been identified, new security procedures have been enacted in organizations, and better screening devices are in place to identify applicants who may be prone to violence. Nevertheless, workplace violence continues to be a problem in the crisis management landscape, as a number of such events have occurred across the nation. One of the more common scenarios is for a disgruntled or recently terminated employee to return to the workplace and seek revenge on a former supervisor. Unfortunately, such scenarios often result in multiple fatalities.

Human Error and the Normal Accident Theory Problem

In addition to unethical decisions and the "bad behaviors" described, human-induced crises also include employee or operator errors, which are a major contributor to industrial accidents. Errors of this kind occur when the work environment is both complex and "tightly coupled." Charles Perrow (1999) suggested that such a scenario can lead to a "normal accident." Tight coupling can be understood by considering the interdependence that exists among departments, units, teams, and other groups within an organization. The higher the interdependence (i.e., the more the departments depend on each other in order to function), the more tightly the departments are coupled. If the departments can exist within the organization but are not highly interdependent, then they are loosely coupled. For example, in a restaurant, the service staff and the cooking staff are tightly coupled because one group cannot adequately function without the other. If the chef and several cooks were suddenly to become ill, a major crisis would ensue, and the restaurant might have to close, albeit temporarily. However, the relationship between the cooks and the cleaning staff of dishwashers is more loosely coupled. The restaurant can survive if there is a shortage of dishwashers, even if the cooks have to take over this function temporarily.

This example considered the notion of interdependence within an organization. However, the concept of coupling also involves entities outside of the organization, a phenomenon that has increased with the notion of partnerships and strategic alliances. Consider that some of the organization's suppliers are more tightly coupled with the company than others. Tightly coupled suppliers must be available to make regular deliveries with the full order and in a timely fashion if the business is to perform well. In a restaurant, food suppliers are tightly coupled to the organization, whereas suppliers of paper and cleaning goods, although important, are more loosely coupled. A crisis can develop when an entity that is tightly coupled, either within the organization or outside of it, is temporarily incapacitated. The other groups aligned with that unit are now also part of the crisis. For example, in a just-in-time (JIT) work system, if a major supplier cannot make the delivery, the assembly line will shut down because there is very little slack built into the system. If the delay continues, the company may have to suspend operations temporarily. This is not a hypothetical example, but one that plays itself out every time there is a substantial disruption in a supply chain. Major industrial fires, earthquakes, terrorism, wars, and tsunamis can initiate a crisis of this sort because these events can disrupt supply chains. Indeed, in today's JIT-oriented society, supply chains are vulnerable due to the tight coupling that exists among supply chain partners (Zsidisin, Ragatz, & Melnyk, 2005).

Perrow's original contributions to normal accident theory were aimed at addressing technologies that create both complexity and tight coupling for the user who must operate these technologies. In such a situation, an employee error can create a major crisis. Perrow (1990) believed that user errors of this sort were inevitable in certain facilities, such as chemical and nuclear power plants (Choo, 2008). The March 28, 1979, near-meltdown of a reactor at the Three Mile Island nuclear power facility outside of Harrisburg, Pennsylvania, illustrated how a normal accident might pan out (Hopkins, 2001). In this incident, nuclear plant operators were at a loss to explain both what triggered the accident and what to do about it (Barton, 2001). The plant met the conditions that Perrow had outlined; it was complex and tightly coupled. The sheer complexity of the facility made it difficult to identify actions needed to remedy the problem. The plant was tightly coupled in that changes in one subsystem would affect the rest of the system as well. In fact, one of the initial means used by operators to control the rising temperature in the reactor core was to shut down high-pressure cooling pumps (Hopkins, 2001). Ironically, leaving pressure pumps on would have alleviated the problem, a tight coupling phenomenon. Although this example has its roots in technology, it is also a case study on how human error can intensify a crisis.

Sloppy Management

Previous to Perrow's normal accident theory, Turner (1978) maintained that human-induced crises are caused by what he called "sloppy management." Whereas Perrow (1990) blamed human error on technological factors, Turner maintained that it is ultimately caused by poor management and the systems in which they function. One of the characteristics of sloppy management is the failure to heed warnings from previous problems (Hopkins, 2001). In other words, managers are presented with warning signs, but they fail to act upon them, which ultimately leads to a crisis. The September 11 terrorist attack on the World Trade Center in New York City has been framed in this light (9/11 Commission, 2004). Sloppy management has also been linked with groupthink, a phenomenon in which poor decisions are made by groups because of a desire to appear united and cohesive (Janis, 1982). In fact, failing to heed warnings can be a by-product of groupthink because nobody in the group wants to be viewed as an alarmist.

Choo's (2008) work offers three explanations as to why warnings are not heeded by management: epistemic blind spots, risk denial, and structural impediments. An epistemic blind spot occurs when warnings are not acted on because the information does not fit an existing frame of reference. Put another way, information is selectively interpreted to fit what we generally accept as true. For example, prior to Enron's bankruptcy in 2001, Enron's board evaded the warnings that were surfacing about the means by which the firm was accounting for its assets and holdings on its financial statements. The board's perception, instead, was that this type of disclosure was just a normal part of conducting business (Choo, 2008).

Unlike blind spots where the warning is completely missed, risk denial is a mind-set that acknowledges the reality of the warning, but the norms and culture of the organization dictate that no response is necessary. This is one of the most perplexing matters related to crisis management because so many of the crises that we study could have been avoided if the appropriate decision maker(s) had acted on clear warnings. A common theme that seems to run through the minds of many managers is the "It can't happen to us" mentality. Thus, the top management team thinks its organization is impermeable and crises happen only to other firms.

The third item, structural impediments, prevents management from acting on warnings because there are structural imperfections within the organization. Unlike risk denial, when the warnings are acknowledged but not considered important, structural impediments hinder warnings from being addressed at all, even when management believes they are legitimate. Choo (2008) cites the example of a five-year-old boy who was admitted to a hospital for elective neurosurgery. Despite the surgery going well, the boy developed complications and seizures. Unfortunately, there was a structural impediment in that no single physician was designated to be responsible. The patient care was established with a research physician, a neurological resident, a neurosurgeon, and an attending physician at the hospital, but nobody took ownership of the case (Snook & Connor, 2005). Eventually, the boy's condition worsened to the point where he stopped breathing. In this example, everyone agreed that the warnings were serious, but the structure of the situation meant that nobody was really in charge, a prescription for a crisis.

Environmental Damage and Sustainability of Resources Cause Crises to Have a Global Impact

Two separate but related issues can result in environmental concerns. Sustainability seeks economic growth while ensuring that natural resources are available for the next generation of users (Stead & Stead, 2004). Sustainability is a trend that is to be encouraged in the business environment. But environmental damage due to an accident or deliberate exploitation is to be discouraged. While this may appear obvious, the reality of how many companies, particularly in developing countries, operate seems to contradict what should be clear: Do not destroy the environment needlessly.

Prior to April 2010, the *Exxon Valdez* oil spill was the proverbial poster child for an oil company's worst environmental and public relations nightmare. In 1989, the *Exxon Valdez* tanker hit a reef in Alaska's Prince William Sound, spilling approximately 10.5 million gallons of oil. Although there was no loss of human life, the loss of animal and bird life was extensive, and the negative press was daunting. The company's untested crisis management plan assumed that a spill could be contained in five hours. Unfortunately, due to bureaucratic and weather delays, efforts to contain the spill were not implemented for two days (Hartley, 1993). The onslaught of media coverage was brutal, putting Exxon in a negative light throughout the world.

Unfortunately, BP surpassed Exxon in terms of severity on April 20, 2010, when its deep-water oil well was in the final stages of being capped. A surge of gas emerged from the seabed and blew past the containment apparatus that was supposed to suppress it. The resulting blast killed 11 workers and caused the largest offshore oil spill in U.S. history (Crooks, Pfeifer, & McNulty, 2010). The accident and recovery efforts were quickly known worldwide, and BP remained in the headlines for months afterward. During the capping of the oil spill, viewers on the Internet could watch in real time as efforts were made to stop the flow of oil, a phenomenon that reinforced the power of the Internet and social media.

Some may think that environmental crises only occur in large manufacturing companies or those that process oil. However, service industries are also under scrutiny. Fast-food giant McDonald's found itself in the middle of an environmental quagmire in the early 1990s. The problem was that excessive packaging of menu items was bulky and a potential landfill problem. Fortunately, the company met voluntarily with members of the Environmental Defense Fund (EDF) over a period of a year to discuss what could be done (Sethi & Steidlmeier, 1997). The result was a major revamping of packaging practices that not only reduced the Styrofoam used but also placed McDonald's in a favorable light among environmentalists. What could have been a potential public relations crisis was handled proactively by the company, with a cost savings to the firm as an added benefit (Sethi & Steidlmeier, 1997). This is a critical issue for large firms like McDonalds because industry leaders tend to be targets of efforts designed to promote an environmental agenda.

On a more positive note, sustainable development has been a familiar buzzword within business and government entities since the early 1990s. Proceeding with economic growth while maintaining the integrity and resources of the environment are necessary for the well-being of local societies at the micro level and humankind at the macro level. Two scenarios exist involving crises and sustainable development (Crandall & Mensah, 2008). First, a sudden environmental crisis can impair the sustainability of certain resources in the long term. For example, a crisis event such as an oil spill can negatively influence the long-term survivability of the seafood industry in the affected area. The 2010 BP oil spill in the Gulf of Mexico and the 1989 *Exxon Valdez* spill off the coast of Alaska illustrate this scenario and depict events that are both sudden and unexpected. In the second scenario, the events occur slowly in a more organized fashion. For example, the steady growth of a firm (and on a larger scale, a society) can gradually deplete renewable resources faster than they are being replenished. It is these slower types of economic growth that are of special importance in sustainability. Water, air, and land are noticeable resources that have been used negatively—depleted or contaminated—by various businesses, industries, and even societies.

Sustainable development is likely to become even more newsworthy in the future as continued attention is focused on the depletion of renewable resources. Companies and even countries that are perceived to be detractors to sustainable development will be viewed in a negative light, which can lead to an array of public relations crises. Emerging countries in particular have been the target of criticism because of their ability to hinder sustainability efforts (Parnell, Spillan, & Lester, 2010). One country in particular that has seen its share of negative press is the People's Republic of China, where two concerns have been repeatedly voiced concerning environmental practices. First, its pollution is crossing its borders into Japan and Korea in the form of acid rain. Second, China's inability to enforce basic environmental regulations has resulted in lower production costs for Chinese manufacturers when compared to competitors in other countries. Critics charge that such actions put millions of people out of work and depress wages in other nations that have more stringent regulations (Navarro, 2007).

Concern for the environment remains a high priority in the crisis management landscape. Companies must not only work to prevent environmental damage, but they should also portray to the public their efforts to be champions of sustainable development. Indeed, companies are evaluated to a large extent in terms of how much they support or ignore sustainability management (Coombs, 2010). Even today, McDonald's provides leaflets in their restaurants (on recycled paper) that outline what they are doing to use environmental resources wisely. In addition, municipalities, states, and entire countries will need to do their share to protect the environment and ensure that resources are available for future generations. Indeed, the cost of damaging the environment needlessly while not promoting sustainability will create a twofold crisis. In the short run, a public relations crisis results in which external stakeholders view the offending entity negatively. In the long run there is a deeper problem: damage to the environment and the cavalier attitude that resources exist only for the whims and consumption of the current generation.

Globalization Increases the Risk of Organizational and Societal Crises

Globalization refers to the development of economic interdependence among nations. Its existence is undeniable, although debates abound concerning the extent to which its effects are positive or negative. In practice, globalization creates both positive and negative outcomes. One conclusion is clear: globalization has created an environment in which crisis events are more likely to occur.

Global outsourcing is a strategy associated with the proliferation of globalization. This term refers to contracting out a firm's noncore, non–revenue-producing activities to organizations in other nations primarily to reduce costs. Many consumers and activists have become increasingly disturbed about job losses that occur when a firm moves a production facility abroad or a retailer stocks its shelves with imported products (Ansberry & Aeppel, 2003). A number of American firms have closed production facilities in the United States and opened new ones in Mexico, China, India, and other countries where labor costs are substantially lower (Dean, 2004; Luhnow, 2004; Millman, 2004; Morse, 2004). For example, China, Mexico, Honduras, Bangladesh, and El Salvador account for a substantial amount of imported apparel in the United States. Analysts also suggest that differences in wages could spark increased global outsourcing in a broad array of professional and technical fields, such as architecture, medical transcribing, and accounting (Buckman, 2004; Maher, 2004).

In the discussion that follows, we focus primarily on the impact that global outsourcing has on causing crisis events. The scope of the coverage looks at outsourcing's relation to operational control problems, fragile supply chains, reputational crises, and a new development, the movement toward bringing production back to the host country, a process known as *reshoring*.

Operational Control Problems

When an organization chooses to allow business functions to be completed by other organizations, it inevitably loses some control over these functions. In addition, when outsourcing involves partner firms across borders, the organization must contend with the political, legal, and other international influences associated with its partners. Union Carbide's Bhopal, India, disaster was one of the first crisis events to illustrate what can happen when partners in other countries do not maintain the same standards as those in the home company. In 1984, gas leaked from a methyl isocyanate (MIC) tank at a Union Carbide plant in Bhopal, initially killing more than 2,500 people and injuring another 300,000. The plant was jointly owned and operated by parties in India and in the United States (49.1 percent was owned by the Indian stakeholders, the rest by Union Carbide in the United States). Inadequate safety practices, equipment failures, and careless operating procedures contributed to the disaster, which was caused when water accidentally entered Tank 610, which held the deadly gas (Hartley, 1993).

Herein lay the heart of the dilemma: outsourcing relinquishes control of the production of a product (Zsidisin, Meinyk, & Ragatz, 2005). This can be beneficial when the outsourcer has expertise in the field and is better equipped to perform a particular task, but one of the dilemmas of any outsourcing relationship is the potential gap between the quality that is expected and the quality that is provided. When cultural differences between partners create different expectations of quality, this gap becomes problematic. Clarifying specifications in purchasing contracts can reduce—but not always eliminate—this problem of quality. There are other issues that may not be addressed in an outsourcing relationship, such as how well the outsourced facility is maintained in terms of cleanliness and equipment functioning abilities. In other words, purchasing contracts usually look at the final product, but not necessarily the functional capabilities of the production facility.

The accident at Bhopal illustrates how a push for globalization and outsourcing can lead to a devastating crisis. Safety standards were not being met in the manufacturing of the deadly MIC gas. Control of these standards and equipment maintenance at the plant were in the hands of the Indian owners, under an elaborate arrangement called Union Carbide (India) Limited (Sethi & Steidlmeier, 1997). One might liken this situation to giving a toddler a loaded gun. As business ethicist Robert Hartley (1993) states, "A laissez-faire decentralization is not appropriate in underdeveloped countries when safety and environmental degradation are at stake" (p. 156).

The Problem of Fragile Supply Chains

There are two subtrends that have been occurring in the world's supply chains. The first is global outsourcing; the second is the movement toward lean management and its accompanying emphasis on leaner supply chains and single sourcing (Crandall, Crandall, & Chen, 2010). Both trends make supply chains more vulnerable to external shocks that can interrupt a firm's supply lines. "Specifically, today's lean supply chains are becoming increasingly—'fragile'—that is, less able to deal with shocks and disruptions that can have a significant, if not catastrophic, impact on the firm" (Zsidisin, Ragatz, & Melnyk, 2005, p. 46). Because companies are carrying less inventory, interruptions in the supply chain due to a crisis event can grind production to a standstill.

Single sourcing is another important practice. Unfortunately, when a company's key vendor is hit with a crisis, the companies it supplies will be affected as well. The same is true with vendors that supply daily deliveries of product. An interruption in the delivery schedule can halt production immediately. For a dramatic example of the impact of a crisis on a single supplier, consider the fire that took out the main production facilities of Philips Electronics in early 2000. Philips supplies radio-frequency chips (RFCs) to cellular phone makers. The crisis caused a $400 million revenue loss for the telecommunications company, Ericsson, and eventually led to its exit from the cellular telephone industry altogether (Rice & Caniato, 2003).

Cisco, the San Jose, California–based provider of networking and communication systems, appears to understand the risks of supply chain disruptions, because 95 percent of its production is outsourced (Harrington & O'Connor, 2009). Because most of its supply chain is global in nature, the company has adopted a program to move away from single sourcing (a common practice with many companies) to multiple sourcing. Indeed, such planning was important when on May 12, 2008, a 7.9 magnitude earthquake hit the Sichuan province of China, a region at the heart of Cisco's supply chain for that region of Asia.

Reputational Crises

A number of American firms—including Nike and Wal-Mart—have been fighting crisis events of their own, such as negative publicity and boycotts resulting from their ties to countries where labor costs are much lower. Wal-Mart critic Arindrajit Dube suggested that Wal-Mart's relatively low wages emanating from its promotion of outsourcing result in an annual wage loss in the retail sector of almost $5 billion. Hollywood's Robert Greenwald produced a movie about the giant retailer—WAL-MART: *The High Cost of Low Price*—chronicling the plight of an Ohio-based hardware store when Wal-Mart moved to town (York, 2005). The net effect of this sentiment against Wal-Mart is unclear, and not all press has been negative. As Jason Furman of New York University notes, Wal-Mart's economic benefits cannot be ignored; the retailer saves its customers an estimated $200 billion or more on food and other items every year (Mallaby, 2005).

Public opposition to outsourcing can harm public sentiment and weaken customer loyalty for firms directly or indirectly involved. Wal-Mart is often the brunt of criticism from politicians, activists, and union leaders. Detractors, for example, contend that the retailer giant's aggressive negotiating tactics ultimately decimate American manufacturers and send American jobs overseas (Fishman, 2006). Some critics charge that Wal-Mart seeks to destroy small businesses in the communities in which it operates (Edid, 2005; Quinn, 2000). Others, however, cite positive influences, noting such factors as job creation and the benefits of low prices to consumers (Etter, 2005; York, 2005).

Outsourcing from firms in the United States has resulted in a substantial number of U.S. jobs going overseas. Consider the case of India. General Electric's (GE) Jack Welch was instrumental in one of the earliest partnerships with the populous Asian nation. Welch first met with the Indian government in 1989, and GE formed a joint venture to develop and market medical equipment with Wipro Ltd. in 1990. By the mid-1990s, much of GE's software development and maintenance activities had been shifted to Indian companies. GE Capital Services (GECIS) established the first international call center in India in 1999. GE sold 60 percent of GECIS for $500 million in 2004, freeing it to compete against IBM, Accenture, and Indian firms. In 2005, India received more than $17 billion from foreign corporations seeking to outsource a variety of jobs (Solomon & Kranhold, 2005). The number of legal outsourcing firms in India has grown from 40 in 2005 to more than 140 at the end of 2009. Revenue at India's legal outsourcing firms is expected to grow to more than $1 billion by 2014 (Timmons, 2010). The argument for such outsourcing is simple: reduced operational costs. According to one analyst, the cost of developing a particular legal database for contracts might be about $60,000 in the United States, but only about $5,000 in India (Bellman & Koppel, 2005).

Of course, it is inappropriate to note the job losses associated with outsourcing from a given nation without also considering job gains that come from outsourcing that occurs in other nations. Nonetheless, the outsourcing debate illustrates how strategic decision making can later lead to an organizational crisis. The pressure to lower costs is overwhelming. Global competition has forced many businesses to look for ways to cut costs, and global outsourcing is one such option. But there is a dark side to this decision that can backfire on the organization: negative publicity. Entire books have been written on the subject, and emotions often run high because outsourcing does lead to a loss of jobs, at least in the short run. Television commentator Lou Dobbs has charged that corporate greed is behind the job losses because it is the company that purposely chooses to outsource jobs overseas (Dobbs, 2004). While it is convenient and simplistic to invoke the "corporate greed" argument, the reality is more complex. In the long run, social critics must acknowledge that consumer demand is what generates revenues, and consumers want low prices (Shell, 2010). While it may sound noble and patriotic to retain jobs in a country like the United States, these jobs will not exist if the company cannot survive in the long run. To do so, cost cutting must occur because consumers demand low prices and competition is intense; this results in strategic decisions in favor of global outsourcing. Hence, like it or not, global outsourcing is a trend that is utilized to ensure long-term company survival based on the consumer's desire for low-cost goods.

Some firms have attempted to avoid the publicity crises associated with the outsourcing controversy. A number of companies have become more sensitive to the public disapproval that outsourcing can bring to their companies or organizations. An interesting case occurred in 2004 when e-Loan announced that customers would be given a choice to have their loan applications processed in Delhi, India, or Dallas, Texas. Although Dallas was considered the more patriotic choice for American consumers, it would also take two days longer than the Delhi option (Drucker & Brown, 2004). Hence, the outsourcing debate remains a key consideration for consumers and organizations alike, and its potential for creating publicity-oriented crises should not be underestimated. However, despite the enthusiasm for global outsourcing among many businesses, there are some who are viewing the cost factor in a different light, as the next section illustrates.

The Reshoring Movement

Within the external landscape, there is a movement afoot to bring manufacturing back to the United States from countries where it is currently outsourced, a process called *reshoring*. This movement acknowledges the weaknesses of the current offshoring model, but with one significant addition: The dollar costs of offshoring are not always calculated well when managers make their decisions to move production overseas to begin with. When one considers the declining value of the dollar in the late 2000s and early 2010s, it becomes clear that manufacturers that use global outsourcing may be paying more than they initially anticipated (Cable, 2011).

A key player in the reshoring movement is Harry Moser, who maintains that the costs of global outsourcing should follow a total cost of ownership model (Markham, 2011). The model includes calculating all costs associated with making the product, including costs that are often overlooked by managers. These include risk factors such as the stability of the country, the loss of business due to poor quality, the economic stability of the supplier, and loss due to lack of innovation. More traditional costs are also included such as transportation and holding costs, damage to product while en route, and duty fees. An Archstone Consulting 2009 survey revealed that 60 percent of manufacturers use "rudimentary total cost models" and ignore 20 percent of the cost of offshoring (Moser, 2011). As a result, Moser claims that most companies that offshore consider only the price of the product, and perhaps three or four other cost factors (Markham, 2011). He argues that such a perspective is incomplete.

One factor that also must be considered is the convergence of labor rates in the United States and other countries, such as China. As labor costs rise in popularly outsourced countries, the playing field levels when the total cost of ownership is compared across countries. Over time, the cost gap between a product produced in the United States and one produced in China narrows (Sprovieri, 2011). As more people become aware of the non–job-related costs of moving production overseas, additional pressure may be put on companies to bring production back to the home country. Hence, the cost of reshoring is about *both* costs and patriotism, at least in the eyes of those who support the reshoring initiative.

As we can see, globalization in general and the global outsourcing strategy in particular have spawned a number of crisis threats. In production management, the move to outsource at the local level has traditionally been motivated by locating a vendor with a complementary strategic capability. For example, many companies outsource the food service function to a specialty firms better equipped to provide the service. Likewise, they may outsource the manufacture of a particular component to a nearby firm with appropriate expertise. This has been the model in the auto industry for years. However, when a company resigns its role as a manufacturer in favor of outsourcing production to a company in an emerging country, the motivation is usually associated with costs. As Shell (2010) contends, however, what is often at stake is more than just lower costs, but quality, safety, environmental responsibility, and human dignity.

Summary

This chapter examined six major trends in the crisis management landscape, each of which contributes to the proliferation of crisis events that organizations must face. For each trend, a tradeoff exists between the external environment and the degree of influence that management can exert in its strategic planning efforts. Management has the most strategic influence in its decisions to undertake globalization initiatives. The least amount of control can be seen in addressing transboundary crises. Understanding these trends is useful as we examine the origins of crises, the topic of the next chapter.

Questions for Discussion

1. What is a transboundary crisis?
   - What are the four characteristics of a transboundary crisis?
   - What are some examples of transboundary crises?

2. How far should companies go in preparing for acts of terrorism? How much preparation is too much? Explain.

3. How can the Internet add to the severity of a crisis? Provide examples.

4. What types of human-induced crises have occurred where you work?

5. What is a normal accident? What conditions can contribute to this type of event?

6. What is sustainable development? What is its association with crisis events?

7. How has globalization contributed to an increase in crisis events?

8. What can companies do to decrease the risk of a crisis involving global outsourcing?

Chapter Exercise

The six trends in this chapter have been carefully researched to reflect the latest factors that lead to organizational crises in the strategy landscape. Although the trends are discussed individually, they overlap as well. In this exercise, the class should form six groups, with each group representing one of the trends discussed in the chapter.

Each group should create a list of examples of crises that originate from its respective trend. (This part can be done outside of class.) The lists should then be posted in the classroom so that members of all six groups can view each group's examples. Once the class has reconvened, identify the examples that seem to transcend other categories. For example, a transboundary crisis can also have roots in the globalization movement, and so on.

Discuss as a class how the organization can exert more strategic control in mitigating a future crisis that is linked to multiple trends.

Opening Case, Part 2:
How a Distance of 10 Feet Can Be Fatal

The U.S. Chemical Safety and Hazard Investigation Board investigated the accident at the Little General Store in September 2008 and issued an 84-page report on the incident. Not surprisingly, the board found that the location of the propane tank adjacent to the building contributed to the explosion (CSB, 2008). However, the propane tank under question had been allowed to remain in its location for 11 years. Records indicate that the tank was installed in late 1994 against the back wall of the Little General Store by the then-Southern Sun Company (CSB, 2008). It was not until that fateful day on January 30, 2007, when the old tank was to be decommissioned, that a new tank would be located at the required 10-foot distance level. Ironically, it was this move to secure a safer location that led to the explosion.

The board identified a second factor in the accident. The junior technician was not properly trained to conduct a liquid propane transfer. In addition, he was working alone when he attempted to remove the plug from the propane tank. OSHA regulations require that an attendant be present during the transfer and that the technician be properly trained to undertake such a transfer (Busick, 2010).

The report also noted that although propane had seeped into the store and was noticed by employees because of its odor, no evacuation ever took place. Propane is an odorless liquid and must be given a characteristic odor so it can be detected at one-fifth of its explosive limit (Busick, 2010).

The board also uncovered a defect in the propane tank itself; a withdrawal valve positioned underneath the outer plug was stuck in the open position. Hence, when the junior technician attempted to remove the outer plug, the propane escaped unabated. Under normal circumstances, removing the plug should not release any propane. However, as a safety requirement, the plug has a slot that releases a small amount of propane when the plug is partially opened. This device is meant to signal to the technician that the valve underneath is stuck and the outer plug must be replaced. Unfortunately, the junior technician had not been trained on how to remove the outer plug properly, or to note that a small amount of escaping gas indicates a problem with the withdrawal valve. Instead, the technician completely removed the plug, which allowed the propane to escape under high pressure (CSB, 2008). At that point, it was not possible to replace the outer plug, and the gas escaped freely for nearly 20 minutes.

A complete evacuation of the building and the surrounding area should have occurred. Instead, emergency personnel and employees were located in areas laden with propane fumes. At 10:53 A.M., the propane encountered a flame from a pizza oven, an electrical spark, or another source of ignition. The trigger to the explosion was never identified.

An added irony in this case was that Appalachian Heating was working with a competitor's tank. That tank, owned by Ferrellgas, had to be disconnected so that Appalachian could connect its tank to the building. Ideally, a liquid transfer by which the propane is transferred safely to another tank should be done in a bulk plant. However, that process can be done in the field if the proper safety precautions are met and the technicians are trained (Johnston, 2008). Unfortunately, that was not to be the case in this incident.

Greg Darby is the owner of the Little General Stores and acknowledges it was one of the worst days of his life. "It was a tough day. We went out there, and it was completely gone. It was scary. We didn't know what happened or who died. It was the most difficult thing" (Lannom, 2012, p. 9). Darby grew up in Beaver, West Virginia, only a few miles from the ill-fated Little General Store. He graduated from West Virginia University with a degree in accounting. His first job was with Little General as an accountant, and he has remained there for his entire career. When he first started with the company, the chain had only eight stores; today, it has more than 100. Today, a memorial to the victims of the tragedy sits in the location where the Little General once operated.

Opening Case Part 2 Case Discussion Questions

1. What steps should be taken to ensure that proper training occurs for employees working with hazardous substances?

2. In this accident, which organizations are potentially liable for the explosion? List these in order of priority and discuss your reasons.

Opening Case Part 2 References

Busick, J. (2010, October 1). Propane: This common fuel can be uncommonly deadly. *Safety Compliance Letter,* Issue 2518, 5–6.
CSB. (2008, September). *Investigation Report: Little General Store—Propane Explosion.* U.S. Chemical Safety and Hazard Investigation Board. Retrieved July 29, 2012, from http://www.csb.gov/assets/document/CSBFinalReportLittleGeneral.pdf.
Johnston, J. (2008). Know the safety situations. *LP/Gas, 68*(11), 32.
Lannom, A. (2012). Darby's stores have gone through triumphs, tragedy. *Who's Who in West Virginia Business Award Winner,* 8–9.

References

Ali, S., & Ali, A. (2010). A conceptual framework for crisis planning and management in the Jordanian tourism industry. *Advances in Management, 3*(7), 59–65.
Ansberry, C., & Aeppel, T. (2003, October 6). Surviving the onslaught. *Wall Street Journal,* pp. B1, B6.
Ansell, C., Boin, A., & Keller, A. (2010). Managing transboundary crises: Identifying the building blocks of an effective response system. *Journal of Contingencies and Crisis Management, 18*(4), 195–207.
Barton, L. (2001). *Crisis in organizations II.* Cincinnati: South-Western.
Bellman, E., & Koppel, N. (2005, September 28). More U.S. legal work moves to India's low-cost lawyers. *Wall Street Journal,* pp. B1, B2.
Bernstein, J. (2006). Who are those bloggers and why are they saying those terrible things? *Associations Now, 2*(11), 58–61.

Birchall, J. (2010, May 27). Criticism that spread like a rash. *Financial Times,* p. 10.

Boin, A. (2009). The new world of crises and crisis management: Implications for policy-making and research. *Review of Policy Research, 26*(4), 367–377.

Buckman, R. (2004, March 22). Apparel's loose thread. *Wall Street Journal,* pp. B1, B8.

Cable, J. (2011). The Pied Piper of manufacturing. *Industry Week, 260*(8), 29–30.

Carroll, A., & Buchholtz, A. (2003). *Business and society: Ethics and stakeholder management* (5th ed.). Cincinnati: Thompson South-Western.

Cheung, C., & Law, R. (2006). How can hotel guests be protected during the occurrence of a tsunami? *Asia Pacific Journal of Tourism Research, 11*(3), 289–295.

Choo, C. (2008). Organizational disasters: Why they happen and how they may be prevented. *Management Decision, 46*(1), 32–45.

Conlin, M. (2007, April 16). Web attack. *Business Week,* 54–56.

Coombs, T. (2010). Sustainability: A new and complex "challenge" for crisis managers. *International Journal of Sustainable Strategic Management, 2*(1), 4–16.

Crandall, R., Crandall, W., & Chen, C. (2010). *Principles of supply chain management.* Boca Raton, FL: Taylor and Francis.

Crandall, W., & Mensah, E. (2008). Crisis management and sustainable development: A framework and proposed research agenda. *International Journal of Sustainable Strategic Management, 1*(1), 16–34.

Crooks, E., Pfeifer, S. & McNulty, S. (2010, October 7). A sea change needed. *Financial Times,* p. 9.

Dean, J. (2004, February 17). Long a low-tech power, China sets its sight on chip making. *Wall Street Journal,* pp. A1, A16.

Diefendorff, J., & Mehta, K. (2007). The relations of motivational traits with workplace deviance. *Journal of Applied Psychology, 92*(4), 967–977.

Dobbs, L. (2004). *Exporting America: Why corporate greed is shipping American jobs overseas.* New York: Time Warner.

Drucker, J., & Brown, K. (2004, March 9). Latest wrinkle in jobs fight: Letting customers choose where their work is done. *Wall Street Journal,* pp. B1, B3.

Edid, M. (2005). *The good, the bad, and Wal-Mart.* Ithaca, NY: Cornell University Institute of Workplace Studies.

Etter, L. (2005, December 3–4). Gauging the Wal-Mart effect. *Wall Street Journal,* p. A9.

Fishman, C. (2006). *The Wal-Mart effect: How the world's most powerful company really works—and how it's transforming the American economy.* New York: Penguin.

Glaesser, D. (2005). *Crisis management in the tourism industry.* Oxford, UK: Butterworth-Heinemann.

González-Herrero, A., & Smith, S. (2008). Crisis communications management on the Web: How Internet-based technologies are changing the way public relations professionals handle business crises. *Journal of Contingencies and Crisis Management, 16*(3), 143–153.

González-Herrero, A., & Smith, S. (2010). Crisis communications management 2.0: Organizational principles to manage in an online world. *Organizational Development Journal, 28*(1), 97–105.

Green, W., III. (2004, Fall). The future of disasters: Interesting trends for interesting times. *Futures Research Quarterly,* 59–68.

Greenberg, D., Clair, J., & Maclean, T. (2002). Teaching through traumatic events: Uncovering the choices of management educators as they respond to September 11th. *Academy of Management Learning and Education Journal, 1*(1), 38–54.

Greenberg, J. (2002). September 11, 2002: A CEO's story. *Harvard Business Review, 80*(10), 58–64.

Grégoire, Y., Tripp, T., & Legoux, R. (2011). When your best customers become your worst enemies: Does time really heal all wounds? *New Insights, 3*(1), 27–35.

Griffin, R., & Lopez, Y. (2005). "Bad behavior" in organizations: A review and typology for future research. *Journal of Management, 31*(6), 988–1005.

Harrington, K., & O'Connor, J. (2009). How Cisco succeeds. *Supply Chain Management Review, 13*(5), 10–17.

Hartley, R. (1993). *Business ethics: Violations of the public trust.* New York: Wiley.

Hopkins, A. (2001). Was Three Mile Island a "normal accident"? *Journal of Contingencies and Crisis Management, 9*(2), 65–72.

Institute for Crisis Management. (2011). *Annual ICM crisis report: News coverage of business crises during 2010.* Retrieved April 8, 2012, from http://crisisconsultant.com/images/2010CrisisReportICM.pdf.

Janis, I. (1982). *Groupthink: Psychological studies of policy decisions and fiascoes.* Boston: Houghton Mifflin.

Kovoor-Misra, S., & Misra, M. (2007). Understanding and managing crises in an "online world." In C. Pearson, C. Roux-Dufort, & J. Clair (Eds.), *International handbook of organizational crisis management* (pp. 85–103). Thousand Oaks, CA: Sage.

Lagadec, P. (2009). A new cosmology of risks and crises: Time for a radical shift in paradigm and practice. *Review of Policy Research, 26*(4), 473–486.

Lee, G., & Thurman, E. (2008, September 30). Southeast retail deals with gas shortage. *Women's Wear Daily,* p. 17.

Luhnow, D. (2004, March 5). As jobs move East, plants in Mexico retool to compete. *Wall Street Journal,* pp. A1, A8.

Maher, K. (2004, March 23). Next on the outsourcing list. *Wall Street Journal,* pp. B1, B8.

Mallaby, S. (2005, November 29). Wal-Mart: A progressive dream company, really. *Fayetteville Observer,* p. 11A.

Markham, D. (2011). Reshoring initiative challenges assumptions about overseas cost advantages. *Metal Center News, 51*(13), 4–6.

Millman, J. (2004, March 3). Blueprint for outsourcing. *Wall Street Journal,* pp. B1, B4.

Morse, D. (2004, February 20). In North Carolina, furniture makers try to stay alive. *Wall Street Journal,* pp. A1, A6.

Moser, H. (2011). From selfishness to citizenship. *Material Handling and Logistics, 66*(6), 48.

Navarro, P. (2007). *The coming China wars: Where they will be fought, how they can be won.* Upper Saddle River, NJ: Financial Times.

Nickerson, R. (2011). Roles of human factors and ergonomics in meeting the challenge of terrorism. *American Psychologist, 66*(6), 555–566.

The 9/11 Commission. (2004). *The 9/11 Commission report: Final report of the National Commission on Terrorist Attacks Upon the United States.* Washington, DC: Government Printing Office.

O'Leary-Kelly, A., Griffin, R., & Glew, D. (1996). Organization-motivated aggression: A research framework. *Academy of Management Review, 21*(1), 225–253.

Parnell, J., Spillan, J., & Lester, D. (2010). Crisis aversion and sustainable strategic management (SSM) in emerging economies. *Internal Journal of Sustainable Strategic Management, 2*(1), 41–59.

Pedahzur, A., Eubank, W., & Weinberg, L. (2002). The war on terrorism and the decline of terrorist group formation: A research note. *Terrorism and Political Violence, 14*(3), 141–147.

Perliger, A., Pedahzur, A., & Zalmanovitch, Y. (2005). The defensive dimension of the battle against terrorism: An analysis of management of terror incidents in Jerusalem. *Journal of Contingencies and Crisis Management, 13*(2), 79–91.

Perrow, C. (1999). *Normal accidents: Living with high risk technologies.* Princeton, NJ: Princeton University Press.

Quinn, B. (2000). *How Wal-Mart is destroying America.* Berkeley, CA: Ten Speed Press.

Rice, J., & Caniato, F. (2003). Building a secure and resilient supply network. *Supply Chain Management Review, 7*(5), 22–30.

Robinson, S., & O'Leary-Kelly, A. (1998). Monkey see, monkey do: The influence of work groups on the antisocial behavior of employees. *Academy of Management Journal, 41*(6), 658–672.

Schaefer, N. A. (2004). Y2K as an endtime sign: Apocalypticism in America at the fin-de-millennium. *Journal of Popular Culture, 38*(1), 82–105.

Sethi, S., & Steidlmeier, P. (1997). *Up against the wall: Case in business and society* (6th ed.). Upper Saddle River, NJ: Prentice Hall.

Shappell, B. (2012). Falling Sun. *Business Credit, 114*(3), 10–12.

Shell, E. (2010). *Cheap: The high cost of discount culture.* New York: Penguin.

Snook, S., & Connor, J. (2005). The price of progress: Structurally induced inaction. In W. H. Starbuck & M. Farjoun (Eds.), *Organization at the limit* (pp. 178–201). Oxford, UK: Blackwell.

Solomon, J., & Kranhold, K. (2005, March 23). In India's outsourcing boom, GE played a starring role. *Wall Street Journal,* pp. A1, A12.

Spillan, J. E., Parnell, J. A., & de Mayoro, C. A. (2011). Exploring crisis readiness in Peru. *Journal of International Business and Economy, 12*(1), 57–83.

Sprovieri, J. (2011). Bringing it all back home. *Adhesives and Sealants Industry, 18*(4), 14–18,

Stallard, M. (1999). *Y2K: Mass hysteria or prophetic event?* Faculty Forum, Baptist Bible Seminary, Clarks Summit, PA. Accessed December 7, 2010, from http://faculty.bbc.edu/mstallard/wp-content/uploads/2009/10/y2k.pdf.

Stead, W., & Stead, J. (2004). *Sustainable strategic management.* Armonk, NY: ME Sharpe.

Timmons, H. (2010, August 5). Outsourcing to India draws Western lawyers. *New York Times*, p. B1.

Turner, B. (1978). *Man-made disasters.* London: Wykeham.

Wachtendorf, T. (2009). Trans-system social ruptures: Exploring issues of vulnerability and resiliency. *Review of Public Research, 26*(4), 379–393.

York, B. (2005, November 23). Panic in a small town. *National Review.* Retrieved April 15, 2012, from http://www.nationalreview.com/articles/216070/panic-small-town/byron-york.

Ziemnowicz, C., Harrison, G., & Crandall, W. R. (2011). The new normal: How social media is changing the way organizations manage a crisis. *Central Business Review, 30*(1–2), 17–24.

Zsidisin, G., Melnyk, S. & Ragatz, G. (2005). An institutional theory perspective of business continuity planning for purchasing and supply management. *International Journal of Production Research, 43*(16), 3401–3420.

Zsidisin, G., Ragatz, G., & Meinyk, S. (2005, March). The dark side of supply chain management. *Supply Chain Management Review,* 46–52.

CHAPTER 3

Sources of Organizational Crises

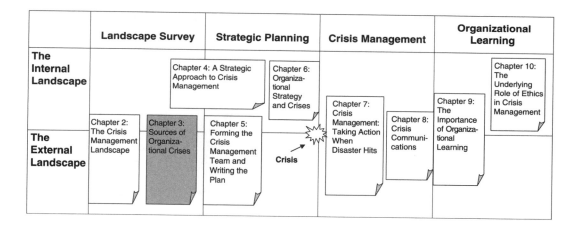

Opening Case: Kleen Energy Gets Into a Dirty Explosion

February 7, 2010, was supposed to be a countdown day for the opening of the Kleen Energy power generation plant in Middletown, Connecticut. Instead, an explosion rocked the facility, leaving six workers dead and 50 more injured. The cause of the explosion was traced to a controversial practice known as a "gas blow," a process whereby natural gas is pumped under high pressure through pipes that feed the turbines that generate electricity (Smith, 2010). As the natural gas was pumped through the pipes, it was vented outside into the open air, a practice that is highly dangerous if there is an ignition source in the area such as an open flame or an electrical spark. During the operation, welding and other construction work was taking place near the area where the gas was dispersed. The fatal explosion occurred at 11:15 A.M., when the gas encountered an ignition source.

The facility was one of a new generation of power plants that utilize gas instead of coal to generate electricity. Such plants use a "combined cycle" approach to power generation, combusting natural gas to run the turbines while any heat generated is retrieved and used to run a steam turbine. The Kleen Energy plant is equipped with two gas and one steam turbine (U.S. Chemical Safety Board [CSB], 2010). The advantage of this type of plant is lower pollution.

When a new gas-operated power plant is constructed, a procedure to clean the gas lines that feed into the large turbines is necessary because the turbine blades are delicate and cannot come into contact with dust and debris. When construction occurs and the gas lines are new, however, it is common for sediment to reach the blades. The makers of turbines require that gas lines be cleaned as a condition of honoring the warranty (Smith, 2010).

There are several ways that lines can be cleaned. The most popular method is to use natural gas because it is readily convenient and does not require purging the lines before final installation. In a survey conducted by the U.S. Chemical Safety Board, 37 percent of the respondents indicated they used natural gas as the preferred method of cleaning lines (CSB, 2010). However, this method is also the most dangerous because of the risk of encountering an ignition source. Other alternative methods of cleaning gas lines include using water, steam, nitrogen, or compressed air, all of which are safer and not flammable (Benner, 2010).

An article in *Fortune* ("Anatomy," 2010) unfolds the chronology of the events that fateful morning of the accident:

6:00 A.M. to 7:00 A.M.: The construction company, O&G Industries, does not hold a safety meeting to indicate that a series of gas blows will be conducted during the morning. As a result, potential ignition sources such as open-flame heaters, welding equipment, and electricity are all left operating near the area where the gas will be vented.

7:00 A.M. to 9:00 A.M.: The gas lines that run to Turbine 2 are cleared out using a series of eight gas blows. Each blow is preceded by a warning horn. The gases are vented outside in the open air and no incidents are reported.

10:30 A.M. to 11:15 A.M.: Workers in the area notice a strong smell of natural gas, perhaps indicating that the gas is not dissipating well.

11:00 A.M.: The gas blow begins on Turbine 1, but no warning horn is sounded. The gases are vented within 15 feet of the ground.

11:15 A.M.: An explosion occurs, followed by a fire.

Although the cause of the accident was natural gas encountering an ignition source, the source was never identified.

Two different organizations investigated the accident, and although their findings were identical as to the cause, their recommendations were different. Both the U.S. Chemical Safety Board and the Occupational Safety and Health Administration (OSHA) found the practice of using natural gas to clean out pipes as hazardous to the safety of nearby workers. However, while the CSB advised prohibiting the practice altogether, OSHA stopped short of making the same recommendation. OSHA has the legal power to issue fines, while the CSB does not.

OSHA levied a $16.6 million fine on the companies involved and identified 371 workplace violations at the worksite. The largest fine of $8.35 million went to O&G Industries for 119 willful and 17 serious violations (Smith, 2010). According to Dr. David Michaels, assistant secretary of labor for OSHA, "These employees blatantly disregarded well-known and accepted industry procedures and their own safety guidelines in conducting the gas blow operation in a manner that exposed workers to fire and explosion hazards. . . . We see this time and time again across industries when companies deliberately ignore safety precautions in the interest of completing jobs quickly, and workers end up being killed or seriously hurt" ("$16.6 million in fines," 2010, p. 16). Completing the job quickly, as mentioned by Dr. Michaels, was indeed a consideration in the accident. Stipulated in the contract was a $14 million bonus to O&G Industries if the plant was completed early (Benner, 2010).

Opening Case Discussion Questions

1. Are you aware of other examples in which a contractor sacrificed worker safety in the building of a construction project?

2. The U.S. Chemical Safety Board can only make recommendations and not issue fines. Why, then, is this board considered to be influential in the industry?

3. This case mentions that completing a project early can result in a bonus to the contractor. How does the use of gas blowing speed up the completion of a project like this one? Discuss the appropriateness of financial payoffs in contracts that are linked to completing projects ahead of time.

Opening Case References

Anatomy of a catastrophe. (2010, September 27). *Fortune,* 101.

Benner, K. (2010, September 10). The fatal deal. *Fortune,* 99–106.

Chemical Safety Board. (2010, May 19). Pipe cleaning practices that led to Kleen Energy explosion are common across gas energy industry, survey data shows. Retrieved July 28, 2012, from http://www.csb.gov/newsroom/detail.aspx?nid=319.

$16.6 million in fines for fatal Connecticut explosion. (2010, September 26). *Industrial Safety and Hygiene News, 44*(9), 16.

Smith, R. (2010, August 6). "Unsafe" cleaning with gas allowed. *Wall Street Journal,* p. A4.

Introduction

Crisis events such as the one at Kleen Energy have sources; they are not merely random events. One must understand these sources before steps can be taken to avoid subsequent crises. Likewise, practitioners and management scholars often view the external environment in terms of general forces that originate from four areas: political–legal, economic, social, and technological (PEST). These four areas are not only consistent in strategic analysis but also lay the groundwork for examining the external landscape for crises. In this chapter, we examine each of these four forces in detail and discuss their relationships to origins of a crisis. We also review the industry and organizational life cycles and their applicability to effective crisis management.

Crises and the External Environment

Every organization exists within a complex network of political–legal, economic, social, and technological forces, as depicted in Figure 3.1. Together, these elements make up the organization's external environment, also called the *macroenvironment*. Changes in any of these realms can increase the likelihood of a crisis.

Political–Legal Forces

Political–legal forces include the outcomes of government leader decisions, the impacts of existing and new legislation, and judicial court decisions, as well as the decisions rendered by various regulatory commissions and agencies at all levels of government. As with the other forces, political–legal factors sometimes affect different firms in the same industry in different ways.

Politically Motivated Events

The terrorist attacks of September 11, 2001, were followed by a number of political decisions on the part of the United States that created both crises and opportunities. Following the sharp decline in air travel in the United States, airlines on the verge of bankruptcy campaigned for and received $15 billion in government

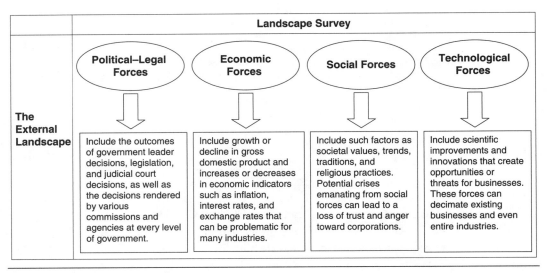

Figure 3.1 Crises and the External Landscape

support in 2002 and an additional $2.9 billion in 2003 (Sevastopulo, 2003). The subsequent war in Iraq created a number of crises for organizations, especially those with tight global ties. For example, during the early part of the military conflict, when Allied forces were marching toward Baghdad, many firms modified their advertising campaigns, fearing that their television promotions might be considered insensitive if aired alongside breaking coverage of the war. This move was intended to avoid a potential public relations crisis. At the same time, other firms viewed the war as an opportunity for revenue growth and began planning for Iraq's future needs in the areas of cell phones, refrigerators, and automobiles. After Saddam Hussein's regime was ousted in mid-2003, American firms began to compete vigorously for lucrative reconstruction contracts. Overall, the war created crises for some firms but opportunities for others (Cummins, 2003; King, 2003; Trachtenberg & Steinberg, 2003).

Laws and Regulations

Most societies have laws and regulations that affect business operations. Table 3.1 summarizes some of the major legislation in the United States over the past century. Although the details surrounding major legislation are always complicated, most of these laws can be viewed as responses to an industry or organizational crisis that already existed (Hartley, 1993). For example, the passage of the Foreign Corrupt Practices Act was in response to the infamous Lockheed bribery case. In this incident, Lockheed paid $12.5 million in bribes and other commissions to secure a sale of $430 million in commercial aircraft to All-Nippon Airways in Japan (Carroll & Buchholtz, 2003). At the time, the president of Lockheed argued that paying bribes was an accepted way of doing business in Japan.

Table 3.1 Examples of U.S. Legislation and the Crises That Led to Its Enactment

Legislation	Purpose	Crises That Led to Its Enactment
Title VII of the Civil Rights Acts (1964)	Prohibits discrimination against protected employment groups based on factors such as age, religion, race, and gender	Numerous cases involving discrimination against specific groups
Occupational Safety and Health Act (1970)	Requires employers to provide a hazard-free working environment	A response to a number of workplace safety issues that had occurred in the previous decades
Federal Mine Safety and Health Act (1977)	Seeks to ensure a safe working environment for miners	Accidents emanating from the hazardous working environment that miners face

(Continued)

Table 3.1   Continued

Legislation	Purpose	Crises That Led to Its Enactment
Foreign Corrupt Practices Act (1978)	Outlaws direct payoffs and bribes of foreign governments or business officials	A response to the early 1970s Lockheed bribery incident, in which the company paid bribes to secure contracts to sell aircraft to All-Nippon Airways, a Japanese airline
Oil Pollution Act (1990)	Mandates that oil storage facilities and vessels provide a detailed plan of how they will respond to a large oil spill	A response to the 1989 *Exxon Valdez* oil spill in Prince William Sound, off the coast of Alaska
Aviation and Transportation Security Act (2001)	Created the Transportation Security Administration to help ensure the safety of the nation's air travel system	A response to the terrorist attacks on the World Trade Center in New York on September 11, 2001
Sarbanes-Oxley Act (2002)	Makes businesses more accountable by requiring them to adhere to higher standards of financial disclosure	A response to a number of corporate scandals involving inappropriate bookkeeping, including the most famous one, the Enron Corporation
CAN SPAM Act (2003)	The Controlling the Assault of Non-Solicited Pornography and Marketing Act prescribes regulations for e-mail spammers	A response to the proliferation of unwanted e-mail that has glutted cyberspace
Food Allergen Labeling and Consumer Protection Act of 2004 (FALCPA)	Requires the labeling of known allergens on food labels	Various cases concerning illness or death from ingesting a food substance
Patient Protection and Affordable Care Act (2010)	Increases regulation of health care providers and insurance companies in an effort to lower costs and expand coverage	Some organizations offered health insurance to their employees but others did not
Dodd-Frank Wall Street Reform and Consumer Protection Act (2010)	Outlines comprehensive regulation of U.S. financial markets and credit rating agencies	The mortgage/financial crisis of 2008

Organizations are often affected by legislation and other political events specific to their lines of business. For example, changing legislation that concerns food safety and health can lead to organizational crises. Consider the appearance of variant Creuztfeldt-Jakob disease (vCJD), better known as Mad Cow Disease. This ailment is a rare malady of the brain passed through tainted meat. When it began to surface in the United Kingdom in 1996, most European nations responded by banning the import of British beef. Firms in the industry were not able to ensure safety, and financial losses were staggering (Higgins, 2001). Although measures were implemented to stop the spread of the disease, collateral damage affected other stakeholders in the beef and food-related industries. For example, the economic impact in Canada was around $10 billion in lost trade and compensation, despite the fact that very little is known about the disease (Fortier, 2008). As an example, a single diseased cow in northern Alberta in 2003 led to a widespread closing of the borders, with thousands of cattle slaughtered and sales of Canadian beef falling to crisis levels, from $1.10 per pound to 30 cents (Fortier, 2008). While the disease itself can be considered a crisis, the reaction to it created a secondary crisis.

Economic Forces

Economic forces can also be a source of organizational crises. Growth or decline in gross domestic product (GDP) and shifts in economic indicators such as inflation, interest rates, and exchange rates can be problematic for many companies. Other factors such as an overexpansion of credit and surges in energy prices and health care costs can also create challenges for firms in many industries.

The Overexpansion of Credit

An overexpansion of credit, particularly in the subprime mortgage industry, created an economic crisis in the United States that had a ripple effect around the world. Extending credit can have its advantages when the debt is paid back in a timely manner. However, when excessive debt causes normal spending to decrease, the economy slows. To offset this problem, central banks like the Federal Reserve often extend additional credit, initiating a continuous cycle of debt, spending, and more debt. Hence, expanding credit can create what appears to be economic growth in the short term, but it can also create a "bubble" and economic stagnation in the long term (Kline, 2010). In other words, once that "demand" is actually consumed, a void awaits at the end of the tunnel—an economic slowdown, or worse, a recession. When a recession results, a crisis is created for many organizations because spending decreases and budget cuts typically follow. Sometimes these cutbacks occur in vulnerable areas, such as safety and equipment overhaul. When safety is compromised or equipment is not repaired or replaced in a timely manner, accidents will be the result.

On a personal level, much can be gleaned from observing the link between consumerism and credit. When consumers do not have what they want, they attempt to buy it. However, if they do not have the means to pay, they seek credit. Consumers with poor or marginal credit histories represent substantial payback risks, especially if the economy declines. Backed by Federal Reserve policies, these consumers were granted mortgages for relatively expensive homes, often with escalating interest rates, balloon payments, and other characteristics that sparked the financial crisis.

An interesting side note on the credit discussion is the role of the positive thinking industry and its relation to the economic crisis. The positive thinking industry is comprised of motivational speakers, self-help books, and an endless array of CDs and DVDs that compel individuals to view themselves and their abilities with more confidence. This increased sense of self may have contributed to an increased desire for material goods, amplifying a cycle of consumerism that is not based on adequate financial resources. Instead, individuals spend today and hope to pay later. Ehrenreich (2009) surmised that this type of irrational exuberance might have contributed to the crisis.

Hence, the positive thinking movement offers some insight on the consumer end of the mortgage problem that occurred during the recession. Many consumers believed they were "entitled" to own homes beyond their economic means. The Federal Reserve, government policy promoting home ownership, and entities like Fannie Mae and Freddie Mac flooded the market with excessive funds at artificially low interest rates. Likewise, the mortgage companies that promoted these loans were overly optimistic as well. The result was not only a crisis for the mortgage companies and the recipients of their loans, but a worldwide recession that jolted service and manufacturing industries alike.

The Surge in Oil Prices

Although many shifts in economic forces can create crises that permeate an industry, some firms may be better situated to withstand them than others. When oil prices spiked in 2005, for example, firms in oil-intensive industries such as airlines and carmakers began to experience severe cost pressures (Michaels & Trottman, 2005). These hikes in fuel prices did not have the same effect on all airlines, although specific effects are difficult to determine because of other, simultaneous environmental and competitive changes in the industry. Weak players like Delta seemed to have been hit the hardest, while budget carriers like Southwest and Ryanair experienced mild gains. This advantage occurred because fuel represents a lower percentage of operating costs on short-haul flights such as those championed by budget carriers, and these increases can be spread over more customers when occupancy rates are higher (Michaels & Trottman, 2005).

Fuel economy standards can require that producers develop new vehicles or modify existing ones so that average fuel economy goals are met. This can be a costly venture. When the George W. Bush administration proposed that the smallest trucks reach 28.4 miles per gallon and the largest trucks reach 21.4 miles per gallon by 2011, it estimated that the industry would spend $6.3 billion over four years to comply, adding $275 to the price tag of a large truck by 2011 (Meckler & Lundegaard, 2005). When President Barack Obama announced an additional increase in the corporate average fuel economy (CAFE) standards to 55 miles per gallon by 2025, some analysts estimated that production costs would rise by as much as an additional $3,000 per vehicle (Tennant, 2011). Although proponents of the higher standards argued that fuel savings would more than compensate for the additional costs if the target can be achieved, the new regulation, a political–legal force, influenced an economic force and had the potential to create a crisis for automobile manufacturers.

When oil prices spiked in 2008, however, firms in the automobile industry faced a different kind of crisis, one sparked by an economic factor. Expectations that gasoline prices would remain high over the long term affect demand for automobiles, as consumers shifted from sport utility vehicles (SUVs), large cars, and trucks to smaller, more fuel-efficient alternatives, as well as hybrids and electric vehicles (EVs). Hence, the cost of complying with the regulations was no longer a consideration because producers were required to alter both their research and development and their production priorities to address these new demand patterns. Ford and General Motors (GM) acknowledged this reality early in 2008, while start-up firms around the world began the race to develop vehicles that consume less fuel or eschew gasoline altogether (Stewart, 2008; Taylor, 2008). As a result, what began as a potential crisis with political–legal origins was transformed into a more substantial crisis with an economic impetus.

The downturn in the economy and the unpredictability of oil prices contributed to ongoing problems for the industry as well. Indeed, automobile sales dipped during the economic downturn of 2009 but recovered in 2010, prompted by gains in more fuel-efficient vehicles. The rise in gasoline prices has created long-term challenges for manufacturers that rely on trucks, large vehicles, and SUVs. Small cars accounted for about one-third of new vehicle sales globally in the early 2010s, but forecasting fuel prices is very difficult, especially in the short term. The trend reversed temporarily in the 2010 when average fuel prices in the United States consistently remained below $4 per gallon, as sales of SUVs and pickup trucks increased or exceeded car sales at many automakers. When $4 gasoline returned in early 2012, however, consumer demand shifted back to automobiles boasting 30 or more miles per gallon, as well as updated SUVs engineered for better fuel economy.

Unfortunately, the automobile industry crisis spilled over into other related industries as well. U.S. automobile parts suppliers were forced to realign their workforces and production schedules to meet the overall decline and the shift toward more fuel-efficient vehicles. In addition, suppliers typically must absorb lower margins when their customers experience a downturn in sales (Bennett, 2008).

Social Forces

Social forces can trigger a variety of crises and include such factors as societal values, trends, traditions, and religious practices. Societal values are beliefs that citizens tend to hold in high esteem. In the United States, major values include individual freedom, fairness, concern for the environment, diversity, consumer rights, and equality of opportunity. Potential crises emanating from social forces can lead to a loss of trust and anger toward corporations, and to various forms of social disapproval including boycotts, negative websites, and bad publicity. When these negative feelings are expressed through social media, the word can spread in a matter of hours.

Distrust of Corporate America

One social force of keen interest is the anti-corporate sentiment shared by many consumers. Although the reasons for this phenomenon are beyond the scope of this book, evidence can be found in the "Occupy Wall Street" movement launched in 2011. Distrust is manifested when ordinary people believe unfounded rumors. One of the more fascinating instances in consumer history revolved around Procter & Gamble in the early 1980s. The rumor concerned the widespread belief that its corporate logo was a satanic symbol and its chief executive officer (CEO) was a devil worshiper, a claim the CEO allegedly made on the *Merv Griffin* television program (Cato, 1982). What followed was the distribution of literature urging consumers to boycott Procter & Gamble. Although there was no truth to the rumor, the company expended legal resources in efforts to stop those who were spreading the literature, mostly in the form of photocopied flyers. In the early 1990s, another such rumor surfaced, this time claiming that the popular Cabbage Patch Dolls were possessed by the devil (Steele, Smith, & McBroom, 1999).

Unfortunately, corporate America does not always live up to society's ethical standards. The coal mining industry is famous for ongoing management–labor strife. The safety record for coal mining is abysmal, despite the fact that a reduction of fatalities has occurred over the past century. However, 2010 was one of the worst years on record. In one notable case, an April 5 methane explosion at a Massey Energy coal mine near Beckley, West Virginia, killed 29 miners. An independent investigation found the explosion to be completely preventable had Massey Energy followed basic safety standards of the mining industry ("WV governor's report," 2011).

Distrust of Massey Energy is not a recent occurrence. In fact, the company has been widely cited as having a culture of disregard of worker safety (Barrett, 2011; Ceniceros, 2011). From 2005 to May 2010, the Mine Safety and Health Administration (MSHA) issued 1,342 safety violations totaling $1.89 million in fines. Rather than address the safety violations, Massey chose to contest these citations in court by challenging the regulations (Smith, 2010). Massey's former CEO, Don Blankenship, has come under much criticism for his role in promoting production at the expense of worker safety. A *Rolling Stone* feature article on Blankenship labeled him "The Dark Lord of Coal Country" (Goodell, 2010).

Preoccupation With "the Bargain"

The distrust of corporate America also extends to other industries like discount retail, where a heavy premium is placed on low prices. Some Americans believe workers in this industry are underpaid and treated unfairly (Ehrenreich, 2001). Indeed, in order to sell goods at low prices, the big box retailers must control costs. Keeping labor costs low is a necessity, and benefits such as health care can be expensive (Shell, 2010).

The preoccupation with the bargain extends into quality as well. Consumer pressures can prompt retailers to sacrifice quality. Many appliances and electronics are built at rock-bottom costs, and consumers often discard them after a short period of time and purchase a replacement. This preference for low price over high quality can be viewed as a crisis of sorts. Craftsmanship and quality were valued as far back as the founding of the United States, and citizens were willing to pay a higher price for higher-quality goods (Crawford, 2009).

To recap, the societal emphasis on bargains has contributed to a loss of dignity of rank-and-file workers in retail establishments as well as a decline in quality of finished goods. But another crisis has also been initiated: the movement of manufacturing jobs overseas. While "corporate greed" is often blamed for the displacement of jobs, consumer preferences for low prices ultimately drive corporate behavior (Fishman, 2006; Shell, 2010). Large firms like Wal-Mart that provide low prices are often blamed for the problem as well. Wal-Mart's depression of wages by buying products made by low-wage earners in developing nations has had a major impact on the U.S. manufacturing sector, has reduced the standard of living of many people, and has removed a major source of jobs (manufacturing) from the American business environment. This has created a crisis in that the alternative employment for displaced workers has not grown as fast as the outsourcing has developed. Low-paying jobs create a negative multiplier effect that depresses the entire economy. This is a major crisis for unskilled or lower-skilled workers.

Social Equality

One of the more visible social trends in the United States is the movement away from racial discrimination, including efforts by companies to provide equal access to all customers, regardless of race. The Denny's restaurant discrimination case is an example of how an incident of racism on the part of a large company can result in a strong public backlash. The incident began in 1993 when a waitress at an Annapolis, Maryland, restaurant purportedly refused to serve six African American Secret Service agents (Chin et al., 1993). The result was a major media frenzy that eventually became a key story on the *CBS Evening News*. As a result of the crisis, Denny's changed many of its human resource practices.

The appearance of racism, even if not intended, can result in serious public scrutiny. Cracker Barrel, the family-oriented restaurant chain based in Lebanon, Tennessee, found itself in a crisis when Rose Rock, mother of comedian Chris Rock, visited the Murrells Inlet Cracker Barrel (near Myrtle Beach, South Carolina) on May 16, 2006. Ms. Rock and her daughter waited for 30 minutes without service while white customers were served (Fuller, 2006). The incident eventually led to a news conference, held in the parking lot of the restaurant, which included Al Sharpton and officials from the restaurant's headquarters. The official statement made by Cracker Barrel was that the incident was a service issue, not a racial issue. Apparently, Rock and her daughter had been seated but not assigned a server (Fuller, 2006).

But social equality does not necessarily include those workers who produce textiles, appliances, and other goods in other countries. Americans are quick to criticize firms that appear to facilitate so-called sweatshops, and many are willing to boycott certain companies to address their concerns.

The Health and Fitness Trend

Social forces can result in an opportunity for companies in one industry while simultaneously creating crises in another industry. For example, the health and fitness trend that emerged in the 1990s has spawned growth in a number of industries including health and fitness centers, sport drinks, nutritional supplements, and low-fat foods. The reality television show *The Biggest Loser* encourages people to lose weight and stay fit. The popular series was launched in October 2004 and has received high ratings and a loyal fan base (Siegler, 2010). However, this same trend for health and fitness has hurt a number of businesses in less health-friendly industries such as tobacco, alcohol, and fast-food restaurants. The fast-food industry, and particularly McDonald's, has been the target of much criticism concerning the health qualities of their menu offerings (Copeland, 2005). High-fat content and large servings are common in this industry.

Sometimes social factors appear to conflict with each other. During the past several years, many fast-food restaurants have been "supersizing" their meal combinations by adding extra fries and larger drinks, while at the same time expanding alternatives for items such as grilled chicken sandwiches and salads (Ellison & Steinberg, 2003). In 2004, Coca-Cola and PepsiCo began to emphasize smaller cans and bottles (McKay, 2004), while McDonald's introduced low-carb menu items (Leung, 2004). Sometimes a company will appear to buck the social trend and offer products that seem counter to society's higher-road wishes. With the introduction and reported success of products like Hardee's Monster Thickburger, with 107 fat grams and 1,418 calories, the extent to which many American consumers consider health factors when purchasing fast food is not always clear (Gray, 2005). In this instance, what one firm considers to be a potential crisis might be seen as a business opportunity by another.

Recent criticism of the McDonald's Happy Meals illustrates conflicts that can exist between consumers and interest groups. In late 2010, the San Francisco board of supervisors voted to disallow restaurants like McDonald's from including toys as part of a meal unless the accompanying food complied with prescribed limits on calories, sugar, sodium, and fat content. Although this measure was ostensibly aimed at curbing childhood obesity, it clearly targeted McDonald's Happy Meals. Shortly after the vote, the advocacy group Center for Science in the Public Interest filed a lawsuit accusing McDonald's of deceptive advertising practices to attract children to their restaurants. The center alleged that Happy Meals contain amounts of fat, sodium, and calories much higher than government-recommended levels. Responding to the attacks, CEO Jim Skinner attacked what he called the "food police," charging the legislation prohibits families from making their own decisions about menu items (Farrell, 2010; Farrell & Weitzman, 2010).

The beer industry has been in a public relations crisis of sorts for several decades:it is continually hounded by charges of contributing to poor health, alcoholism, and drunk driving. Recognizing the controversial nature of the industry, many beer companies now promote responsible drinking in their advertisements. Some have even advocated the health benefits of beer. In the mid-2000s, Anheuser-Busch teamed up with noted Harvard epidemiologist Meir Stampfer to tout the potential medical benefits of beer consumption. Stampfer cites a number of studies suggesting that moderate consumption of alcohol may reduce the risk of heart attack, diabetes, and other ailments (Hellier & Ellison, 2005).

Concern for the Environment and Sustainable Development

A major social force, particularly in the United States and the European Union, is the heightened concern for the environment and the need to practice sustainable development, specifically "development that meets the need of the present world without compromising the ability of future generations to meet their own needs" (Brundtland Commission, 1987, p. 54). Hence, the pursuit of sustainability has both short- and long-term implications. Of course, sustainability efforts can involve an investment of resources, an opportunity cost dilemma that balances profits with funds to protect and sustain resources. Nonetheless, consumers expect firms to engage in sustainable practice; those that do not risk a public relations crisis.

Stakeholders do not always agree on appropriate actions with regard to sustainability. A prominent ecological concern for many industries—particularly those involved in heavy manufacturing—is the ongoing debate over anthropogenic (human-induced) climate change. Proponents contend that carbon dioxide produced by human activity is the impetus for substantial changes in global climate patterns. If unchecked, these changes will influence life on Earth in dramatic ways. Critics of the anthropogenic climate change hypothesis question the causal link between carbon dioxide in the atmosphere and global temperatures. While the two appear to be positively correlated—to the extent that average global temperatures can be measured and computed accurately—shifts in temperature appear to precede changes in carbon dioxide levels, not the other way around. Although this debate is complex and beyond the scope of this text, governments frequently attempt to manage economic development or address ecological concerns. For example, various plans have been proposed to tax carbon emissions, require firms to buy and sell carbon permits in order to engage in production, or restrict certain manufacturing activity altogether. While the ecological impact of such measures is open to debate, the economic ramifications of such measures would be significant, especially in manufacturing industries.

Technological Forces

Technological forces include scientific improvements and innovations that create both opportunities and threats for businesses. The rate of technological change varies considerably from one industry to another and can affect a firm's operations as well as its products and services. Firms have used advances in technology such as computers, satellites, and fiber optics to perform their traditional tasks at lower costs and higher levels of customer satisfaction.

New Technology Pitfalls

Technological forces not only create opportunities for firms, but they can also be a source of crises. These forces can decimate existing businesses and even entire industries by shifting demand from one product to another. Examples of such changes include the shifts from vacuum tubes to transistors, from steam locomotives to diesel and electric engines, from fountain pens to ballpoints, from propeller airplanes to jets, and from typewriters to computers (Wright, Kroll, & Parnell, 1998).

Technological change can create its own opposition, such as has occurred with the production of batteries for electric vehicles. Although considerable progress has been made, producers of such vehicles have not been free of crises. For example, as mentioned in Chapter 1, General Motors (GM) encountered a crisis in 2011 when crash testing by the National Highway Traffic Safety Administration (NHTSA) revealed that the battery utilized in the Chevy Volt could cause fires. In response, GM made loaner cars available to the 6,000 owners of Volt owners while the problem was resolved (Terlep, 2011). Indeed, the effects of the information technology (IT) revolution have not always been positive. Information theft though hacking, pirating, and unauthorized entry into company information systems has created huge problems and crises for companies and organizations across the economy. The trust and credibility of everyone is now questioned in almost any organization and in any industry.

Resistance to Technology

History is replete with examples of those who have shunned technology. For some, technology itself was the crisis. The Luddites, for example, carried out violent attacks on technology in the early 1800s by smashing machines in industrial settings. However, the attacks, which originated in England during the Industrial Revolution, were more of a social protest against falling wages, unemployment, and rising food prices (Malcolm, 1970; Wren, 1987). In such an environment, the threat that machines would displace jobs seemed realistic. Unfortunately for the Luddites, their actions went too far, even to the point of burning down the houses of machine inventors John Kay and James Hargreaves (Wren, 1987).

An American group that even today shuns most technology, particularly electricity, is the Amish. Their rationale is that traditional Amish culture and social customs may be diluted (Berry, 1977). It can be argued that the Amish represent "the truest geniuses of technology, for they understand the necessity of limiting it, and they know how to limit it" (p. 212). It is not that the Amish oppose technology per se, but rather, they argue that it must be used only when it promotes the goodness of the people and the community (Rheingold, 1999; Schultze, 2002). The Amish, then, have reasoned that technological advances carry negative consequences as well and must be carefully evaluated when adopting a lifestyle.

From a crisis management perspective, the implications of such suspicions of technology are noteworthy. Although not to the degree of the Luddites and the Amish, many people today still fear technology and the change it can bring about. They work in our organizations, and their resistance can spawn a crisis. Consider these common examples (all of which have been encountered by the authors of this book) seen in various forms throughout a number of organizations today:

■ A supervisor in a department creates problems for the IT department when new software is introduced to replace the existing one. The result is poor morale in the resisting department and a headache of implementation for the IT department. The situation reaches a crisis when the department supervisor and the IT manager get in a shouting match in the company cafeteria.

■ A group of teachers in a public school district refuse to access their e-mail accounts from their school-issued computers placed in the classrooms. This older group of teachers lacks technical savvy and still feels that "the old ways are the best ways," a veiled reference to their resistance to learning how to use personal computers. As a result, the school district sends e-mails to all teachers and print hard copies for those who resist the change. Two minicrises are present in this situation. First, the printing of hard copies and the subsequent unnecessary use of paper is a needless waste of resources. Second, the very group of people responsible for teaching our children and inspiring a love of learning are resistant to learning new things themselves.

■ A senior accounting instructor in a small four-year college refuses to use spreadsheets as part of his instruction. The reason he gives is that "accounting is at the tip of the pencil," an obvious reference to the thinking skills required of every accountant. The real reason, however, is that this instructor does not know how to use computer spreadsheets, despite the fact that their usage has become mainstream in the field. This instructor had been resisting technology for years, and when he announces his retirement, the department finally advances into the 21st century in the delivery of its accounting instruction.

■ A supply chain manager who has kept up to date in the field is resisted by the company finance director when he proposes changes in how the company can place orders with its suppliers. The changes involve upgrading to electronic interfacing, already a common practice in many organizations. Each time the proposals are made, the finance director blatantly states that it costs too much. Again, two crises are present. First, the company misses out on a chance to make a much-needed upgrade to its purchasing function. Second, the supply chain manager seriously considers leaving his present employer for work in a more progressive organization.

Resistance to changes in technology remains prevalent. In the examples given, the overlap between strategic challenges and crisis events is evident. What begins as a strategic challenge ends up as a mild to moderate crisis because of some form of resistance to technology.

The advent of the Internet has created both opportunities and potential crises for government agencies. On the one hand, local governments can utilize the Internet to collect fees, disseminate information, and even provide some limited services to citizens. These types of arrangements emanate from strategic planning that seeks to serve a wider number of citizens in the most efficient and cost effective means possible. On the other hand, governments are charged with securing large amounts of data and protecting it from thieves. Indeed, the Internet has opened a new arena of organizational crises created by hackers, disgruntled consumers and employees, and others. Criminals throughout the world can extort thousands of dollars from organizations fearful of a Web crash. So-called cyber-blackmailers may have the ability to disrupt or even halt Internet activity associated with certain sites (Bryan-Low, 2005).

Crises and the Industry Life Cycle

Industries develop and evolve over time. Competitors within an industry change continually, and as a result, the nature and structure of the industry can also change as it matures and its markets are redefined. Strategy scholars have long known that an industry's developmental stage influences the nature of competition and potential profitability among competitors (Hofer, 1975; Miles, Snow, & Sharfman, 1993). Likewise, the stage of the industry life cycle can serve as a breeding ground for certain type of crises. In theory, each industry passes through five distinct phases of an industry life cycle: introduction, growth, shakeout, maturity, and decline.

Introduction Stage

In a young industry, demand for the industry's outputs is low while product and/or service awareness is still developing. Most purchasers are first-time buyers and tend to be relatively affluent, risk tolerant, and innovative (Parnell, 2013). Process technology is a key concern because firms are seeking ways to improve their production and distribution efficiencies. Product technology is also important because of the need to introduce new and innovative products. Crisis situations can develop with a new firm whose viability is linked to a developing technology or innovative product design that may be particularly vulnerable to imitation and even copyright infringement.

The untested domain of a new industry can also create a potential crisis, as we can see in the realm of transportation. As commercial air travel grew during the 1940s and 1950s, a string of aviation accidents also occurred. The causes of these accidents included pilot error, weather conditions, and flaws in the design of the aircraft. Two aircraft in particular that had their share of fatal crashes during these early years were the British-made de Havilland Comet and U.S.-built Lockheed Electra. Both of these suffered from structural defects in their earlier models. The de Havilland Comet was the world's first commercial jet, beginning service in 1952. Unfortunately, a string of fatal crashes revealed a structural flaw in the aircraft that eventually led to major changes in its design (Winchester, 2010). Likewise, the Lockheed Electra was one of the first commercial turboprop aircraft. It also had two major crashes involving a loss of a wing during the 1950s. Lockheed spent $25 million to modify and strengthen the design of the plane, which later went on to have a successful tenure in commercial aviation history (Magnuson, 1985). As for the de Havilland Comet, it also enjoyed success. However, unlike the Electra, which had existing aircraft retrofitted with safety and structural improvements, the Comet was improved by building later versions from the first-generation aircraft.

Growth Stage

The second industry stage, growth, is characterized by rising customer demand. Technological issues are addressed so that higher production can take place. The industry grows rapidly until market demand approaches saturation. Fewer first-time buyers remain, and most purchases tend to be upgrades or replacements. Many competitors are profitable, but they may be cash poor since available funds are heavily invested in new facilities or technologies (Parnell, 2013).

Some industries have been around for decades but are currently enjoying a new wave of growth. One example is the cruise ship industry, which is entering a surge of growth as baby boomers and their families seek out vacation retreats. At present, existing ships are being renovated and newer, larger vessels are joining the fleets of many of the cruise lines. But with more people hitting the seas, there is also a greater potential for accidents and crises. There have been several high-profile cruise ship fires in recent years, most notably the 2006 Carnival Cruise incident involving the *Star Princess,* a ship carrying 3,813 passengers and crew when it caught fire while bound for Jamaica. Two people suffered significant smoke inhalation, and one person died of a heart attack (Hayhurst, 2006).

In 2009, Princess Cruises experienced a fire in the engine room on its MS *Royal Princess,* a small ship that was cruising off Port Said, Egypt. Fortunately there were no fatalities, but the ship had to cancel its remaining cruise time as it was assisted back to port. In this fire, a special carbon dioxide flooding system was used to extinguish the blaze. Ship firefighting is different in that every gallon of water used to fight a fire must be pumped off the ship lest the vessel sink. Using carbon dioxide has been successful with smaller fires in confined spaces, a situation that exists on ships (Rielage, 2010). Although cruise ship fires are rare, it is an industry-wide threat because there is a fire potential on any cruise vessel (Coombs, 2007).

Another incident common to the entire industry is that of missing passengers who apparently fall overboard. In 2004 and 2005, for example, a total of 13 passengers disappeared from cruise ships (Martinez, 2005). Inevitably, such events can result in wrongful death lawsuits. Royal Caribbean faced this crisis in December 2005 when passenger George Smith disappeared on his honeymoon while in the Mediterranean. His parents filed a wrongful death lawsuit, claiming Royal Caribbean, the world's second largest cruise ship company, did not take sufficient action to prevent his disappearance (Martinez, 2005).

Although rare, a cruise ship accident can constitute a major crisis. A high-profile accident occurred on January 13, 2012, when the cruise ship *Costa Concordia* hit a rock close to shore off Giglio Island, Italy. The accident caused the ship to take on water and become partially submerged. Eleven of the ship's 4,200 passengers were confirmed dead and another 24 were missing (Mouawad, 2012). The *Costa Concordia* is owned by Costa Cruises, a part of Carnival Corporation, the world's largest cruise line. The accident occurred when the ship deviated from its normal course and sailed close to the shore. The reason for the change in course was widely disputed, but the captain of the ship, Francesco Schettino, claimed that he was ordered to do so by company officials (Pianigiani, 2012).

Shakeout Stage

As growth slows, the industry may enter a shakeout stage. At this point, industry growth is no longer strong enough to support the increasing number of rivals. Competitive crises become common, as firms take advantage of economies of scale. As a result, some of the industry's weaker competitors may not survive (Parnell, 2013).

A shakeout of a particular business may occur if a marginally performing firm encounters a crisis. Such was the case with the Mexican restaurant chain Chi-Chi's when it was struck with an outbreak of hepatitis A in September 2003. The sudden crisis sickened more than 660 people and caused three deaths. To make matters worse, the chain was already in Chapter 11 bankruptcy when the illnesses hit (Veil, Liu, Erickson, & Sellnow, 2005). Unfortunately, the impact of the crisis was enough to put the company out of business permanently.

Maturity Stage

Industry maturity occurs when the market demand for the industry's outputs is completely saturated. Virtually all purchases are upgrades or replacements, and industry growth may be slow if it is growing at all. Industry standards for quality and service have been established, and customer expectations tend to be more consistent than in previous stages (Parnell, 2013). When an industry reaches maturity, its remaining firms tend to be large and are more likely to become targets of interest groups, trade unions, and the like.

Because industry leaders tend to be larger, high-profile companies, they can also be targets for criticism from various stakeholders. A large company may be singled out for questionable practices, while smaller companies in the same industry may go unnoticed. Nestlé was targeted for a massive boycott in the 1970s for marketing infant formula to third world countries. However, smaller companies followed the same marketing strategy but were not attacked. Union Carbide was targeted by the newly created Environmental Protection Agency in 1970 not only for its large size but for the extent of its pollution in the Ohio Valley area in West Virginia. Fast forward to today, and one can see industry leaders like Wal-Mart, Starbucks, PepsiCo, and Coca-Cola under the gun for various alleged misdeeds.

Decline Stage

Sales decrease if and when an industry approaches the final stage, decline. This trend often begins when consumers turn to more convenient, safer, or higher-quality offerings from firms in substitute industries. Some firms may divest their business units in this stage, whereas others may seek to "reinvent themselves" and pursue a new wave of growth associated with a similar product or service (Parnell, 2013). As companies in these industries become weaker, they may also become more prone to crises.

The tobacco industry is one that has seen its share of crises, including product sales declines in the United States (although not in all parts of the world), as well as aggressive antismoking campaigns and lawsuits. Certainly, this is an industry in decline, at least in the United States. However, another less obvious example is the regional shopping mall industry. Early instances of indoor mall closings began in larger cities such as Chicago, Dallas, Los Angeles, San Francisco, and Milwaukee (Kilborn, 2003). Replacing regional mall shopping is the push for one-stop shopping at supercenters and power center retailers that offer one-stop shopping for food and other items (Ryan, 2008). Prices at these outlets are often lower because of correspondingly lower overhead costs.

Although retail sites have always been prone to some threat of robbery, some shopping malls have attracted a criminal element. Consider the once-famous Mall of Memphis in Tennessee. The two-level mall featured a larger than average food court, a five-screen movie theater, an indoor ice skating rink, and a safe atmosphere. However, the mall became a target for robberies and violent crime in the late 1990s and early 2000s. In one high-profile example, a 71-year-old shop manager was shot in the parking lot during a robbery (Kilborn, 2003). As crime engulfed the mall and the surrounding neighborhood, anchor stores Dillard's and J.C. Penney departed, triggering an exodus of smaller retailers. The Mall of Memphis closed in December 2003 after 22 years of operation. The facility was a victim of crime, declining neighborhoods, and changing customer shopping habits (Maki, 2006). This mall, along with hundreds of others, closed down after many years of successful service. The last years of many of these malls were full of crises, sometimes culminating in serious security and crime problems.

Crises and the Organizational Life Cycle

While the sources of crisis events can be linked to common factors in a given industry; many others are a function of an organization's unique attributes and business processes. Organization-specific factors may be linked to a firm's stage in the organizational life cycle, the most common description of which is a five-stage model based on the work of several researchers (Lester & Parnell, 2006; Lester, Parnell, & Carraher, 2003; Miller & Friesen, 1984). The following discussion looks at the relationship of the life cycle as a source of different crisis events.

Stage 1: Existence

Stage 1, also known as the existence or entrepreneurial stage (Quinn & Cameron, 1983), marks the beginning of an organization's development (Churchill & Lewis, 1983). The focus is on identifying a sufficient number of customers who will desire the firm's products or services. Decision making and ownership are in the hands of one or only a few individuals.

Most firms in this stage are small; however, many young organizations are launched with a significant amount of venture capital and may be quite large (Starbuck, 2003). The existence stage is characterized by long hours and diverse responsibilities on the part of employees. Because sufficient resources are not always available to hire staff specialists, employees may have to share responsibilities and even perform duties with which they might lack familiarity.

Sources of crises for organizations in the existence stage are often associated with resources and specialization. A new firm may lack the resources to protect itself from acts such as copyright infringement and may not be able to hire the specialists necessary to perform critical functions. Because employees often perform multiple roles, the potential for mental errors and/or physical accidents may also be greater during this stage.

When companies are young, the emphasis on formalized employee safety may be lacking. The inexperience and lack of maturity in making decisions can affect the approach to operating a business. The preoccupation with reaching the top without regard for the entire organization can facilitate vulnerabilities that expose the organization to a variety of crises. As an example, Film Recovery Systems, Inc., experienced a crisis early in its history. The company was formed in late 1979 with the purpose of extracting silver from used film. Two years later, however, an employee died from what was later determined to be acute cyanide poisoning. The medical examiner ruled that the victim died from breathing cyanide fumes at the Film Recovery Systems facility (Sethi & Steidlmeier, 1997). After several court cases, three company officials were sentenced for involuntary manslaughter. Eventually, the firm went bankrupt.

Stage 2: Survival

The survival stage is characterized by firm growth (Adizes, 1979). Formalization of structure (Quinn & Cameron, 1983) and establishing distinctive competencies—special abilities that distinguish a firm from its competitors (Miller & Friesen, 1984)—are sought during this stage. Firms in this stage typically focus on generating sufficient cash flow to survive (Churchill & Lewis, 1983).

The growth of the company is often due to a unique differentiating feature that makes it attractive to consumers. Odwalla, Inc., a 25-year-old company that makes fruit juices, is an example of a firm that was in the growth stage when a major crisis hit. The company had enjoyed success based on marketing its juices as fresh, with as little processing as possible. In October 1996 an *E. coli* outbreak in its unpasteurized apple juice product contributed to the death of a 16-month-old girl and caused 61 other children to become ill (Lawrence, 1999). Prior to the crisis, Odwalla made its juices without preservatives or any artificial ingredients. In addition, the juices were not pasteurized because the process changed the flavor as well as depleted important vitamins and enzymes. This differentiating factor led to the company's success and, ultimately, to a major crisis as well. Odwalla survived the crisis, but in the process switched to the flash pasteurization of its juice in order to prevent another *E. coli* outbreak (Lawrence, 1999).

Stage 3: Success

Organizations in the success stage have passed the survival test, growing to a point at which top management focuses on planning and strategy and leaves daily operations to middle managers and unit managers. Formalization and bureaucracy are the norm in the success stage, as can be seen through written job descriptions, the adoption of official policies and procedures, standardization of work, a clear division of labor, and hierarchical reporting relationships (Quinn & Cameron, 1983). However they must be vigilant because overconfidence and complacency as a result of their hubis is dangerous and a source of vulnerability. Managers need to keep their eye on the prize yet understand that no one is invincible.

When an organization succeeds, it may become the target of various forms of extortion attempts. Cracker Barrel, the Lebanon, Tennessee-based restaurant chain, was the victim in 2004 of such an attempt. In this plot, a mother and son planted a mouse in a bowl of soup at one of the Virginia stores. The two family members were later convicted of attempted extortion (Lockyer, 2007). Likewise, hamburger chain Wendy's faced an unusual crisis in March 2005 when a San Jose, California, customer, Ann Ayala, allegedly found a human finger in her chili. Law enforcement officials quickly got involved and attempted to identify the fingerprint. The finger was also autopsied and was determined to have been inserted after the chili was cooked. This clue led investigators to suspect product tampering. It was later discovered that Mrs. Ayala and her husband planted the finger in the chili in an attempt to collect monetary damages from the company. Nonetheless, Wendy's lost millions of dollars in sales in the Northern California market during the ordeal (Coombs, 2006).

Extortion attempts also target successful companies via the Internet. Such online extortionists have made threats against big-name companies, including Microsoft and Google. Although these firms have been able to successfully fight off such attacks, not all companies have been as fortunate. A credit card–processing company, 2Checkout, received an online extortion threat that it promptly rebuffed. It was later hit with a denial-of-service attack that put the company offline for more than a week (Fogarty, 2005).

Stage 4: Renewal

The renewing organization displays a desire to recreate a leaner organization that can respond more quickly and effectively to environmental changes (Miller & Friesen, 1984). In effect, the renewal stage can be viewed as one in which a firm seeks to regain control over how it responds to crisis-creating shifts in its environment. Firms in the renewal stage are trying to recapture a spirit of collaboration and teamwork that fosters innovation and creativity.

In an effort to renew itself, an organization may take radical steps to boost its market share. The sport entertainment genre of professional wrestling is one that has enjoyed success, downturns in popularity, and more recently, a resurgence of interest. In a renewal effort, elaborate stunts have been part of the shows.

Unfortunately, on May 23, 1999, pro wrestler Owen Hart fell 78 feet to his death in a stunt that went awry (Gegax & Adler, 1999). The resulting lawsuits and bad publicity were setbacks for World Wrestling Entertainment (WWE), the promoters of the event.

Despite the popularity and resurgence of professional wrestling, it has also encountered another crisis, a high death rate of wrestlers under the age of 45. One study found that wrestlers had a death rate seven times higher than the general population and were 12 times more likely to die of heart disease (Applebome, 2010). At the core of the problem is the use of steroids to enhance bodybuilding and the abuse of prescription drugs to treat painful injuries. The unusual circumstances surrounding the death of wrestler Chris Benoit in 2007 raised national attention. Benoit committed suicide by hanging himself after choking his wife and son to death in their Atlanta home. An autopsy report found he had significant levels of steroids and the painkiller hydrocodone in his system (Walton & Williams, 2011). This event and others led to calls for Congress to regulate the industry (Red, 2009).

Stage 5: Decline

Firms may exit the life cycle at any stage by going out of business, but those that progress through the stages and are unable to achieve renewal eventually reach the final stage of the life cycle. The decline stage embodies an internal environment characterized by politics and power (Mintzberg, 1984) as organization members become more concerned with personal goals rather than organizational goals. For some organizations, the inability to meet the external demands of a former organizational stage leads them to a period of decline when they experience lack of profit and loss of market share. Control and decision making have a tendency to return to a handful of people as desire for the power and influence of earlier stages erodes the viability of the organization. This is a stage at which the management is unable to sustain the momentum, the competitive edge that is critical to success. Lack of energy or interest causes the company to make too many mistakes, become complacent, and sometimes give up. This is a crucial stage that needs to be evaluated continually.

Sometimes, a single crisis can put an organization out of business permanently. Such was the case with Chalk's Ocean Airways, a niche-oriented carrier that flew flights from the port of Miami, Florida, to the Bahamas in vintage seaplanes. The company had been going through some rough financial times when, on December 19, 2005, one of its planes crashed, killing all 18 passengers and both pilots. The accident, flight 101 from Miami to Bimini, occurred about a minute after takeoff from the waterway. The right wing separated from the fuselage of the plane, causing it to crash in the shallow waters below. The age of the plane—a Grumman Turbo Mallard (G-73T) manufactured in 1947—and structural cracks in the wing contributed to the accident (National Transportation Safety Board [NTSB], 2007).

The airline was founded by A. B. "Pappy" Chalk in 1917. Its beginnings were humble, operating on Miami's Flagler Street under a beach umbrella with a desk and a phone number nailed to a nearby utility pole (Stieghorst, 2007). After World War I, when Chalk returned after flying for the military, he renamed the airline

Chalk's Flying Service in 1919 to fly tourists and fisherman to the Bahamas. Over the years, a number of different owners operated the airline, including the late television talk-show host Merv Griffin (Stieghorst, 2007). In 1980, a hotel and casino development company bought the airline. This company sold it to several South Florida investors, who used the operating name Pan Am Air Bridge (NTSB, 2007). James Confalone, owner of the company at the time of the accident, bought the airline in 1999 in bankruptcy court (Goodnough, Wald, & Lehren, 2005).

The airline was headquartered in Watson Island, a small island adjacent to the Port of Miami where the planes would takeoff from the waterway, the same channel where the ships also arrive and depart. At the time of the accident, Chalk's operated three G-73T aircraft offering six to eight flights daily to the Bahamas. On the day after the accident, Chalk's operated one more flight, after which it ceased operations (NTSB, 2007). Unlike most airline crashes, the Chalk's Flight 101 accident proved to be fatal to the company.

Firms in the decline stage function with some sort of disadvantage. Whether it is a struggle against stiff competition, a problem with cash flow, or an internal battle for control of the organization, the resolution of a crisis inevitably determines the survival or failure for the organization. The organizational life cycle is summarized in Figure 3.2.

Summary

Crisis events can originate from a number of sources external to the organization. These forces can be analyzed by examining the firm's macroenvironment, including political–legal, economic, social, and technological forces. Political–legal forces

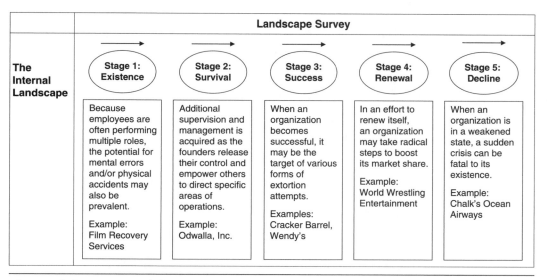

	Landscape Survey				
The Internal Landscape	**Stage 1: Existence**	**Stage 2: Survival**	**Stage 3: Success**	**Stage 4: Renewal**	**Stage 5: Decline**
	Because employees are often performing multiple roles, the potential for mental errors and/or physical accidents may also be prevalent. Example: Film Recovery Services	Additional supervision and management is acquired as the founders release their control and empower others to direct specific areas of operations. Example: Odwalla, Inc.	When an organization becomes successful, it may be the target of various forms of extortion attempts. Examples: Cracker Barrel, Wendy's	In an effort to renew itself, an organization may take radical steps to boost its market share. Example: World Wrestling Entertainment	When an organization is in a weakened state, a sudden crisis can be fatal to its existence. Example: Chalk's Ocean Airways

Figure 3.2 Crises and the Organizational Life Cycle

include politically motivated events such as terrorism, the outcomes of elections and legislation, as well as the decisions rendered by various commissions and governmental agencies. Economic forces include growth or decline in gross domestic product and increase or decrease in economic indicators such as inflation, interest rates, and exchange rates. The overexpansion of credit and the surge of oil prices sparked a number of organizational crises. Social forces include societal values, trends, traditions, and religious practices. Social forces specific to crises include a general distrust of corporate America, the preoccupation of consumers with low prices, social inequality and unrest, the health and fitness trend, and concern for the environment and sustainable development. Technological forces include scientific improvements and innovations that create opportunities or threats for businesses, as well as resulting technological pitfalls and resistance to technology on the part of the public. Each of these forces can create crises for organizations.

Organizational crises can also be examined in terms of the industry life cycle. This life cycle affects many firms that offer similar products or services. With each stage of this cycle—introduction, growth, shakeout, maturity, and decline—certain crisis vulnerabilities are more prominent. Likewise, the organizational life cycle, and its corresponding stages of existence—survival, success, renewal, and decline—can also breed specific types of crises.

Questions for Discussion

1. Identify political trends in your area (city, county, or state) that have contributed to or could contribute to a crisis in a particular industry.

2. How do political and economic events comingle to create a crisis?

3. What crisis events are discussed the most on the blogs and Internet sites that you visit?

4. What examples of resistance to technology have you seen where you work? Have you seen resistance at your school? If so, do you think this resistance constitutes a crisis?

5. Identify the life cycle stage in which your organization functions. What specific crises are associated with this stage of development?

6. How can the stage in the industry life cycle affect crises in individual organizations?

7. What industries are most vulnerable to crises in the near future? Explain.

Chapter Exercise

The class should form four groups, each representing one of the four factors discussed in the chapter: political–legal, economic, social, and technological. Each group creates a list of crises that originate from its respective factor. Display these lists in the classroom and identify the ones that seem to transcend multiple categories, such as crises that have both political and economic dimensions. Conclude the session by addressing trends in the four categories that could spawn future crises.

Mini-Case: Sony Gets Hacked

The name LulzSec probably does not mean much to the majority of the students reading this book. But to Sony, it represents an Internet crisis that cost them an estimated $173 million (Saporito, 2011). LulzSec is a group of hackers who broke into Sony's network and shut down its PlayStation Network on April 20, 2011. After Sony thought it had fixed the problem, LulzSec hacked their system again and Sony was unable to resolve the problem. During the months of April and May, the company's network was invaded a total of 20 times (Greenberg, 2011b).

The damage to the company was devastating. The PlayStation Network was down for about a month, leaving Sony in an embarrassing situation. Kazuo Hirai, a Sony executive who many people believe will be next in line as CEO, made the traditional Japanese bow and expressed his regrets to the public (Greenberg, 2011a). In addition, more than 100 million users' information had been exposed to hackers (Saporito, 2011). Sony's stock price dropped 23 percent in the months following the crisis (Greenberg, 2011b), and a class action lawsuit was filed in federal court in Los Angeles, charging that Sony was negligent in allowing the theft of consumer data (Wakabayashi, 2011).

Sony's chief executive, Howard Stringer, has advocated linking the firm's hardware products to online revenue options such as the PlayStation Network. Competing in the stand-alone hardware industry is no longer a highly profitable venture, and online venues are seen as way to supplement revenues. Apple follows a similar approach, linking its hardware with its iTunes media software (Wakbayashi, 2011). Unfortunately, what appeared to be an attractive strategic alternative also engendered a crisis.

What makes the Sony case particularly interesting is the motive of the hackers. Most cyber-attackers are motivated by money and have sometimes been given the informal term *black-hat hacker*. In contrast, a *white-hat hacker* is one who is hired by a company to see if its network can breached. Their motives are strictly to help the firm improve its cyber-security. In between the white- and black-hat groups one finds the *gray-hats*. This group preys on an organization's computer network as a form of protest or entertainment. When gray-hats have strong political messages or agendas, they are termed "hacktivists" (Rashid, 2011). In the case of Sony, the hackers were gray-hats, a group of six individuals calling itself LulzSec. *Lulz* implies entertainment and comes from the familiar LOL (laugh out loud) acronym. *Sec* is short for security. When the two are put together, it becomes apparent the hackers saw their work as a form of satire. LulzSec claimed to hack into Sony multiple times to expose the company's lax security (Saporito, 2011).

Unlike the black-hats, who seek to steal data quietly, gray-hats like LulzSec seek publicity to promote an agenda. In one hacking incident, Aaron Barr, then-CEO of cyber-security firm HB Gary Federal, boasted how his company was about to reveal the identities of several hacktivists from a group known as Anonymous. In retaliation, members of Anonymous hacked in HB Gary's system and stole e-mail and other sensitive documents (Rashid, 2011).

Mini-Case Discussion Questions

1. Why do you think Sony was targeted for attacks by LulzSec?

2. What other examples of hacking are you aware of?

3. Have you or your employer ever been the target of a hacking attempt? If so, what happened and how did your organization recover?

Mini-Case References

Greenberg, A. (2011a, May 24). Sony goes silent as its hacking spree snowballs. *Forbes, 34.*
Greenberg, A. (2011b, June 20). In Sony's 20th breach in two months, hackers claim 177,000 email addressed compromised. *Forbes, 21.*
Rashid, F. (2011, August 15). Hackers shift from vandalism to data theft. *eWeek,* 15–16.
Saporito, B. (2011, July 4). Hack attack. *Time,* 50–55.
Wakabayashi, D. (2011, April 28). Sony plan for network takes a blow. *Wall Street Journal,* p. B5.

References

Adizes, I. (1979). Organizational passages: Diagnosing and treating life cycle problems. *Organizational Dynamics, 8*(1), 3–24.
Applebome, P. (2010, August 26). Politics, wrestling and death. *New York Times,* p. 19.
Barrett, P. (2011, August 29). Cleaning America's dirtiest coal company. *Bloomberg Businessweek,* 48–55.
Bennett, J. (2008, June 23). Auto-parts firms face trouble as carmakers retool production. *Wall Street Journal,* p. B3.
Berry, W. (1977). *The unsettling of America: Culture and agriculture.* San Francisco: Sierra Club Books.
Brundtland Commission. (1987). *Development and International Economic Co-operation: Environment, Report of the World Commission on Environment and Development,* 54.
Bryan-Low, C. (2005, May 5). Tech-savvy blackmailers hone a new form of extortion. *Wall Street Journal,* pp. B1, B3.
Carroll, A., & Buchholtz, A. (2003). *Business and society: Ethics and stakeholder management.* Mason, OH: Thomson South-Western.
Cato, F. (1982). Proctor & Gamble and the devil. *Public Relations Quarterly, 27*(3), 16–21.
Ceniceros, R. (2011). Game changer for mine safety? *Business Insurance, 45*(48), 1–2.
Chin, T., Naidu, S., Ringel, J., Snipes, W., Bienvenu, S., & DeSilva, J. (1993). Denny's: Communicating amidst a discrimination case. *Business Communication Quarterly, 61*(1), 180–197.
Churchill, N., & Lewis, V. (1983). The five stages of small business growth. *Harvard Business Review, 61*(3), 30–50.
Coombs, W. (2006). *Code red in the boardroom: Crisis management as organizational DNA.* Westport, CT: Praeger.
Coombs, W. (2007). *Ongoing crisis communication: Planning, managing, and responding* (2nd ed.). Thousand Oaks, CA: Sage.

Copeland, M. (2005). Ronald gets back in shape. *Business 2.0, 6*(1), 46–47.

Crawford, M. (2009). *Shop class as soulcraft: An inquiry into the value of work.* New York: Penguin Press.

Cummins, C. (2003, March 24). Business mobilizes for Iraq. *Wall Street Journal,* pp. B1, B3.

Ellison, S., & Steinberg, B. (2003, June 20). To eat, or not to eat. *Wall Street Journal,* pp. B1, B4.

Ehrenreich, B. (2001). *Nickel and dimed: On (not) getting by in America.* New York: Henry Holt and Company.

Ehrenreich, B. (2009). *Bright-Sided: How the relentless promotion of positive thinking has undermined America.* New York: Henry Holt and Company.

Farrell, G. (2010, December 16). McDonald's sued over toys with meals. *Financial Times,* p. 20.

Farrell, F., & Weitzman, H. (2010, December 14). McDonald's chief attacks children's meal "food police." *Financial Times,* pp. 18, 20.

Fishman, C. (2006). *The Wal-Mart effect: How the world's most powerful company really works—and how it's transforming the American economy.* New York: Penguin.

Fogarty, K. (2005). Your money or your network. *Baseline.* Retrieved April 21, 2012, from http://www.baselinemag.com/c/a/Projects-Security/Your-Money-Or-Your-Network/1/.

Fortier, J. (2008). U of O research examines risks of mad cow disease. *Ottawa Business Journal, 13*(33), 14.

Fuller, K. (2006, October 19). Restaurant: Poor service wasn't bias: Rock speaks to media on Cracker Barrel incident. *Sun News* (Myrtle Beach, SC). Retrieved October 28, 2006, from Ebscohost database.

Gegax, T., & Adler, J. (1999, June 7). Death in the ring. *Newsweek,* 64–65.

Goodell, J. (2010, November 29). The Dark Lord of Coal Country. *Rolling Stone.* Retrieved April 17, 2012, from http://www.rollingstone.com/politics/news/the-dark-lord-of-coal-country-20101129.

Goodnough, A., Wald, M., & Lehren, A. (2005, December 22). Airline grounds fleet after seaplane crash. *New York Times,* p. 27.

Gray, S. (2005, January 27). For the health-unconscious, era of mammoth burger is here. *Wall Street Journal,* pp. B1, B3.

Hartley, R. (1993). *Business ethics: Violations of the public trust.* New York: Wiley.

Hayhurst, L. (2006, March 31). Princess offers full refunds. *Travel Weekly,* 10.

Hellier, K., & Ellison, S. (2005, December 9). Anheuser wants world to know beer is healthy. *Wall Street Journal,* pp. B1, B4.

Higgins, A. (2001, March 12). It's a mad, mad, mad-cow world. *Wall Street Journal,* pp. A13–A14.

Hofer, C. (1975). Toward a contingency theory of business strategy. *Academy of Management Journal, 18*(4), 784–810.

Kilborn, P. (2003, January 24). An enormous landmark joins the graveyard of malls. *New York Times,* p. 12.

King, N., Jr. (2003, April 11). The race to rebuild Iraq. *Wall Street Journal,* pp. B1, B3.

Kline, S. (2010). Not your father's recession. *Production Machining, 10*(10), 56.

Lawrence, A. (1999). Odwalla, Inc., and the E. coli outbreak (A), (B), (C). *Case Research Journal, 19*(1).

Lester, D., & Parnell, J. (2006). *Organizational theory.* Cincinnati: Atomic Dog Publishing.

Lester, D. L., Parnell, J. A., & Carraher, S. (2003). Organizational life cycle: A five-stage empirical scale. *International Journal of Organizational Analysis, 11,* 339–354.

Leung, S. (2004, January 28). McDonald's makeover. *Wall Street Journal,* pp. B1, B10.

Lockyer, S. (2007). Scams: Communication and crisis plans guard restaurants against cons and crooked insiders. *Nation's Restaurant News, 41*(21), 78–80.

Magnuson, E. (1985, February 4). Crash of a troubled bird. *Time,* 19.

Maki, A. (2006, September 20). Wal-Mart may put store at once-proud Memphis, Tenn., shopping location. *Commercial Appeal.* Retrieved April 21, 2012, from EBSCOhost Newspaper Source Plus Database.

Malcolm, T. (1970). *The Luddites: Machine breaking in Regency England.* Hamden, CT: Archer Books.

Martinez, A. (2005, December 10). RCL incident adds to safety debate. *Miami Herald.* Retrieved April 20, 2012, from http://www.redorbit.com/news/technology/328146/rcl_incident_adds_to_safety_debate/.

McKay, B. (2004, January 27). Downsize this! *Wall Street Journal,* pp. B1, B5.

Meckler, L., & Lundegaard, K. (2005, August 24). New fuel-economy rules help the biggest truck makers. *Wall Street Journal*, pp. B1, B2.

Michaels, D., & Trottman, M. (2005, September 7). Fuel may propel airline shakeout. *Wall Street Journal*, pp. C1, C5.

Miles, G., Snow, C., & Sharfman, M. (1993). Industry variety and performance. *Strategic Management Journal*, *14*(3), 163–177.

Miller, D., & Friesen, P. H. (1984). *Organizations: A quantum view.* Englewood Cliffs, NJ: Prentice Hall.

Mintzberg, H. (1984). Power and organization life cycles. *Academy of Management Review*, *9*(2), 207–224.

Mouawad, J. (2012, January 18). Industry weighs effect of ship accident. *New York Times*, p. 1.

National Transportation Safety Board. (2007). In-flight separation of right wing, Flying Boat, Inc. (doing business as Chalk's Ocean Airways) Flight 101, Grumman Turbo Mallard (G-73T), N2969, Port of Miami, Florida, December 19, 2005. *Aircraft Accident Report NTSB/AAR-07/04*. Washington, DC.

Parnell, J. A. (2013). *Strategic management: Theory and practice* (4th ed.). Thousand Oaks, CA: Sage.

Pianigiani, G. (2012, January 26). Captain of doomed cruise ship says course change was an order. *New York Times*, p. 12.

Quinn, R., & Cameron, K. (1983). Organizational life cycles and shifting criteria of effectiveness: Some preliminary evidence. *Management Science*, *29*(1), 33–41.

Red, C. (2009, January 2). *New York Daily News*. Retrieved April 23, 2012, from http://articles.nydailynews.com/2009-01-02/sports/17914359_1_drug-testing-wwe-total-nonstop-action.

Rheingold, H. (1999). Look who's talking: The Amish are famous for shunning technology, but their secret love affair with the cell phone is causing an uproar. *Wired*. Retrieved April 21, 2012, from http://www.wired.com/wired/archive/7.01/amish.html.

Rielage, R. (2010, July). Shipboard firefighting is a different animal. *Fire Chief*, 19–20.

Ryan, T. (2008). The future of the regional mall. *SGB*, *41*(10), 22.

Schultze, Q. (2002). *Habits of the high-tech heart: Living virtuously in the information age.* Grand Rapids, MI: Baker Academic.

Sethi, S., & Steidlmeier, P. (1997). *Up against the corporate wall: Case in business and society* (6th ed.). Upper Saddle River, NJ: Prentice Hall.

Sevastopulo, D. (2003, October 2). US airlines are on life support. *Financial Times*, p. 15.

Shell, E. (2010). *Cheap: The high cost of discount culture.* New York: Penguin Group.

Siegler, B. (2010). Bob Harper: Demands actions and takes no excuses. *American Fitness*, *28*(4), 34–36.

Smith, S. (2010). A "Massey"ive catastrophe. *EHS Today*, *3*(5), 8.

Starbuck, W. H. (2003). The origins of organization theory. In H. Tsoukas & C. Knudsen (Eds.), *The handbook of organization theory: Meta-theoretical perspectives* (pp. 143–182). Oxford, UK: Oxford University Press.

Steele, T., Smith, S., & McBroom, W. (1999). Consumer rumors and corporate communications: Rumor etiology, background, and potential devastating consequences. *Journal of Marketing Management*, *9*(2), 95–106.

Stewart, J. B. (2008, May 28). Auto makers can find opportunity in $4 gasoline. *Wall Street Journal*, p. D3.

Stieghorst, T. (2007, October 23). Chalk's Airlines loses flight license; its airport lease could be cancelled. Retrieved March 13, 2012, from http://www.aviationpros.com/news/10384737/chalks-airlines-loses-flight-license-its-airport-lease-could-be-canceled.

Taylor, E. (2008, May 6). Start-ups race to produce "green" cars. *Wall Street Journal*, p. B1.

Tennant, M. (2011, September 23). Obama's automobile standards could drive industry over a cliff. *New American*. Retrieved September 23, 2012, from http://www.thenewamerican.com/economy/sectors/item/4372-obama%E2%80%99s-automobile-standards-could-drive-industry-over-a-cliff.

Terlep, S. (2011, November 29). GM scrambles to defend Volt. *Wall Street Journal*, p. B1, B2.

Trachtenberg, J., & Steinberg, B. (2003, March 20). Plan B for marketers. *Wall Street Journal*, pp. B1, B3.

Veil, S., Liu, M., Erickson, S., & Sellnow, T. (2005). Too hot to handle: Competency constrains character in Chi-Chi's green onion crisis. *Public Relations Quarterly, 50*(4), 19–22.

Walton, L., & Williams, K. (2011). World Wrestling Entertainment responds to the Chris Benoit tragedy: A case study. *International Journal of Sport Communication, 4,* 99–114.

Winchester, J. (2010). *Civil aircraft—Passenger and utility aircraft: A century of innovation.* London: Amber Books.

Wren, D. (1987). *The evolution of management thought* (3rd ed.). New York: Wiley.

Wright, P., Kroll, M., & Parnell, J. (1998). *Strategic management: Concepts.* Upper Saddle River, NJ: Prentice Hall.

WV Governor's report places blame for Upper Big Branch explosion on Massey, agencies. (2011, June). *Coal Age, 116*(6), 10.

CHAPTER 4

A Strategic Approach to Crisis Management

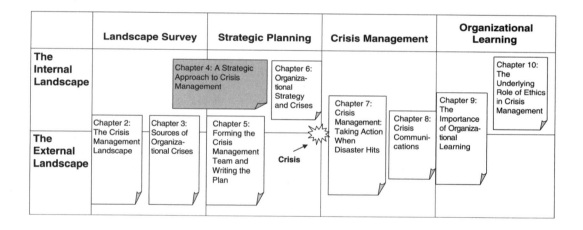

	Landscape Survey		Strategic Planning	Crisis Management		Organizational Learning
The Internal Landscape			Chapter 4: A Strategic Approach to Crisis Management	Chapter 6: Organiza-tional Strategy and Crises		Chapter 7: Crisis Management: Taking Action When Disaster Hits	Chapter 9: The Importance of Organiza-tional Learning	Chapter 10: The Underlying Role of Ethics in Crisis Management
The External Landscape	Chapter 2: The Crisis Management Landscape	Chapter 3: Sources of Organiza-tional Crises	Chapter 5: Forming the Crisis Management Team and Writing the Plan	**Crisis**	Chapter 8: Crisis Communi-cations	

Opening Case, Part 1: The Professor, "Arrogant Amy"

Dr. Amy Bishop arrived on the campus of the University of Alabama at Huntsville (UAH) in 2003 with impeccable credentials. She had a Ph.D. from Harvard and was by all means a rising star in the field of neurobiology. Her new position was that of a tenure-track assistant professor, a job that would require her to teach and conduct research. A tenure-track professor at UAH has six years to make a case for the long-term stint known as tenure. An assistant professor who is not deemed to be a good fit may be denied tenure, at which time the assistant professor begins anew at another institution.

In general, a tenure-track faculty member must be a good teacher and provide a steady stream of research scholarship in the form of peer-reviewed publications. In addition, *being collegial* is a term used frequently on university campuses. Albeit subjective, the notion of collegiality means that faculty members are respectful of their students and peers. Put a bit differently, a faculty member must be likeable, although agreement with everything that is said at the university is not required. Indeed, one can disagree with another colleague's viewpoint but still be respectful and courteous to that colleague. Professors who are overly confrontational or arrogant may find it hard to attain tenure at some institutions. Amy Bishop's arrogant and abrasive style rubbed many people the wrong way, earning her the informal nickname "Arrogant Amy." She was even known for introducing herself as "Dr. Amy Bishop, Harvard-trained" (Wallace, 2011).

Bishop's personal style of carrying herself did not go over well at UAH. Initially, she was described by colleagues and students as funny and extroverted, but she was not universally liked. Students complained that her exam questions went beyond what was covered in the course. A petition was circulated by students complaining about her exams (Dewan, Saul, & Zezima, 2010).

Her relationship with graduate students was also volatile. It was generally known that most students simply did not last long working for her in the laboratory, and many transferred to another lab before completing their degrees. One student was dismissed from her lab in May 2006. The student promised to return notebooks and keys the next day, but Bishop called the campus police to address the situation (Dewan et al., 2010).

Her erratic behavior was noted by a member of her tenure committee, who commented in a report that she was literally "crazy." When given a chance to restate the word *crazy*, the faculty member did not change his stance, stating "I said she was crazy multiple times and I stand by that. . . . The woman has a pattern of erratic behavior. She did things that weren't normal. . . . She was out of touch with reality" (Wallace, 2011).

In March, 2009, the university decided not to accept her application for tenure. Bishop's research was cited as being a low point. She had published one peer-reviewed paper in each of 2004, 2005, and 2006, but none in 2007 and 2008. Then, in 2009, she had three peer-reviewed papers, although one of them was published in a journal that was not considered of very high quality. In addition, her teaching failed to measure up to the standards desired by UAH (Bartlett, Wilson, Basken, Glenn, & Fischman, 2010).

At this point in her career, it would be expected that Amy Bishop would need to move on to another institution. The career prospects, though, can be difficult for some professors, as many in the higher education industry see not getting tenure as being the ultimate rejection from that colleague's peers (Wallace, 2011). In addition, career mobility for a faculty member who teaches and researches in a very specialized field can be limited. For some professors, there may be only one or two positions each year for which they are truly qualified (Bartlett et al. 2010). Dr. Bishop decided to appeal the tenure decision and requested that various faculty members write letters of support on her behalf. She was the main source of income for her family and she desperately needed the job; the family was already experiencing financial problems and had discussed declaring bankruptcy (Wallace, 2011). Despite her efforts to appeal the tenure decision, her request was still denied. Dr. Bishop would need to seek employment elsewhere.

Opening Case Part 1 Discussion Questions

1. What can colleges and universities do to help their new faculty be successful in their jobs?

2. Some take the viewpoint that the institution is at fault if a faculty member fails to attain tenure. Discuss this statement in terms of its merits.

3. Faculty members who are not granted tenure are often given a final one-year contract before they are required to leave. What potential crisis could emerge during that person's last year on campus?

Opening Case Part 1 References

Bartlett, T., Wilson, R., Basken, P., Glenn, D., & Fischman, J. (2010, February 26). In Alabama, a scientist's focus turns deadly. *Chronicle of Higher Education,* pp. A8, A12.

Dewan, S., Saul, S., & Zezima, K. (2010, February 20). For professor, fury just beneath the surface. *New York Times.* Retrieved July 26, 2012, from http://www.nytimes .com/2010/02/21/us/21bishop.html?pagewanted=all

Wallace, A. (2011, February 28). What made this university researcher snap? *Wired.* Retrieved July 26, 2012, from http://www.wired.com/magazine/2011/02/ff_bishop/.

Introduction

Effective crisis management requires that managers understand both the sources of crisis events and the strategies needed to identify and plan for them. A crisis event rarely occurs "out of the blue." Instead, it usually follows one or more warning signs. Typically, a series of precondition events occur before a crisis can commence. These events eventually lead to the "trigger event" that ultimately causes the crisis (Shrivastava, 1995; Smith, 1990). Recall that in 1984, deadly methyl isocyanate gas leaked from a storage tank at a Union Carbide plant in Bhopal, India, initially killing more than 2,500 people and injuring another 300,000. The trigger event for this crisis was the entry of water into a storage tank that subsequently caused the unit's temperature and tank pressure to rise. Numerous preconditions contributed to the origin of this accident. These included shutting down a refrigeration system designed to keep the gas cool, failing to reset the tank temperature alarm, neglecting to fix a nonfunctioning gas scrubber, and not performing the maintenance and repair on an inoperative flame tower designed to burn off toxic gases (Hartley, 1993). Each of these four systems was designed to help alert plant workers and contain the toxic effects of a gas leak. Each of them was inoperable the day of the accident.

In the evolution of a crisis, the warning signs may not be identified until it is too late, either because decision makers are not aware of them or because they do not recognize them as serious threats. Sometimes managers are simply in denial. Some assert that a crisis cannot happen to their organization or that the probability of it occurring is so low that it does not warrant spending the time and resources required to prevent it (Nathan, 2000; Pearson & Mitroff, 1993). In some cases, the warning signs are ignored altogether, even though these preconditions are signaling an impending crisis. For example, Toyota's unintended acceleration problem with its Camry model was preceded by a year's worth of problems with stuck accelerators (Institute for Crisis Management, 2011). All of this underscores the importance of assessing crisis vulnerability, the practice of scanning the environment and identifying those threats that could happen to the organization.

In this chapter, we examine crisis management from a strategic point of view. First we overview the challenges managers face as they assess the external environment, particularly in terms of its uncertainty. We then proceed to the heart of identifying potential crises and employ the SWOT (strengths, weaknesses, opportunities, and threats) analysis, a tool that is widely used in strategic planning. We close this chapter with a short discussion on the link between organizational culture and crisis planning.

A Strategic Approach to Crisis Management

Crisis management requires a *strategic* mind-set or perspective (Chong & Park, 2010; Preble, 1997; Somers, 2009). Therefore, understanding effective crisis management requires that we first understand the four key distinctions of a strategic orientation perspective.

1. It is based on a systematic, comprehensive analysis of internal attributes, also referred to as strengths and weaknesses; and of factors external to the organization, commonly referred to as opportunities and threats. Readers familiar with strategic management recognize this process as the SWOT analysis. Approaching this process in a systematic manner is important because it ensures that potential crises are not overlooked. Thus, we must look both inside and outside the organization as we determine the risk factors that must be confronted.

2. A strategic orientation is long term and future oriented—usually several years to a decade into the future—but also built on knowledge of events from the past and present.

3. A strategic orientation is distinctively opportunistic, always seeking to take advantage of favorable situations and avoiding pitfalls that may occur either inside or outside the organization.

4. A strategic orientation involves choices, and very important ones at that. Because preparing for every conceivable crisis can be costly, priorities must be established. For example, resources must be spent to ensure safety in the workplace. The expenditure of resources, however, does take money directly off the bottom line. Because this approach is strategic, the expenditure may ensure the overall well-being of the firm in the long run. Therefore, some expenditures should not be viewed solely as cost items, but as investments in the future longevity (and safety) of the company.

Because of these distinctions, the overall crisis management program must include the top executive and members of his or her management team. The chief executive is the individual ultimately accountable for the organization's strategic management, as well as any crises that involve the organization. Except in the smallest companies, he or she relies on a *team* of top-level executives, all of whom play instrumental roles in the strategic management of the firm (Carpenter, 2002; Das & Teng, 1999).

Strategic decisions designed to head off crises are made within the context of the strategic management process, which can be summarized in five steps (Parnell, 2013):

1. *External analysis.* Analyze the opportunities and threats or constraints that exist in the organization's macroenvironment, including industry and external forces.

2. *Internal analysis.* Analyze the organization's strengths and weaknesses in its internal environment; reassess the organization's mission and its goals as necessary.

3. *Strategy formulation.* Formulate strategies that build and sustain competitive advantage by matching the organization's strengths and weaknesses with the environment's opportunities and threats.

4. *Strategy execution.* Implement the strategies that have been developed.

5. *Strategic control.* Engage in strategic control activities when the strategies are not producing the desired outcomes.

Crisis management is an important consideration in each step, in different ways. In the first step, managers identify the sources of crises that exist in the firm's external environment. Typically, the organization's external opportunities and threats are identified to determine specific vulnerabilities of concern. The threat of online viruses and other denial-of-service (DoS) attacks, for example, may suggest that the firm invest in upgrading firewall and virus protection measures so that its website is not taken offline by hackers (Robb, 2005). Also related to technology is a new opportunity: the use of social media outlets in addition to the company's regular Web page. Facebook pages for organizations are common as firms seek to demonstrate their human side to the public. This move can be important when a crisis does strike, because the company can use more personalized media outlets to communicate its side of the story (Jacques, 2009).

Government regulations, formed in response to a previous crisis, are part of the external environment. Following a salmonella outbreak and subsequent recalls of tomatoes in 2008, the U.S. Food and Drug Administration strengthened inspection and other measures to reduce the likelihood of a similar crisis in the future. Initially, the agency focused on tomatoes as the culprit. Later, various types of peppers were also part of the investigation (O'Rourke, 2008). Food-related firms from growers to producers to restaurants should consider how this crisis evolved and what strategic changes might be appropriate (Zhang, 2008). Ultimately, those in the food manufacturing industry must be knowledgeable concerning what is now labeled *food traceability*, a term that requires all parties processing food to have the ability to track inputs through the entire supply chain (Schrader, 2010).

The second step focuses on vulnerabilities within the organization that may result in a crisis event. Typically, the organization's internal strengths and weaknesses are identified to determine what vulnerabilities may be present. A poorly trained workforce, for example, could lead to a workplace accident. Likewise, dubious advertising claims about one's competitors could result in litigation. Aging equipment is another common area of weakness.

The Chalk's Ocean Airways crash mentioned in Chapter 3 is an example of a company with certain strengths that made it a popular small airline over many decades. In 2003, the airline had been cited in the *Guinness Book of World Records* as the world's oldest continuously operating airline (Scammell, 2003). The company was a novelty in south Florida because it flew vintage seaplanes to the Bahamas, a feature that made it popular with local Bahamians who found the arrangement convenient when returning home. Indeed, flying in seaplanes in a time of modern aviation was a strength that the airline possessed. It was a visit back to nostalgic times. Unfortunately, the vintage seaplanes also embodied a weakness that was not apparent to its mechanics: structural fatigue cracks caused by years of use. "This accident tragically illustrates a gap in the safety net with regard to older airplanes," said Mark Rosenker, National Transportation Safety Board (NTSB) chairman. "The signs of structural problems were there—but not addressed. And to ignore continuing problems is to court disaster" (Vines, 2007, p. 14).

The third and fourth steps concern the development and execution of the firm's strategies at the various functional levels. Indeed, some strategies are more prone to crisis events than others. For example, a strategy that emphasizes global expansion into less stable emerging nations engenders a greater risk of crisis than one that has a strong domestic market orientation. This is not to suggest that potential crisis-laden strategies be avoided, but rather that they be evaluated closely within the strategic decision-making process.

The final step involves strategic control. This is an evaluative process through which the organization's managers engage in a serious assessment of the outcomes that are occurring or have occurred in the organization. Once the assessment is completed, the organization must take action to counter undesirable or unanticipated outcomes that emanate from the strategy's implementation. When a strategy is executed as planned, control may be minimal. When execution difficulties exist or unforeseen problems arise, however, the nature of strategic control may need to change to crisis prevention or even crisis response. Monitoring mechanisms must be established so that corrective action can be initiated when necessary. Strategic control is useful in crisis management because it often signals that a problem may be forthcoming. For example, accounting controls can signal whether there is embezzlement taking place in the organization. Figure 4.1 depicts how these five strategic steps fit within the crisis management framework. Note that Chapter 3 provided the foundation for the second step in the process—examining the external landscape. This chapter builds on that discussion and also focuses on Steps 2 and 3. In the next section, we examine the nature of environmental uncertainty as it pertains to the strategic and crisis management process.

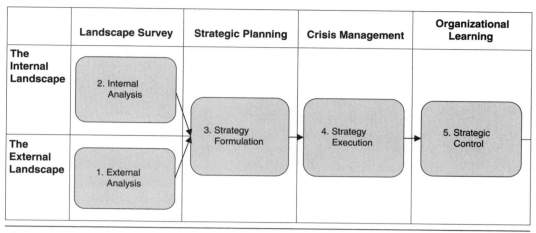

Figure 4.1 A Strategic Approach to Crisis Management

Understanding Environmental Uncertainty

Chapter 3 discussed a number of external sources of crises: political–legal, economic, social, and technological forces. Preventing crises would probably not be so complex if the top management team always had perfect information. Unfortunately, this is not the case. An important step in the strategic management process—analyzing the external environment—presents one of the most critical challenges for preventing crises: understanding and managing environmental uncertainty.

Managers must develop a systematic process to obtain information about the organization's environment. Ideally, top managers should be aware of the multitude of external forces that influence an organization's activities. Uncertainty occurs when decision makers lack current, sufficient, or reliable information and cannot accurately forecast future changes. In practice, decision makers in any organization must be able to render decisions when environmental conditions are uncertain.

Environmental uncertainty is influenced by three key characteristics of the organization's environment. First, the environment can be classified along a simple–complex continuum. Simple environments have few external factors that influence the organization, and the strength of these factors tends to be minimal. Complex environments are affected by numerous external factors, some of which can have a major influence on the organization. Most organizations fall somewhere between these two extremes.

Second, the environment can be classified along a stable–unstable continuum. Stable environments are marked by a slow pace of change. City and county municipalities typically fall under the category of stable environments. Unstable environments are characterized by rapid change, such as when competitors continually modify strategies, consumer preferences change quickly, or technological forces develop rapidly. The computer hardware and software industries reside in unstable environments.

Third, environmental uncertainty is a function of the quality or richness of information available to decision makers (Starbuck, 1976). This information function usually does not present a problem for established firms operating in developed countries. In these settings, information sources are of higher quality and richness; they include business publications, trade associations, and well-developed governmental agencies. In emerging economies, however, reliable data on items such as market demand, economic forces, and consumer preferences may not be as readily available.

Considering these three environmental characteristics, uncertainty is lowest in organizations with simple and stable environments, and where the quality of available information is high. In contrast, uncertainty is highest in organizations whose environments are complex and unstable, and where the quality of information is low (Duncan, 1972). The relationship between uncertainty and the prevalence of organizational crises can now be seen: as uncertainty increases in organizations, so does the likelihood of crises. Hence, organizations whose core competencies are tied closely to technology tend to experience the greatest complexity and instability. Following the terrorist attacks of September 11, 2001, airlines were added to this category because of increased regulatory pressure and fears of further attacks.

Organizations in environments marked by low uncertainty should be managed differently from those marked by high uncertainty. When uncertainty is low, greater formality and established procedures can be implemented to increase predictability, improve efficiency, and lessen the frequency of crisis events. When uncertainty is high, however, procedures are difficult to develop because processes tend to change more frequently. In this situation, decision makers are often granted more freedom and flexibility so that the organization can adapt to its environment as it changes or as better information on the environment becomes available. While this freedom and flexibility may be necessary, it can create a crisis-prone environment. The reason is the possibility of experiencing what management scholar Karl Weick (1993) labels as "cosmology episodes." Such episodes are characteristic of many crisis events in which the stakeholders involved have encountered a situation unlike any that has been experienced before. Indeed, one of the characteristics of a crisis is its low probability of occurring, and yet, if it does occur, it can appear to be unique and unparalleled. The term *cosmology episode* was originally applied to the 1949 forest fire at Mann Gulch, Montana, that resulted in the deaths of 13 smokejumpers. The event consisted of a unique interaction of weather, fire, and geography that trapped the smokejumpers fighting the fire (Weick, 1993). Despite the fact that the smokejumpers were experienced and the original fire was not considered large, the events that unfolded were new to those involved and ended in tragedy.

A number of techniques are available for managing uncertainty in the environment. The first consideration, however, is whether the organization should adapt to its environment or, in some cases, attempt to influence or change it. Urban hospitals represent a classic example of adapting to their environments when the surrounding neighborhoods where they are located become crime ridden, a common problem for many urban facilities. Moving the hospital is usually not an option because, geographically, it is located to serve a specific community. To keep it safe from the crime in the external neighborhoods (and hence, free of specific crises), measures are taken to ensure the safety of the buildings and the patients. Employing extra security guards, installing perimeter lighting, using security cameras, and utilizing metal detectors are all methods of adapting to the environment.

Occasionally, a business may seek to change its environment to protect it from a crisis. Farmers have been known to use special cannons to ward off approaching hail that might damage crops. These anti-hail cannons send a loud popping noise into the air, directed squarely at the storm at hand. Although the practice stems back to the 1890s—and is not entirely validated by science—a resurgence of this practice has occurred in both Europe and the United States (Griffith, 2008). Even automaker Nissan has used this unusual method for dealing with hail. The company has a production facility in Canton, Mississippi, with a storage area of 140 acres. Hail is a major concern because of the body damage it can cause to an automobile. To respond to this threat, Nissan installed its anti-hail system using sound-producing hail cannons. Using weather-sensing equipment—when conditions are right for hail—a sonic wave is fired into the air every five and a half seconds to prevent the forming of hail (Foust & Beucke, 2005). Not everybody is happy with the arrangement, however, as the cannons have created a secondary crisis: local neighbors have been complaining about the excessive noise and have petitioned the Madison County Board of Supervisors to make Nissan stop the practice. However, county officials have not found Nissan in violations of existing laws, although they did ask the company to explain to the board how the cannons are supposed to work (Chappell, 2005).

Other techniques for managing uncertainty can also be used. One is buffering, a common approach whereby organizations establish departments to absorb uncertainty from the environment and thereby buffer its effects (Thompson, 1967). Purchasing departments, for example, perform a buffering role by stockpiling resources for the organization lest a crisis occur if they become scarce. Likewise, even companies that follow lean management practices are learning that some buffering is necessary lest there be an interruption within their supply chains (Ganguly & Guin, 2007). Of course, establishing a crisis management team and engaging in formal planning is also a form of buffering. If a crisis occurs, the team takes on a mitigating role by managing the ordeal.

Another technique is imitation, an approach whereby the organization mimics a successful key competitor. Presumably, organizations that imitate their competitors reduce uncertainty by pursuing "safety in numbers." The concept of imitation is paramount in crisis management as companies seek to learn what other organizations are doing to avoid crises. The literature on high-reliability organizations (HROs) has helped to achieve this goal by extolling how those in high-risk environments manage to stay incident free (Bourrier, 2011; Roberts & Bea, 2001).

Imitating the successful crisis management techniques of other organizations can be advantageous as well. The crisis management plans for many universities and government agencies are publicly available on their websites. One can learn much by studying the examples of these plans. However, imitation must be undertaken with an understanding of the differences that exist between the two organizations. Managers must account for the specific internal and external factors unique to their own organizations, which is why assessing crisis risks must begin with an examination of the organization's internal and external environments. Imitating an ineffective strategy or structure can also reduce the effectiveness of crisis management (Bertrand & Lajtha, 2002).

Environmental Scanning

Keeping abreast of changes in the external environment that can lead to crises presents a key challenge. *Environmental scanning* refers to collecting and analyzing information about relevant trends in the external environment. A systematic environmental scanning process reduces uncertainty and organizes the flow of current information relevant to organizational decisions. In addition, scanning provides decision makers with an early warning system about changes in the environment. This process is also an important element in risk identification. Because organization members often lack critical knowledge and information, they may scan the environment by interacting with outsiders, a process known as *boundary spanning*.

Environmental scanning is meant to be future oriented in that it provides a basis for making strategic decisions. It also must not be too general in nature (Kumar, Subramanian, & Strandholm, 2001), but specific to the needs of the organization. Hence, the goal is to provide *effective* environmental scanning to produce information relevant to the firm (Groom & David, 2001). Although managers may possess information that could mitigate a crisis or prevent it from occurring, they still need to act on that information and make the appropriate decisions.

The infamous crisis that erupted between Royal Dutch Shell and the environmental activist group Greenpeace illustrates that important cues can still be ignored by management. In fact, this incident has been labeled a "predictable surprise," one that had plenty of warning indicators, yet still caught the company off guard (Watkins & Bazerman, 2003). The incident involved Shell's plan to sink an obsolete oil platform, the *Brent Spar,* in the North Sea. On April 29, 1995, however, Greenpeace activists boarded the platform and announced they would block its sinking because of radioactive contaminants that were stored on the structure. Shell responded by blasting the protestors and their boats with water cannons, a move that turned out to cause a major public relations crisis for the company. After the water cannon incident, opposition to Shell's plans grew in Europe, leading to a boycott of Shell service stations in Germany. Protestors damaged 50 German gas stations, firebombing two of them and riddling one with bullets (Zyglidopoulos, 2002). Less than two months after the initial Greenpeace protest, Shell gave in and abandoned its plan to sink the *Brent Spar.*

Watkins and Bazerman (2003) note that Royal Dutch Shell was surprised by the turn of public opinion against it. This occurred despite the fact that the company had an abundance of information indicating that protests by Greenpeace likely would involve the physical occupation of the platform by activists. Even other oil companies protested Shell's plans. The case illustrates that misreading external signals can still occur even when those signals prove to be reliable.

Environmental scanning should be viewed as a continuous process (Herring, 2003). Top managers must plan for and identify the types of information the organization needs to support its strategic decision making. A system for obtaining this information is then developed. Information is collected, analyzed, and disseminated to the appropriate decision makers, usually within the functional areas of the firm. This information must be acted on, however, as the A. H. Robins case illustrates.

In the early 1970s, A. H. Robins manufactured the Dalkon Shield, a plastic intrauterine contraceptive device (IUD). More than 4 million IUDs were implanted in women by doctors who were swayed by the optimistic research reports offered by the company (Hartley, 1993). However, warnings from the external environment began to surface almost immediately after the product was introduced. Women were afflicted with pelvic infections, sterility, septic abortions, and in a few cases, death (Barton, 2001; Hartley, 1993). An analysis of information coming in from the external environment would have prompted most companies to shut down production of the IUD, but A. H. Robins persisted in marketing the product. It continued to promote the device as safe, even though management knew there were problems. In the end, the company was sued by thousands of victims. Eventually, the firm's poor financial standings resulting from lawsuit payoffs led to a sale of the company to American Home Products in 1989 (Barton, 2001).

Large organizations may engage in environmental scanning activities by employing one or more individuals whose sole responsibility is to obtain, process, and distribute important environmental information to their organization's decision makers. These individuals continually review articles in trade journals and other periodicals and watch for changes in competitor activities. They also monitor what is being said about the company on the Internet, including blogs and other social media outlets. Alternatively, organizations may contract with a research organization that offers environmental scanning services and provides them with real-time searches of published material associated with their organizations, key competitors, and industries. In contrast, decision makers at many smaller organizations must rely on trade publications or periodicals such as the *Wall Street Journal* to remain abreast of changes that may affect their organizations.

A potential lack of objectivity can be a concern when managers evaluate the external environment because they perceive selectively through the lens of their own experiences, professional expertise and operating departments. Managers with expertise in certain functional areas may be more interested in evaluating information pertaining to their functions. The problem with this viewpoint is that key elements from the environment may be ignored—elements that may pose future risks that could develop into a crisis. For example, cutting the budget of a human resource (HR) department to trim overall costs may sound tempting to the chief executive officer (CEO), but lapses in HR can lead to poor training and loosely enforced safety rules, both of which can lead to industrial accidents (Sheaffer & Mano-Negrin, 2003).

In an example of functional bias based on CEO background, Massey Energy has long suffered from a tarnished reputation based on its disregard for safety regulations set forth in the coal mining industry (Barrett, 2011). Under the direction of its former CEO, Don Blankenship, the company performed well financially, but apparently at the expense of miner safety (Fisk, Sullivan, & Freifeld, 2010). The result was a string of mining accidents, some involving fatalities. According to David McAteer, a governor-appointed investigator of the company's mining accidents between 2000 and 2010, "No United States coal company had a worse fatality record than Massey Energy" (Barrett, 2011, p. 51). During that decade, Massey had 54 mining fatalities. The company did not respond effectively to the external environment for cues to prevent a crisis. Rather, Massey responded by alerting mine staff when inspectors were about to descend on the mine (Fiscor, 2011) and by keeping separate books to cover up safety violations from in-mine safety reports required by federal law (Ward, 2011).

A key problem associated with environmental scanning is determining which available information warrants attention. This is why developing sensitive indicators that trigger responses is so important. Consider the December 2004 Asian tsunami. Although an earthquake had been detected, scientists were unsure of the exact size of the resulting tsunami and were unable to share their observations with countries that would soon be affected because the governments in those countries lacked environmental scanning systems (Coombs, 2006).

Identifying Potential Crises Using the SWOT Analysis

The first step in assessing the likelihood of a crisis specific to a particular organization is to conduct a survey of the internal and external environments. This process involves the collection of data and perspectives from various stakeholders. The data are then integrated into an overall assessment of specific crisis threats that appear to be most prominent. Typically, each threat is ranked in terms of its likelihood and potential impact on the organization. Those crisis threats at the top of the list become the focus of prevention and mitigation efforts.

In strategic planning, the SWOT analysis is the tool used to determine an organization's strengths, weaknesses, opportunities, and threats. The SWOT analysis should also be used to assess crisis vulnerability during the strategic planning process (Chong, 2004). For example, in 2003, the Pacific Area Travel Association (PATA) provided a framework for its members to use to identify crisis threats to their organizations, most of which are involved with destination tourism. The use of the SWOT analysis to identify such threats is a major planning tool in assessing crises vulnerability (Parnell, 2013; Pennington-Gray, Thapa, Kaplanidou, Cahyanto, & McLaughlin, 2011). In the sections that follow, we identify the four facets of the SWOT analysis and how they are linked to potential crises.

Strengths

Typically, internal strengths would not be thought to contribute to a potential crisis. As Veil (2011, see p. 125) notes, however, a track record of organizational successes can blind management to perceiving warning signals from potential crises.

Location is a key strength in some organizations, particularly those in destination tourism. Certainly, lodging establishments can be worthy retreats for tourists when they are located in exotic places, such as on islands and beaches. However, a coastal location can turn into vulnerability when a hurricane, typhoon, or tsunami occurs. Such was the case for many tourist hotels in South Asia when an earthquake occurred off the coast of the island of Sumatra in Indonesia. This event triggered a devastating tsunami that caused widespread damage and up to 250,000 fatalities in the South Asian region. Many of the victims were staying at resort hotels that were unprepared for such an event (Cheung & Law, 2006).

Management researchers Gilbert Probst and Sebastian Raisch identified a number of organizational strengths that can eventually lead to problems. For example, excessive growth, what many would deem is a desirable performance outcome, can be offset by problems with high debt and an overemphasis on expanding through company acquisitions. In this respect, strength can lead to a crisis. Likewise, a strong leader in the organization can lead to a top-down culture in which the followers put blind faith in the leader and fail to approach the leader's strategies with skeptical questioning (Probst & Raisch, 2005). This situation is further exasperated when boards of directors rubber-stamp the CEO's agenda, often failing to challenge top management with tough questions and instead exhibiting groupthink, further putting the balance of power dangerously in favor of the CEO (Zweig, 2010).

Table 4.1 provides examples of internal organizational strengths that could conceivably result in organizational crises.

Table 4.1   Examples of Internal Organizational Strengths and Potential Crisis Events

Internal Strength	Corresponding Potential Crises
Extremely fast company growth	■ Loss of managerial control over operations can occur, particularly when the company has multiple locations over a wide geographic area. This condition can eventually result in defective products and/or poor service quality. Franchises are especially prone to this type of crisis. ■ Rapid growth can also lead to high debt and cash flow problems.
Unique differentiating product or service characteristic	■ If the product or service offering is new, its uniqueness could later result in a product or service defect. For example, some types of elective or unique surgeries (such as gastric bypass) can later lead to physical problems. Dietary supplements have also come under attack.
Charismatic organizational leader	■ Some charismatic leaders have led their organizations into financial ruin because their boards did not challenge them. ■ Some leaders become so influential that they take on a godlike status and are not challenged by stakeholders. Some successful athletic coaches exemplify this behavior.
Company both large and successful	■ Employees may feel they are not compensated enough, particularly if the company is recording "record profits."

(Continued)

Table 4.1   Continued

Internal Strength	Corresponding Potential Crises
	■ Environmental activists search for any evidence that suggests the company is harming the natural environment. Large companies make good targets because they are more visible to the general public.
	■ Social-minded stakeholders claim the company does not share its wealth with those who are in need.
	■ The government will watch the company more closely and look for ways that it may be hiding income, polluting the environment, harming natural resources, or hiring or firing employees illegally.
	■ Lawmakers will look for *any* wrongdoing on the part of the company so they can establish a reputation among their constituents.

Weaknesses

While the link between crises and strengths may not be obvious at first glance, the connection between organizational weaknesses and crises is both intuitive and well established. Weaknesses identified in the SWOT should be examined in light of their potential for breeding crises in the organization. For example, an emphasis on the human resource management (HRM) function is directly related to the potential for crisis events in the organization (Lockwood, 2005). Specifically, when good human resources (HR) practices are ignored by an organization, a crisis is more likely to occur. The infamous Rent-A-Center case illustrates how the link between HRM and employee lawsuits can develop. In this example, Rent-A-Center eliminated its HR department when its new CEO, J. Ernest Talley, took over in August 1998. The company also changed to a less female-friendly workplace, according to depositions from more than 300 company officials over a 47-state region. Talley's own anti-female policy became well known within the company, including several quotes indicating that women should not be working at Rent-A-Center (Grossman, 2002). Without an HR department, women who felt discriminated against had no internal recourse. Charges of discrimination began to increase, plunging the company into a class action lawsuit on behalf of female employees, eventually resulting in a $47 million verdict against Rent-A-Center (Grossman, 2002).

A related HR issue is the decision by some companies, particularly in the retail and service sector, not to offer fringe benefits to their hourly employees. Typically, this strategy is followed by companies that employ a cost leadership strategy, an approach that seeks to offer basic, no-frills products and services to a mass market of price-conscious consumers (Parnell, 2013). Hence, efforts are made to keep costs as low as possible in the production and service-offering process. In the manufacturing sector, companies typically have achieved lower costs via economies of scale and automation of processes through technology innovation (Crandall & Crandall, 2008; Parnell, 2013).

There are potential crises associated with this strategy. For one, there is the irony that these same employees are on the front lines every day and offer the first contact a customer has with the products and services of the company. Ceteris paribus, organizations are better off when these employees are well trained, loyal, and reasonably satisfied with their employment. In addition, large and successful companies are more likely to be criticized for their wages and benefits, as the example of Wal-Mart so often illustrates (Ehrenreich, 2001; Fishman, 2006; Institute for Crisis Management, 2011).

Table 4.2 provides examples of internal weaknesses that could conceivably result in organizational crises.

Table 4.2   Examples of Internal Organizational Weaknesses and Potential Crisis Events

Internal Weaknesses	*Corresponding Potential Crises*
Poorly trained employees	■ Industrial accidents in the workplace
	■ Poor service to the customer
	■ In manufacturing settings, defective products
Poor relationship with a labor union	■ Labor strikes during contract negotiations as well as a larger amount of grievances resulting from day-to-day operations
	■ A secondary crisis: negative publicity in the media
Poor ethical orientation of top management	■ White-collar crime and cash flow problems
	■ If the organization is large, potential publicity problems
Aging production facilities and equipment	■ A greater number of machine breakdowns, resulting in lost productivity and higher operating costs
	■ Likely industrial accidents and poor product quality
Understaffed or nonexistent Human Resource Department	■ Discrimination against protected groups and sexual harassment charges
	■ Higher operating costs due to industrial accidents (a result of poor training), employee absenteeism, and turnover
Not offering a competitive fringe benefit package to employees	■ Negative publicity from both internal and external stakeholders

(Continued)

Table 4.2   Continued

Internal Weaknesses	Corresponding Potential Crises
	■ Lack of employee loyalty, which could lead to hiring only marginal employees and a cycle of turnover
Haphazard safety inspections	■ Industrial accidents coupled with increased workplace injuries
	■ The larger the organization, the more likely negative publicity may result
Employee substance abuse	■ Increased industrial accidents, workplace injuries, and product quality problems
Lack of a crisis management team and plan	■ Slow and ineffective response to crisis events
	■ Negative public perception because the firm is seen as being unprepared

Opportunities

A SWOT analysis also looks at the organization's opportunities existing in the external environment. While it may not seem readily apparent that organizational opportunities could be a potential source of crises, a closer examination suggests otherwise. The assessment of opportunities can generate strategic alternatives a company may pursue to expand its market share. Problems can surface and escalate into a crisis, particularly as the firm considers globalization options.

One opportunity that most businesses, both small and large, have acted on is the expansion of the Internet, both technologically and socially. Many have responded to this opportunity by shifting to an online sales format. Numerous firms have evolved to assist companies in making this transition, as the learning curve can be quite steep. However, companies that generate online sales are open to crises associated with cybersecurity, including theft of personal records of consumers as well as denial of service attacks (DOS) by hackers.

Table 4.3 outlines three possible scenarios in which a strategic response to opportunities may breed a crisis.

Threats

External threats are a common source of crisis. Some of these factors can be opportunities in some organizations but threats in others. Consider the example of location discussed earlier in this chapter. In some organizations, threats emanate from geographical considerations. For example, in parts of the United States such as Florida, weather concerns such as hurricanes are included as part of the risk assessment (Kruse, 1993). Other regions of the United States such as California are vulnerable to earthquakes. Urban areas of any country can be subject to crises that are different from less populated areas. Events such as riots, power outages, and bad weather can be especially hard on more populated regions.

Certain industries also face external threats. One industry that may be on the horizon for a host of health-related crises is the indoor tanning industry.

Table 4.3 Examples of External Organizational Opportunities and Potential Crisis Events

Strategic Alternatives That Emanate From Opportunities	Corresponding Potential Crises
Expand product availability by moving from a brick-and-mortar to a "brick-and-click" arrangement	▪ Offering products online can lead to denial-of-service cyberattacks by hackers. ▪ Hackers are usually external to the organization, but a disgruntled employee could become one as well.
Expand company manufacturing facilities to another part of the world (greenfield venture)	▪ Here, the company builds and owns its manufacturing facility in a host country. While the quality and process can be more controlled than through a licensing approach (see the next option), there is also the risk of outside interference from the host country. ▪ In some cases, companies have been taken over by the host country's government and become state owned.
Outsource to another company outside the home country	▪ Because jobs in the home country are usually lost, the company could incur negative publicity from external stakeholders, particularly former employees, labor unions, politicians, and municipalities that hosted the business. ▪ If the outsourcing is through a licensing agreement, there is the possibility that parties in the host country may pirate proprietary information. ▪ The product from the outsourced company may be defective. This situation creates a two-pronged crisis. First, the defective product itself creates problems received by the final consumer. Second, there is the public image problem because of the firm's decision to outsource overseas in the first place.

Evidence is growing of the health risks associated within this industry ("Indoor Tanning," 2005). In addition, there is an emphasis on keeping teenagers out of tanning booths altogether because of the long-term risk of developing skin cancer (Johnson, 2004; Rados, 2005). The industry has been likened to the tobacco industry, which has a history of denying that cigarettes were harmful to the consumer's health, despite a long string of research indicating otherwise. Like the tobacco industry, the indoor tanning industry has been working hard to dispel any links to skin cancer (Loh, 2008). As with tobacco processors, executives in the indoor tanning industry downplay the health risks associated with moderate usage. Nonetheless, the warning signs for crises are clear for this industry, with a dawn of litigation about to begin.

Table 4.4 overviews various external threats that can evolve into a crisis.

Table 4.4   Examples of External Organizational Threats and Potential Crisis Events

External Threat	*Corresponding Potential Crises*
Changing demographics of the surrounding neighborhood	■ The organization may become a target for crime, such as vandalism or robbery.
	■ Sales revenue may decline.
Severe weather	■ The building and facilities where the organization is located may be damaged by wind, snow, or flooding.
	■ Sales revenue may be interrupted while the building is being repaired.
Dysfunctional customers or employees	■ There could be an incident of workplace violence.
Poor-quality components from a supplier	■ The components that are assembled into the final product will cause that product to be defective as well.
	■ If the component was outsourced to an overseas supplier, negative publicity is likely to follow.
Consumer activism due to poor products or some other activity of the company	■ Consumer lawsuits may develop in the case of poor-quality products.
	■ Boycotts of the company's products and services can result.
Extortionists	■ Product tampering may occur.
	■ Online extortionist may threaten the company's website with a denial-of-service attack.
Earthquake, wildfire, or other natural disaster	■ Structural damage to the building and information technology systems can occur.
	■ Injuries and fatalities could occur to employees and customers.
Rumors/Negative publicity	■ Loss of revenues due to boycotts and negative company publicity may result.

Table 4.4   Continued

Terrorism	■ Negative attention could appear on the Internet through hate sites, blogs, and other social media outlets including Facebook and YouTube.
	■ Direct physical attacks on buildings can result in damage, injuries, and fatalities.
	■ In addition to the items mentioned, attacks outside the organization may disrupt the supply chain.

Organizational Culture and Crisis Planning

Despite the fact that crisis planning is an important part of the strategic management process, not all managers are convinced that its role is important. And yet, an organization's crisis vulnerability is linked to its cultural norms and assumptions (Smith & Elliott, 2007). In other words, being diligent about crisis planning involves a cultural shift. As a result, organizations often do not have effective crisis management plans because their managers have not cultivated a mind-set that values this process (Weick & Sutcliffe, 2001). Many managers are engrossed with "putting out today's fires" and do not think they have time to plan for tomorrow's contingencies. Therefore, they have not developed the critical tools needed for a comprehensive crisis management plan (Simbo, 2003).

Thus, not all establishments have adopted a culture of crisis preparedness. At one end of the scale, many managers carry an "It can't happen to us" mentality (Nathan, 2000; Pearson & Mitroff, 1993). Coupled with this attitude is the notion that "nobody gets credit for fixing problems that never happened" (Repenning & Sterman, 2001). Other managers are reactive concerning crisis events by contemporaneously planning and managing as the problems unfold. Some organizations, because of their cultures, seem to develop blind spots and completely miss the cues that signal a crisis is on the move (Smallman & Weir, 1999).

Other managers are more proactive in their conduct. They plan for future potential crises by presupposing what could be their worst-case predicaments. Yet another group of managers includes battle-scarred victims who have experienced organizational crises and are now involved in proactive planning so they can manage future crises more effectively (Carmeli & Schaubroeck, 2008).

Indeed, there is a "way of thinking" and a "way things are done" in every organization. Long-term members understand it well and newcomers usually learn it quickly. Organizational theorists refer to this phenomenon as *organizational* or *corporate culture*. *Culture* refers to the commonly held values and beliefs of a particular group of people (Weitz & Shenhav, 2000). Organizational culture is a more specific concept in that it refers to the shared values and patterns of belief and behavior that are accepted and practiced by the members of a particular organization (Duncan, 1989).

An organization's culture exists at two levels. At the *surface level,* one can observe specific behaviors and artifacts of the organization such as accepted forms of dress, company logos, office rituals, and specific ceremonies such as awards banquets. These outward behaviors reflect the second level of organizational culture—a deeper, *underlying level* that includes shared values, belief patterns, and thought processes common to members of the organization (Schein, 1990). The underlying level is the most critical to understand because it lies at the core of how organizational members think and interpret their work. Embracing a culture of crisis planning must occur at the underlying level first before it will be evident at the surface level. Indeed, as crisis expert Timothy Coombs (2006) put it, crisis management must become the DNA of the organization.

An organization's culture serves as the basis for many day-to-day decisions in the organization. For example, members of an organization whose culture values innovation are more likely to invest the time necessary to develop creative solutions to complex problems than will their counterparts in organizations whose cultures value short-term cost containment (Deal & Kennedy, 1982). An innovative organization is more likely to "do its homework" and take the steps necessary to prevent crises from occurring. This homework includes setting up crisis management teams, developing plans, and practicing mock disasters, which are drills to help the organization learn how to manage a crisis more effectively. Of course, culture also contributes to the success of the firm's crisis management response. Indeed, as Marra (2004) points out, organizational culture helps determine the success of crisis communications, a main facet of the overall crisis management process.

In the realm of crisis management, there appear to be "crisis-prepared" cultures that support crisis planning, as well as those that do not, sometimes labeled "crisis prone" (Pearson & Mitroff, 1993). Managers should seek to develop and support crisis-prepared cultures in their organizations.

Summary

The entire crisis management process should be viewed from a strategic perspective and should be part of the organization's overall strategic planning process, including (1) an external analysis of its opportunities and threats, (2) an internal analysis of the firm's strengths and weakness, (3) a strategy formulation stage, (4) a strategy execution stage, and finally, (5), a strategic control emphasis.

Analyzing the external environment presents a critical challenge for preventing crises because it involves assessing environmental uncertainty. Uncertainty occurs when decision makers lack current, sufficient, reliable information about their organizations and cannot accurately forecast future changes. Uncertainty is lowest in organizations whose environments are simple and stable and where the quality of available information is high. It is highest in organizations whose environments are complex and unstable and where the quality of information is low.

Environmental scanning refers to collecting and analyzing information about relevant trends in the external environment. A systematic environmental scanning process reduces uncertainty and organizes the flow of current information relevant to organizational decisions while providing decision makers with an early warning system for changes in the environment.

The SWOT analysis enables management to identify the crisis threats that are specific to their organization. Ironically, it is not just organizational weaknesses and external threats that can lead to crises. The firm's internal strengths and external opportunities, under the right circumstances, can breed crises as well.

Finally, the organization's culture influences the enthusiasm that exists for crisis management. Developing a crisis management plan may involve changes to the company's culture, including changing the way management and staff view crises in general.

Questions for Discussion

1. Why should crisis management be part of an organization's strategic planning process?

2. What are the four types of uncertainty that exist in the external environment? How is each one linked to a potential set of crises?

3. What is environmental scanning? What tools are available to help management scan the environment in such a way that it would yield information useful to identify potential crises?

4. How can an organization's strengths be a source of crises?

5. How can organizational opportunities be a useful tool in identifying potential crises?

6. How can a company change its organizational culture to better embrace enthusiasm for crisis management?

Chapter Exercise

Identifying potential threats to an organization is an effective method to prepare for future crises. Consider the college or university that you are attending and perform a crisis vulnerability assessment of your institution.

Using the SWOT analysis approach, identify potential crises that reside in each of the four areas of strengths, weaknesses, opportunities, and threats. Assess each crisis threat in terms of its likelihood and potential impact.

Opening Case, Part 2: The Professor, "Angry Amy"

On February 12, 2010, Amy Bishop attended one of her last department meetings at the University of Alabama at Huntsville. She had been denied tenure and felt betrayed by her peers and department dean. She sat silently while various routine agenda items were discussed, including the course schedule for the upcoming semesters. Thirty minutes into the meeting, Dr. Bishop stood up and abruptly began shooting her colleagues across the table. Using her 9-millimeter handgun, she fired first at department chairman Dr. Gopi K. Podila, killing him instantly. She then shot and killed professors Maria Ragland and Adriel D. Johnson Sr. Three others in the room were wounded in the shootout (Bartlett et al., 2010). When Dr. Bishop's gun jammed, she left the conference room, throwing the revolver and her blood-splattered jacket into the trash in the restroom. She called her husband and instructed him to pick her up (Wallace, 2011). Those who survived the shooting moved the conference room table to the door so she could not regain access. Within minutes, though, Bishop was apprended by the police and taken away in a squad car.

A Checkered Past

After Bishop's arrest, information began to surface about her past. Of particular significance was the fact she had shot and killed her 18-year-old brother in 1986. At the time she was 21 and a student at Northeastern University. According to the story given by her mother to the police, Amy accidently shot her brother while they were in the kitchen of their home. After the shot was fired, Bishop ran out of the house with the shotgun and headed toward town. At a Ford dealership, she pointed her gun at an employee and told him she needed a car because she had been in a fight with her husband and that he was looking for her. Bishop quickly left the dealership, though, and police found her near a newspaper distribution agency, still holding the gun. Police ordered her to drop the gun, which she refused to do. Another officer snuck up behind her and disarmed Bishop. When she was taken into custody, she told police that she had a fight with her father earlier in the day, which was true (Dewan et al., 2010).

A fateful sequence of events then transpired. Police officers of the Braintree (Massachusetts) Police Department began the questioning process as to what had happened with the "accidental shooting." During the questioning, her mother arrived and told Amy not to answer any more questions. The booking process was stopped, and the investigation was never continued. Amy Bishop was never charged with a crime, and for 24 years, the event remained a secret to her employers. That fact that it was her shotgun blast that killed her brother has never been disputed. However, a formal investigation into the death was never conducted either, leading some to believe that the incident may not have been just an accident. On June 16, 2010, the case was reopened by the Norfolk District Attorney's office in Canton, Massachusetts, and a grand jury indicted Bishop on a charge of first-degree murder in the death of her brother, Seth (Wallace, 2011).

While the death of her brother occurred in 1986, another bizarre event involving Bishop occurred in 1993. A pipe bomb was sent to Paul Rosenberg, a former supervisor of Bishop's at the Children's Hospital Boston. Rosenberg had been in charge of the lab where Bishop was working and felt that she was not up to the standards of the workplace. He was instrumental in her departure from the lab, leaving both

Bishop and her husband angry with him. Bishop was on the verge of a nervous breakdown, and her husband James wanted to seek revenge against Rosenberg, according to records from the Bureau of Alcohol, Tobacco, and Firearms, which was looking into the investigation.

Bishop departed from her job on November 30, 1993. On December 19, 1993, a suspicious package, which the house sitter found inside the front storm door, arrived at Rosenberg's home. The package showed six 29-cent stamps but no postal markings on them. The white cardboard box was a foot square and 3 inches deep. Ironically, Rosenberg had been to a seminar on letter bombs earlier and suspected the package might be a bomb. He called police and they confirmed his suspicions (Wallace, 2011). Bishop and her husband Paul were both questioned but were never charged due to lack of evidence.

An incident at an International House of Pancakes in Peabody, Massachusetts, also revealed a tendency for dysfunctional behavior. Another woman in the restaurant had taken the last booster seat when Bishop approached her and demanded the seat for one of her children. Bishop shouted profanities at the customer and then physically struck her in the head. When the manager asked her to leave she responded, "I am Dr. Amy Bishop." Bishop was charged with assault and battery and disorderly conduct. She pled guilty and was given six months probation (Herring & Levitz, 2010).

The Problem of Background Checks

What is troubling about Bishop's past is that none of it was uncovered in the background check that was conducted by UAH as part of her hiring process. This is not to say that UAH was negligent, however; rather, the institution lacked the information that would have revealed a troubling past. Normal background checks in academia usually reveal employment history, job responsibilities, tenure in the prior position, reason for separation, and names of references. When it comes to a candidate's criminal history, it may be more difficult to uncover. This is because the federal Fair Credit Reporting Act and many state laws restrict revealing a candidate's criminal history. Furthermore, criminal records are kept on the state and country levels, which makes information more difficult to find (Cadrain & Minton-Eversole, 2010).

For Bishop, the history of her past was even more elusive. No arrests or convictions were ever made in the death of her brother or the questioning in the pipe bomb case. The incident at the International House of Pancakes did not appear on her record either. Police ran their own background check on Bishop after she had been apprehended, which also came up empty (Jonsson, 2010).

Opening Case Part 2 References

Bartlett, T., Wilson, R., Basken, P., Glenn, D., & Fischman, J. (2010, February 26). In Alabama, a scientist's focus turns deadly. *Chronicle of Higher Education*, pp. A8, A12.

Cadrain, D., & Minton-Eversole, T., (2010). Campus violence reveals background screening flaws. *HR, 55*(5), 13.

Dewan, S., Saul, S., & Zezima, K. (2010, February 20). For professor, fury just beneath the surface. *New York Times*. Retrieved July 26, 2012, from http://www.nytimes .com/2010/02/21/us/21bishop.html?pagewanted=all.

Herring, C, & Levitz, J. (2010, Feb). Alabama suspect had erratic history. *Wall Street Journal*, p. A3.

Jonsson, P. (2010, February 17). Amy Bishop case: Why no red flags were waved before shoot-ing spree. *Christian Science Monitor*, p. 1.

Wallace, A. (2011, February 28). What made this university researcher snap? *Wired*. Retrieved July 26, 2012, from http://www.wired.com/magazine/2011/02/ff_bishop/.

Opening Case Part 2 Questions

1. If a criminal background check can only be conducted in certain states, how can a university protect itself from a prospective professor with a violent past? Research the state (or county) laws where you reside and determine the process of conducting background checks in your locale.

2. As of the writing of this book, Bishop's case had not gone to trial. Provide an update as to the status of her case.

References

Barrett, P. (2011, August 29). Cleaning America's dirtiest coal company. *Bloomberg Businessweek*, 48–55.

Barton, L. (2001). *Crisis in organizations II*. Cincinnati: Southwestern.

Bertrand, R., & Lajtha, C. (2002). A new approach to crisis management. *Journal of Contingencies and Crisis Management*, 10(4), 181–191.

Bourrier, M. (2011). The legacy of the high reliability organization project. *Journal of Contingencies and Crisis Management*, 19(1), 9–13.

Carmeli, A., & Schaubroeck, J. (2008). Organisational crisis preparedness: The importance of learning from failures. *Long Range Planning*, 4, 177–196.

Carpenter, M. A. (2002). The implications of strategy and social context for the relationship between top management heterogeneity and firm performance. *Strategic Management Journal*, 23, 275–284.

Chappell, L. (2005, August 22). Nissan's booming, neighbors fuming. *Automotive News*, 4, 36.

Cheung, C., & Law, R. (2006). How can hotel guests be protected during the occurrence of a tsunami? *Asia Pacific Journal of Tourism Research*, 11(3), 289–295.

Chong, J. (2004). Six steps to better crisis management. *Journal of Business Strategy*, 25(2), 43–46.

Chong, J., & Park, J. (2010). A conceptual framework and research propositions for integrat-ing TQM into crisis planning. *Review of Business Research*, 10(2), 69–74.

Coombs, W. (2006). *Code red in the boardroom: Crisis management as organizational DNA*. Westport, CT: Praeger.

Crandall, R. E., & Crandall, W. R. (2008). *New methods of competing in the global market-place: Critical success factors from service and manufacturing*. Boca Raton, FL: Taylor and Francis.

Das, T. K., & Teng, B. (1999). Cognitive biases and strategic decision processes: An integrative perspective. *Journal of Management Studies*, 36, 757–778.

Deal, T. E., & Kennedy, A. A. (1982). *Corporate cultures: The rites and rituals of corporate life*. Reading, MA: Addison-Wesley.

Duncan, R. B. (1972). Characteristics of perceived environments and perceived environmen-tal uncertainty. *Administrative Science Quarterly*, 17, 313–327.

Duncan, W. W. (1989). Organizational culture: "Getting a fix" on an elusive concept. *Academy of Management Executive, 3,* 229–236.

Ehrenreich, B. (2001). *Nickel and dimed: On (not) getting by in America.* New York: Henry Holt and Company.

Fiscor, S. (2011). MSHA provides update on UBB explosion. *Coal Age, 116*(7), 30–34.

Fishman, C. (2006). *The Wal-Mart effect: How the world's most powerful company really works—and how it's transforming the American economy.* New York: Penguin.

Fisk, M., Sullivan, B., & Freifeld, K. (2010, April 25). The accountant of coal. *Business Week,* 48–51.

Foust, D., & Beucke, D. (2005, October 5). Heading off storms. *Business Week,* 16.

Ganguly, K., & Guin, K. (2007). A framework for assessment of supply-related risk in supply chain. *Icfai Journal of Supply Chain Management, 4*(4), 86–98.

Griffith, M. (2008). The return of the anti-hail cannons. *Weatherwise, 61*(4), 14–18.

Groom, J. R., & David, F. (2001). Competitive intelligence activity among small firms. *SAM Advanced Management Journal, 66*(1), 12–29.

Grossman, R. (2002). Paying the price: Events at Rent-A-Center prove that when employers don't respect HR today, they'll pay tomorrow. *HRMagazine, 47*(8), 28–37.

Hartley, R. (1993). *Business ethics: Violations of the public trust.* New York: Wiley.

Herring, J. (2003). The future of competitive intelligence: Driven by knowledge-based competition. *Competitive Intelligence, 6*(2), 5.

Indoor tanning: Unexpected dangers. (2005, February). *Consumer Reports,* 30–33.

Institute for Crisis Management. (2011). *Annual ICM crisis report: News coverage of business crises during 2010.* Retrieved April 8, 2012, from http://crisisconsultant.com/images/2010CrisisReportICM.pdf.

Jacques, A. (2009). Domino's delivers during crisis. *Public Relations Strategist, 15*(3), 6–10.

Johnson, D. (2004, June 28). States to teens: We'll ban the tan. *Newsweek,* 44.

Kruse, C. (1993). Disaster plan stands the test of hurricane. *Personnel Journal, 72*(6), 36–43.

Kumar, K., Subramanian, R., & Strandholm, K. (2001). Competitive strategy, environmental scanning, and performance: A context specific analysis of their relationship. *International Journal of Commerce and Management, 11,* 1–33.

Lockwood, N. (2005). Crisis management in today's business environment: HR's strategic role. *SHRM Research Quarterly, 4*(4), 1–9.

Loh, A. (2008). Are artificial tans the new cigarette? How plaintiffs can use the lesson of tobacco litigation in bringing claims against the indoor tanning industry. *Michigan Law Review, 107*(2), 365–390.

Marra, F. (2004). Excellent crisis communication: Beyond crisis plans. In D. P. Millar & R. L. Heaths (Eds.), *Responding to crisis: A rhetorical approach to crisis communication* (pp. 311–325). Mahwah, NJ: Erlbaum.

Nathan, M. (2000). The paradoxical nature of crisis. *Review of Business, 21*(3), 12–16.

O'Rourke, M. (2008). Some say tomato, some say jalapeno. *Risk Management, 55*(9), 14–16.

Parnell, J. A. (2013). *Strategic management: Theory and practice* (4th ed.). Thousand Oaks, CA: Sage.

Pearson, C., & Mitroff, I. (1993). From crisis prone to crisis prepared: A framework for crisis management. *Academy of Management Executive, 71,* 48–59.

Pennington-Gray, L., Thapa, B., Kaplanidou, K., Cahyanto, I. & McLaughlin, E. (2011). Crisis planning and preparedness in the United States Tourism Industry. *Cornell Hospitality Quarterly, 52*(3), 312–320.

Preble, J. (1997). Integrating the crisis management perspective into the strategic management process. *Journal of Management Studies, 34*(5), 769–791.

Probst, G., & Raisch, S. (2005). Organizational crisis: The logic of failure. *Academy of Management Executive, 19*(1), 90–105.

Rados, C. (2005). Teen tanning hazards. *FDA Consumer, 39*(2), 8–9.

Repenning, N., & Sterman, J. (2001). Nobody ever gets credit for fixing problems that never happened. *California Management Review, 43*(Summer), 64–88.

Robb, D. (2005). Defending against viruses, worms and DoS attacks. *Business Communications Review, 35*(12), 24–27.

Roberts, K., & Bea, R. (2001). Must accidents happen? Lessons from high-reliability organizations. *Academy of Management Executive, 15*(3), 70–78.

Scammell, H. (2003). Chalk's Ocean Airways. *Air and Space Magazine.* Retrieved May 14, 2012, from http://www.airspacemag.com/history-of-flight/cit-scammell.html.

Schein, E. H. (1990). Organizational culture. *American Psychologist, 45,* 109–119.

Schrader, R. (2010). Six actions to enable efficient traceability. *Food Logistics, 121,* 34–35.

Sheaffer, Z., & Mano-Negrin, R. (2003). Executives' orientations as indicators of crisis management policies and practices. *Journal of Management Studies, 40*(2), 573–606.

Shrivastava, P. (1995). Industrial/environmental crises and corporate social responsibility. *Journal of Socio-Economics, 24*(1), 211–217.

Simbo, A. (2003). Catastrophe planning and crisis management. *Risk Management, 40*(2), 64–66.

Smallman, C., & Weir, D. (1999). Communication and cultural distortion during crises. *Disaster Prevention and Management, 8*(1), 33–41.

Smith, D. (1990). Beyond contingency planning: Towards a model of crisis management. *Industrial Crisis Quarterly, 4*(4), 263–275.

Smith, D., & Elliott, D. (2007). Exploring the barriers to learning from crisis: Organizational learning and crisis. *Management Learning, 38*(5), 519–538.

Somers, S. (2009). Measuring resilience potential: An adaptive strategy for organizational crisis planning. *Journal of Contingencies and Crisis Management, 17*(1), 12–23.

Starbuck, W. H. (1976). Organizations and their environments. In M. D. Dunnette (Ed.), *Handbook of industrial psychology* (pp. 1069–1123). Chicago: Rand McNally.

Thompson, J. D. (1967). *Organizations in action.* New York: McGraw-Hill.

Veil, S. (2011). Mindful learning in crisis management. *Journal of Business Communications, 48*(2), 116–147.

Vines, M. (2007). Intelligence. *Business and Commercial Aviation, 101*(1), 13–26.

Ward, K. (2011, June 29). MSHA: Massey covered up Upper Big Branch safety hazards. *Charleston Gazette.* Retrieved May 17, 2012, from http://wvgazette.com/News/201106290959.

Watkins, M., & Bazerman, M. (2003). Predictable surprises: The disasters you should have seen coming. *Harvard Business Review, 81*(3), 72–80.

Weick, K. (1993). The collapse of sensemaking in organizations: The Mann Gulch disaster. *Administrative Science Quarterly, 38,* 628–652.

Weick, K., & Sutcliffe, K. (2001). *Managing the unexpected.* San Francisco: Jossey-Bass.

Weitz, E., & Shenhav, Y. (2000). A longitudinal analysis of technical and organizational uncertainty in management theory. *Organization Studies, 21,* 243–265.

Zhang, J. (2008, June 12). Food-safety measures faulted. *Wall Street Journal,* p. A4.

Zweig, D. (2010). The board that couldn't think straight. *Conference Board Review, 47*(2), 40–47.

Zyglidopoulos, S. (2002). The social and environmental responsibilities of multinationals: Evidence from the Brent Spar case. *Journal of Business Ethics, 36,* 141–151.

CHAPTER 5

Forming the Crisis Management Team and Writing the Plan

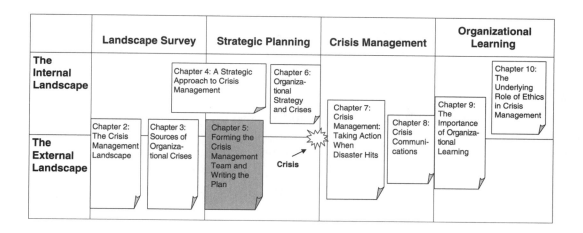

	Landscape Survey		Strategic Planning	Crisis Management		Organizational Learning
The Internal Landscape		Chapter 4: A Strategic Approach to Crisis Management	Chapter 6: Organizational Strategy and Crises			Chapter 10: The Underlying Role of Ethics in Crisis Management
The External Landscape	Chapter 2: The Crisis Management Landscape	Chapter 3: Sources of Organizational Crises	Chapter 5: Forming the Crisis Management Team and Writing the Plan	Crisis	Chapter 7: Crisis Management: Taking Action When Disaster Hits	Chapter 8: Crisis Communications	Chapter 9: The Importance of Organizational Learning

Opening Case: Roof Party at Local College Goes Terribly Wrong

Years ago an odd and obscure event occurred at Concord College, a small public institution nestled on top of a mountain in southern West Virginia. Four students somehow gained access to the roof of the student union building and proceeded to have a small party of their own. With lawn chairs, a bit of music, and of course, some alcohol, the little get-together seemed harmless and uneventful until two of the students got a little too close to the edge of the roof, and fell. Although the ground was only 12 feet below, both students were knocked unconscious and lay motionless, just underneath a window to the faculty dining room.

Almost immediately, emergency providers were on the scene tending to the injured students. Meanwhile, another student who was passing by noticed the commotion and became very distraught, as she knew one of the victims. This student was in her third trimester of pregnancy and suddenly began to have contractions. With the emotional excitement of the events, and her impending delivery of her own baby, it appeared she had gone into labor. Now, three students—not two— were receiving attention from emergency providers. Because of the commotion, traffic began to move slowly on the road in front of the student union. Campus police moved to the area and redirected traffic.

The college's crisis management team arrived on the scene and was looking into matters as well. After confirming the identities of the students involved, they began to monitor the activities of the emergency providers. The situation was highly unusual. To make matters even more perplexing, one of the two remaining students who had been on the roof of the student union had disappeared. Emergency providers and the police were told of this missing student, but he could not be found. It turned out that he had become distraught and was sitting by himself at the stairs of the administration building, some 300 feet away. The head of the crisis management team—not the police—eventually found this student.

But there was more to come. Approximately one hour after the students had fallen off the roof, the two student victims, the pregnant student, and the distraught student suddenly appeared perfectly functional again. The police and firefighters left the scene and the crisis management team calmly went back to their normal duties. Concord College had just completed its annual mock disaster training exercise.

Opening Case Discussion Questions

1. Could this crisis have been averted if the university had an effective security management system?

2. What is your reaction to the crisis management team's response?

3. What improvements could you suggest for future incidents like this one?

4. What crisis management insights can we gather from this incident?

Introduction

The crisis management team (CMT) and the crisis management plan (CMP) are the core of an organization's crisis planning efforts. The team meets together first and then develops the plan. Later, the plan can be tested through mock disaster drills such as the one discussed in the opening case. This chapter explores all three of these processes in detail. We begin with the mechanics involved in forming the crisis management team. Next, the crisis management plan is outlined. We close the chapter by examining the components of crisis management training, including guidelines on how to conduct a mock disaster.

Forming the Crisis Management Team

Before any crisis planning can occur, the crisis management team must be formally organized. While discussion about crises can take place at any time without a team, the CMT is the most effective and appropriate starting point for serious crisis planning.

Goals of the CMT

The basic mission of the CMT is to plan for potential crises and manage the ones that eventually occur. Encompassing this mission involved five specific goals. These are overviewed in Figure 5.1.

1. *The CMT identifies the crisis threats the organization is facing.* Every organization faces threats that are unique to its industry and in some cases, to its geographical location. The CMT considers these factors as it evaluates the specific risks that are likely candidates for a crisis. In planning for a crisis, the team cannot formulate a response for every potential crisis, so it must be flexible (Clark & Harman, 2004). Most threats cluster into crisis families (Coombs & Holladay, 2001; Pearson & Mitroff 1993). This understanding can simplify the threat assessment phase because managers can plan responses to potential families (categories) of crises rather than to each individual crisis that might erupt.

2. *The CMT develops the crisis management plan.* The CMT develops a crisis management plan that addresses the potential crisis threats identified in the first step. The plan also contains key contact information of vendors and other important stakeholders. In many cases, the plan is posted on the organization's website.

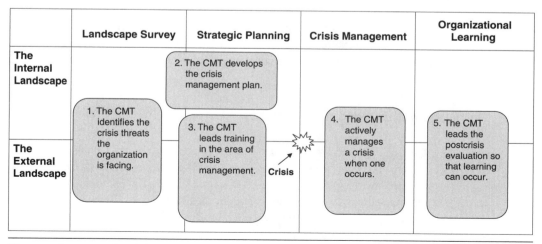

Figure 5.1 Goals of the Crisis Management Team (CMT)

3. *The CMT leads training in the area of crisis management.* The CMT oversees the crisis training efforts in the organization. Two levels of training are made available, one for the CMT, and one for the organization members at large. Team training should occur at regular scheduled intervals. The content of training usually revolves around reviewing the crisis management plan and conducting simulated drills (Coombs, 2007). Simulated drills are necessary because the team really does not know how well it can function in a crisis unless the plan is tested periodically (Clark & Harman, 2004). Training activities need to be coordinated between the internal and external landscapes. For example, it is necessary when setting up a mock disaster drill to contact stakeholders in the external landscape, such as fire departments and emergency medical service (EMS) organizations.

4. *The CMT actively manages a crisis when one occurs.* When a crisis does occur, the CMT is activated and placed in charge of managing the event. This phase of the team's experience is most crucial because it reveals performance levels in two areas: (1) How well was the crisis handled, and (2) how well did members of the team work together? The evaluation of these two areas is addressed in the fifth goal, mentioned next.

5. *The CMT leads the postcrisis evaluation so that learning can occur.* After the crisis, a postevaluation session is recommended to determine how well the crisis was managed. Specifically, the CMT seeks to find answers to the following questions:

   - What did we learn from this crisis that will help us prevent a similar one in the future?
   - If the same crisis did occur again, what could we do differently to mitigate its impact?
   - What aspects of the crisis response were performed well?
   - What aspects of the crisis response need improvement?

Scheduling the evaluation sessions is the most important factor in the postcrisis evaluation phase. Such sessions must be held soon after the event while the details of the crisis are still familiar to everyone. Waiting too long can lead to forgetfulness (Kovoor-Misra & Nathan, 2000). This forgetfulness can lead to the loss of valuable insights on how to make crisis management function better in the future.

Team Member Characteristics

The CMT has been referred to as the "nerve center of the crisis management process" (Gilpin & Murphy, 2008, p. 134). As a result, CMT members must have a specific and complementary set of individual characteristics that allow them to work well in a group setting. To accomplish this difficult task, a team is necessary, one whose composition is diverse and includes members from different parts of the organization (Barton, 2001). The characteristics of an ideal CMT member are discussed next.

Ability to Work in a Team Environment

CMT members must like people and enjoy working in a group. This is not an assignment for an employee who prefers to work on projects independently. Above all, CMT members must realize they are part of a team working toward shared goals (Coombs, 2007).

Ability to Think Under Pressure

CMT members should be able to think under pressure (Clark & Harman, 2004). Employees react to stress in different ways, and some do not manage it effectively. For CMT members, however, stress should be a motivator, a sort of adrenaline shot that makes them want to manage a crisis environment (Chandler, 2001).

Ambiguity Tolerance

We always prefer to make decisions when all needed information is readily available. However, in a crisis situation, decisions are typically made in conditions of uncertainty. Ambiguity tolerance enables a decision maker to be effective, even when desired information is not available (Chandler, 2001).

Good Listening Skills

Team members need to be able to listen effectively to the stakeholders and victims presenting their sides of the crisis story. Listening for what is said is important, but being intuitive and listening for the untold story is equally critical.

Verbal Skills

Good speaking skills are a must. Some of the team members may be assigned to talk to members of the media, an assignment that requires excellent verbal skills. Among team members, communication intentions should also be clear. This ability goes back to stress tolerance, because some team members may not communicate as effectively when they are under stress.

Critical Thinking Skills

This characteristic includes the ability to analyze problems and evaluate alternatives by examining the pros and cons of each option (Coombs, 2007; Gilpin & Murphy, 2008). Understanding the accumulation of details to an event and how they lead to a crisis is essential (Roux-Dufort, 2009). Critical thinking is a savvy skill that implies one does not believe everything he or she hears. Instead, combined with the skill of good listening, one is able to understand the hidden messages that many people convey in their verbal and written communications.

Team Composition

Team members should represent the major functional areas (e.g., marketing, production, finance, etc.) of the organization (Coombs, 2007). Representatives from the following areas are recommended:

Company Chief Executive Officer or President

The chief executive officer (CEO) or president should always have an active interest in the CMT, although the size of the organization will dictate the capacity in which the top executive should serve. In smaller organizations, this person would be on the CMT. In larger organizations, a vice president for administration or operations may serve as the representative of upper management (Barton, 2001). Podolak (2002) advocates that this person should also serve as the team leader; however, not all crisis management experts agree on this. The CEO does not always serve as the company spokesperson during a crisis, although that is certainly an option. This role is often held by a member of the public relations department or the designee who typically communicates with the media. The CEO might not need to address the media if a better-trained staff person is available. "Only in the most egregious of crises—when lives are lost, when the story remains on the front pages for days—does the media and the public even expect to see the CEO" (Pines, 2000, p. 15).

Human Resources

It is always advisable to have a representative from human resources (HR) serving on the CMT. First, HR serves as the liaison with employees. Individual employees can be affected by a crisis in a number of ways, and HR is there to ensure their interests are represented in the crisis management process (Lockwood, 2005). Second, HR has knowledge areas that can be useful during a crisis. These areas include next-of-kin details, number of employees in each site of the facility, and language and cultural barrier knowledge that is especially important if the company operates globally (Millar, 2003). HR should also have a network of trauma counselors on contract in the event of a major crisis involving injuries and/or a loss of life.

Accounting and Finance

A crisis can have affect on cash flow, stock valuation, and cash disbursement, so a representative from finance is appropriate. There may also be a need to secure funds quickly for relief operations. This accountability becomes particularly critical if funds are to be disbursed abroad.

Security

The head of the organization's security or police force should be a member of the CMT. Many crises will involve the services of this department, such as in the case of a workplace violence incident. This department also serves as a liaison with law enforcement departments outside the company whose help may be needed.

Public Relations

This functional area goes by different names in different organizations, such as public information, public affairs, or community outreach. During the crisis, this department relays the information and viewpoints of the organization to its public stakeholders. Hence, the official company spokesperson to the media usually resides in this department. The public relations department also works to help predict public perception of the organization and issues related to the specific crisis at hand. Usually, these departments have established ties with various media outlets so that a crisis event is not the first time the spokesperson and the media will have had contact.

Legal Counsel

An attorney should be a member of the CMT to provide legal expertise, particularly when deciding how much information should be disclosed to outside stakeholders during a crisis. With this in mind, the legal counsel and public relations director must work together and be in agreement about how much disclosure is appropriate.

Operations

The core operations of the organization should be represented on the team. In a manufacturing facility, the plant manager would be the logical choice. At a major university, several core areas require representation, including food service, housing, registrar and records, the director of plant and facilities, and the academic departments.

Outside Consultant

Some organizations may opt to employ an outside consultant during the initial start-up of the CMT and the subsequent plan. The rationale is that a learning curve exists for those organizations new at crisis planning, and a consultant can help ease the learning process. In other cases, a consultant may be brought in to offer advice concerning certain types of crises. For example, in cases involving workplace violence, a psychologist with appropriate experience can advise the CMT on both mitigation and prevention of such a crisis (Simola, 2005).

Virtual Crisis Management Teams

Virtual teams are now quite common in organizations, especially among multinational corporations (MNCs). A 2010 survey of MNCs found that 80 percent of the respondents were members of a virtual team (Sadri & Condia, 2012). Virtual teams face a number of challenges that need to be addressed. Table 5.1 provides an overview of these challenges.

Table 5.1   Understanding the Challenges of Virtual Teams

Trends That Encourage the Use of Virtual Teams	*Challenges Confronting Virtual Teams*
■ Company strategies moving toward outsourcing and strategic alliances ■ Widespread use of Internet technologies ■ Shorter project and product cycle times ■ Need for faster, high-quality decisions ■ Restrictions on corporate travel accounts ■ Threat of terrorism	*Loss of nonverbal cues.* Communicating over the Internet, through meeting software, or teleconferencing reduces the richness of communication. Cues gained in face-to-face communication are lost in virtual environments. *Reduced opportunities to establish working relationships.* With a reduction of face-to-face time with colleagues, it is more difficult to build working relationships. *Time zone differences.* Work schedules of organizational members are different from each other. Even the assigning of timed deadlines will need to be accounted for from one time zone to another. *Complicated and unreliable technology.* Although companies should have a standardized intranet system, the performance may vary from location to location. Moreover, the quality of system performance and power availability may be compromised in some locations. *Difficulty in building consensus.* The lack of communication richness, the distance of organizational members from each other, the asynchronous nature of virtual communications and the unreliability of the intranet system will cause decision making to take longer. The process could also be more frustrating as well to organizational members. *Different cultures.* For MNCs, cultural differences are always a challenge, even in face-to-face communications. Ironically, in the virtual environment some of these challenges may be minimized because communication relies more on the written language. However, differences in meanings of words and expressions must still be accounted for.

Source: Adapted from Nunamaker et al. (2009), 114.

Given the growth of virtual teams and the expansion of the boundaries of organizations in general, CMTs must also be prepared to operate in a virtual manner. One of the first challenges that must be addressed is the location of the command center. Will it be at company headquarters or close to the origins of the crisis? A backup command center should also be designated in case the main command center becomes inoperative. This situation occurred during the September 11, 2001, terrorist attack when the New York City Office of Emergency Management lost its state-of-the art center. After the first tower caught fire and collapsed, the emergency operations center was unusable because of its location across the street from the tower (Davis, 2002).

Trust can enhance the effectiveness of virtual teams (Kimble, 2011). Trust building must occur before a major crisis develops. Hence, virtual teams of any type should engage in regularly scheduled activities that help team members work together and establish their expected roles (Nunamaker, Reinig, & Briggs, 2009; Sadri & Condia, 2012). Another recommendation for virtual teams is to utilize videoconferencing if facilities are available. The rationale is that richer forms of communication are possible such as the ability to observe verbal and visual cues (Chandler & Wallace, 2009).

Potential Problems Within CMTs

As in any group or team that works together, problems can arise. As previously mentioned, care should be taken to select team members who have good interpersonal skills and can work effectively as a unit. "If a team is dysfunctional before a crisis occurs, that team will have a dysfunctional response during an incident" (Barton, 2001, pp. 17–18). A number of problems can occur within the CMT. Bertrand and Lajtha (2002) summarize the common problems faced by the team:

Not Understanding the Symbolic and Sacred Aspects of a Crisis

A crisis is more than just an event; it is an attack on a specific stakeholder or institution, whether inside or outside the organization. Crises are perceived as "symptoms of underlying problems" and, as such, can be viewed as "policy fiascos" (Bovens & 't Hart, 1996). Crises "challenge the foundation of organizations, governmental practice and even societal cohesion" (Lagadec, 2004, p. 167). As a result, certain stakeholders may feel threatened by these events and perceive them to have deeper significance. For example, when a large company is involved in an environmental accident, the event is not just "an accident." It is perceived to be a big corporate giant exploiting the natural environment for its own gain.

Bertrand and Jajtha maintain that CMT training needs to include understanding the symbolic impact of a crisis. Hence, when media and community stakeholders appear to act irrationally, the CMT should seek to understand the reasons why they act that way. Put differently, most stakeholders do not try to act irrationally. From their point of view, their behavior is reasonable.

Not Being Able to Make Decisions Because of a Lack of Information

Many managers are effective at making some decisions when key information is lacking. Although complete information is preferred, decisions are frequently made under conditions of high uncertainty. When the organization is thrust into a crisis, the CMT must be able to make difficult decisions. This reality is a part of the charge that comes with their service on the CMT.

Lack of Interest and Involvement of Senior Management

It is difficult to promote a crisis preparedness atmosphere if the senior managers are not on board. As Bertrand and Lajtha (2002) lament, "Why do many top managers devote so little time to crisis management planning and training when the return on the small investment may be huge—and even commercially life-saving?" (p. 185). A central theme of this book is that crisis management is a key part of the strategic management process; top management must be supportive and involved.

Lack of Psychological Preparation Provided to CMT Members

Crisis team members bring their own emotional baggage to the meetings. Some are more adept than others at handling the stresses and fears of working on the team. The fatigue factor will also play a role, earlier for some members, later for others. In most cases, however, there is no forewarning as to what the CMT is about to face. Training for the psychological aspects of these assignments should be included.

In summary, "Crises are characterized by the absence of obvious solutions, the scarcity of reliable information when it is needed, the lack of adequate time to reflect on and debate alternative courses of action" (Bertrand & Lajtha, 2002, p. 185). While it is easy to list the functional departments that should be represented on the CMT, it is much more sobering to realize the intensity of the challenges team members must face.

Several other challenges can surface with the CMT, including groupthink, operating in different time zones, verbal aggressiveness, and the presence of a Machiavellian personality.

Groupthink

Janis (1982) identified *groupthink* as a problem in the decision-making process of groups and teams. Groupthink occurs when the team does not consider all of the alternatives and potential scenarios associated with a problem. While group cohesiveness can be a positive, too much can foster an atmosphere of groupthink. The rationale is that group members, unwilling to speak up and question the status quo or the leader or the conventional wisdom, remain passive so as not to upset the equilibrium of the group. Groupthink can be particularly present in crisis situations (Chandler & Wallace, 2009). In the crisis management literature, Lintonen (2004) discusses how groupthink influenced the European Union's (EU) adopting sanctions against Russia during the Chechnya crisis.

There are several ways to combat groupthink on the CMT (Simola, 2005). Crisis teams can benefit from an outside consultant who can offer crisis management expertise and also challenge the group on erroneous assumptions. The team leader should be impartial, being careful not to state his or her personal preferences before a decision has been made (Cho, 2005). Above all, alternative viewpoints should be fostered as a means of combating poor decision making. "The presence of team members who view the problem differently may stimulate others in the team to discover novel approaches that they would not have considered, thereby leading to better decisions" (Gomez-Mejia & Balkin, 2012, p. 323).

Practicing in Different Time Zones

When a crisis spans times zones, coordination problems can surface. For the multinational corporation with locations worldwide, it is necessary to negotiate different time zones and languages. Perhaps a key factory has been hit by a typhoon, tsunami, or earthquake. Or a facility on the other side of the world has caught fire. Coordinating relief efforts to get the facility back on line is made more difficult because of the obvious logistic and time complications. One remedy is using the partially distributed or virtually distributed crisis management team discussed earlier.

Verbal Aggressiveness

Chandler (2001) warned of team members who can become overbearing or even hostile. Such people should be screened out as CMT candidates early in the team selection process because they can obstruct group decision making and hamper open communication. Specific criteria should be established for membership on a CMT.

Machiavellian Personality

This person's main goal is simply trying to look good and advance his or her personal agenda. Chandler (2001) also recommends avoiding this person and instead looking for a team player who has the heart for solving problems. If the rest of the CMT is especially compliant, groupthink could possibly result if the Machiavellian type is present.

The Crisis Management Plan

Once the CMT is in place, efforts can be made to construct the crisis management plan. The CMP is not just a plan that exists on a company website or is stored in a notebook on a shelf; it is a systematic way of thinking about organizational crises. Top management support is also important in the development of the CMP (Pennington-Gray, Thapa, Kaplanidou, Cahyanto, & McLaughlin, 2011).

In managing a crisis, flexibility is favored over a rigid step-by-step procedure. In technical operations, such an approach is necessary for the diagnosis and remedy of certain problems. In a crisis, however, when human, technical, and other unknown elements are integrated, some degree of flexibility is required to discern and act on the situation. Having a standard operating procedure (SOP) manual is essential for all members of the team. Moreover, it should be compiled and put into a pocket-sized book that can be readily available for immediate use when a crisis occurs.

Plans should not be compiled just for the sake of meeting a compliance regulation (Bertrand & Lajtha, 2002). While this provides motivation to write the plan, it does not set the proper tone. Ultimately, a plan should encourage the crisis team to think critically about what could happen and plan for mitigation efforts for a crisis that does occur. The problem with writing a plan just to have one is that it may not be reviewed on a regular basis, if at all. An outline of what should be included in a CMP is provided in the Appendix at the end of this book.

Basic Components of the Plan

The CMP is likely to be found on the organization's Web page as well as in a hard copy notebook. The degree of detail can vary, but a concise plan is usually preferable to a longer one (Barton, 2001; Coombs, 2007). Again, this ensures that an element of flexibility is present in the crisis response. The following components are recommended for the CMP.

Cover Page

The cover page includes the name of the organization, general contact information, date of distribution, and the company logo. The page also labels the document as the crisis management plan. A disclaimer may be added stating that the document is confidential, and unauthorized use is prohibited.

Table of Contents

Although the document should not be too lengthy, a table of contents should be included. Crisis plans that are located on the organization's website should include appropriate links to sections within the document, as well as to appropriate websites for emergency providers and other crisis websites that could be useful.

Crisis Management Team Members

Team members should be listed along with their respective departments and contact information, including e-mail addresses, office phone, home phone, and cell phone numbers.

Team Member Responsibilities

This section will vary in its degree of detail. Larger and more complex organizations such as a research university should include more detail than a small organization such as a community high school. CMT members are selected as representatives from their functional areas of the organization, so it is expected they will be operating within their areas of expertise during the crisis. Two decisions that need to be determined before a crisis are (1) Who is in charge of the team, and (2) who are the designated company spokespersons to the media? It is also important to keep the team format flexible so it can adapt to the particular crisis at hand.

Activation of the CMT

The crisis management plan should include the procedures for activating the CMT. While some may view this as a formality, it is important to plan even this part of the event. Usually, the team will be activated by a team member or at the request of a key internal stakeholder. It is important that employees in the organization know who the CMT members are, as well. In some cases, employees may contact a team member instead of the police if they are not sure if an event is really a crisis. It would then be up to the CMT to determine whether police involvement is necessary.

Command Center Locations

The command center is a prearranged meeting location where the CMT gathers in the event of a crisis. The plan should clearly label both this location (the primary command center) and the alternate command center in case the primary one is damaged in some way—perhaps due to weather or a fire. Care should be taken not to locate the alternate command center too close in physical proximity to the primary one lest an event such as a flood or fire causes both centers to be unusable.

If the crisis involves a crime or physical damage to some aspect of the building facilities, an incident command center may be set up near the location of the actual crisis. This would be the case when emergency response providers are working a particular event while the CMT is meeting at the command center. With this type of arrangement, clear communication links will be needed between the incident command center and the CMT at the primary command center. Such a scenario could occur if there is a hostage situation in one location of the complex while the CMT is meeting in another part. It is common for these types of separate command center arrangements to occur on college and university campuses because the sprawling complex of buildings that exist.

Response Plans for Specific Crisis Situations

The CMP will have a list of prospective crisis events that could likely occur at the organization. This section is the longest in the CMP because specific crises are identified and a response plan is offered for each of these events. The plan should list the potential crisis at the top of the page and then follow with a series of bulleted steps on how to manage that event. For example, most CMPs have a response page for a bomb threat that is called in to the organization. Hotels are required to have an evacuation plan for their guests and employees. In fact, for hotels, a fire is typically the most serious crisis because mass causalities are possible (Gonzalez, 2008).

The length of the response plan will vary according to the crisis. Individuals who write response plans should attempt to be thorough yet concise, remembering that too many steps in the response plan can limit flexibility. Table 5.2 lists common crisis events addressed in CMPs at colleges and universities.

Table 5.2   Potential Crises for American Colleges and Universities

Type of Crises	Past Examples
Fires	2007: An off-campus fire at an Ocean Isle, North Carolina, beach condominium kills seven university students during their fall break. 2000: A Seton Hall University residence hall fire kills three students.
Athletics scandals	2011: A former Penn State football coach is accused of sexually molesting young boys within the campus athletic facilities. 2006: Three members of the Duke University lacrosse team are falsely accused of sexual offenses against a young woman at a team party. Although the charges were unfounded, the scandal proved damaging to the university and the students. 2004: The University of Colorado football program is plagued with a scandal involving sex, drugs, and alcohol for new recruits.
Safety of overseas students	2011: A Michigan State University student refuses to leave Egypt when the university formally made plans to evacuate its students in February during the political unrest. The student even achieves a short-lived celebrity status when her hometown media seeking her observations of the uprising interviewed her. After the evacuations are complete and the student realizes the impending danger, she threatens to report to the media that she "had been abandoned" by her university (Friend, 2012).
Major crimes	2010: A disgruntled biology professor, Amy Bishop, kills three of her colleagues in a department meeting at the University of Alabama at Huntsville. 2007: Four Delaware State University students are shot, three fatally, in a schoolyard near the university. 2007: Virginia Tech massacre results in 32 fatalities; victims include both faculty and students.
Floods: Because colleges and universities sprawl over a large geographical area, they are especially prone to flooding.	2009: A threatening flood closes the campus of Valley City State University in North Dakota. With three weeks left in the semester, the university has to deliver all remaining face-to-face courses online. 2003: Floods cause almost $2 million worth of damage at the University of Georgia's College of Veterinary Medicine. 1977: A flood ravages Toccoa Falls College, also in Georgia, killing 39 people and injuring another 60.

(Continued)

Table 5.2   Continued

Contagious diseases	College and university students are commonly cited for being at a higher risk for influenza and meningitis because of the close living conditions associated with residence halls.
Building mold	A number of colleges and universities throughout the United States have been affected by building mold problems. The university where the authors reside had a mold outbreak in the 2003. The result was the complete evacuation of the building for an entire semester while the building was cleaned and the problem resolved.
Weather-related crises	2005: A number of colleges and universities in New Orleans, Louisiana, and the surrounding region are closed long term after Hurricane Katrina devastates southern Louisiana and Mississippi. 2008: A tornado rips through the campus of Union University in Jackson, Tennessee, destroying several residence halls and trapping 13 students in the rubble (Penny, 2011).
Alcohol-related deaths	A major problem at many colleges and universities is the abuse of alcohol among students, sometimes resulting in binge-related deaths.

Distribution of the CMP

The CMP should be made available throughout the organization. There was once a time when distribution was often limited to CMT members. Unless there is proprietary information or confidentiality concern, however, the plan should be posted on the company's intranet at a minimum. For example, many colleges, universities, and school districts post their plans online for public viewing as well.

Crisis Management Training

The CMT is charged with the oversight of training in the area of crisis management. Training can range from simple meetings that review the CMP to providing classroom instruction on certain aspects of crisis management. Training can also include conducting smaller disaster drills that test a segment of the crisis response to taking part in elaborate mock disasters when a crisis is simulated so the team can practice its response. If the organization is large, the human resource management department (also referred to as *human resource development* in some organizations) may be better equipped to lead training exercises in crisis management (Moats, Chermack, & Dooley, 2008).

Regular CMT Meetings

The CMT should meet on a scheduled basis several times a year. Such meetings provide training opportunities as well as opportunities for team members to interact and bond. Both academic institutions and business organizations should consider meeting at least twice a year, although more meetings will be necessary in the initial stages of team development. Also, specific crises that may be threatening the firm will warrant more frequent meetings. Potential training activities that can be held during meetings include reviewing the CMP, conducting tabletop exercises, planning for larger-scale disaster exercises or mock disasters, and presenting new material on crisis management.

Reviewing All or a Part of the CMP

Reading the CMP refamiliarizes team members with the material. In addition, if editing errors are discovered, they can easily be corrected during the meeting if the document file is projected on a screen for all to see. When changes are necessary, they should be carried out during the meeting with the new plan revised and posted on the organization's website the same day. A hard copy of the CMP should also be kept up to date in case electronic access to the plan is not possible during a crisis.

Conducting Tabletop Exercises

This type of training occurs in the meeting room and involves a discussion of how the team would respond to a specific crisis. It is a form of a disaster drill, but without the realistic scenarios that are characteristic of a mock disaster. A tabletop exercise can be an inexpensive way to rehearse for a real disaster (Careless, 2007). Of course, the term *tabletop* is important because the training never leaves the meeting room; hence, there are some limitations in such an exercise. Still, their use is common and the benefits are clear.

A training workshop can be held in conjunction with a tabletop exercise. Workshops may last for several days and address a specific type of crisis. For example, workshops combined with tabletop exercises have been used for training against coastal terrorism (Richter et al., 2005). Cognitive mapping has also been used as a tabletop exercise. In this exercise, participants are asked to draw spatial maps of a developing crisis and then develop scenarios for managing the event (Alexander, 2004). Such an exercise is useful for those involved in disaster response activities.

Presenting New Material on Crisis Management

This training approach can be flexible. A video can be shown, a guest speaker brought in, or the team can take part in a video conference. The objective is to learn new material that will assist the team in its response to a crisis.

Disaster Drills

While a mock disaster is more comprehensive and tests the overall team response, a disaster drill is a smaller exercise that addresses one aspect of the crisis response (Coombs, 2007). Drills are meant to test a part of the crisis response. Examples of training drills include:

■ *Sending an emergency phone message and e-mail to all the employees in the organization.* This drill is practical because an alert of a crisis may need to be sent at a moment's notice. Perhaps a tornado has been spotted in the area or an individual with a gun is seen in the facility. The drill should also include sending text or voice messages to each employee's cell phone.

■ *Conducting a building evacuation drill.* This is perhaps the most common drill; it reminds many of us of the standard fire drill. Building evacuations frequently occur in schools as part of their regular scheduled training.

While evacuations are relatively simple in schools and other settings, they can be more complicated elsewhere, such as in a nursing home. Residents of nursing homes may also need to leave the area after a building evacuation, especially if there is threatening weather, such as a hurricane or flooding. An inadequate evacuation of a nursing home can result in patient deaths. Indeed, after Hurricane Katrina, two nursing homes in Louisiana were charged with negligent homicide in the deaths of 34 residents (Dewan & Baker, 2005). Two items essential to an effective nursing home evacuation include clear travel routes and adequate hydration provisions for the patients (Castle, 2008).

■ *Testing a procedure that is unique to the facility.* A library is an example of a facility with unique crisis scenarios. Libraries house collections of materials that are at risk for roof leaks, pest infestations, fire, theft, mold, security problems, and accumulations of dust and dirt (Yeh, McMullen, & Kane, 2010).

A common crisis scenario for a library is the loss of documents and books due to water damage. In light of this possibility, some libraries practice unique water drills. The Stetson University Law Library held a drill scenario in which a water sprinkler head had malfunctioned and was spraying water onto shelves of books. The personnel practiced draping the shelves with plastic tarps as quickly as possible (Rentschler & Burdett, 2006).

■ *Conducting an active shooter exercise.* These drills involve the simulation of an armed individual on the premises of the facility. They need to coordinate with local law enforcement agencies and other emergency providers to assist in the drill. Shopping malls are often utilized for this type of exercise, and for good reasons. On October 21, 2010, a man claiming to have a gun barricaded himself in a store at the Roseville Galleria in California, later resulting in a fire that caused substantial damage to the mall. On January, 8, 2011, a gunman killed six people at a strip shopping center in Tucson, Arizona (Bell, 2011).

One mall operator, the Cafaro Company out of Youngstown, Ohio, has conducted six active shooter exercises at its facilities, including one at the Meadowbrook Mall, in Bridgeport, West Virginia, in January 2011. The event involved two "recently fired employees" who demanded to see the mall manager. The role-playing involved shots being fired. Participants included nearly 200 volunteer shoppers, the West Virginia State Police, the county sheriff's department, a local hospital, and teams from the U.S. Federal Bureau of Investigations (FBI) (Bell, 2011).

■ *Accessing and using firefighting equipment.* Such equipment is required in all buildings, but training employees to use the equipment properly may be inconsistent. Local fire departments are usually willing to provide such training onsite. In addition, the fire department can also learn more about the unique features of the building, helping it compile a "preplan," a prearranged response to a fire in that particular building.

■ *Conducting a lockdown drill:* Securing the classroom(s) or building by locking the doors and requiring students (or employees) to stay inside, rather than exiting the building as in a fire drill. The intended purpose of a real lockdown is to protect the occupants of the room (building) in the event of a shooting or related incident. Lockdown drills became more frequent after the Columbine, Colorado, massacre (Kass & Marek, 2005), and their practice has increased as a result of the Virginia Tech massacre and other incidents of school violence. Such drills are not limited to schools, however. Incidents of workplace violence also require that employees be in a secure place in the event of a shooting. Thus, a lockdown drill would be advisable in nonschool settings as well.

■ *Activating sheltering in place.* A variation of the lockdown drill involves not only securing the building, but moving occupants to a more central location for additional security. In the United States, this type of drill, called "sheltering in place," has been practiced in school systems close to the nation's ports (Jacobson, 2003). Because ports have been identified as potential terrorist targets, population centers near these ports need to be prepared. Sheltering-in-place drills can include the shutting down of heating and air conditioning systems as well as sealing air inflow openings near windows. Such a move would be likely in response to a chemical or biological terrorist attack.

■ *Conduct shower drills.* In a very specialized drill, companies that use hazardous chemicals are being encouraged to conduct "shower drills" (Hayes, 2011). The danger in these environments is that a dangerous chemical may come in contact with a worker, resulting in the need to flush the chemical off the skin as quickly as possible. Shower units that offer privacy can be positioned in work areas and should offer adequate water pressure at comfortable temperatures for 15 minutes, the required Occupational Safety and Health Administration (OSHA) standard.

The Mock Disaster

A mock disaster is a scenario that is recreated so that a number of crisis management participant–stakeholders can respond to it. It operates in real time, in a setting that is as realistic as possible to a real crisis. A mock disaster is more comprehensive than a disaster drill. Mock disasters are widely recognized as essential in testing an organization's disaster plan (Perry, 2004).

Purpose of a Mock Disaster

A mock disaster can serve a number of purposes. Its practicality is enhanced by the number of people who can participate, the media attention that is received, and the usefulness of testing the organization's crisis response. The following section explains the intended purposes of the mock disaster:

To activate and test the working of the CMT. This type of exercise involves the full activation of the CMT as well as the appropriate emergency providers in the community, such as law enforcement, fire departments, and emergency medical services. One of the most important goals is to ensure that the CMT is alerted to a crisis in a timely manner. The working dynamics of the team can also be evaluated. Do team members work effectively as a unit? Are there any interpersonal problems that need to be addressed? Is there anyone who is not a good fit to serve on the team?

To test communication networks and equipment. A mock disaster should test the communication systems that will be used during an actual crisis. Telephone systems, mobile radios, the intranet, social media messaging, and the Internet should all be activated and used during the drill. In addition, local fire and police departments may have special equipment they need to test. For example, robots are used in certain firefighting situations and in bomb removal and detonation. A mock disaster is an excellent opportunity for testing this type of specialized equipment.

Banks should test their crisis readiness on a regular basis. Several years ago, the Farmington Savings Bank (FSB) staged a mock disaster to test the components of its backup information systems arrangement. The bank has 13 branches in central Connecticut. The scenario involved working with its disaster recovery provider; which supplied a trailer, a power generator, and 20 personal computers (Arnfield, 2009). After conducting the training exercise, bank executives learned that if more than 10 phone lines were in use, the satellite link did not function properly. In addition, slow bandwidth affected the printing of documents stored on the disaster recovery server. Remedying these problems was relatively easy, but identifying them through the disaster drill was the only way to identify them in the first place.

To test the effectiveness of the command center. If the command center has never been used for an actual crisis, it should be activated during the mock disaster. When Concord College held its first mock disaster (see the opening case for this chapter), a major shortcoming was discovered with its primary command center. The problem was that all radio communications were funneled into one large room, the same general area where the media were also assembling. When mock reporters heard the reports coming in from the incident command center, they demanded an explanation from the president of the college, who just happened to be listening to the same reports in the command center (Crandall, 1997). After the drill, a new command center in a different building was designated with a separate room for media briefings.

To develop working relationships with local fire and police departments. In the event of a real emergency, the local fire and police departments will be the first responders to the event. Developing relationships with these agencies before a crisis occurs is recommended. The mock disaster is an excellent vehicle for accomplishing this goal.

To build team cohesiveness and camaraderie. A CMT may actually function quite well in a noncrisis setting. Regularly scheduled meetings and training sessions are low-stress contact points. A mock disaster, however, adds a sense of urgency and purpose to the working relationships of the CMT. After working together on a large-scale exercise, which can be physically and emotionally challenging, team members may find they are more cohesive and appreciative of each other.

To learn where the organization's crisis response needs improvement. A well-designed mock disaster should test the key areas of crisis response and be rigorous enough to expose weak points. At the Stetson University Law Library, the mock disaster discussed previously revealed that response times to a water leak emergency needed to be improved (Rentschler & Burdett, 2006). A mock disaster at the Arco Chemical plant in South Charleston, West Virginia, revealed that media briefings were being rushed; not a good situation given the fact that this particular drill involved a sinking barge full of chemicals spilling its contents into the Kanawha River (Swift, 2004).

Another common area of weakness during a crisis is message overload; too much information going through the system can be hard for employees to interpret. "A common failure is basic system overloads. . . . Are too many messages being sent? Are people not understanding all the messages? Are they not coming in chronological order?" (Morton, 2011, p. 26).

A mock disaster can also alert the CMT where additional training is needed. For example, all mock disasters should include holding a staged press conference and answering hypothetical questions from reporters. Training other employees in this function in addition to the official spokesperson is recommended. The company spokesperson may not be available during a crisis that requires a response to the media. Mock disasters can be useful in determining how "polished" these backup spokespersons are and whether they need additional training.

Guidelines for Setting Up a Mock Disaster

A mock disaster should be planned like any other project. There should be a person in charge, a set of goals and objectives, a delegated list of duties, and a timeline for scheduling the drill. Specific considerations are discussed next.

Determine the objectives of the drill. A mock disaster tests some response systems, but not the organization's entire crisis response capability. The CMT should determine several key areas that need to be tested and include those in the plan. All mock disasters should test communication capabilities and interviews by the media.

If specific equipment is part of the crisis response, then it should be tested as well. The *Exxon Valdez* oil spill in Alaskan waters is known for the massive amounts of oil that damaged the environment. What is less well known is that Exxon had a response plan for an oil spill in that area. Unfortunately, the boat that was designated to set up perimeter booms around the spill was being repaired at the time of the spill (Hartley, 1993). The role of equipment, then, is paramount in certain areas of crisis response. Testing that equipment should be part of the mock drill.

Develop a scenario that represents a potential crisis at your organization. As addressed in previous chapters, crisis assessment activities reveal potential crisis events that could occur in the organization. Some of these crises have geographic considerations, such as earthquakes along the whole west coast of the United States, volcano activity at Mount St. Helens and Mount Rainier, hurricanes in the southeastern United States, terrorism at various targets throughout the world, and wildfires in drier locations in the western United States. Some potential crises are industry specific: chemical spills (production industries), *E. coli* outbreaks (food industries), school violence (education), and computer hacking and viruses (any industry that depends on online sales). Thus, the mock disaster should involve a scenario that represents a real crisis the organization might face.

Be sure the top leaders in your organization are supportive and involved in the drill. Without their support, the project will not reach its full potential. Support and participation in the mock disaster shows employees that management takes these activities seriously. In the opening case, the president of the college was a member of the CMT and active in the mock disasters and training held at the school. His enthusiasm helped carry the drills through to successful implementation and completion. It also showed that he cared about instilling a culture in the organization that supported crisis planning.

Include as many parties as possible in planning the mock disaster. Despite their seriousness and intensity, mock disasters also have a social aspect to them in that groups of people are working together on a common project. This is not to imply that such drills are meant to be festive or partylike, but they are social gatherings even if the objective is serious. Hence, including as many individuals as possible who have a link to the drill is advisable. Enthusiasm for the drill can be high because participants are taking part in a social exercise while engaging in activities outside of their normal routines. Participating toward a common goal is also a satisfying experience.

Include local police, fire, and other emergency services. Fire and police departments spend a great deal of time in training activities. Most will be receptive to taking part in a mock disaster because it serves as a training opportunity for their departments as well. It is also beneficial in that CMT members can become acquainted with some of the key players within the emergency services departments.

Use mock reporters. Mock reporters are standard in any disaster exercise of this scope. The realistic scenario of being interviewed by the media can be unexpected and intimidating. Local university journalism students make a good source of mock reporters, because many will be working for the media in the future.

Sometimes the experience of working in a disaster exercise can lead to working on a real disaster. Mock reporters are used regularly at Syracuse University in disaster training. In 2002, however, the simulated chemical spill that was supposed to occur was replaced by the real thing. Two hours before the mock disaster, a real crisis developed when brown puddles of unknown origin formed inside the university's biological research center. The real crisis resulted in the building being evacuated and the arrival of a hazardous material team, along with police and fire personnel (Strupp, 2002).

Use mock victims. Including mock victims with injuries is also useful in this type of exercise. Once again, local colleges and universities may be helpful (Crandall, 1997). The drama or theater department can supply "victims" who can be made up to look injured. This activity provides useful practice for these students who work both on and off stage.

Invite the media to come to your drill. In addition to using mock reporters, inviting the local media is an excellent idea as well. The training event can be featured in the local newspaper and on the television evening news. The publicity generated is usually well received because it shows the organization is being proactive in its crisis management efforts. In addition, local reporters can offer advice from their perspectives, some of which may be quite useful to the CMT.

Be sure all of the employees and local community are aware of the drill. The mock disaster should be well publicized to all employees and the local community so that citizens do not mistake the drill for a real crisis. One of the authors lives near a large military base that occasionally conducts mock exercises in the community. One such drill involved the use of a military team descending on an abandoned motel. Helicopters were flying overhead and soldiers were maneuvering around the facility. The drill was so extensive that spectators gathered across the street to watch. Fortunately, advance notice had been given to the community, and many were expecting this event as a form of entertainment for the evening. Several years later, the local fire department torched the entire facility in a dramatic blaze as a training exercise. Again, the community knew to expect a spectacular fire that night.

Guidelines While the Mock Disaster Is in Progress

Planning a mock disaster is an extensive process. The actual drill should proceed well if the guidelines presented here are applied. In addition, it is important that care be taken not to create a real crisis during the drill. Such events do occur and can result in injuries. If the fire department is involved, it will likely have a safety officer who helps ensure that injuries do not occur. Nonetheless, problems can develop, and anyone planning such an exercise should be aware of such possibilities. Case in point: in 2007, an elaborate search-and-rescue drill involving about 400 people was held off the coast of Newfoundland. The objective of the drill was to respond to a scenario in which a ferry was on fire. The drill involved evacuating passengers from the ferry into lifeboats. The drill took a realistic turn, however, when several passengers on one of the lifeboats were overcome by exhaust fumes and had to be airlifted by helicopter to a hospital (Brautigam, 2007).

A second consideration during a mock disaster is to remember that mistakes will be made during the drill. This is not a bad thing as long as serious damages and injuries are avoided, because one of the purposes is to identify crisis response weaknesses. Those involved should record any mistakes and discuss them during the debriefing meeting held after the mock disaster. One animal shelter staged a mock disaster involving the evacuation of all animals from the facility. Such an incident would be required if a natural disaster such as a hurricane was threatening. A number of small problems developed during the drill, including a fight between two dogs that were being held by volunteers in the waiting queue and a cat that escaped from its cage. Moreover, the volunteers who helped with the mock drill were plentiful but untrained in how to carry out their required roles, complicating the process considerably (Irvine, 2007). Hence, formal training for the volunteers was warranted.

A third guideline, which may be useful for catching mistakes, is to record the drill. When Concord College staged its first mock disaster, two photographers made video recordings. One cameraperson was at the incident command center, where the disaster scenario took place. The other recorded the meetings in the main command center, where most of the CMT was meeting. This arrangement was later useful for evaluation because CMT members at the command center could view what was happening at the incident area, and vice versa (Crandall, 1997).

Guidelines for After the Mock Disaster

Immediately after the drill, food and refreshments should be provided for all of those who participated. This step is highly recommended, as most participants will be exhausted. This social gathering also gives individuals time to reflect, relax, and build camaraderie.

Within one week of the drill, it is recommended that a debriefing meeting be held to discuss what was learned. Some teams may choose to debrief immediately after the mock disaster. This may be feasible if the drill did not last too long. Otherwise, it may be better to debrief on another day when the CMT is refreshed and mentally alert. Care should be taken not to wait too long after the event, however, lest team members forget some of the finer learning details of the drill. The lessons learned from the mock disaster may result in changes to the crisis management plan. These changes should be made soon in the master document and in any additional associated locations such as the organization's website.

Summary

This chapter emphasized the importance of forming the crisis management team and writing the crisis management plan. The CMT is charged with developing a list of threats that face the organization and overseeing the compilation of the CMP. The CMP revolves around addressing these threats as well as providing other guidelines for how the organization should respond to a crisis.

The CMT also leads the training needed for crisis response. Regular meetings should be held to keep members familiar with the crisis plan, as well as to provide training for specific crisis events. Testing the crisis response of the organization is also important. Tabletop drills are short and confined to usually one room. A disaster drill is larger in scope and involves testing a single component of the organization's crisis response. A mock disaster is larger in its inclusion of stakeholders and the number of crisis components being tested. All of these exercises fine-tune the CMT so that it is ready if and when a crisis occurs.

Questions for Discussion

1. Discuss how groupthink can be a problem for a crisis management team. What can be done to prevent groupthink?

2. How are problems associated with the crisis management team different from those associated with other committees?

3. If you were the crisis management team leader, how would you ensure that the team members regularly review the crisis management plan?

4. Why is it a good idea to require your suppliers to have a crisis management plan?

5. What types of disaster drills are regularly practiced at your place of employment? If none are used, what would you propose for a disaster drill exercise?

6. What scenarios would make a good mock disaster where you work or go to school?

Chapter Exercise

All students and practitioners in the area of crisis management should be able to write a crisis management plan. In addition, the ability to organize a training program and a mock disaster is desirable. This course exercise is designed to be a comprehensive project that accomplishes each of these goals.

General Guidelines

1. Students in the class should be assigned to teams of four to six members. Each team should work with the management team of a local organization to compile a crisis management plan. For this first step, the instructor should serve as the liaison between the organization and the student team.

2. Employed students already have an entry into their organizations. These are potential companies for the project also and can be pursued with the approval of the instructor.

3. Each team should design a mock disaster for that particular organization. Keep in mind that the purpose of this drill is to test the organization's CMP and its crisis response capabilities.

4. Each team should formulate a crisis training program schedule for the organization.

   - Indicate how often meetings should be held and what training modules should be provided.
   - Designate which training is for the CMT only and which should be company-wide.

5. Each team should present its CMP, mock disaster plan, and training program schedule to the class. If possible, a representative from the respective organization should also be present.

Specific Guidelines

1. In organizing the CMP, remember that many such plans are already posted on the Internet. College and university plans are readily available for review and can provide useful insights on how to organize your team's plan. In addition, the Appendix at the end of this book provides an outline of areas that should be addressed in your CMP.

2. Remember that a landscape survey of the internal and external environment is necessary to assess that organization's crisis vulnerability. This is performed with a SWOT analysis (see Chapter 4). Include this information in the plan as well.

3. Be sure the plan is realistic for the organization you have selected. Do not address crisis scenarios that are unrealistic.

4. Designate a backup command center in your plan and explain how a virtual command center would be arranged.

5. Be sure to prepare a timeline for the mock disaster. Identify what should occur two months before the drill, one month before, two weeks, two days, and so on. Use a timeline that is feasible for your particular mock disaster.

Mini Case: Industrial Accident

On April 2, 2010, an explosion and fire erupted at the Tesoro Corporation, a refining company in Washington State. The explosion killed five workers immediately, while two died later in the hospital. The resulting fire took 90 minutes to extinguish and at times reached the height of the refinery tower ("U.S. oil refiner fined," 2010). The accident occurred while workers were performing maintenance on a heat exchanger. Because heat exchangers contain highly combustible material, they can easily explode if not properly inspected and managed.

The company conducted an internal investigation and blamed the accident on a chain of events that caused hydrogen to react with the carbon in the steel pipes. The occurrence, also called a hydrogen attack, eventually caused the pipe in the heat exchanger to crack (Pipken, 2010). The incident was also investigated by the Washington Department of Labor and Industries. The six-month investigation resulted in the issuing of 44 citations and a $2.38 million fine for safety and health violations ("Washington state fines Tesoro," 2010). Specifically, the department concluded that Tesoro had:

- Disregarded a number of workplace safety regulations
- Continued to operate equipment that was failing and should have been replaced
- Purposely postponed maintenance
- Inadequately tested for potential damage to equipment, including the heat exchanger that exploded
- Failed to protect workers from injury and death

The Tesoro Corporation refinery in Anacortes, Washington, had been previously fined $85,700 in April 2009 by the Washington Department of Labor and Industries. The agency found the company guilty of 17 serious safety and health violations that had the potential to cause a worker death or serious injury. In addition, the state inspectors found 150 other deficiencies that did not ensure that the company adhered to safe work practices ("U.S. oil refiner fined," 2010).

Accidents are no stranger to the refining industry. In 2010, the U.S. Chemical Safety and Hazardous Investigation Board were examining 18 major accidents in refineries and chemical plants. Of these cases, seven of the accidents were at refineries. There are in excess of 10,000 chemical plants in the United States, but only 150 refineries ("U.S. oil refiner fined," 2010). The high concentration of accidents in the industry is alarming. According to John Bresland, chairman for the Chemical Safety and Hazardous Investigation Board, "This is a significant and disturbing trend that the refining industry needs to address immediately" ("Six workers die," 2010, p. 3).

One of the problems in the refinery industry (as well as other industries, such as coal mining) is the lack of effective enforcement of existing regulations. What results is a situation in which companies challenge citations from regulatory agencies, often for years ("Regulatory flaws," 2011). The company then is not required to make any changes while the citation is in the appeal process. In essence, the company does not have to upgrade older or unsafe equipment that might have been the target of a citation. This practice becomes a bit of a game; the company hedges that it can postpone equipment upgrades and eventually pay fines instead of buying new and safer equipment, which can be costly. The first option results in less cash expenditures than the second option. Unfortunately, as we found in this case, it can also compromise worker safety and lead to fatalities.

Mini-Case Discussion Questions

1. It was noted that Tesoro conducted its own internal investigation. From a legal standpoint, why do you think this was an important item to note?

2. Postponing maintenance and operating older equipment can result in an accident to a worker. What examples are you aware of when an accident occurred because of these factors?

3. Companies often contest a government agency when they are cited for safety violations. This practice occurs in the refinery industry, as well as in coal mining. Instead of paying the fine or fixing the problem, the company fights the agency in an effort to stall the process of making improvements to equipment. What can be done to address this problem?

Mini-Case References

Pipken, W. (2010, August 28). BRIEF: Tesoro: Hydrogen reaction caused fireball. *Skagit Valley Herald* (Mt. Vernon, WA). Retrieved on July 24, 2012, from Newspaper Source Plus.

Regulatory flaws, repeated violations put oil refinery workers at risk. (2011, February 28). *iWatch News,* The Center for Public Integrity. Retrieved July 24, 2012, from http://www.iwatchnews.org/2011/02/28/2111/regulatory-flaws-repeated-violations-put-oil-refinery-workers-risk.

Six workers die in Washington refinery fire. (2010, June). *Loss Prevention Bulletin,* Issue 213, 2–4.

U.S. oil refiner fined before deadly blaze. (2010, April 3). *Toronto Star,* p. A19.

Washington state fines Tesoro more than $2 million after refinery explosion that killed seven workers. (2010, October 15). *OSHA Quick Takes.* Retrieved July 24, 2012, from http://www.osha.gov/as/opa/quicktakes/qt10152010.html#3.

References

Alexander, D. (2004). Cognitive mapping as an emergency management training exercise. *Journal of Contingencies and Crisis Management, 12*(4), 150–159.

Arnfield, R. (2009). Dress rehearsals reveal holes. *Bank Technology News, 22*(5), 26.

Barton, L. (2001). *Crisis in organizations II.* Cincinnati: South-Western.

Bell, J. (2011). Mayhem at the mall: Cafaro training exercises prepare teams for crisis. *Chain Store Age, 87*(4), 72.

Bertrand, R., & Lajtha, C. (2002). A new approach to crisis management. *Journal of Contingencies and Crisis Management, 10*(4), 181–191.

Bovens, M., & 't Hart, P. (1996). *Understanding policy fiascos.* New Brunswick, NJ: Transaction.

Brautigam, T. (2007, September 28). Mock disaster turns real. *Toronto Star,* p. A03.

Careless, J. (2007). Practice, practice, practice. *Mobile Radio Technology, 25*(3), 46–49.

Castle, N. (2008). Nursing home evacuation plans. *American Journal of Public Health, 98*(7), 1235–1240.

Chandler, R. (2001). Crisis management: Does your team have the right members? *Safety Management, 458,* 1–3.

Chandler, R., & Wallace, J. (2009). The role of videoconferencing in crisis and emergency management. *Journal of Business Continuity and Emergency Planning, 3*(2), 161–177.

Cho, C. (2005). Information failures and organizational disasters. *MIT Sloan Management Review, 46*(3), 8–10.

Clark, J., & Harman, M. (2004). On crisis management and rehearsing a plan. *Risk Management, 51*(5), 40–43.

Coombs, W. (2007). *Ongoing crisis communication: Planning, managing, and responding* (2nd ed.). Thousand Oaks, CA: Sage.

Coombs, W., & Holladay, S. (2001). An extended examination of the crisis situation: A fusion of the relational management and symbolic approaches. *Journal of Public Relations Research, 13,* 321–340.

Crandall, W. (1997, April). How to choreograph a disaster. *Security Management,* 40–43.

Davis, S. (2002). Virtual emergency operations centers. *Risk Management, 49*(7), 46–52.

Dewan, S., & Baker, A. (2005, September 14). Owners of nursing home charged in deaths of 34. *New York Times.* Retrieved May 22, 2012, from http://www.nytimes.com/2005/09/14/national/nationalspecial/14storm.html?pagewanted=all.

Friend, J. (2012). Learning from the recent challenges in education about crisis management. *International Educator, 21*(1), 56–59.

Gilpin, D., & Murphy, P. (2008). *Crisis management in a complex world.* New York: Oxford University Press.

Gomez-Mejia, L., & Balkin, D. (2012). *Management: People, performance, change.* Upper Saddle River, NJ: Prentice Hall.

Gonzalez, G. (2008). Hotel disaster plans must consider an array of exposures. *Business Insurance, 42*(24), 12–13.

Hartley, R. (1993). *Business ethics: Violations of the public trust.* New York: Wiley.

Hayes, C. (2011). Be proactive: Conduct emergency shower drills. *Facility Safety, 46*(1), 60.

Irvine, L. (2007). Ready or not: Evacuating an animal shelter during a mock emergency. *Anthrozoos, 20*(4), 355–364.

Jacobson, L. (2003, April 30). Disaster drills emphasize plans to "shelter" pupils at school. *Education Week, 22*(33), 6–7.

Janis, I. (1982). *Groupthink: Psychological studies of policy decisions and fiascoes* (2nd ed.). Boston: Houghton Mifflin.

Kass, J., & Marek, A. (2005, April 4). What happened after Columbine. *U.S. News & World Report,* 28–29.

Kimble, C. (2011). Building effective virtual teams: How to overcome the problems of trust and identity in virtual teams. *Global Business and Organizational Excellence, 30*(2), 6–15.

Kovoor-Misra, S., & Nathan, M. (2000, Fall). Timing is everything: The optimal time to learn from crises. *Review of Business,* 31–36.

Lagadec, P. (2004). Understanding the French 2003 heat wave experience: Beyond the heat, a multi-layered challenge. *Journal of Contingencies and Crisis Management, 12*(4), 160–169.

Lintonen, R. (2004). Understanding EU crisis-making: The case of Chechnya and the Finnish presidency. *Journal of Contingencies and Crisis Management, 12*(1), 29–38.

Lockwood, N. (2005). Crisis management in today's business environment: HR's strategic role. *SHRM Research Quarterly,* no. 4, 1–10.

Millar, M. (2003, October 28). HR must be at forefront of crisis management plans. *Personnel Today,* 7.

Moats, J., Chermack, T., & Dooley, L. (2008). Using scenarios to develop crisis managers: Applications of scenario planning and scenario-based training. *Advances in Developing Human Resources, 10*(3), 397–424.

Morton, J. (2011). Practice makes perfect. *Buildings, 105*(2), 26.

Nunamaker Jr., J., Reinig, B., & Briggs, R. (2009). Principles for effective virtual teamwork. *Communications of the ACM, 52*(4), 113–117.

Pearson, C., & Mitroff, A. (1993). From crisis prone to crisis prepared: A framework for crisis management. *Academy of Management Executive, 71,* 48–59.

Pennington-Gray, L., Thapa, B., Kaplanidou, K., Cahyanto, I., & McLaughlin, E. (2011). Crisis planning and preparedness in the United States tourism industry. *Cornell Hospitality Quarterly, 52*(3), 312–320.

Penny, J. (2011). Crisis averted? *Buildings, 105*(9), 50–54.

Perry, R. (2004). Disaster exercise outcomes for professional emergency personnel citizen volunteers. *Journal of Contingencies and Crisis Management, 12*(2), 64–75.

Pines, W. (2000). Myths of crisis management. *Public Relations Quarterly, 45*(3), 15–17.

Podolak, A. (2002). Crisis management teams. *Risk Management, 54*(4), 54–57.

Rentschler, C., & Burdett, P. (2006, Spring). Mock disaster at Stetson Law Library prepares staff for a real one. *Florida Libraries,* 13–15.

Richter, J., Livet, M., Stewart, J., Feigley, C., Scott, G., & Richter, D. (2005, November). Coastal terrorism: Using tabletop discussions to enhance coastal community infrastructure through relationship building. *Journal of Public Health Management Practice,* S45–S49.

Roux-Dufort, C. (2009). The devil lies in details! How crises build up within organizations. *Journal of Contingencies and Crisis Management, 17*(1), 4–11.

Sadri, G., & Condia, J. (2012). Managing the virtual world. *Industrial Management, 54*(1), 21–25.

Simola, S. (2005). Organizational crisis management: Overview and opportunities. *Consulting Psychology Journal: Practice and Research, 57*(3), 180–192.

Strupp, J. (2002, September 2). Chemical scare tests reactions. *Editor and Publisher,* 4.

Swift, K. (2004). Crisis stage. *ABA Journal, 90*(1), 75.

Yeh, F., McMullen, K. & Kane, L. (2010). Disaster planning in a health sciences library: A grant-funded approach. *Journal of the Medical Library Association, 98*(3), 259–261.

CHAPTER 6

Organizational Strategy and Crises

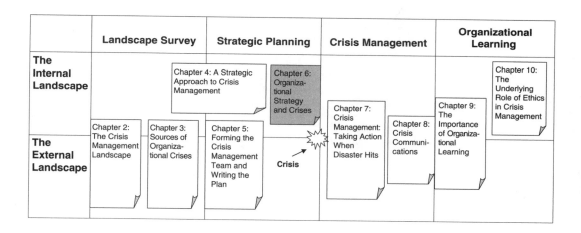

	Landscape Survey		Strategic Planning	Crisis Management		Organizational Learning
The Internal Landscape		Chapter 4: A Strategic Approach to Crisis Management	Chapter 6: Organizational Strategy and Crises			Chapter 10: The Underlying Role of Ethics in Crisis Management
The External Landscape	Chapter 2: The Crisis Management Landscape	Chapter 3: Sources of Organizational Crises	Chapter 5: Forming the Crisis Management Team and Writing the Plan	Chapter 7: Crisis Management: Taking Action When Disaster Hits	Chapter 8: Crisis Communications	Chapter 9: The Importance of Organizational Learning

Crisis

Opening Case, Part 1: The BP Gulf of Mexico Oil Spill

On April 20, 2010, British Petroleum's (BP) offshore drilling rig, the *Deepwater Horizon,* exploded in the Gulf of Mexico and caused the largest accidental marine oil spill in history. The ruptured oil well spewed nearly 5 million barrels of oil into the sea over three months (Friedman & Friedman, 2010). Eleven men working on the project were fatally injured, and 17 others were severely injured. This crisis resulted in major destruction to marine wildlife, and extensive economic harm was inflicted on the fishing and tourism industries. For BP, it was a public relations crisis nightmare.

Offshore Versus Deep-Water Drilling

Starting in the 1980s, the United States looked for a solution to its energy and national security needs through offshore oil production. Since World War II, the Gulf of Mexico has been a major area for offshore drilling. Most of the wells in this area were in shallower waters with depths around 200 feet or less (Schneider, 2011). However, as these wells were depleted, oil companies moved their efforts to deeper waters that were several thousand feet in depth. At the time of the BP oil spill, the Gulf of Mexico was estimated to hold 19 percent of the U.S. oil reserves (Griggs, 2011).

Deep-water drilling is a promising alternative for extracting oil reserves, but there are drawbacks. The most obvious difficulty is to drill and operate a well at such tremendous depths. The U.S. government defines a deep-water well as one that involves drilling in excess of 500 feet. In 2010, there were about 600 deep-water wells in the Gulf of Mexico (Tankersley, 2010). Because of the excessive depths of the wells, they are not accessible by human divers and must be reached by robots if there is a maintenance problem.

A special drilling rig is needed to bore an oil well in deep waters. Two types exist: the drillship and the semi-submersible (Cook, 2010). A drillship resembles an actual ship, with the drilling apparatus located in the center. The semi-submersible rig has large pontoons that can be filled with ballast so the rig can be partially submerged. This feature also helps the rig remain more stable amid the waves (Cook, 2010). The *Deepwater Horizon* was a semi-submersible rig that was used to dig the well on the Macondo slope of the Gulf of Mexico. Once the well was dug and capped, the rig would move on to a different site to dig another well. A different rig would arrive afterward at the Macondo well and extract the oil. Companies like BP do not own or operate these rigs; instead, they lease them from specialized companies such as Transocean, the largest offshore drilling contractor in the world (Barrett, 2011).

The Deepwater Horizon

The *Deepwater Horizon* was built in Korea and literally sailed to the United States, arriving for service in the Gulf of Mexico in 2001. The original price tag was $365 million and included a 28,000-ton drilling package (Elkind, Whitford, & Burke, 2011). But the rig was also designed for the use of its employees who would be working there on an extended basis. Amenities such as a movie room, a gym, maid service, a smoking cave, berths with carpeting, in-room Internet, and a 24-hour mess hall were all provided. When one is out at sea, a workplace needs to resemble home as much as possible.

The rig was a multi-use facility that included the drilling apparatus, monitoring facilities, a heliport, and accommodations for the employees. The most important function, however, was to drill for oil. Extracting the oil would be performed by a different rig; hence the *Deepwater Horizon* was better termed a drilling rig.

Understanding the Macondo Well

The Macondo oil well in the Gulf of Mexico was sunk 18,360 feet below sea level. BP leased the *Deepwater Horizon* at a cost of $533,000 a day from Transocean (Crooks, Pfeifer, & McNulty, 2010). Since the accident, critics have questioned BP's cost-cutting efforts. At a charge of a half a million dollars a day, it is easy to see why the company was concerned about expenses. Moreover, drilling the Macondo well had been fraught with problems, causing the project to fall behind schedule by some 45 days and resulting in a $58 million overrun of the budget (Elkind et al., 2011).

The Blowout Preventor

One of the key devices on a deepwater well is the blowout preventer (BOP). The BOP is a 40-foot stack of valves that sits on top of the well on the sea bed (McNulty & Crooks, 2010). It is designed to stop the flow of oil and gas from the well in the event of an emergency. If the BOP were to fail, dangerous oil and gases could spew from the well and move up the riser, which is located in the water and serves as the connection tube between the rig and the well. Once the gases have moved up the riser, they are emitted at the oil rig itself, which creates a volatile situation because the gases are highly flammable. A sufficient amount of gas and an ignition source could ignite an explosion. Because oil is rising up uncontrollably as well, the resulting fire would be fueled by the oil, creating a burning inferno that could last as long as the fire has a fuel source.

Because of the importance of the BOP, it must be built well and checked periodically. The maker of the BOP for the Macondo well was Cameron International, a company known for reliability. Indeed, the BOP must work perfectly because it is the main barrier protecting human life, capital equipment, and the environment (Hoyos, 2010). However, there was an incident involving the BOP after it had been installed. Four weeks before the night of the explosion, a worker had accidently bumped a control switch that moved a portion of pipe through the BOP. Later, chunks of rubber were found in the drilling fluid, indicating that "something" had been compromised in the BOP. However, no further action was taken on the matter (Cook, 2010).

Cementing the Drill Casing

The process of drilling a well involves boring a hole first, then inserting a metal casing into the hole so that the shaft has structural integrity. In other words, the metal casing keeps the bored hole from falling in on itself. Before a well can be capped, the area between the bored hole and the outside of the casing must be filled with cement. Filling this gap helps to center the casing in the hole, and it prevents dangerous hydrocarbon gases from entering the shaft (Cook, 2010). In addition, the bottom of the well where the shaft is still open is filled with cement to keep these gases from entering. Thus, the shaft is now protected with cement from the sides and the bottom. The goal is to seal the shaft tightly so nothing can enter it until the next oil rig arrives to extract the oil. At that point, the shaft is reopened to allow oil to flow up to the rig. Until then, the shaft must not become a conduit for hydrocarbon gases and oil.

The cementing process also accomplishes another goal, to keep the metal casing of the drill shaft completely centered in the bore. However, cement alone is not enough to keep the long shaft in place. Carbon-steel liners are also used to correctly position the metal casing in the hole. The design of the well called for 21 centralizers, but only six were available for installation. Instead of waiting for more to arrive, BP decided to work with six. It should be noted BP officials made this decision, although another company, Halliburton, was contracted to do the cement work. Although a Halliburton official warned that not using the full 21 centralizers could cause a problem with the integrity of the shaft, the work proceeded with only six (Elkind et al., 2011).

The Negative Pressure Test

Before the *Deepwater Horizon* was allowed to move to its next job, a negative pressure test had to be conducted on the well. This test measures whether or not the well is sealed completely. If the well has a good seal, then no change in pressure should occur. An increase in pressure from the well indicates that a good seal has not been attained, meaning that hydrocarbon gases and oil could leak into the shaft. When the test was conducted, the results were confusing. What added to the problem was that BP did not have a standard procedure in place on how to conduct the negative pressure test, nor was there guidance on how to interpret the results (Cook, 2010).

When the test was first run, the well was exerting pressure on the drill pipe, indicating that hydrocarbons were leaking into the pipe. The test was run again just to make sure it was not a mistake, but the same results occurred—pressure was occurring, which meant a good seal was not attained. Somewhere, the cement had not done its job. Or had it? A discussion ensued among BP, Halliburton, and Transocean staff. One engineer suggested that it might be a false reading. A third test was run, this time a line that connected to the main drill shaft. The crew theorized that this line should also show an increase in pressure if there was indeed a leak because the entire setup was a closed system (Elkind et al., 2011). The feeder line showed normal pressure. The BP staff concluded the system was not leaking, a decision that would prove to be fatal in just a few hours.

Opening Case Part 1 Discussion Questions

1. Even though BP did not directly own the oil rig in question, why do you think it received the most blame in the media?

2. What are the advantages and disadvantages of outsourcing?

3. This case illustrates that a testing procedure may not always produce reliable results. Have you experienced problems at work where established testing procedures were not adequate and led to problems?

Opening Case Part 1 References

Barrett, P. (2011, July 4). Success is never having to say you're sorry. *Bloomberg Businessweek,* 54–62.

Cook, N. (2010). Deepwater Horizon. *RoSPA Occupational Safety and Health Journal, 40*(12), 13–17.

Crooks, E., Pfeifer, S., & McNulty, S. (2010, October 7). A sea change needed. *Financial Times,* p. 9.

Elkind, P., Whitford, D., & Burke, D. (2011, February 7). An accident waiting to happen. *Fortune,* 105–132.

Friedman, H., & Friedman, L. (2010). Lessons from the twin mega-crises: The financial meltdown and the BP oil spill. *Journal of Business Systems, Governance and Ethics, 5*(4), 34–45.

Griggs, J. W. (2011). BP Gulf of Mexico oil spill. *Energy Law Journal, 32*(1), 57–79.

Hoyos, C. (2010, May 7). Safety equipment: The rig's blow-out preventer holds the key to what went wrong and why. *Financial Times,* p. 7.

McNulty, S., & Crooks, E. (2010, May 7). A spreading stain. *Financial Times,* p. 7.

Schneider, R. (2011). Ethics and oil: Preventing the next disaster. *Journal of Emergency Management, 9*(3), 11–22.

Tankersley, J. (2010, June 10). A closer look at deep-water drilling. *Los Angeles Times.* Retrieved July 30, 2012, from http://articles.latimes.com/2010/jun/10/nation/la-na-oil-spill-qa-20100610.

Introduction

Effective crisis management requires a strategic mind-set; top managers must be alert to the crisis vulnerabilities that may occur. This chapter examines the links between organizational strategies and crisis planning. The relationship between these two functions is reciprocal. Crisis management should be part of the strategic management process, but the strategies selected can influence the frequency and types of crises that follow. This chapter begins by examining the strategy–crisis nexus. We then explore the intricate relationships between corporate-level strategy and crises, and between businesses-level strategy and crises. The chapter concludes with a discussion on strategic control and how it can be used to forecast and prevent future crises.

Strategy and Crises

Strategy refers to top management's plans to develop and sustain competitive advantage so that the organization's mission is fulfilled. *Strategic management* is a broader term and involves top management's analysis of the environment the organization operates in, as well as the plan for implementation and control of the strategy (Parnell, 2013). Much of this analysis is similar to what must be done to heighten crisis preparedness in an organization. Hence, there is a strong and necessary link between the strategic management process and crisis management (Pauchant & Mitroff, 1992; Preble, 1997; Smith, 1992).

The prevalence of organizational crises can be related to a firm's strategy. Simply stated, some strategies are more crisis prone than others. For instance, a company following a corporate strategy of growth through acquisitions may be setting itself up for certain types of calamities (Probst & Raisch, 2005). Hence, a firm's strategy can foreshadow the type of crisis that may occur.

The Multiple Levels of Strategy

Organizational strategy can be examined from corporate and business levels. The corporate strategy (also called the *firm strategy*) reflects the broad strategic approach top management formulates for the organization. Specifically, corporate strategy answers the questions: (1) In which industries will the firm compete, and (2) what growth pattern will be followed? The business strategy (also called the *competitive strategy*) outlines the competitive pattern for a business unit—an organizational entity with its own mission, set of competitors, and industry. These strategies are crafted so that each business unit can attain and sustain competitive advantage, a state whereby successful strategies cannot be easily duplicated by rivals (Cockburn, Henderson, & Stern, 2000; Parnell, 2013). As we will see, the choice of strategies can influence the types of crises the organization may face.

Corporate-Level Strategies

There are two steps involved in corporate strategy development. The first is to assess the markets or industries in which the firm operates. The second is to identify a strategy to manage the firm's size, an approach that often—but not always—incorporates growth. Both of these dimensions and their links to crisis planning are discussed next.

Industry Dimension

At the corporate level, top management defines the corporate profile by identifying the specific industries in which the organization will operate. Three basic profiles are possible: (1) operate within a single industry, (2) operate in multiple, related industries, or (3) operate in multiple, unrelated industries. Each profile has its own inherent advantages and disadvantages and also brings with it the potential for different types of crises.

Single industry

An organization that operates in a single industry can benefit from the specialized knowledge that it develops by concentrating its efforts in one business area. McDonald's, for instance, continually changes its product line while maintaining a low per-unit cost of operations by concentrating exclusively on restaurants. Wal-Mart benefits from discount retail expertise derived from keeping its cost structures low, as well—a benefit that is passed on to consumers. Both of these companies are successful and play leadership roles in their respective industries. However, a drawback to their success is that they are easy targets for critics and, as a result, can be subject to negative public opinion. For McDonald's, critics in the 1990s pointed to bulky packaging practices (Adams, 2005; Sethi & Steidlmeier, 1997), and more recently, to concerns about nutrition (Morrison, 2012).

Wal-Mart's impressive growth has created a love–hate relationship with its external stakeholders. The company's obsession with cost containment has also resulted in lower prices, but with lower wages and limited benefits for employees. Wal-Mart pressures its suppliers to keep their costs down as well, promising them volume if they meet specific targets. However, many suppliers struggle to meet the cost targets, and some choose other options. Snapper, the maker of quality lawn equipment, pulled out of its partnership with Wal-Mart, fearing that it would ultimately reduce the quality of its products because of cost trade-offs. The irony is that despite the many benefits Wal-Mart provides to the economy and society, many people simply do not like the company (Fishman, 2006). Because Wal-Mart operates only in discount retail, its high visibility makes it vulnerable to crises, particularly those associated with public relations.

Multiple, Related Industries

Because firms operating in a single industry are more susceptible to sharp downturns in business cycles that cannot be offset by other business units in the firm, they can be prone to economic crises. As such, an organization may operate in more than one industry to reduce uncertainty and risk. It may diversify by developing a new line of business, or acquire other businesses with complementary product or service lines, a process known as *related diversification.* The key to successful related diversification is the development of synergy among the related business units. Synergy occurs when the two previously separate organizations join to generate higher effectiveness and efficiency than each would have generated separately. This is not always easy, however, particularly if one of them has experienced a major crisis, such as that which occurred when Dow Chemical acquired Union Carbide in 1999. Union Carbide's Bhopal, India, gas leak disaster in 1984 created a "guilt by association" crisis for Dow, which immediately became the target of protests from groups that wanted to clean up the old Bhopal facility because of groundwater contamination (Baldauf, 2004).

Consider the case of Atlanta-based ValuJet, one of the first budget airlines in the United States. On May 11, 1996, Flight 592 plunged into the Florida Everglades, killing all passengers and crew. Safety violations in the cargo area mistakenly allowed the introduction of oxygen containers that exploded in flight. The airline blamed its Miami subcontractor, SabreTech, for loading full oxygen containers that should have been empty (Englehardt, Sallot, & Springston, 2004). Not surprisingly, SabreTech blamed ValuJet for the mistake, while the Federal Aviation Administration (FAA) and the National Transportation Safety Board (NTSB) put the scrutiny on ValuJet. In fact, the airline was already under an FAA safety review prior to the crash.

The investigation of the crash cause was headed by the NTSB and revealed that safety practices existed, particularly in terms of subcontracting maintenance to

SabreTech. Immediately after the crash, the FAA forced the airline to ground half of its flights while it looked into the airline's day-to-day operations. The agency also found deficiencies in maintenance and ordered the airline to stop flying on June 17, just over a month after the crash of Flight 592. In August 1997, the NTSB found ValuJet at fault for not overseeing the work of its subcontractor, SabreTech. The final NTSB report produced four years later blamed ValuJet, SabreTech, and even the FAA for lax oversight (Englehardt et al., 2004).

The background of this case is important because it shows why ValuJet, seeking survival and growth, merged with AirTran and adopted a new name as part of its rebuilding effort (Beirne & Jensen, 1999). Changing the name of a company can palliate some of the negative crisis associations from the past. In the instance of ValuJet, the crisis was removed even further when Southwest Airlines acquired AirTran in 2010. Such transformations have also been carried out by Philip Morris, now Altria, and Anderson Consulting, now Accenture (Keating, 2012).

Another interesting example is Alpha Natural Resources, a coal company based in Abingdon, Virginia. On June 1, 2011, Altria acquired Massey Energy, a company with a less-than-stellar reputation (see Chapter 3). Massey Energy was notorious for safety violations and incorporating a culture in which wrongdoing was overlooked (Barrett, 2011). The challenge for Alpha was to remain profitable, protect miner safety, and assimilate the cultures of the two companies. The decision to acquire Massey was a strategic one, and industry watchers hope that Alpha's oversight will put an end to the string of mining accidents experienced under previous leadership. As part of the deal, however, Alpha also acquired the liability from Massey's negligence associated with the accident at Upper Big Branch that killed 29 miners in 2005. In the largest settlement ever for a mine accident, Alpha accepted the obligation to pay a total of $209 million, a figure that includes $1.5 million for each of the 29 victims who died and for two other miners who were injured (Tavernise & Krauss, 2011). Clearly, this acquisition has been an expensive one for Alpha.

Multiple, Unrelated Industries

A business may choose to operate in unrelated industries because its managers wish to reduce company risk by spreading resources across several markets. These firms pursue an unrelated diversification strategy by acquiring businesses not related to the core domain. In terms of potential crises, this strategy also has its challenges. By attempting to expand their core competencies, firms may find themselves in unfamiliar territory, thereby heightening crisis potential. This scenario happened to the once-respected A. H. Robins Company when it departed from its core product line to pursue the marketing of the ill-fated Dalkon Shield, an intrauterine contraceptive device known as an IUD. The product was later associated with health problems and was ultimately withdrawn from the market. The legal fallout was so devastating that A. H. Robins had to enter bankruptcy and was later acquired by Wyeth (D'Zurilla, 1998).

Problems can arise when firms are diversified simply to achieve short-term bumps in stock value. A host of abuses can result, but most notably, ethical issues whereby managers seek to artificially inflate the value of the firm, as in the cases of Enron and Tyco (Hosmer, 2011). Table 6.1 summarizes this discussion on industry involvement and crisis risk factors.

Growth Dimension

After an organization's corporate profile is determined, its corporate strategy must be established. Three possibilities exist: an organization may attempt to increase its size significantly (growth), remain about the same size (stability), or become smaller (retrenchment).

Growth Strategies

Most firms seek to grow, but this strategy can be realized in several ways. Internal growth is accomplished when a firm increases revenues, production capacity, and workforce. This type of growth can occur by expanding the business or creating new ones. External growth is accomplished when an organization merges with or acquires another firm. Mergers are generally undertaken to improve competitiveness by sharing or combining resources.

Table 6.1 Industry Dimension Involvement and Risk Factors

Industry Dimension Involvement	Risk Factors	Examples
Operate in a single industry	High visibility of the company makes it a "target" for criticism from external stakeholders.	• McDonald's • Wal-Mart
Operate multiple businesses in related industries (related diversification)	The acquiring company must be careful when it acquires a company previously damaged by a crisis.	• Union Carbide/Dow Chemical • ValuJet/AirTran • Massey Energy/Alpha Natural Resources
Operate multiple businesses in unrelated industries (unrelated diversification)	Potential exists to operate outside of the company's original core area, thus opening it up to a crisis. Business may be viewed as a portfolio, creating an incentive to falsify income statements and balance sheets so that it will look attractive to investors while driving up stock prices and bringing in bonuses for top executives.	• A. H. Robins • Tyco • Enron

When a company increases in size, it becomes more noticeable to the public. A surge in popularity means the public generally likes the product or service being offered. However, it also means the company is more vulnerable. Growth strategies include the potential for becoming a target of social media or even extortion because the firm is larger and more visible. The Wendy's severed finger incident (see Chapter 3) illustrates such an extortion attempt. Although no payment was made, Wendy's suffered a 2.5 percent decline in sales for the quarter (Langston, 2006).

Another type of crisis can occur when a company enters into a strategic alliance as part of its growth strategy. Strategic alliances—often called "partnerships"—occur when two or more firms agree to share the costs, risks, and benefits associated with pursuing new business opportunities. Such arrangements include joint ventures, franchise or license agreements, joint operations, joint long-term supplier agreements, marketing agreements, and consortiums. Strategic alliances can be temporary, disbanding after the project is finished, or can involve multiple projects over an extended period of time (Parnell, 2013). Many strategic alliances fall under the category of global outsourcing, thereby creating a unique set of crisis vulnerabilities.

The late 1990s and early 2000s witnessed a sharp increase in strategic alliances (Reuer, Zollo, & Singh, 2002). There are many examples of partnerships, especially when technology and global access are key considerations. IBM and Apple Computer have exchanged technology in an attempt to develop more effective computer operating systems. General Motors (GM), Ford, and Chrysler are jointly conducting research to enhance battery technology for electric and alternative fuel cars powered by electricity, hydrogen, and other sources of alternative energy. Perhaps the most dramatic example of strategic alliances is occurring in China, where every major automobile manufacturer in the world is working with firms in the Chinese auto market to build vehicles (Casey, Zamiska, & Pasztor, 2007; Chu, 2011).

Strategic alliances enable a firm to expand its reach into new markets while utilizing the expertise of a partner firm and risk as well. Yet, strategic alliances can also be vulnerable to crises, especially if the partner firms do not agree explicitly on the contribution each will make to the alliance or if they do not have an agreed-upon approach to identify vulnerabilities and an action plan to address crisis management. For example, in 2000, Amazon.com and Toys"R"Us signed a 10-year deal to join forces in a strategic alliance. Amazon agreed to devote a portion of its website to Toys"R"Us products, while the toy retailer agreed to stock certain items on Amazon's virtual shelves. Although the arrangement was supposed to be an example of how Internet retailers can work effectively with their traditional counterparts, the deal deteriorated several years later and ended up in court in 2006. Toys"R"Us argued that Amazon broke its original commitment to use its company as its sole provider of toys and related products, while Amazon contended the toy retailer did not maintain an appropriate selection of toys (Mangalindan, 2006).

Stability Strategies

There are times when a company may seek to retain its present size, at least on a temporary basis. A stability strategy may be pursued temporarily when there is significant political and/or economic stability. Many firms in the United States adopted a wait-and-see approach in the early 2010s when the economy struggled to recover from the mortgage crisis and the regulatory environment became more cumbersome. Such a path may also be taken after a period of excessive growth. Early in its history, computer maker Dell pursued a period of stability strategy after achieving a 285 percent growth over a two-year period so that the company could address needs for new facilities and managers (Burrows & Anderson, 1993). Indeed, growing too fast can create its own set of crises, including potential for the premature demise of the company (Probst & Raisch, 2005).

A stability strategy may also be advisable in other instances. If a firm's industry is not growing, then internal growth must come at the expense of rivals, a difficult proposition. The costs associated with growth may not justify the benefits. Moreover, a small firm known for quality and excellent service may choose to remain small so it can provide a high level of personal customer attention. While growth is usually desirable, stability may be pursued temporarily or even over the long term in certain instances (Parnell, 2013).

Retrenchment Strategies

Retrenchment strategies seek to decrease the size of the organization and usually follow a downturn. Certainly, an economic crisis—a significant decline in sales—represents one such scenario. However, a retrenchment strategy often follows an acute crisis. For example, a major fire, negative publicity, product recall, or a breach of ethics by management can all be factors that lead to a decrease in revenue and therefore the need to retrench.

Consider Enron's ethical malaise. The company eventually imploded, although one could argue the demise occurred in a series of stages; hence some degree of retrenchment was evident. But the more typical scenario involves a partial retrenchment in response to a crisis that does not lead to the ultimate dissolution of the company. Instead, after a period of retrenchment, a buyer may come along and rescue the company from its deteriorated condition, after which a period of growth may occur.

Retrenchment can take one of three forms: turnaround, divestment, or liquidation. A turnaround is the most conservative approach, whereas liquidation is the harshest. A turnaround seeks to transform the corporation into a leaner, more efficient firm and includes such actions as eliminating unprofitable outputs, pruning assets, reducing the size of the workforce, cutting costs of distribution, and reassessing the firm's product lines and customer groups (Parnell, 2013). From a crisis management perspective, a turnaround strategy also includes any strategic initiative that management deems necessary to improve the company's performance in a specific area.

Denny's restaurants needed a turnaround—particularly in its human resource management practices—after agreeing to pay $54 million to resolve several racial discrimination lawsuits stemming from incidents in the early 1990s. Although social media outlets were not yet popular, the late-night television comedians at the time were poking fun at the chain on a regular basis. Show hosts Arsenio Hall and

Jay Leno attacked the company as an example of southern bigotry and intolerance. The crisis that gathered the most news coverage involved the poor service that six black Secret Service officers received at an Annapolis, Maryland, Denny's in 1993. The agents alleged humiliating and discriminatory service while their white colleagues enjoyed hearty breakfasts (Adamson, 2000). However, these setbacks illustrate how a company can not only withstand a crisis, but can benefit from it in the long run. "A decade ago, the restaurant chain Denny's was nearly synonymous with racism," according to Ray Hood-Phillips, chief diversity officer at Denny's. After the devastating lawsuit, the company viewed its turnaround as requiring "a holistic approach to diversity" (Brathwaite, 2002, p. 28). This move involved changing the culture of the company through intensive diversity training, better recruiting practices, and a more valid performance appraisal system.

Some turnaround strategies may result in a reduction in the size of the workforce. If layoffs are implemented, management must be prepared to address their effects on both departing employees and survivors. Employees may be given opportunities to leave voluntarily—generally with an incentive—to make the process as congenial as possible. When this occurs, those departing can be the top performers who are most marketable, leaving the firm with a less competitive workforce. When layoffs are simply announced, morale is likely to suffer considerably. For this reason, turnarounds involving layoffs are often more difficult to implement than anticipated (Murray, 2001). Furthermore, layoffs should not always be an option of first choice because of the devastating consequences they can have on employees, their families, and the local community (Macky, 2004). Instead, the decision to reduce the workforce should be based on the long-term cost adjustments that are needed at the firm (Gandolfi, 2008).

If layoffs are utilized, several actions can mitigate some of the negative effects. Top management is encouraged to communicate honestly with all employees, explaining why the downsizing is necessary and how terminated employees were selected. Everyone, including those employees who remain in the organization (i.e., the survivors) should be made aware of how departing employees will be supported. Employees should also be encouraged to partake of services available to them, including educational retraining funds through the government and company outsourcing services. Although these measures will not eliminate all the harsh feelings associated with layoffs, they can help keep the process under control.

A number of executives are widely recognized as "turnaround specialists" and may be brought in as temporary chief executive officers (CEOs) to lead the process and orchestrate such unpopular strategic moves as layoffs, budget cuts, and reorganizations. In addition, crisis management consulting firms are abundant and can advise on the specifics of crisis management planning and communicating with the media. Robert "Steve" Miller, a major player in the Chrysler turnaround, has served as CEO of Waste Management and the automobile parts supplier Federal-Mogul, as well as a consultant on turnaround issues to such companies as Aetna. According to Miller, the CEO in a company seeking turnaround should be honest with employees from the outset and seek their input. He or she should also spend time with customers. As Miller put it, "Listen to your customers. [They] are usually more perceptive than you are about what you need to do with your company" (Lublin, 2000).

Divestment—selling one or more business units to another firm—often occurs when a firm's leaders believe the organization is facing a crisis. Divestment may be necessary when the industry is in decline or when a business unit drains resources from more profitable units, is not performing well, or is not synergistic with other corporate holdings. During the aforementioned Denny's turnaround effort, the firm also pursued a degree of divestment by selling its Coco's and Carrows restaurants (Kruger, 2004).

Liquidation terminates the business unit by selling its assets. Liquidation is by definition a last-resort response to a severe crisis. In effect, it can be viewed as a divestment of *all* the firm's business units and should be adopted only under extreme conditions. Shareholders and creditors experience financial losses, managers and hourly employees lose their jobs, suppliers lose a customer, and the local community suffers an increase in unemployment and a decrease in tax revenues. Hence, liquidation should be considered only when other forms of retrenchment are not feasible.

Business-Level Strategies

Whereas the corporate-level strategy addresses industries in which a firm competes, the business-level strategy focuses on whom the company should serve, what needs should be satisfied, and how a business should develop core competencies and be positioned to satisfy customer needs. The challenging task of formulating and implementing a strategy for each business unit is based on a number of factors (Parnell, 2013).

The first step in formulating a business strategy is to select a broad or generic strategy to compete with rivals and then fine-tune it to accentuate the organization's unique set of resource strengths (Campbell-Hunt, 2000; Parnell, 2013). Porter's (1980) generic strategy framework serves as a good starting point for assessing business strategies. According to Porter, a business unit must address two basic competitive concerns. First, managers must determine whether the business unit should focus its efforts on an identifiable subset of the industry in which it operates or seek to serve the entire market (i.e., the industry) as a whole. For example, many specialty clothing stores in shopping malls adopt the focus concept and concentrate their efforts on limited product lines primarily intended for small market niches. In contrast, most chain grocery stores seek to serve the "mass market"—or at least most of it—by selecting an array of products and services that appeal to the general public. Second, managers must determine whether the business unit should compete primarily by minimizing its costs relative to those of its competitors (what Porter calls a "low-cost strategy") or through differentiation, distinguishing itself by offering unique and/or unusual products and services (Parnell, 2006).

Low-Cost Strategies

Businesses that utilize low-cost strategies produce basic, no-frills products and services. They provide their products and services to an entire market and appeal primarily to price-sensitive consumers (Parnell, 2013). High-profile companies that follow low-cost strategies include Wal-Mart and Southwest Airlines. Businesses using low-cost strategies are susceptible to price competition from other firms, particularly large rivals. This continuous pressure to reduce costs may cause a firm to cut corners, ultimately leading to a crisis situation.

Trimming costs can create crisis challenges for companies that follow low-cost strategies. For example, regional or commuter airlines typically pay lower wages and require less cockpit time than their national and international counterparts. Pilots at United and other major airlines are required to log 5,000 to 7,000 flight hours before stepping into the cockpit. However, smaller airlines like JetBlue require 4,000, and some commuter airlines hire pilots with fewer than 1,000. Relaxing this requirement creates a cost advantage for commuter airlines but can also create safety concerns. As of 2010, seven of the past eight U.S. crashes resulting in fatalities involved small carriers (Pasztor & Carey, 2009). The experience factor in the cockpit is a major factor in several recent commuter crashes and has prompted the FAA to take a stronger look at the safety practices of these airlines.

While this example illustrates how the low-cost strategy can translate into low prices, it also reminds the customer that there can be a "high cost to low prices," an adage that author Charles Fishman (2006) made famous in his book on Wal-Mart. Fishman's critique of the big box was intense:

> Wal-Mart's brilliant, obsessive focus on a single core value—delivering low prices—created what became the largest and most powerful company in history. And yet the drive for low prices is also the cause of the troubling elements of the Wal-Mart effect: low wages, unrelenting pressure on suppliers, products cheap in quality as well as price, offshoring of jobs. (Fishman, 2006, p. 14)

We do not seek to debate Fishman's claims in detail. Instead, we point out that all strategies, including the low-cost strategy, carry with it certain crisis vulnerabilities. Companies that follow a given strategy can learn how to hedge against these crisis vulnerabilities accordingly.

One of the strategies associated with cost containment is to engage in global outsourcing. As Fishman (2006) notes, the suppliers to Wal-Mart, as well as to most of the big box discount stores, have also engaged in global outsourcing. Companies that utilize global outsourcing usually do so to take advantage of labor cost differentials between the home country, where company headquarters resides, and other nations with lower production costs. However, the potential for crisis is ever present. Consider the case of Mattel in the late 2000s. Following a string of defective toys imported from China, Mattel issued recalls for millions of Chinese-made toys, many of which contained small magnets or lead paint. Shortly after announcing one of the recalls, an owner of a Chinese toy factory involved in much of the production committed suicide at a factory warehouse (Casey et al., 2007).

China has been recognized largely for its ability to produce products at low costs (Buehlmann, Bumgardner, Lihra, & Frye, 2006). Quality has improved markedly over the past two decades, however, thanks to modernization in both equipment and production practice. Nevertheless, some quality concerns in toys, tires, and agricultural products remain. In the Mattel case, the company initially blamed faulty Chinese workmanship but later accepted responsibility for the problems and suggested that a design flaw was a contributing factor. Critics charged that Mattel's excessive efforts to control costs placed children at risk. Although this might be an overstatement, it is clear that the cost control dimension of Mattel's competitive strategy created a breeding ground for this type of crisis.

Differentiation Strategies

Businesses that utilize differentiation strategies tend to be larger firms that are seeking to meet the demands of an entire industry. The key characteristic of a differentiator is its ability to produce products and services that can be readily distinguished from those of competitors (Parnell, 2013). As a result, differentiators, although cost conscious, place a greater emphasis on quality than those companies following low-cost strategies. Competing on the basis of cost and/or price is not as high a priority.

Businesses emphasizing differentiation may be more threatened by abrupt shifts in consumer tastes. When oil prices spiked in 2008, consumer preferences shifted away from sport utility vehicles (SUVs), large cars, and trucks to smaller, more fuel-efficient alternatives. Carmakers like Ford and GM developed and emphasized vehicles that were stylish and fun to drive, not necessarily fuel efficient. When the average price of gasoline hit $4 a gallon in the United States in 2008, they faced a strategic crisis. At the same time, venture capital began pouring into start-up firms around the world, racing to develop vehicles that consume less gas or utilize alternative, cleaner, and cheaper fuels (Stewart, 2008; Taylor, 2008).

When gasoline prices spiked to $4 a gallon again in 2012, carmakers had begun to develop plug-in hybrids and fully electric vehicles (EVs). With the introduction of new vehicles, however, a new array of crises can ensue. As mentioned in Chapter 1, the Chevy Volt has had problems with battery fires after accident testing, forcing GM to offer loaner cars to Chevy Volt owners while the company worked to fix the problem (Terlep, 2011). Differentiation implies going into new territories, and with that will come new crises as well.

Johnson & Johnson (J&J) has long been the example for excellent corporate social responsibility and crisis management savvy. Indeed, it could even be considered a differentiator in that it used its corporate credo as a basis for guiding the company through a difficult crisis in the 1980s. J&J responded effectively to product tampering crises in 1982 and 1986, creating a response standard against which other firms would be judged. However, J&J's stellar reputation for corporate responsibility was drawn into question in 2009 and 2010. On April 14, 2009, the company learned that some of the raw materials used to make children's and infant Tylenol formulas were tainted with *Burkholderia cepacia* bacteria. Although J&J denied using these materials, the company used other raw materials that were part of the same batch. Nonetheless, J&J continued shipping the medicines until June 4, the day that Food and Drug Administration (FDA) investigators cited the firm for violating good manufacturing practices. J&J did not launch a recall of the bottles until August 21 and did not make the recall public until September. J&J internal testing revealed no contamination, and the FDA linked no side effects to the products in question (Rockoff, 2010a).

In September 2010, U.S. officials charged J&J with failing to swiftly and adequately inform regulators about a nationwide withdrawal of the over-the-counter pain reliever, Motrin. Rather than issuing a product recall, J&J instigated a "phantom recall" by commissioning a contractor to secretly purchase all stocks of the product (Brewster, 2011). Federal Drug Administration deputy commissioner Joshua Sharfstein acknowledged that pharmaceutical companies have no legal obligation to inform the FDA when recalls are initiated, nor does the FDA have any legal authority to dictate the procedure utilized by the company. Nonetheless, J&J head Bill Weldon acknowledged that the company "let the public down" and "should have handled things differently" (Jack, 2010). In the end, the recall cost J&J an estimated hundreds of millions of dollars in lost sales alone (Rockoff, 2010b).

The first children's Tylenol products returned to the shelves in mid-November 2010, but J&J had to address a decline in consumer confidence, encroachment of rival brands, and cheaper private-label brands that had thrived during the recession. According to an annual survey administered by Brand Keys, consumer loyalty to Tylenol dropped 7 percent during the year. Perrigo, a leading manufacturer of store-brand nonprescription drugs, gained nearly 20 percent in market share during the crisis (Rockoff, 2010b). Clearly, the damage had been significant to J&J, which was once held in the highest esteem.

Focus–Low-Cost Strategies

A focus strategy literally "focuses" on a specific niche in an industry. The focus strategy can take a low-cost or differentiation direction. The focus–low-cost strategy seeks low overall costs while meeting the needs of consumers in a narrow segment of the market (Parnell, 2013). Businesses following a focus–low-cost strategy tend to be smaller than those adhering to a low-cost strategy. The reason is that more resources are needed by a company to successfully reach an entire industry; therefore, smaller companies are not equipped for such an endeavor. However, smaller companies can be successful operating in market niches.

Like the low-cost strategy, the focus–low-cost can also result in customer complaints on the quality of products and services. If there is a perception that the company is being "cheap," a backlash may result. Consider the case of Spirit Airlines, a budget carrier based in Miramar, Florida. This company operates in the ultra-low-cost niche of the airline industry. Specifically, the strategy involves the "unbundling" of services, which means options to the passenger are priced separately. The ticket is one price, carryon bags that go in the overhead bin are $45, water is $3, there are fees to change reservations, and so on (Nicas, 2012). However, despite the fact that their prices are lower compared to other carriers, passengers often feel nitpicked by the company for all of the hidden charges, a problem that has been voiced by many passengers via social media outlets.

In 2012, Spirit found itself in a crisis when it refused to refund a $197 ticket to a passenger with cancer. The incident received national attention on the Internet when his doctor told the passenger, Jerry Meekins, who has esophageal cancer, that he could not fly. Meekins had booked a ticket from St. Petersburg, Florida, to

Atlantic City, New Jersey, but had not bought insurance, thinking he would be able to make the flight (Watson, 2012). When the airline refused to refund the ticket, the story went viral and made the airline look like an unfeeling company pitted against the small consumer. A "Boycott Spirit Airlines" page appeared on Facebook with more than 21,000 "likes" (Miller, 2012). Public perception was not in favor of the airline and even resulted in two Atlantic County, New Jersey, assemblymen asking Spirit Airlines to change its refund policy (Watson, 2012). After considerable attention from the media, CEO Ben Baldanza reversed his decision and allowed the refund (Nicas, 2012). Still, damage had been done to the airline's reputation.

It should be noted, though, that the Spirit Airlines' refund policy is similar to that of other airlines. What made the Spirit Airlines case so noticeable stemmed from three factors. First, the victim was a veteran of the U.S. Marine Corps. A strict business decision to deny a refund to a member of the armed forces seemed anti-patriotic to many. Second, Spirit has had a high number of customer complaints in the past. Kate Hanni, the executive director of FlyersRights, commented on Spirit's approach to customer service: "They're the worst airline in the U.S. They put no money back into customer service, which is a black hole at Spirit. Spirit Airlines has a history of cruelty toward their passengers, but they continue to treat them like meat in a seat because their fares are so low they are confident people will continue to fly with them" (Miller, 2012).

Finally, Baldanza tried to justify his decision to not refund the ticket, maintaining that it would not be fair to the other passengers who fly with the airline. Public relations consultant and author Fraser Seitel commented that the airline could simply have transferred the ticket to Mr. Meekins's daughter, whom he was flying to see, a move that might have generated positive publicity for the airline (Miller, 2012). All three of these factors created a recipe for disaster and explain why the media and public for a public relations crisis targeted Spirit Airlines.

In terms of crisis management, Spirit Airlines may have more at risk than some of its rivals in the airline industry because the nature of a focus strategy implies that the company is relatively small and therefore has more at stake. As one *Wall Street Journal* writer stated, "Spirit is still small—carrying just one percent of the nation's fliers—and one public relations fiasco, such as a plane crash or lengthy labor strike, could damage its profitability and growth, according to industry analysts" (Nicas, 2012, p. A1).

Focus-Differentiation Strategy

Because companies pursuing a focus strategy tend to be relatively small, there is more at stake in terms of the overall risk to the firm when a crisis occurs. Put differently, larger companies such as Wal-Mart have more buffering power than do their smaller rivals to counter the jabs of a crisis. Hence, a major crisis can decimate a company following a focus strategy.

The Chalk's Ocean Airways case addressed in Chapter 4 illustrates how one major crisis can put a company out of business permanently. This company followed a focus-differentiation strategy in that it offered vintage seaplane flights between the Bahamas and south Florida. The selective nature of its strategy made it vulnerable to a crisis, and when Flight 101 went down just minutes after takeoff, it ended the life of what was once the nation's oldest airline.

Odwalla is another company that follows the focus-differentiation strategy (see Chapter 3). In 1996, a nonpasteurized fruit juice it marketed caused the death of an infant and made dozens of people violently ill (Levick & Slack, 2011). Fortunately, the company overcame the crisis by offering an immediate apology and promised to fairly compensate all of the families affected. It also changed its juice processing to include flash pasteurization, a process that kills any bacteria that may be present in the juice. Even Bill Marler, the attorney representing the victims and their families, had good things to say about Odwalla: "If you look at what people remember (from the case), everyone remembers the positive stuff about what Odwalla did" (Levick & Slack, 2011, p. 15). Odwalla not only survived but has performed well since the crisis.

Crises can threaten restaurants operating in a market niche. Established in 1951, Bullock's Bar-B-Q is a popular eatery and the longest-operating restaurant in Durham, North Carolina. Famous patrons include Dolly Parton, Garth Brooks, Kris Kristofferson, and Joe Biden. On April 20, 2010, more than a dozen patrons reported ill effects later determined to be salmonella. Business declined 80 percent shortly after the outbreak. Sam Poley, Durham Convention and Visitors Bureau's marketing director and a former chef himself, recruited an overflow crowd of chefs and restaurant owners for lunch at Bullock's on May 7 to show their support. Steps can be taken to reduce the likelihood of salmonella poisoning, but it is virtually impossible to eliminate the possibility of an outbreak. As Poley put it, "Every chef knows, there but for the grace of God go I" (Wise, 2010).

After the investigation of the incident, the Durham County Health Department said the likely cause of the salmonella bacteria was a commercial product, pasteurized egg whites, and not improper food handling by employees. However, tests by the North Carolina Department of Agriculture and Consumer Services could not confirm that the egg product was contaminated with salmonella. According to several blog comments also related to the story, the people who were sickened were not eating at the restaurant but consumed the food as a takeout order ("Officials," 2010). In cases like this, the product might have been held at an improper temperature before it was consumed, thus creating an environment for bacteria growth. Restaurants that offer takeout options must consider this reality as one of their crisis vulnerabilities. The Bullocks example illustrates how a small niche-oriented business can be affected by a crisis outside of its control. Fortunately, Bullocks recovered and is doing well.

The case of Chi-Chi's restaurants did not have a happy ending. As mentioned in Chapter 3, Chi-Chi's suffered a major crisis when its Beaver Valley Mall location near Pittsburgh, Pennsylvania, was identified as the source of a hepatitis A outbreak. Chi-Chi's was a differentiator focused on Mexican food, a difficult niche to serve effectively (Lockyer, 2004). The crisis erupted rather innocently and was completely unnoticed. Employees were chopping green onions for the salsa, not knowing that the ice packed with the product had melted and soaked the onions for hours. The ice, unfortunately, was laden with the hepatitis A virus (Veil, Liu, Erickson, & Sellnow, 2005). What resulted was the sickness of more than 660 people and three fatalities. This crisis, along with severe competition and bankruptcy, sealed the fate for the 27-year-old chain (Lockyer, 2004). Another focus-oriented business had become a victim of a crisis.

Combining Low-Cost and Differentiation Strategies

Porter suggested that combining low-cost and differentiation strategies is not advisable and leaves a business "stuck in the middle" because actions designed to support one strategy could work against the other. Indeed, differentiating a product can be costly, and doing so can erode a firm's basis for cost leadership. Moreover, some cost-cutting measures may be directly related to quality and/or other bases of differentiation. Following this logic, a business should choose *either* low-cost *or* differentiation, but not both. Although combining the two approaches can be challenging, some businesses do so successfully.

Consider two examples. McDonald's was originally known for consistency from store to store, friendly service, and cleanliness. These bases for differentiation catapulted McDonald's to market share leader, allowing the firm to negotiate for beef, potatoes, and other key materials at the lowest possible cost. JetBlue Airways was launched in 2000 to provide economical air service among a limited number of cities. JetBlue has minimized costs by such measures as squeezing more seats into its planes, selling its tickets directly to customers, and shortening ground delays. Although commonly thought of as a discount airline, JetBlue has also distinguished itself by providing new planes, satellite television on board, and leather seats (Parnell, 2013).

Businesses that pursue a combination strategy also share the crisis vulnerabilities associated with pursuing either low costs or differentiation. Put another way, companies like McDonald's and JetBlue are susceptible to crises associated with attempts to lower costs and provide distinctive service. Hence, the combination strategy is not only more difficult to execute from a strategic standpoint, but it can also place greater strains on crisis management.

Strategic Control

Just as strategic control is a part of the overall strategic management process, it should also be a tool in the crisis management process. The goal of strategic control is to determine the extent to which the organization's strategies are successful in attaining its goals and objectives. The strategy implementation process is tracked, and adjustments to the strategy are made as necessary (Picken & Dess, 1997). It is during the process of strategic control that gaps between the intended and realized strategies (i.e., what was planned and what really happened) are identified and addressed.

Overview

The process of strategic control can be likened to that of steering a vehicle. After the accelerator is pressed (executing the strategy), the control function ensures that everything (the organization) is moving in the right direction. When a simple steering adjustment (managerial decision) is not sufficient to modify the course of the vehicle, the driver can resort to other means, such as applying the brake or shifting gears (other managerial decisions). In a similar manner, strategic managers can steer the organization by instituting minor modifications to prevent crises or resort to more drastic changes in response to an ongoing crisis, such as altering the strategic direction altogether (Parnell, 2013).

The need for strategic control is brought about by two key factors. First, there is a need to know how well the firm is performing. Without strategic control, there are no clear benchmarks and ultimately no reliable measurements that indicate how the company is doing. A second key factor supporting the need for strategic control is uncertainty. Because managers are not always able to forecast the future accurately, strategic control highlights when environmental uncertainties have upset the performance of the organization. For example, one of the authors of this book found himself in a crisis when a major weather event shut down the facility he was managing. The result was a significant loss of revenue for about a week. The strategic control system in place was able to identify the financial extent of the crisis and its impact on the firm. Although a loss of revenue was recorded, the control mechanism was able to show that the poor performance was not the fault of the manager, but the weather.

The extent of that crisis was easily measured by comparing the results to those of the previous year's revenues for the same time period. Because the manager was being held accountable for sales and profits based on a projected budget, provisions were made not to penalize him because of the inclement weather. Indeed, in some environments managers are told to "suck it up" and work that much harder so that the *original* forecast can be reached. This practice is not reasonable and penalizes managers for forces beyond their control. In fact, it ignores the important role that strategic control can add to understanding the situation better.

The Strategic Control Process

The strategic control process generally follows five steps (Parnell, 2013):

1. Top management determines the focus of strategic control by identifying the internal factors that can serve as effective measures for the success or failure of the chosen strategy. In addition, the external factors that could trigger responses from the organization are identified.

2. Benchmarks are established for the internal factors with which the performance of the organization can be compared after the strategy is implemented.

3. Management measures and evaluates the company's performance, both quantitatively and qualitatively.

4. Performance evaluations are compared with the previously established standards.

5. If performance meets or exceeds the standards, corrective action is usually not necessary. If performance falls below the standard, then management typically takes remedial action.

Step 1: Identify Factors to Track

First, strategic control encompasses external and internal dimensions. Although individual firms usually exert little or no influence over the external and industry forces (see Chapters 2 and 3), they must be continuously monitored because their shifts can have strategic ramifications. Specifically, strategic control consists of modifying the company's operations so it can be defended more effectively against external threats that may arise or become known before a crisis emerges. Recall the six broad trends in the crisis management landscape identified in Chapter 2:

1. Crises have become more transboundary in nature.

2. Terrorism remains an ongoing threat.

3. Social media and the Internet intensify the effects of a crisis.

4. Human-induced missteps are at the core of the majority of crises.

5. Environmental damage and sustainability of resources cause crises to have a global impact.

6. Globalization increases the risk of organizational and societal crises.

A major shift in one or more of these factors can alter the strategy of the firm and, therefore, its crisis management preparedness. In Chapter 3 we reviewed the concept of the PEST analysis, a tool in the strategic management toolkit that looks at the political, economic, social, and technology trends in the macroenvironment. Understanding these external factors is necessary in devising a firm's corporate and business strategies.

Step 2: Develop Standards or Benchmarks for the Factors

Top management must identify factors that serve as surrogates of company performance. These indicators often include factors related to revenue, expenses, and profitability, but may also include machine breakdowns (if applicable), quality scores, and indicators involving employee well-being such as accident rates, tardiness, absenteeism, number of sick days taken, and workplace injuries. Predesignated goals or benchmarking against other companies should be established for each of these items. Assessing these performance indicators can help identify early warning signs that a crisis may be looming.

Step 3: Measure Performance Both Quantitatively and Qualitatively

Firm performance may be evaluated in a number of ways. Management can compare current operating results with those from the preceding quarter or year. A key problem with performance measurement is that one measure can be pursued to the detriment of another. The common goals of growth and profitability versus safety concerns come to mind. Many crises in organizations are caused by accidents due to poor training and faulty equipment. Expenditures in these areas decrease short-term profits, yet a single accident can severely hurt the long-term viability of the firm or even close it down.

A number of companies have begun using a *balanced scorecard* approach to measuring performance; measurement is not based solely on traditional quantitative factors but on an array of quantitative and qualitative factors, such as return on assets, market share, customer loyalty and satisfaction, speed, and innovation (Kaplan & Norton, 1996, 2000). A weight and specific means of measurement is assigned to each indicator. For example, customer satisfaction may receive a weight of 10 percent and may be determined by the average score in a survey. The key to employing a balanced scorecard is selecting a combination of performance indicators and measures tailored specifically to the firm and its strategic position. Including indicators that can predict potential crises, such as level of customer satisfaction, accident rates, or product quality measures, should be considered. A list of possible indicators is presented in Table 6.2.

Table 6.2   Balanced Scorecard Indicators and Potential Crises

Indicator to Include on the Balanced Scorecard	Potential Crises That It Represents
Number of accidents in a work section or unit	Accident and safety issues; potential employee lawsuits
Absenteeism by employee in a work section or unit	Motivational problems; substance abuse; abusive supervision
Number of grievances (union setting) or employee complaints in a non-union work environment	Morale problems; abusive supervision; potential for workplace violence
Employee satisfaction survey	Problems with morale, supervision
Machine or work section downtime	Major production interruption due to accidents, fire, or major machine breakdown
Percentage of defective products	Potential for recalls; negative publicity
Negative media reports on the Internet and social media outlets	Adverse publicity; consumer boycotts
Customer complaints	Negative media attention; future loss of revenue
Returned or defective product rates	Negative media attention; injured customers

Step 4: Compare Measurements With Predesignated Goals or Benchmarks

The process of comparing results with predesignated goals or benchmarks can help identify an impending crisis. For example, a common item to monitor in industrial settings is the presence of dust. Under some conditions, dust can cause an explosion that can level a building. West Pharmaceuticals in Kinston, North Carolina, experienced a dust-related blast that killed six people and injured many others in 2003. The irony of this explosion was that the company had a regular cleanup program for dust in the processing area. However, a suspended ceiling installed several years before had accumulated a large amount of dust that lay out of sight of the regular cleanup. It was this dust that fueled the fatal explosion (Dawson, 2003).

Because of the threat of dust explosions, industrial and pharmaceutical companies are continually aware of the dangers that can occur. Hence, dust levels are regularly monitored to ensure an explosion does not occur. At chemical plants, temperature and pressure are continually monitored against established norms. An increase in temperature can cause a gas to expand, ultimately increasing the pressure of that gas in its holding tank. Hence, a pressure gauge on a tank holding a lethal chemical is a mechanism for control. When the gauge indicates that the pressure is above the normal range, the operator must make a decision on how to prevent the release of the chemical that is contained in the tank. Several options are available: the temperature of the tank can be lowered, or the chemical can be moved to another tank.

In a well-maintained chemical plant, control mechanisms such as pressure and temperature indicators can signal employees to take measures so the release of the dangerous chemical does not occur. Suppose that the same scenario exists, except that the temperature of the chemical starts to rise and there is no way to move it or alter the temperature of the tank. After a period of time, the tank pressure release valve opens and the dangerous chemical spews into the atmosphere as a lethal gas. At this point, strategic control enters a more acute phase during which the factory must now contain the leak, protect the employees, and warn members of the community that a gas leak has occurred. Unfortunately, the scenario just described is exactly what happened at the Union Carbide plant in Bhopal, India, when methyl isocyanate spewed out of its holding tank after reaching a pressure that the tank could not contain. This incident, discussed in Chapter 3, is an example of control mechanisms that had gone awry. It remains the worst industrial accident on record (Carroll, & Buchholtz, 2012).

While certain industrial measures must be made to help prevent accidents, it is also important that financial controls be measured and taken seriously so that managerial fraud can be prevented. Tyco offers one of the most vivid examples of managerial fraud by a CEO. Although the company had controls in place, they did not stop the theft of $600 million from within the company in 2002. Tyco CEO Dennis Kozlowski abused his power, and managerial controls failed to stop his "spider spinning a web of deceit" (Coombs, 2006, p. 56) in the following areas:

- Kozlowski hid transactions from the board of directors, but then told lower-level managers that the board had approved those same actions.

- He gave a $1 million party for his wife. The party was held in Sardinia and featured an ice sculpture of David (the statue) urinating high-priced vodka. The party was charged to Tyco.
- He misused the Tyco compensation program by exploiting relocation, bonuses, and automobile expenses. (Coombs, 2006)

It is not enough just to have controls. Controls must be taken seriously, as this now infamous case illustrates.

Step 5: Take Corrective Action

Strategic control emphasizes continuous improvement whereby managers seek to improve the long-term efficiency and effectiveness of the organization. In other words, control is not viewed as an action necessary only when a firm is in crisis. Rather, managers should think critically when considering what strategic controls to enact and look for opportunities to enhance performance even when operations seem to be going well. In this regard, crisis management can be viewed as an outgrowth of strategic control. In Chapter 9 we discuss an outgrowth of this type of strategic control: organizational learning.

The notion of strategic control highlights the link between a firm's strategy and the subsequent crisis events that may occur. When a crisis occurs, the top management team should not only address the situation but should consider strategic changes that may lessen the likelihood or severity of similar crises in the future. Hence, the public relations dimension is important when a crisis occurs, but a serious look at the appropriateness of existing strategies is also in order (Guiner, 2008).

Identifying crisis events in the early stages is not always easy. Acknowledging the sales declines brought about by a product boycott is not difficult to realize, but sensing the early warning signals so that action can be taken to mitigate their effects can be. Some warning signs are universal, such as product return rates. Others are more organization specific, such as absenteeism levels and number of grievances.

Exercising strategic control requires that performance be measured, compared with previously established standards, and followed by corrective action, if necessary. Not meeting a performance indicator is often an early warning sign that a potential crisis may exist. Generally speaking, corrective action should be taken at all levels if performance is less than the standard unless extraordinary causes of the discrepancy can be identified, such as a halt in production when a fire shuts down a critical supplier. Whenever possible, it is desirable for managers to anticipate possible corrective measures *before* a strategy is implemented. Doing so lowers the likelihood that threats and problems turn into crises.

Summary

A strategy is a top management plan to develop and sustain competitive advantage so that the organization's mission is fulfilled. Organizational crises can be related to a firm's strategy. The corporate strategy of the firm seeks to define the industries in which the company should compete and the growth trajectory that should be pursued. The decisions the organization makes in these areas will influence the types of crises it may face in the future.

The business strategy defines how the firm will operate given its chosen industry. The generic strategy framework is a useful starting point for crafting a competitive strategy. Low-cost, differentiation, and focus strategies carry embody unique crisis vulnerabilities.

The strategic control process is necessary to signal when a crisis may be eminent. By design, controls communicate to management when something is wrong. However, management must be willing to take controls seriously and abide by the rules of control parameters. This chapter illustrates how failure to abide by controls can lead to industrial accidents and management fraud.

Questions for Discussion

1. What crisis vulnerabilities exist when a company competes in:
   - A single industry?
   - Multiple, but related industries?
   - Multiple, and unrelated industries?

2. What types of crises can occur when a company is following a growth strategy?

3. What relationships exist between retrenchments strategies and crises?

4. What types of crises might a company encounter when it is following:
   - A low-cost strategy?
   - A differentiation strategy?
   - A focus-low-cost strategy?
   - A focus-differentiation strategy?

5. What are some examples of when controls failed in an organization and a crisis erupted?

6. What would a balanced scorecard look like where you work?

Chapter Exercise

The low-cost strategy has linkages to crisis vulnerabilities that have been widely publicized in the media. Several examples were given in this chapter on how a low-cost strategy can create its own set of crises. In this exercise, form teams of three to four students and propose a balanced scorecard for a company following a low-cost strategy.

To begin, select one of the following companies:

- Wal-Mart
- Spirit Airlines
- Motel 6
- IKEA
- Aldi
- Nucor Steel

Each of these companies follows a predominantly low-cost strategy. Conduct an Internet search and determine the types of crises these companies have faced in the past. Check YouTube and other social media outlets as part of your effort.

From your research, prepare a balanced scorecard for your company. In addition, list the types of crises the company might face. Use the example of the balanced scorecard found in this chapter as a guide for the one you develop.

Opening Case, Part 2: The BP Gulf of Mexico Oil Spill

Shortly before 10:00 P.M. on April 20, 2010, a series of unusual events took place aboard the *Deepwater Horizon*. The lights started to glow so brightly that some of them burst. The generators were speeding up their revolutions, giving the rig a strange humming sound. Computer monitors began to shatter and the gas alarms were buzzing. Something was amiss. A dangerous gas cloud had surrounded the rig, followed by a series of explosions and a violent shaking of the rig. It lost power, an intense fire soon developed, and orders were given to abandon the ship. After years of successful drilling service, the *Deepwater Horizon* had encountered a fatal crisis. Only a few months before, the *Horizon* had set a new world record, drilling down 35,000 feet to another BP well in the Gulf (Cook, 2010). Now it was about to be completely destroyed.

Abandoning the Ship

According to *Transocean Investigation Report* (2011), there were 126 people onboard the rig. These included the *Deepwater Horizon* crew (employed by Transocean), the BP well site team, employees from other contractors, and visitors from both Transocean and BP, who ironically, were there to celebrate the rig's safety record. Some of the crew proceeded to the lifeboats as instructed. Others had to jump 100 feet to the waters below. Eleven workers probably died immediately or soon after the explosion and fire began.

The *Deepwater Horizon* had a prearranged plan in place for the crew to exit the vessel in the event of an accident. As is with most sea vessels, in the event of an emergency, the crew is to meet in designated areas (called "muster stations") so that their exit can be arranged. On the night of the explosion, the crew proceeded to their muster stations, at least as best they could. Some muster stations such as the galley and the movie room had been damaged in the explosion. Upon learning this, orders were given for those affected to arrive at the lifeboat stations instead (*Transocean Investigation Report,* 2011).

The *Deepwater Horizon* was equipped with four lifeboats, each capable of holding 73 people. In addition, there were six self-inflating rafts that could accommodate 25 people each. With this capacity, the rig was well equipped to evacuate everyone, even if some of the lifeboats and rafts were damaged. In fact, on the night of the accident, only two lifeboats and one raft were utilized (*Transocean Investigation Report,* 2011). The other two lifeboats were not accessible because of the fire. According to the Transocean Report, four people jumped before the lifeboats were launched, 100 abandoned the vessel using two of the lifeboats, seven exited on one inflatable raft, and four jumped after the raft was launched. After the crew abandoned the *Deepwater Horizon,* they proceeded to a nearby ship, the *Damon B. Bankston,* a supply vessel that assists the rig. Once onboard, 17 of the survivors were airlifted to nearby hospitals for treatment.

The Fire

The resulting fire burned intensely for 36 hours. Feeding the fire was a column of oil and hydrocarbons rising from the well, past the BOP and into the riser. From there the volatile mixture made its way to the rig, where it fueled an intense fire that could not be extinguished with conventional water streams. In fact, the only way to stop the fire was to find a way to disconnect the fuel source. Locating it was not difficult, but finding a way to stop the flow would prove impossible. The BOP was the mechanism in place that was supposed to be the last resort of safety. When all else fails, the BOP is designed to cut off the flow of oil and gas by severing the pipe casing using a mechanism called a "blind sheer ram." This piece works by cutting through the metal pipe and sealing it shut (Schneider, 2011). However, the BOP had failed.

While the fire burned, relief ships nearby directed streams of water on the rig to try to cool the vessel and extinguish the blaze. Efforts to shut down the fuel source never materialized. After 36 hours of burning, the *Deepwater Horizon* slowly began to list to one side and then slid into the sea. The Gulf of Mexico had extinguished the blaze. But the Gulf was not spared from what was to happen next. As the rig sank, another new crisis unfolded: crude oil began gushing into the Gulf and would continue for some 87 days.

What Went Wrong?

What had malfunctioned to cause the conflagration? It appeared that a dangerous hydrocarbon gas had permeated the area around the rig. This gas then encountered an ignition source, causing the explosion. Because oil was also feeding up through the riser, the fire had a continuous fuel source. But why did the gases escape? The suspect points in the investigations that followed would focus on the BOP and the integrity of the cementing process on the well casing. Had mistakes been made in the sealing of the well? Had safety issues been compromised? During the investigations that followed, each of the three major companies involved in the disaster blamed the other. In Chapter 7, we examine this blame game in more detail.

Opening Case Part 2 Discussion Questions

1. Describe a time when a major appliance at home or a piece of machinery at work malfunctioned. What warning signs occurred before the machine ceased to work properly? Was it because a faulty repair had been completed earlier or was it simply because of the age of the machinery?

2. If you have taken a cruise on a ship, describe the training you received on how to find your muster station and what you needed to know in case of an emergency.

3. Describe a time when you had to exit a building, a ship, or some other structure, either for a drill or because of an actual emergency. Was the exit well planned on the part of the authorities? Was there anything that could have been done differently?

Opening Case Part 2 References

Cook, N. (2010). Deepwater Horizon. *RoSPA Occupational Safety and Health Journal, 40*(12), 13–17.

Schneider, R. (2011). Ethics and oil: Preventing the next disaster. *Journal of Emergency Management, 9*(3), 11–22.

Transocean Investigation Report. (2011, June). Macondo Well Incident, Vol. 1. Retrieved August 1, 2012, from http://www.deepwater.com/fw/main/Public-Report-1076.html.

References

Adams, R. (2005). Fast food, obesity, and tort reform: An examination of industry responsibility for public health. *Business and Society Review, 110*(3), 297–320.

Adamson, J. (2000). How Denny's went from icon of racism to diversity award winner. *Journal of Organizational Excellence, 20*(1), 55–68.

Baldauf, S. (2004, May 4). Bhopal gas tragedy lives on, 20 years later. *Christian Science Monitor,* p. 7.

Barrett, P. (2011, August 29). Cleaning America's dirtiest coal company. *Bloomberg Businessweek,* 48–55.

Beirne, M., & Jensen, T. (1999). AirTran continues its comeback. *Adweek, 40*(30), 4.

Brathwaite, S. (2002). Denny's: A diversity success story. *Franchising World, 34*(5), 28–29.

Brewster, P. (2011). Johnson & Johnson and the "phantom" recall: Practical advice to prevent risk management and quality systems from failing to identify and address sentinel events. *Health Lawyer, 23*(6), 1–12.

Buehlmann, U., Bumgardner, M., Lihra, T., & Frye, M. (2006). Attitudes of U.S. retailers toward China, Canada, and the United States as manufacturing sources for furniture: An assessment of competitive priorities. *Journal of Global Marketing, 20*(1), 61–73.

Burrows, P., & Anderson, S. (1993, July 12). Dell Computer goes into the shop. *Business Week,* 138–140.

Campbell-Hunt, C. (2000). What have we learned about generic competitive strategy? A meta-analysis. *Strategic Management Journal, 21,* 127–154.

Carroll, A., & Buchholtz, A. (2012). *Business and society: Ethics, sustainability, and stakeholder management.* Mason, OH: South-Western Cengage Learning.

Casey, N., Zamiska, N., & Pasztor, A. (2007, September 22). Mattel seeks to placate China with apology. *Wall Street Journal,* pp. A1–A7.

Chu, W. (2011). How the Chinese government promoted a global automobile industry. *Industrial and Corporate Change, 20*(5), 1235–1276.

Cockburn, I. M., Henderson, R. M., & Stern, S. (2000). Untangling the origins of competitive advantage. *Strategic Management Journal, 21,* 1123–1145.

Dawson, B. (2003, June 30). Powder causes West explosion. *Rubber and Plastics News, 32*(24), 1.

D'Zurilla, W. (1998). Reflections of a Dalkon Shield arbitrator. *Dispute Resolution Journal, 53*(1), 13–15.

Englehardt, K., Sallot, L., & Springston, J. (2004). Compassion without blame: Testing the accident decision flow chart with the crash of ValuJet flight 592. *Journal of Public Relations Research, 16*(2), 127–156.

Fishman, C. (2006). *The Wal-Mart effect: How the world's most powerful company really works—and how it's transforming the American economy.* New York: Penguin.

Gandolfi, F. (2008). Cost reductions, downsizing-related layoffs, and HR practices. *SAM Advanced Management Journal, 73*(3), 52–58.

Guiner, T. (2008, May 25). Dealing with a PR crisis takes planning and truth. *Wall Street Journal,* Special Insert.

Hosmer, L. (2011). *The ethics of management: A multidisciplinary approach* (7th ed.). New York: McGraw-Hill/Irwin.

Jack, A. (2010, October 1). J&J criticized over cough remedy action. *Financial Times,* p. 19.

Kaplan, R., & Norton, D. (2000). *The strategy-focused organization.* Boston: Harvard Business School Press.

Kaplan, R., & Norton, D. (1996). *The balanced scorecard: Translating strategy into action.* Boston: Harvard Business School Press.

Keating, C. (2012, April 30). Famous rebrandings. *Fortune,* 15.

Kruger, D. (2004, June 21). Short-order chef. *Forbes,* 106–108.

Langston, R. (2006). Just good business. *Communication World, 23*(5), 40–41.

Levick, R., & Slack, C., (2011). Owning up to error is a safeguard, not a liability. *Of Counsel, 30*(7), 15–17.

Lockyer, S. (2004). Chi-Chi's shuts all units; Outback buys site rights. *Nation's Restaurant News, 38*(40), 5, 170, 172.

Lublin, J. S. (2000, December 27). Tips from a turnaround specialist. *Wall Street Journal,* p. B1.

Macky, K. (2004). Organizational downsizing and redundancies: The New Zealand workers' experience. *New Zealand Journal of Employment Relations, 29*(1), 63–87.

Mangalindan, M. (2006, January 23). How Amazon's dream alliance with Toys "R" Us went so sour. *Wall Street Journal,* pp. A1, A12.

Miller, J. (2012). Spirit Airlines boss calls complaints "irrelevant," says dying veteran should've bought insurance. Retrieved May 28, 2012, from http://www.foxnews.com/us/2012/05/03/spirit-airlines-outpaces-competitors-regarding-passenger-complaints-statistics/.

Morrison, M. (2012, May 24). McDonald's shareholders defeat proposal to weigh impact on obesity. *Advertising Age.* (Retrieved June 4, 2012, from http://adage.com/article/news/mcdonald-s-shareholders-defeat-obesity-impact-proposal/234961/.

Murray, M. (2001, March 13). Waiting for the ax to fall. *Wall Street Journal,* pp. B1, B10.

Nicas, J. (2012, May 12). A stingy spirit lifts airline's profits. *Wall Street Journal,* p. A1.

Officials: Eggs, not employees caused illnesses at Durham restaurant. (2010, July 16). *WRAL.com.* Retrieved May 30, 2012, from http://www.wral.com/news/local/story/7975607/.

Parnell, J. A. (2013). *Strategic management: Theory and practice* (4th ed.). Thousand Oaks, CA: Sage.

Parnell, J. A. (2006). Generic strategies after two decades: A reconceptualization of competitive strategy. *Management Decision, 44,* 1139–1154.

Pasztor, A., & Carey, S. (2009, December 1). Commuter airlines: Questions of safety. *Wall Street Journal,* pp. A1, A16.

Pauchant, T., & Mitroff, I. (1992). *Transforming the crisis-prone organization.* San Francisco: Jossey-Bass.

Picken, J. C., & Dess, G. G. (1997). Out of (strategic) control. *Organizational Dynamics, 26*(1), 35–48.

Porter, M. E. (1980). *Competitive strategy.* New York: Free Press.

Preble, J. (1997). Integrating the crisis management perspective into the strategic management process. *Journal of Management Studies, 34*(5), 669–791.

Probst, G., & Raisch, S. (2005). Organizational crisis: The logic of failure. *Academy of Management Executive, 19*(1), 90–105.

Reuer, J. J., Zollo, M., & Singh, H. (2002). Post-formation dynamics in strategic alliances. *Strategic Management Journal, 23,* 135–152.

Rockoff, J. (2010a, September 29). J&J's quality control draws scrutiny. *Wall Street Journal,* pp. B1, B2.

Rockoff, J. (2010b, November 18). Tylenol for kids returns to shelves. *Wall Street Journal,* p. B3.

Sethi, S., & Steidlmeier, P. (1997). *Up against the corporate wall: Cases in business and society.* Upper Saddle River, NJ: Prentice Hall.

Smith, D. (1992). Commentary: On crisis management and strategic management. In P. Shrivastava (Ed.), *Advances in strategic management* (pp. 261–269). Greenwich, CT: JAI Press.

Stewart, J. B. (2008, May 28). Auto makers can find opportunity in $4 gasoline. *Wall Street Journal,* p. D3.

Tavernise, S., & Krauss, C. (2011, December 7). Mine owner will pay $209 million in blast that killed 29 workers. *New York Times,* p. 16.

Taylor, E. (2008, May 6). Start-ups race to produce "green" cars. *Wall Street Journal,* pp. B1, B7.

Terlep, S. (2011, November 29). GM scrambles to defend Volt. *Wall Street Journal,* B1.

Veil, S., Liu, M., Erickson, S., & Sellnow, T. (2005). Too hot to handle: Competency constrains character in Chi-Chi's green onion crisis. *Public Relations Quarterly, 50*(4), 19–22.

Watson, S. (2012, May 2). Atlantic County assemblymen call on Spirit Airlines to change refund policy. *The Press of Atlantic City.* Retrieved May 30, 2012, from http://www.pressofatlanticcity.com/news/press/atlantic/atlantic-county-assemblymen-call-on-spirit-airlines-to-change-refund/article_18d30f1a-948c-11e1-9211-0019bb2963f4.html.

Wise, J. (2010, May 8). Chefs' eat-in bolsters Bullock's. *News and Observer,* p. 3B.

CHAPTER 7

Crisis Management: Taking Action When Disaster Hits

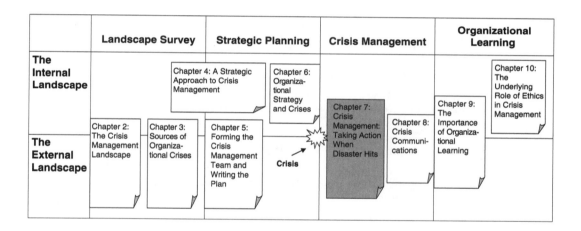

Opening Case, Part 3:
The BP Gulf of Mexico Oil Spill

Before the *Deepwater Horizon* incident in 2010, British Petroleum (BP) was already under scrutiny for some of its maintenance and safety practices. Two incidents that had occurred only a few years earlier had gained much attention. An accident involving worker fatalities occurred in 2005 at a Texas City refinery. In addition, a large amount of oil had spilled in Alaska due to the faulty maintenance of pipes in 2006. Both events would be relived again as the public demanded accountability on the part of the oil giant.

Previous Incidents

In 2005, a large explosion occurred at a BP refinery in Texas City, Texas, killing 15 employees and injuring another 170 workers. BP was found to be in violation of the Clean Air Act and was the first company to be prosecuted under a section of the act that was designed to prevent injuries to employees. The company was fined $50 million (Sawayda & Jackson, 2011).

BP acquired the Texas City refinery in 1999 from Amoco. Upon purchase, the refinery was in need of a major overhaul; Amoco had neglected maintenance and safety upgrades for years. Unfortunately, BP headquarters was in the midst of a 25 percent budget cut (Elkind, Whitford, & Burke, 2010), meaning such upgrades would be slow. The at-risk plant eventually had a malfunction on a cooking tank processing gasoline additives. The tank boiled over, sending a vapor cloud over the refinery. A pickup truck in the parking lot backfired, igniting the vapor cloud (Elkind et al., 2010). The accident attracted a lot of negative attention for BP as the refinery declined further, making it vulnerable to this type of accident.

In 2006, BP pipelines leaked in the Prudhoe Bay region of Alaska. The leaks were due to years of neglect in maintaining the lines and addressing corrosion. The pipeline failures triggered a 200,000-gallon oil leak and resulted in another violation of the Clean Air Act. BP was ordered to pay a total of $45 million in fines, $12 million in criminal fines, $4 million to the National Fish and Wildlife Foundation, $4 million in criminal restitution to the state of Alaska, and $25 million for violating clean air and water laws (Sawayda & Jackson, 2011).

The Arrival of Tony Hayward

To help address its safety problems, BP enlisted Tony Hayward as chief executive office (CEO) in 2007. Hayward had joined the company in 1982, working as a geologist and traveling the globe, helping the company find new sources of oil. At the time, John Browne was a charismatic, celebrity-style CEO who had led the company through growth by acquisitions (Elkind et al., 2010). Under Browne's reign, BP took on more risks but also slashed budgets, creating an atmosphere of vulnerability in the area of field operations. Texas City and the Alaskan oil pipe problems were examples of how cost cutting created problems for the company.

Hayward's role was to improve safety and get the company in "silent running" mode, a term used to indicate "a quiet, methodical, trouble-free operation, with no problems, no surprises, and high productivity" (Campbell, 2008, p. 18). Hayward went to work instituting expansive changes to improve safety, including the implementation of a common management system with precise safety rules and training for all facilities (Mouawad, 2010). Under his reign, Hayward has been given credit for improving the safety culture of BP and for its operational performance (Orwall, Langley, & Herron, 2010).

Individual Safety Versus Process Safety

Despite the improvements in the safety culture at BP, critics charged that too much emphasis was placed on ensuring individual worker safety, and not enough attention was devoted to process safety. Individual safety in the workplace focuses on ensuring that employees do not commit unsafe acts, such as lifting a heavy object incorrectly. As a result, workplace rules such as requiring employees to wear eye protection when working around machinery are established. At BP, strict guidelines were in place that prohibited employees from carrying a cup of coffee unless it had a lid (Elkind et al., 2011). While these kinds of rules can decrease accidents, they do not address the hazards that can occur on a drilling rig or in a refinery such as the one at Texas City.

Process safety is much broader and does not assume that employee error is the primary cause for workplace accidents. Instead, it emphasizes the "process" that caused the employee to commit the error in the first place. For example, poor training of an employee—a process—can contribute to that employee's involvement in a workplace accident. Process safety does not blame an individual employee or equipment failure (Schreiber, 2012). Instead, if equipment did fail, the process that caused the failure would be examined. Perhaps poor maintenance—a process—caused failure. The process approach to safety seeks to identify root causes, at which time safety issues and the prevention of accidents can be addressed from a more holistic perspective.

For BP, one process in particular was suspect: conducting of a negative pressure test on a well. A correct understanding of the test results was necessary, because it indicated whether hydrocarbons and oil were entering the drill casing. However, BP had a process problem because it did not have standardized procedure to conduct the test, interpret the results, and respond if the test indicated the well had failed (Crooks, Pfeifer, & McNulty, 2010). The process for checking the integrity of the well was not defined, and therefore flaws compromised the safety of the well, the rig, and its employees. In hindsight, we know now that flammable hydrocarbons and oil entered the drill casing, that the well was indeed compromised, and that a fatal incident occurred.

Opening Case Part 3 Questions

1. Think of an example of an accident that occurred where you work. Assume that you cannot assign the blame to employee error or faulty equipment. Instead, analyze the process that led to the accident, and identify any flaws that existed in the process.

2. Was the *Deepwater Horizon* accident a problem associated more with cost cutting or with a faulty process safety culture?

Opening Part 3 Case References

Campbell, H. (2008). Keep on running. *BP,* Issue 8, 16–23.
Crooks, E., Pfeifer, S., & McNulty, S. (2010, October 7). A sea change needed. *Financial Times,* p. 9.
Elkind, P., Whitford, D., & Burke, D. (2011, February 7). An accident waiting to happen. *Fortune,* 105–132.
Mouawad, J. (2010, May 8). For BP, a history of spills and safety lapses. *New York Times,* p. A22.

Orwall, B., Langley, M. & Herron, J. (2010, July 26). Embattled BP chief to exit—American Robert Dudley to succeed Tony Hayward as head of British oil giant. *Wall Street Journal*, p. A1.

Sawayda, J., & Jackson, J. (2011). BP struggles to resolve sustainability disaster. In O. C. Ferrell, John Fraedrich, & Linda Ferrell (Eds.), *Business ethics: Ethical decision making and cases* (9th ed., pp. 342–354). Mason, OH: South-Western Cengage Learning.

Schreiber, J. (2012). Working with the CSB after a major accident. *Chemical Engineering, 119*(7), 49–51.

Introduction

High-profile events such as the terrorist attacks of September 11, 2001, the Enron scandal in 2001, and Hurricane Katrina in 2005 have highlighted the importance of crisis preparedness. Most organizational crises do not receive as much attention as these examples, but they still constitute major events for the firm and the community. As a result, many organizations have begun to analyze their vulnerabilities. Indeed, anticipating and preparing for crises is much less traumatic and costly than experiencing an unexpected calamity without a plan for managing it. Assuming a company will always remain free from any type of crisis is guesswork at best. For some organizational leaders, this may involve confronting "paradigm blindness," a condition "where people are unable to see information that threatens and disconfirms their worldview" (Wheatley, 2006, p. 18).

There are countless stories about the lack of a plan causing severe or even irreparable damage to a firm. Interestingly, however, there are also examples where proper planning and execution of a crisis plan not only kept the crisis under control but also resulted in positive changes for the business (Borodzicz & van Haperen, 2002). This topic of positive change is explored in depth in Chapter 9, "The Importance of Organizational Learning."

Most crises are, by their very nature, somewhat unexpected and unpredictable. A poorly managed crisis can severely damage a firm's reputation and profitability. As mentioned, proactive organizations should develop crisis management responses for managing an event should it occur. Some businesses encounter "smoldering" crises that start internally and slowly create problems that can be more difficult to resolve in their later stages (Institute for Crisis Management, 2011). Other crises can occur externally and take the organization by surprise. Effective crisis management requires managers to develop strategies that are integrated with the annual corporate planning process (Preble, 1997). Its effectiveness can be enhanced if managers are able to identify a potential crisis and develop appropriate strategies to prevent it, or at least mitigate its effects.

This chapter focuses on the management practices and decision-making activities that should be implemented at the beginning, duration, and conclusion of the crisis event. The first part of this chapter addresses the initial response actions that are critical in the assessment of the crisis during its onset. The next part discusses key issues relating to managing the crisis. Response strategies and mitigation of the crisis are the major concerns here. In this stage, managers must make decisive decisions that will determine the success or failure of their crisis management efforts.

The final part of the chapter discusses what happens after the crisis, including the issues of recovery, reentry, and business continuity. Ultimately, the organization must regroup and return to normal operations or its survival may be in jeopardy.

Strategies at the Beginning of a Crisis

The first step in the formal response to a crisis is to convene the crisis management team (CMT). Recall that the organization should have a preestablished team and a crisis management plan (CMP). Activating the team may be as simple as one member calling the team together. Alternatively, an employee in the organization may alert a member of the CMT to the potential or developing crisis at hand. Once convened, the team begins the process of assessing the situation.

The response to the onset of a crisis depends on the nature of the event. Some crisis situations, such as an industrial accident, the sudden death of a senior executive, the notification of a government investigation, or a chemical spill, can occur quickly and often with little or no warning. Others, such as a hostile takeover, union labor unrest, a consumer boycott, or corporate embezzlement, develop over a longer period of time. The length of time managers have to react to a crisis is related to its impact on the organization and its stakeholders. Having a CMP makes it possible to think and act expediently during the first few hours of a crisis. The CMP is a key strategic organizational tool responsible for initiating the crisis decision-making process by helping to frame the problem, determine the parties responsible for implementing various actions, and develop justifications for the decisions that are made.

Leadership of the CMT

Effective leadership is necessary during a crisis, both by the leader of the CMT and by top management (Wooten & James, 2008). This team is responsible for making and implementing decisions that help the organization resolve the crisis. Three components of the CMT that must be present for crisis leadership to be successful are (1) the right leadership, (2) the structure and resources necessary to accomplish crisis response and containment, and (3) broad public support for the organization (Cavanaugh, 2003).

In a crisis response, CMT members should not only be knowledgeable about their own roles on the team but also willing to accept suggestions presented by members who are experts in other areas. The CMT leader must have an array of both leadership and management skills. Drawing from the experience of the military and the emergency services sector, Crichton, Lauche, and Flin (2005) identified the following skills needed for the CMT leader:

- *Situation assessment*: Being able to identify the problem accurately
- *Decision making*: Deciding what the CMT should do
- *Team coordination*: Getting the CMT and affiliated stakeholders to work together

- *Communicating:* Deciding how to receive and deliver relevant information
- *Monitoring:* Keeping abreast of key developments
- *Delegating:* Assigning tasks to individual CMT members
- *Prioritizing:* Determining the importance of incoming information and what should be done next
- *Planning:* Taking part in the planning process and encouraging task completion

The CMT leader should utilize these competencies by taking charge of the situation, assessing the level of crisis seriousness, determining the level of resources needed, and then making the decisions that will resolve the crisis (Cavanaugh, 2003). Simultaneously, the leader should be in frequent communication with his or her team members to implement the crisis plan. Within the context of this role, the leader must recognize and implement these actions while remaining visible and available. Admiral Thad Allen of the U.S. Coast Guard led the incident command efforts for the *Deepwater Horizon* oil spill in the Gulf of Mexico in 2010. During the crisis, his visibility and availability demanded that he spend half his time in Washington, D.C., briefing members of Congress, the rest of the administration, and the media. The other half of his time was spent on board Coast Guard boats in the Gulf. He commented, "If you're not visible to your people out on the boats who are trying to pull a boon in Barataria Bay in 110-degree heat, then you're not a credible leader, because you don't understand what they're going through" (Berinato, 2010, p. 78).

The leader must have the ability to remain calm and focused on the crisis management process while making decisions under significant pressure. In fact, the CMT leader may be required to make decisions without certain desired information, because a crisis is characterized by high levels of ambiguity and stress (Baran & Adelman, 2010). Moreover, those involved in the crisis are having their assumptions about reality challenged (Pearson & Clair, 1998). Recall that some crises take the CMT to places they have never been before in terms of experiences, what management scholar Karl Weick (1993) labeled as "cosmology episodes."

All crises create tension and stress. Acute stressors for the CMT can include chaotic events, communication problems, time pressure, consequences and accountability, fear of failure, dealing with the media, and information problems including overload, missing, and/or ambiguous information. Maintaining control allows the leader to sustain an objective perspective and see the way through complex and confusing scenarios. Hence, the leader must present an objective perspective quickly and methodically for all stakeholders (Rolston & McNerney, 2003).

One final note should be mentioned concerning the attributes of the CMT leader: there is no one best profile for success. As Schoenberg (2005) noted:

> A crisis leader in one situation may be a follower in a different situation. A crisis leader in a natural disaster will need to demonstrate different skills than a crisis leader of a product recall. A crisis leader dealing with employee sabotage or violence faces an entirely different situation. (p. 3)

Crisis leaders should also mentor less experienced team members. In fact, it is likely that the leader is mentoring without even knowing it (Berinato, 2010).

Situational Assessment

One of the first tasks of the CMT is to assess the situation so that decisions can be made to mitigate the crisis (Wilson, 2004). *Situational assessment* refers to the information processing and knowledge creation aspects of crisis management (Coombs, 2007). Endsley and Garland (2000) describe it as an awareness of knowing what is going on and then predicting how the crisis may evolve. Situational awareness is critical to understanding the crisis and identifying its dimensions and intensity. Unfortunately, the crisis management literature offers extensive examples of how the initial stages of assessing the situation were erroneous. We overview several of these.

The 1989 Hillsborough Soccer Tragedy

A tragic case involving errors in the situational assessment stage of a crisis situation occurred at the 1989 Hillsborough soccer match in Sheffield, England. In this incident, 97 fatalities occurred in a section of the stands that had become thronged with people. Most of the victims were crushed to death (Taylor, 1990). The response by police as a simple case of overcrowding was incorrect; in fact, it had become a major safety issue (Crichton et al., 2005).

The tragedy was triggered by a police decision to open the gates at the Leppings Lane entrance to the stadium so that fans could enter the stands more quickly in advance of the 3:00 P.M. start. There was also concern that the situation outside of the stadium could result in a crush, where fans would be penned against each other or trampled to death. The police decided to open the gates to the stadium at 2:52 P.M. to relieve the pressure. Unfortunately, the sudden rush of supporters into the stadium was funneled into pens (i.e., sections) 3 and 4, which were already overcrowded (Elliott & Smith, 1993). The fans at the front of the stands or at the terrace were pinned against the wall and the fence with nowhere to go, resulting in their suffocation.

Numerous photographs and videos showed an odd display of behavior—fans reaching to be pulled up by other fans on the upper terrace, as well as spectators seeking to climb over the fence just near the pitch (i.e., field). Police mistakenly took this to be a sign of a "pitch invasion" by fans, but it was really a desperate attempt to escape the deadly crush of the crowd. At 3:06 P.M., the police control room became aware of the full extent of the situation and stopped the match. At 3:13, cutting equipment was requested to extract fans penned against the fence. Unfortunately, many of them had already died (Elliott & Smith, 1993). One of the ironies of this tragedy was that a decision to save lives outside of the stadium resulted in the mass casualties inside the stadium. Clearly, the situation had not been assessed properly, and lives were lost.

The 1992 Los Angeles Riots

The Los Angeles riots in 1992 illustrate an erroneous assessment of the crisis situation by the Los Angeles Police Department (LAPD). The riot was rooted in the police beating of Rodney King, an African American motorist who had been stopped by police on March 3, 1991. King had led police on a high-speed chase before being pulled over, and then continued to resist arrest once he was out of his vehicle. Police officers struck King 56 times with batons, in addition to kicking him and stomping on his head. The beating was recorded by an amateur photographer, who sold the tape to a Los Angeles television station (Miller, 2001). Today, such a video would likely appear on YouTube within minutes.

The police officers making the arrest were tried for using excessive force. During the time up to the trial, the video of the beating had been played countless times on television and was fueling contempt for the officers involved, as well as for the LAPD in general. The trigger event for the riots was not the videotape of the beating, but rather the not guilty verdict for the officers. The verdict was announced on April 28, 1992, shortly after 3:15 P.M. By 5:30 P.M., the riots had begun.

The LAPD and the mayor's office were unprepared for what happened next. Mayor Thomas Bradley, fearing that a police presence during the verdict would provoke a negative response from the community, objected to the deployment of police during the verdict decision. Police Chief Daryl Gates was not available during the early stages of the riot but instead was attending a political rally in Brentwood. Hence, at the beginning of the riot, there was little police presence and no central control for managing the eventual deployment of police (Miller, 2001).

Unlike the response of the public sector, private organizations were assessing the situation and quickly making their own crisis preparations. Solomon (1992) overviewed the crisis response of various organizations in the areas where the rioting was worst. Because of the danger of physical harm to employees, companies needed to act quickly. Thrifty Corporation[1] operated 21 pharmacies in these areas. Four of the stores were burned to the ground and the other 17 stores were looted:

> Company executives gave guidelines to managers. If they felt that a group of people approaching the stored looked threatening, or if people came in hordes, they were to close down. In addition, if they could see that neighboring stores were having trouble, or if they could see fires anywhere around, they were to close down. (Solomon, 1992, p. 24)

ARCO service stations responded quickly by closing stations so underground gas tanks would not ignite. Employees were notified via a phone chain (e-mail was not available yet) not to report to work because of the danger. In addition, chain-link fences were quickly erected by ARCO around damaged stores. Company headquarters was located 25 miles southeast of the riot area, but executives at the home office were updated continuously on the status of the riot (Solomon, 1992).

The Los Angeles riots were an example of misreading the original situation. This case serves as an example of the importance of situational assessment. The Hillsborough stadium tragedy and the Los Angeles riots are clearly unusual events that fall outside of the realm of crisis vulnerabilities for many businesses, however. Can situational assessment be as difficult in less dramatic examples? Consider the problem that many companies faced when they tried to assess the impact of Y2K.

The Y2K Crisis

We mentioned the Y2K crisis briefly in Chapter 2. The Y2K crisis was especially interesting because it was difficult for leaders and CMTs to determine how it would affect their organizations. Conducting a situational assessment was difficult as well. This particular crisis was different for three key reasons. First, it was associated with a particular date. At the turn of the century, computers could interpret a two-digit year as 1900 instead of 2000, triggering an array of potential problems. Second, there was an apocalyptic fervor associated with this particular event. A minority of Christians believed that this event would usher in the second coming of Christ, an event associated with biblical prophecy (Powell, Hickson, Self, & Bodon, 2001). Finally, a number of writers, church leaders, and other self-proclaimed experts—some with significant followings—offered their own viewpoints on the issue.

Interestingly, many of these experts lacked any computer background but predicted that the Y2K computer bug would commence a series of events that would ultimately trigger a widespread meltdown of society, including but not limited to social upheaval, riots, food shortages, electric grid malfunctions, airplane crashes, and even nuclear war. Misinformation was widespread, including the story of a 104-year-old woman—presumably identified as four years old by a computer—who had received a note from the local public school system reminding her to enroll in kindergarten. This story was shared by Florida-based televangelist James Kennedy in his booklet on the topic. Kennedy borrowed the story from another doomsday author, Michael Hyatt, who appeared on many Christian radio programs but neglected to tell his audience that it occurred in 1993, not 1999, and was attributed to human error, not computer error. Various versions of the story were propagated, including the use of different locations (Boston, 2000). Why and how this story spread so easily is beyond the scope of this discussion, but it does illustrate the amount of misinformation that was disseminated at the time.

An understanding of how these thought processes developed and progressed is important for crisis management for two reasons. First, we must not presume that the cognitions exhibited during Y2K were simply illogical or conjured up by a small group of uneducated people. While some citizens naively believed what they heard without questioning it, many caught in the Y2K panic were represented a variety of socioeconomic and educational backgrounds, including physicians, attorneys, and professors, some of whom even left their homes and set up isolated communities in rural areas (McMinn, 2001). Second, the fact that a large group of people believed a crisis was eminent runs counter to what we see in the crisis management literature; it is more common for the masses to be in denial.

Y2K was indeed a one-of-a-kind crisis in that so many people both erred and were correct in their situational assessments. The concern over what the computer bug *might* do prompted most companies to simply fix the problem, which in the end, was not very difficult. And yet, the Y2K panic was spreading as if nothing could be done to stop the problem, when in fact computers by the thousands were being fixed every day, well in advance of the fated end of the year. When the new millennium arrived with no major snags, both sides on the Y2K issue were able to claim victory. The doomsdayers claimed that their alarm raised the attention needed to remedy the bug (Cowan, 2003). Those who did not panic suggested that the bug was fixed simply because it was a necessary component of a sound-running management information system (MIS) and would have been done anyway.

Mitigation Strategies

Once the situational analysis is completed, strategies for managing the crisis can be identified and implemented. Not all strategies will work initially, so care must be taken to reassess the situation on a regular basis. Flexibility must be maintained because a crisis situation can change almost hourly. Care should be taken to address the crisis directly and restore confidence with the affected stakeholders.

The Sheetz convenience store chain, based in Pennsylvania and run by members of the Sheetz family, experienced such a crisis in July 2004. Hundreds of customers in western Pennsylvania became sick from salmonella. The source was later found to be Roma tomatoes that Sheetz procured from one of its produce suppliers. Sheetz executives immediately called a press conference to alert their customers and the media that the company would take full responsibility for the crisis. Shortly thereafter, the chain switched to a new type of tomato from a different supplier. In addition, company chairman Steve Sheetz, president Stan Sheetz, and vice president Travis Sheetz personally visited stores to meet with customers and offered to pay medical bills and lost wages to those who had become sick (Donahue, 2004). The company also posted a toll-free number on its website to field any questions that customers or other stakeholders might have. In this example, the mitigating strategies had to begin early and be sustained for several weeks until the crisis was brought under control.

The major goal at the beginning of a crisis is to minimize potential damage to the firm and its reputation. In some cases the objective may even be to turn any potential negatives associated with the crisis into positives for the organization. For example, one of the first successful cases in crisis management involved the 1990 cruise ship fire aboard the *Crystal Harmony,* a vessel owned by Crystal Cruises of Los Angeles, California. The company turned this crisis into a positive situation by immediately convening its crisis management team and implementing its 61-page crisis management plan (Sklarewitz, 1991). The first task was to conduct the situational analysis, which in this case involved assessing the damage to the ship and the extent of injuries. Fortunately, there were no injuries from the fire, which had started in an auxiliary engine room. However, because the ship had only minimal emergency power, it was not able to propel itself in the water. With 920 guests and 540 crew members, it was necessary to transport the vessel back safely to port as soon as possible. The CMT arranged to have tugboats move the ship back.

Sometimes strategies need to be changed after implementation has already begun. In the case of the *Crystal Harmony,* the CMT later learned that the ship was able to regain 80 percent of its power, meaning the tugboats would no longer be needed. Once the safety of the ship was ensured, the CMT went to work preparing statements for the media. The director of public relations, Darlene Papalini, managed the media proactively by issuing these press statements. Because of this forthcoming approach, media coverage of the event was minimal, which is what Papalini had desired (Sklarewitz, 1991). Meanwhile, another part of the CMT was managing the refund process to the passengers. When guests disembarked from the ship, they received a full refund and were offered a $500 credit off any future cruise. The aggressive crisis management had a positive spin: 280 passengers signed a letter expressing their appreciation for the way the company managed the event (Sklarewitz, 1991).

The initial mitigation strategies also begin the long-range quest for managing and surviving the crisis. Decision-making activities are similar to a number of other projects that employees may be part of. What is different here is the nature of the project. In crisis management, the goal is to contain the crisis quickly and return the organization to normal operations. Table 7.1 suggests seven decision-making functions that should take place during the management of a crisis.

Initial Communications

Chapter 5 stressed the importance of designating a spokesperson ahead of time who can manage organizational communications with the media. The major stakeholders in the crisis must be identified and informed, and given both an assessment of what exists and a sense of what is likely to occur next. In some instances, the

Table 7.1   Decision Making During a Crisis

Step 1: Alert and assemble the crisis management team. As soon as the crisis is detected, the CMT should be activated.

Step 2: Collect all relevant information. Learn as much as possible about the situation, including what happened, who was involved, where it took place, and the current status of the crisis. This step not only occurs during the situational analysis but also throughout the duration of the crisis.

Step 3: Assign tasks and continue fact finding. The crisis management team should delegate duties, just like a project management team would.

Step 4: Develop solution alternatives. Identify possible solutions that can be implemented.

Step 5: Implement the chosen solution(s). Implementation is often the most difficult part of the process. It requires competent people, time, and money. Allocation of sufficient resources is important.

Step 6: Communicate with the media. The organization should be proactive in meeting with the media and presenting its side of the story. If the organization does not communicate, the media must find the facts of the story elsewhere, a situation that takes control out of the hands of management.

Step 7: Review what happened. Evaluate the decisions that were made and the results that followed. What was learned, and how might such a crisis be handled differently in the future?

Source: Wilson (2003), 58–61.

organization may have to move quickly to make its first statements to the media. Exxon, a company that has been through its share of crises, experienced a refinery fire in Baton Rouge, Louisiana, on August 2, 1993. The oil company reacted in less than three hours by issuing its first press release at 7:00 A.M. Follow-up statements were issued at 8:00 A.M., 9:00 A.M., 10:00 A.M., 12:15 P.M., 6:00 P.M., and 9:30 P.M. that same day (Duhe & Zoch, 1994). This crisis claimed the lives of three workers and had been preceded by a similar explosion and fire in December 1989, when two employees were killed.

Companies should also use the Internet to communicate to their stakeholders. The organization's website and social media outlets must be activated, communicating what is known about the crisis and what is being done to remedy the situation. The communications aspects of crisis management, including the use of social media tools, are covered more extensively in Chapter 8.

Information Needs

Managers and affected staff from all divisions of the company must share a common and systematic approach to obtaining and utilizing information (Coombs, 2006). It is important to monitor and evaluate the crisis and to make adjustments as needed. It can be difficult to know whether one is making the best decisions during a crisis, however. The CMT must recognize the importance of monitoring the opinions and behaviors of its key publics during a crisis and exercising its own influence when possible. It may be necessary to adjust the message being communicated, the stakeholders being addressed, and the manner in which the leader is communicating (Caponigro, 2000).

Two elements of information are essential in crisis management. First, it must be timely. Timely details of the crisis should be made available to the CMT. An interesting comparison between the private and public sectors before the arrival of Hurricane Katrina illustrates this point. Wal-Mart's emergency operations center began tracking the storm six days before it hit New Orleans. Wal-Mart reacted early to this timely information by sending bottled water, flashlights, batteries, tarps, canned tuna, and strawberry Pop-Tarts to those stores that were likely to be in the path of the storm (Olasky, 2006). In contrast, government agency responses were hampered by late information, slow response, and a general inability to make decisions.

Second, information must be accurate. It must include the precise location, description, and status of the crisis. The Sago Mine disaster in West Virginia illustrates how muddled communications and tired emotions triggered a wave of inaccurate information concerning the fate of 12 trapped miners. In this January 2006 crisis, a mine explosion trapped the miners. They were later found dead, save for one, some 40 hours later by rescuers. The original message originating from the rescuers simply said that "twelve individuals" had been found and one was alive. The radio message was transmitted through five underground relay stations and had to be conveyed through the rescuers' breathing masks, which they were wearing due to the carbon monoxide danger. Unfortunately, the message, muddied by all of the communication "noise," came out "twelve alive" (Langfitt, 2006). The wave of misinformation morphed into a frenzied celebration outside the mine, which would later be silenced by the news that 11 of the miners had in fact died.

Inaccurate information was also exemplified in the Hurricane Katrina disaster. The media displayed a vast amount of information, much of it accurate and dramatic, and some of it useful to those in crisis management capacities. But decision makers seeking new information about the status of the damage or evacuations were often met with media reports of unfounded stories, some of which hindered crisis response. In one instance, a CNN report detailed how two patients had died because rescue helicopters were grounded due to false media reports of sniper fire (Olasky, 2006).

Timely and accurate information is vital to managing a crisis. In addition, crisis managers need systems and resources that ensure a continuous flow of appropriate information. Structures, procedures, and processes for gathering and monitoring information must be established and continuously monitored throughout the crisis. It may be necessary to restructure or modify the information-gathering process as the crisis evolves. Without a well-developed system of gathering information, the success of any crisis management effort is hindered.

Strategies During the Crisis: Response and Mitigation

The mid-crisis stage represents a turning point for all affected stakeholders. Three potential scenarios may emerge at this stage. The first is the belief that the crisis is under control and the damage can be contained. This is a positive sign that the business or organization may be able to continue operating in a close-to-normal capacity. In the second scenario, however, crisis managers must continue to assess the situation and take action to bring it under control. The third scenario suggests that the outcome is hopeless and managers should take steps to salvage whatever they can for the organization.

This third scenario was illustrated when, in early 2012, an unusual crisis occurred within the beef processing industry that proved to be costly to some of the companies involved. One company monitoring the event, AFA Foods, Inc., had to file for bankruptcy as a direct result of the crisis. Customers became aware that ground beef had an additive to it, a substance that had been nicknamed "pink slime." Few were aware that pink slime is actually finely textured beef, a substance that has been used as a filler for ground beef products for two decades (Gleason & Berry, 2012).

For AFA Foods, the crisis added a new dimension to its day-to-day operations because it was already in financial straits. The company processes beef for several of the nation's fast-food chains. Pink slime, or as it is known in the industry, "boneless lean beef trimmings," was ground into its beef products. AFA Foods does not make the filler but purchases it from a supplier. One of them, Beef Products, Inc., experienced a sharp decline in demand and had to close three of its four plants just weeks after the crisis commenced (Gleason & Berry, 2012).

The pink slime case illustrates that during the crisis, unfolding events should be monitored to determine the following:

- Which of the three scenarios appears to be unfolding?
- What resources are available and how long will it take to deploy them?
- How long will it take to execute a decision or solution?
- Who and what are the victims of the crisis? (Leskin et al., 2004)

Regardless of the type of crisis, the organization is usually damaged in some way. Hence, it is important that the CMT do what is feasible to contain the damage inflicted on people, the reputation of the organization, and its assets. This task is the bottom-line goal for all crisis managers.

Damage Containment

Damage containment is the effort to keep the effects of a crisis from spreading and affecting other parts of the business (Mitroff & Anagnos, 2001). Management needs to gather resources such as capital and physical and human resources to help contain the damage (Pearson & Rondinelli, 1998). As a side note, what we call "crisis management" within the four-phase framework of this book is actually the reactive part of the process. From this perspective, the four-step crisis management process is both reactive and proactive. Figure 7.1 illustrates this tradeoff within the four steps of the framework.

With the proper information flowing to the right stakeholders at the right time, damage to people and property can be minimized. In this regard, the main emphasis of crisis management should be focused on three major goals:

1. Gaining complete control of the crisis

2. Conducting frequent damage assessments

3. Restoring normal operations to the organization

	Landscape Survey	Strategic Planning	Crisis Management	Organizational Learning
The Internal Landscape	**Proactive** Seeks to determine the organization's internal strengths and weaknesses and external opportunities and threats that can lead to a crisis.	**Proactive** Seeks to formulate a crisis management team and a crisis plan that can be used to both prevent and mitigate potential crisis events.	**Reactive** Seeks to respond to the crisis events that do occur. Emphasis is on containing the damage and restoring normal operations.	**Proactive** Seeks to learn lessons from the crisis. Emphasis is on future prevention of a crisis and to function better as a crisis management team.
The External Landscape				

Figure 7.1 Proactive and Reactive Perspectives in Crisis Management

Communicating With Internal and External Stakeholders

Although Chapter 8 addresses the subject of communication more deeply, we introduce the topic briefly here. Because organizational crises usually have negative effects on internal and external stakeholders, truthful communication with both groups is crucial (Barton, 2008; Coombs, 2007). Internal stakeholders include the employees and owners of the firm. External stakeholders include customers, suppliers, the local community, and any segment of the general public that is affected by the organization's crisis. A union strike, for example, affects all of the stakeholders mentioned. Suppliers in particular should be informed of a strike and any subsequent picket lines around the organization that may be set up by union members, as delivery trucks in these areas may be subject to vandalism (Crandall & Menefee, 1996). In some cases involving larger facilities, it may be necessary to inform suppliers of alternate delivery routes and gates that may be needed to ensure safe delivery. If any danger is present, such as rock throwing or gunshots fired in the area by strikers, then the organization must communicate these potential dangers to suppliers making deliveries (Herman, 1995).

Crisis communication should meet two goals. First, the organization should initiate communications with the media. This process requires that the CMT have a clear understanding of the issues and the selection of the appropriate response, anticipate the need to communicate, and prepare press releases for the media in advance (Barton, 2008). The second goal of effective crisis communication requires the organizational spokespersons to restore and maintain stakeholder confidence. Sometimes this task may simply involve being at the scene of the crisis and working at a grassroots level to ensure that recovery efforts are being maintained. Former California Governor Arnold Schwarzenegger presided over a state that had its share of crises, from earthquakes and wildfires to urban crime and gang problems. During a string of wildfires, the governor was out in the field both encouraging firefighters and consoling victims (Walsh, 2007). Schwarzenegger earned praise during crisis events for being available to his constituents.

As previously mentioned, communications must occur quickly from the affected firm. Communications can be especially tricky when the crisis transcends several countries, however. In the following example, the trigger event for the crisis occurred at the Cannes Film Festival in France, while the backlash was felt primarily in China.

The Sharon Stone/Karma Comment Crisis

A major earthquake measuring 7.8 on the Richter scale jolted southwest China's Sichuan Province on May 12, 2008, resulting in almost 70,000 deaths. An outpouring of relief efforts from around the world followed to help the victims of this tragedy (Long, Crandall, & Parnell, 2010). However, the tragedy took a strange twist on May 24, less than two weeks after the earthquake, when actress Sharon Stone was asked her feelings on the earthquake during the Cannes Film Festival:

"Well you know it was very interesting because at first, I'm you know, I'm not happy about the ways the Chinese were treating the Tibetans because I don't think anyone should be unkind to anyone else. And so I have been very concerned about how to think and what to do about that because I don't like that. And then I've been this, you know, concerned about, oh how should we deal with the Olympics because they are not being nice to the Dalai Lama, who is a good friend of mine. And then all this earthquake and all this stuff happened and I thought: Is that karma, when you are not nice that bad things happen to you. . . ." (Gardner, 2008)

The karma comment created a wave of criticism on Internet blogs in China because the actress was suggesting that the country's earthquake was retribution for its policies on Tibet (Passariello & Meichtry, 2008). Internet postings said she was ignorant of the Tibet issue and had no sympathy for those who were suffering from the earthquake. One online comment, from a woman calling herself Mariah, summed up the reaction of many Chinese citizens: "These kind of remarks deeply hurt Chinese people's feeling and are totally unacceptable" (Roberts, 2008, p. 12).

The backlash in China was swift and powerful. Media reports described protestors tearing down billboards featuring the actress in advertisements (McLaughlin & Kaiser, 2008). In addition, many cinemas on the Chinese mainland and in Hong Kong cinemas pledged not to show her films again. Ng See-Yuen, the founder of the UME Cineplex chain, said films featuring Stone would be banned from any UME cinema in Hong Kong and the Chinese mainland. Moreover, the Shanghai International Film Festival had also decided to permanently ban Stone and her films (Du, 2008).

Consider the impact this incident had on one particular company, Dior, a French firm that offers upscale clothing, cosmetics, and apparel for women. Stone was representing the company as a model. The karma comment erupted into a crisis for the firm's Chinese branch, Dior China. On May 27, 2008, three days after the Stone comment, Dior China issued the following statement through its Shangahi office: "We absolutely disagree with and cannot understand Sharon Stone's illogical remark" (Xiao & Li, 2012, p. 30).

On May 28, Dior China issued another statement, this time quoting the actress: "I am deeply sorry and sad about hurting Chinese people" (Horyn, 2008). On May 31, Stone issued a formal apology through CNN. However, a survey of 250,000 Chinese citizens found that 69 percent did not accept her apology and vowed to never forgive her (Xinhua, 2008). Many Chinese citizens wrote letters to Dior China to express their opinions, indicating they would never buy any Dior products as long as the company was affiliated with Sharon Stone (Passariello & Meichtry, 2008). Under this pressure Dior China began removing all of its advertisements with Stone's image nationwide (McLaughlin & Kaiser, 2008). On June 2, almost one month after the earthquake, the company issued an official statement indicating it would stop using Sharon Stone as a spokesperson in China (Roberts, 2008).

Evaluating What Is Going Right and What Is Not

The evaluation process is not an activity that occurs only after the crisis ends. Evaluation is a process that begins when the crisis commences and continues throughout its duration. The more the CMT can understand what is and what is not working in the crisis response, the more easily they can adjust their plans in attacking the crisis. Because the evaluation process is so important, the following benchmark questions should be raised:

- How has the crisis affected both internal and external stakeholders' behaviors and opinions?
- To what extent have sales and share prices been affected?
- Which crisis response strategies and tactics were effective and which were not?

In reference to the first benchmark, it is important to note that public opinion can work for or against the company. Human-induced crises are usually perceived more negatively by the general public than those resulting from natural disasters. Hence, human-induced crises such as corporate scandals or other ethical violations can harm the reputation of the company (Pearson & Mitroff, 1993). In the case of a natural disaster, however, the public's perception is often that the company is the victim of an outside threat that could not be controlled. Therefore, public opinion may generally still favor the organization, depending on how the crisis is managed.

The second benchmark is important because revenues and shareholder values often decrease during a crisis (Coombs, 2006). Ralph Erben, CEO for Luby's Cafeteria, Inc., knew immediately after a gunman killed 23 people in a Killeen, Texas, restaurant on October 16, 1991, that a massive selloff of Luby's stock would follow. On his flight to Killeen to address the crisis, he called the New York Stock Exchange and requested that stock sales be suspended (Barton, 2001).

Some crises can leave a lingering impact on an industry for years. Consider the travel and tourism industry; part of the overall crisis management effort is not just to keep guests safe, but to keep them traveling back to tourist destinations (Ali & Ali, 2010). Nonetheless, the September 11, 2001, terrorist attacks, Hurricane Katrina in 2005, and the deadly 2004 tsunami that struck coastal communities along the Indian Ocean have all created both primary crises, the events themselves with their destruction and fatalities, and secondary crises, a loss of tourism in the affected areas (Kondraschow, 2006). Events such as these have created the "tourism crisis," which is "any unexpected event that affects traveler confidence in a destination and interferes with its (i.e., the economic entities that support that destination) ability to continue operating normally" (World Tourism Organisation, 1998).

The third benchmark should be a reminder that not all crisis response strategies will be successful and that changes may be necessary. Even a CMP recommended strategy may need to be altered. In the Luby's case, the company's crisis management plan called for the marketing manager to speak with the media. However, due to the severity of the massacre, CEO Erben decided that it would be better if he served as the spokesperson (Barton, 2001).

Understanding whether the crisis management effort has been effective requires the gathering of necessary information. Methods that can be used to obtain the information necessary include:

- Tracking sales and profits during and after the crisis
- Establishing a special communication avenue for stakeholders to call with questions and comments about the crisis and how it was managed
- Conducting focus groups to obtain information from key stakeholders
- Conducting surveys of external publics to determine their attitudes
- Documenting the information flow to and from the news media
- Documenting the information about those strategies that worked and those that did not work, and investigating why they were or were not effective (Caponigro, 2000)

The End of the Crisis: Getting the Organization Back on Its Feet

After the immediate crisis, the work of picking up the pieces and going forward begins. It is here that advanced planning, perhaps from the CMP, can help accelerate the recovery and minimize the long-term negative effects of the disaster. During the recovery, the CMT needs to take stock, assess the damage, and determine what resources are readily available to the organization. In some ways the struggle is similar to the startup phase for a business in that it must think strategically and take an entrepreneurial approach to solving future crisis matters (Munneke & Davis, 2004). Business continuity focuses on getting the organization back on its feet after a major crisis. This can be viewed as a subarea of crisis management whereby the functions of the business are restored so that day-to-day operations can continue (Herbane, 2010).

Business Continuity

Business continuity refers to the ability of the business to resume or continue activities after a crisis occurs. Essentially, business continuity is about maintaining the important business functions during and after a crisis. Meeting customer demand is important, especially when a company is a key player in a supply chain network (Zsidisin, Melnyk, & Ragatz, 2005). A crisis can affect the core functional areas of marketing, accounting, financial management, human resource management, and manufacturing. Two areas especially prone to an interruption are the organization's management information system and its production operations capabilities.

MIS and Production Operations

There are a number of companies that help organizations restore their MIS when it has been damaged. Such disaster recovery firms can provide backup software and computer equipment in an emergency. Some organizations, in preparation for a major MIS disaster, have alternate worksites prearranged for possible use in the event that a crisis takes down their primary operating facility. A hot site is a facility that has all of the backup equipment and electronic connections required to operate the business. A cold site is a facility that lacks such equipment but is ready to be equipped when needed. Somewhere in between these classifications are warm sites, which offer some but not all of the equipment and connections necessary to operate the business (Bartlett, 2007).

When the crisis is over and the immediate threat has passed, the firm moves from a crisis response mode to a crisis recovery posture. The recovery effort depends on the extent of the damage that has taken place. For example, in the tourism industry, weather and natural disasters are two of the main crises that organizations experience (Pennington-Gray, Thapa, Kaplanidou, Cahyanto, & McLaughlin, 2011). As a result, some firms are closed for months because the business was either totally destroyed or suffered major damage as a result of the crisis. Other firms that have experienced relatively minor damage may be able to open within a few hours or days. Some companies may remain open but have business units that are not operational because of localized damage, a common occurrence after a crisis such as a hurricane. Chain restaurants and retail stores are examples of companies that may have geographically specific damage.

Assessing the state of business operations after the crisis helps determine the decisions that must be made next. Managers must assess whether the firm has the ability to meet the needs of its stakeholders or not. If substantial rebuilding is necessary, it is probably a good time to upgrade the facility. A new and more modern plant may be built, upgraded manufacturing equipment may be secured, and/or a new management information system may be implemented.

Employee Needs After the Crisis

When employees are out of work because of a disaster at the business, there is a good chance that they may not be able to return once the business is functioning again. Employees need to support their families and are likely to secure employment elsewhere if their economic needs are great. As a result, some companies keep displaced employees on the payroll, but this move is feasible only if the company has the resources to do so. The Malden Mills fire is an example of a crisis that took multiple turns as the firm sought to recover from a devastating 1995 fire.

The Malden Mills Fire

A fire in Lawrence, Massachusetts, on December 11, 1995, commenced as an apparent boiler explosion at the Malden Mills complex. The plant manufactured fleece, a textile component in clothing and upholstery fabric, and had about 700 employees at the time. This single explosion led to a series of additional explosions, all of which were believed to be rupturing gas lines. These escalating events caused the fire to spread quickly. More than 200 firefighters fought the blaze, some coming from as far away as New Hampshire and Boston ("December 11, 1995," 2005). Although there were no fatalities, 33 people were injured, eight critically (McCurry, 1997).

CEO Aaron Feuerstein made a decision after the fire that proved to be fateful: (1) to rebuild the manufacturing facilities; and, (2) to pay the employees during the rebuilding process. Both decisions were expensive, especially considering that cash flow was compromised. Feuerstein received positive publicity for his decision to keep the employees on the payroll. His move was touted as a good model of employer–employee loyalty (Fisher, Schoenfeldt, & Shaw, 2003).

However, the decision to pay the employees came at a great cost to the company. While it generated waves of good press, it severely depleted cash reserves. In 2001, the company went through bankruptcy, partly due to the $100 million debt it took on after the fire in 1995. These tough financial times were also influenced by several unexpected factors, including warm weather the previous year (which hurt product sales), the loss of a key customer, and an abundance of fleece knockoffs entering the market (Moreno, 2003). The resulting declines in sales and cash flow devastated the company while it was still reeling from the debt it had incurred after the fire.

In hindsight, CEO Feuerstein may have actually contributed to a second crisis years down the road: bankruptcy. Many textile firms closed, outsourcing their production to companies in China and other nations during this time. Feuerstein not only paid his employees while they were not working but also opened up the plant in the center of an expensive labor market. "While Mr. Feuerstein kept all of his employees on the payroll, using insurance money, in part, the company wound up with $100 million in additional debt, the seed of his subsequent undoing" (Pacelle, 2003). However, it is also true that markets such as the one in which Malden Mills operates can be tough and are subject to environmental jolts, as discussed in Chapter 3.

Feuerstein was eventually forced to retire in 2004 amid a turnaround strategy led by a new wave of management. In 2007, the company became part of Chrysalis Capital Partners and now operates under the name Polartec (Clark, 2007). The complexity of the Malden Mills case and the unusual twists that took place after the fire reinforce the idea that paying for the wages of employees during the reconstruction of a business devastated by a disaster must be taken cautiously.

Summary

Actions when disaster hits occur in three stages. Certain responses and tactics are conducted when the crisis begins, when its effects are most pronounced, and when it is at a closing stage. At the beginning of the crisis, the CMT should meet and begin the situational analysis. As information about the crisis begins to unfold, strategies for how to manage the event can then be developed. Some of these strategies may originate from the crisis management plan, while others may have roots in the plan but need to be adjusted for use in the particular crisis at hand. The company spokesperson should be planning a media strategy.

The mid-crisis stage is focused on response and mitigation. Efforts should be made to contain the damage and to respond to internal and external stakeholders' needs. Assessments should be made as to which crisis response strategies are working and which ones should be altered. As the crisis nears its end, the response is geared to assessing the damage and getting the organization up and running again.

Questions for Discussion

1. What actions should be taken when the crisis is just beginning?

2. What are the desirable leadership traits for the CMT leader?

3. What is meant by situational assessment in crisis management? What problems can be created when mistakes are made in the situational assessment stage?

4. What are the major decisions that should be made during the management of the crisis event?

5. Why is it important to establish and monitor an information-gathering system?

6. What is damage containment?

7. Why is it important to have consistent and continuous communication with the internal and external stakeholders?

8. Why is there a need to evaluate what is going right and what is going wrong in the management of the crisis?

9. What is business continuity and why is it important?

Chapter Exercise

Divide the class into groups of three to five students. Each group will represent a crisis management team that is addressing the following scenario:

Suppose a major snowstorm is about to hit your campus in the next 12 hours.[2] Weather information indicates that widespread power outages are likely and travel will be nearly impossible once the blizzard arrives. It is the first week of February and most students have been back on campus for several weeks following the holiday break. Convene your team and discuss the following questions.

1. What actions should be taken immediately? In other words, within 4 to 6 hours before the arrival of the storm? As you discuss this question, consider the following:

   Who will be the key leader on campus during this crisis?

   Which stakeholders should the communication spokesperson address and what messages should be conveyed?

What type of information-monitoring requirements will your team need during the crisis?

What possible crises could occur during the storm?

2. During the storm, what actions should be taken? Be sure to consider the following items:

How will you monitor the extent of the damage that occurs across the campus? Keep in mind that some communication networks may be compromised due to power outages.

What will be the main objectives of the CMT during the storm?

What social media tools and strategies can you use during the storm?

3. After the storm has passed, what actions should the CMT take? Keep in mind the following items:

What are the main priorities that must be addressed?

How will you assess the damage on campus?

What messages should be communicated to the students, parents, faculty, and staff?

What messages should be communicated to traditional and social media?

Opening Case, Part 4: The BP Gulf of Mexico Oil Spill

The resulting oil spill after the 2010 sinking of the *Deepwater Horizon* created an enormous environmental nightmare in the Gulf of Mexico. Attempts to stop the leak were largely unsuccessful for nearly three months. A number of stakeholders felt the need to comment on the event, including politicians, the general public, the media, and industry experts. One message was consistent from BP's external stakeholders: there was little sympathy for the company. In the section that follows, we examine how each company blamed the other for the accident.

The Blame Game

BP contracted the work of drilling the well to Transocean. BP also contracted Halliburton to seal the well with cement. However, one of the key roles that BP had was in determining the integrity of the well seal through its use of the negative pressure test. The official response of each firm follows.

Transocean

Of the companies involved in the accident, Transocean was the most aggressive in denying blame (Barrett, 2011). In a statement before a Senate panel, Transocean's CEO Steven Newman put the blame on Halliburton, the company contracted to cement the drill casing in place (Holly, 2010). However, in an internal investigative report, the company also blamed BP for its misinterpretation of the negative pressure test on the well (Polczer, 2011). A correct understanding of the test results is essential to determine whether gas is leaking from the well or not. Transocean also blamed BP for its role in creating a "fatally flawed well design" ("Contractors," 2010, p. 24).

Much of the blame for the accident, though, has been directed toward Transocean. One of the key points of criticism has been the company's inspection of the blowout preventer (BOP). The BOP was constructed by another contractor, Cameron International, but Transocean is required to maintain the equipment.

Halliburton

Halliburton was the company contracted to cement the drill casing and seal the well. The firm maintains that the cement it used was stable and was not a factor in the well explosion (Russell, 2010). Stability is an important function of cement, which must be able to withstand the pressures of the deep well environment. In addition, the cement slurry must be nonpermeable, lest hydrocarbon gasses escape from the well and into the drill casing.

BP

Immediately after the accident, an irate Tony Hayward lamented that it wasn't his company's accident, but that it was the fault of the subcontractor, Transocean, and its faulty BOP (Elkind et al., 2011). An internal report completed in September 2010 confirms his initial response, spreads the blame across contractors, and also adds the element of sequential failures to the accident (Cook, 2010). Specifically, BP puts the blame on both the cementing job by Halliburton and the failure of the BOP provided by Transocean. The accident was sequential in their findings; hence, both failures were necessary to cause the disaster.

The U.S. Coast Guard

The U.S. Coast Guard was active in the search-and-rescue efforts immediately after the rig explosion. The Coast Guard also investigates and issues its report whenever there are accidents involving fatalities at sea. Their findings put the blame largely on Transocean, citing the company's poor maintenance of electrical equipment and lack of training on how the crew should shut down engines and disconnect the drilling rig from the well in the event of a gas buildup (Rickman, 2011). In addition, their report expressed concern over why gas alarms and automatic shutdown systems were not operating correctly. Such systems would have been instrumental in powering down equipment that could generate ignition sources that could cause an explosion in the presence of hydrocarbon gasses.

The Obama Administration

President Barack Obama held BP liable for cleanup costs and damages. Estimates for the cleanup costs were around $40 billion (Sawayda & Jackson, 2011). BP divested assets to help finance the cleanup bill, selling assets that were not essential to its core operations. In July 2010, BP sold some oil and gas assets to Apache Corporation for $7 billion to generate necessary cash (Chazan & Chon 2010).

The Departure of Tony Hayward

Tony Hayward became the target of criticism for BP. Many considered his performance as a spokesperson after the accident to be poor. Hayward had become CEO after his predecessor, John Browne, had to step down because of a personal scandal (Elkind et al., 2011). Now, Hayward would have to step down as well. His ability to handle the media hit a low point when he made an infamous gaffe while talking informally about the accident, stating, "I'd like my life back." The comment was viewed by many as being insensitive and became the subject of much debate.

Succeeding Hayward on October 1, 2010, was BP veteran Robert Dudley, an American who was head of U.S. operations. The move to replace Hayward by the BP board was seen as an effort to repair the company's reputation and to restore the confidence of the U.S. market (Orwall et al., 2010).

Opening Case Part 4 Questions

1. What is the responsibility of a general subcontractor such as BP when overseeing the work of its subcontractors?

2. After hearing all of the evidence in this case, what are your conclusions as to which parties are at fault in the cause of this accident?

Opening Case Part 4 References

Barrett, P. (2011, July 4). Success is never having to say you're sorry. *Bloomberg Businessweek*, 54–62.

Chazan, G., & Chon, G. (2010, July 21). The Gulf oil spill: BP sells $7 billion of assets to help fund cleanup. *Wall Street Journal*, p. A7.

Contractors slam "self-serving" BP spill report; Dudley takes charge. (2010, October). *Petroleum Economist*, 24.

Cook, N. (2010). Deepwater Horizon. *RoSPA Occupational Safety and Health Journal, 40*(12), 13–17.

Elkind, P., Whitford, D., & Burke, D. (2011, February 7). An accident waiting to happen. *Fortune*, 105–132.

Holly, C. (2010, May 12). Transocean blames oil spill on cementing: BP cites blowout preventer. *Energy Daily*, Issue 89, 2.

Orwall, B., Langley, M., & Herron, J. (2010, July 26). Embattled BP chief to exit—American Robert Dudley to succeed Tony Hayward as head of British oil giant. *Wall Street Journal*, p. A1.

Polczer, S. (2011). Transocean report blames BP for Macondo blowout. *Petroleum Economist, 78*(6), 34.

Rickman, J. (2011, May 3). Coast Guard spill report raps Transocean "deficiencies." *Energy Daily*, Issue 84, 3.

Russell, P. (2010). Halliburton rebuts contention it botched Gulf mud mix. *Engineering News-Record, 265*(13), 60.

Sawayda, J., & Jackson, J. (2011). BP struggles to resolve sustainability disaster. In O. C. Ferrell, John Fraedrich, and Linda Ferrell (Eds.), *Business ethics: Ethical decision making and cases* (9th ed., pp. 342–354). Mason, OH: South-Western Cengage Learning.

Notes

1. Thrifty operated about 1,000 pharmacies on the West Coast of the United States. Rite Aid acquired Thrifty in 1996.

2. If your campus is not in an area where snow is a problem, then substitute a torrential rainstorm in this scenario.

References

Ali, S., & Ali, A. (2010). A conceptual framework for crisis planning and management in the Jordanian tourism industry. *Advances in Management, 3*(7), 59–65.

Baran, B., & Adelman, M. (2010). Preparing for the unthinkable: Leadership development for organizational crises. *Industrial and Organizational Psychology, 3*, 45–47.

Barnard, B. (1987, March 10). Ferry loss raises questions: Concept of roll-on vessels faces spotlight again. *Journal of Commerce*, 16A.

Bartlett, N. (2007). Ready for trouble. *Credit Union, 73*(2), 38–42.

Barton, L. (2001). *Crisis in organizations II*. Cincinnati: South-Western.

Barton, L. (2008). *Crisis leadership now: A real-world guide to preparing for threat, disaster, sabotage, and scandal*. New York: McGraw-Hill.

Berinato, S. (2010). You have to lead from everywhere. *Harvard Business Review, 88*(11), 76–79.

Borodzicz, E., & van Haperen, K. (2002). Individual and group learning in crisis simulations. *Journal of Contingencies and Crisis Management, 10*(3), 139–147.

Boston, R. (2000, February). False prophets, real profits. *Church and State*, 13–15.

Caponigro, J. (2000). *The crisis counselor: A step-by-step guide to managing a business crisis*. Chicago: Contemporary Books.

Cavanaugh, J. (2003). Coolness under fire: A conversation with James Cavanaugh. *Leadership in Action, 23*(5), 7.

Clark, D. (2007, March 20). Malden exits bankruptcy as Polartec. *Women's Wear Daily*, 10.

Coombs, W. T. (2006). *Code red in the board room: Crisis management as organizational DNA*. Westport, CT: Praeger.

Coombs, W. (2007). *Ongoing crisis communication: Planning, managing, and responding* (2nd ed.). Thousand Oaks, CA: Sage.

Cowan, D. E. (2003). Confronting the failed failure: Y2K and evangelical eschatology in light of the passed millennium. *Nova Religio: The Journal of Alternative and Emergent Religions, 7*(2), 71–85.

Crandall, W., & Menefee, M. (1996). Crisis management in the midst of labor strife: Preparing for the worst. *SAM Advanced Management Journal, 61*(1), 11–15.

Crichton, M., Lauche, K., & Flin, R. (2005). Incident command skills in the management of an oil industry drilling incident: A case study. *Journal of Contingencies and Crisis Management, 13*(3), 116–128.

December 11, 1995: Fire destroys Malden Mills. (2005, December 11). *Mass Moments*. Retrieved June 8, 2012, from http://massmoments.org/moment.cfm?mid=355.

Donahue, B. (2004). True leadership in a crisis. *Convenience Store Decisions, 15*(9), 6.

Du, W. (2008, May 30). Netizens annoyed by Stone's ignorance. *China Daily Online*. Retrieved June 7, 2012, from http://www.chinadaily.com.cn/china/2008–05/30/content_6724266.htm.

Duhe, S., & Zoch, L. (1994). A case study: Framing the media's agenda during a crisis. *Public Relations Quarterly, 39*(4), 42–45.

Elliott, D., & Smith, D. (1993). Football stadia disasters in the United Kingdom: Learning from tragedy? *Industrial and Environmental Crisis Quarterly, 7*(3), 205–229.

Endsley, M., & Garland, D. (2000). *Situation awareness, analysis, and measurement.* Mahwah, NJ: Lawrence Erlbaum.

Fisher, C., Schoenfeldt, L., & Shaw, J. (2003). *Human resource management* (5th ed.). Boston: Houghton Mifflin.

Gardner, D. (2008). Why do we say silly things? *Ottawa Citizen.* Retrieved June 7, 2012, from http://www.canada.com/ottawacitizen/columnists/story.html?id=81b2c80c-ddc3–4f4c-94a3–6f9c98f8f608.

Gleason, S., & Berry, I. (2012, April 3). Beef processor falters amid "slime." *Wall Street Journal,* p. B2.

Herbane, B. (2010). The evolution of business continuity management: A historical review of practices and drivers. *Business History, 52*(6), 978–1002.

Herman, M. (1995). When strikes turn violent. *Security Management, 39*(3), 32–35.

Horyn, C. (2008, June 1). Insensitive, Yes. But sorry? Well . . . *New York Times,* p. 2.

Institute for Crisis Management. (2011). *Annual ICM crisis report: News coverage of business crises during 2010.* Retrieved April 8, 2012, from http://crisisconsultant.com/images/2010CrisisReportICM.pdf.

Kondraschow, R. (2006). The lessons of disaster. *Journal of Retail and Leisure Property, 5*(3), 204–211.

Langfitt, F. (2006). Covering the Sago Mine disaster: How a game of "whisper down the coal mine" ricocheted around the world. *Nieman Reports, 60*(2), 103–104.

Leskin, G. A., Morland, L., Whealin, J., Everly, G., Litz, B., & Keane, T. (2004). *Factsheet: Fostering resilience in response to terrorism for psychologists working with first responders.* Washington, DC: American Psychological Association.

Long, Z., Crandall, W. R., & Parnell, J. (2010). A trilogy of unfortunate events in China: Reflecting on the management of crises. *International Journal of Asian Business and Information Management, 1*(4), 21–30.

McCurry, J. (1997). Loyalty saves Malden Mills. *Textile World, 147*(2), 38–45.

McLaughlin, K., & Kaiser, A. (2008, May 30). Dior China drops Stone after quake comments. *Women's Wear Daily,* 24–25.

McMinn, L. (2001). Y2K, the apocalypse, and evangelical Christianity: The role of eschatological belief in church responses. *Sociology of Religion, 62*(2), 205–220.

Miller, A. (2001). The Los Angeles riots: A study of crisis paralysis. *Journal of Contingencies and Crisis Management, 9*(4), 189–199.

Mitroff, I., & Anagnos, G. (2001). *Managing crises before they happen.* New York: AMACOM.

Moreno, K. (2003, April 14). Trial by fire. *Forbes,* 92.

Munneke, G., & Davis, A. (2004). Disaster recovery for law firms. In *The essential formbook: Comprehensive management tools for lawyers: Vol. IV. Disaster planning and recovery* (pp. 59–67). Chicago: American Bar Association, Law Practice Management Section.

Olasky, M. (2006). *The politics of disaster: Katrina, Big Government, and a new strategy for future crisis.* Nashville: W Publishing Group.

Pacelle, M. (2003, May 9). Through the mill: Can Mr. Feuerstein save his business one last time? *Wall Street Journal,* p. A1.

Passariello, C., & Meichtry, S. (2008, May 30). Dior pulls ads with Sharon Stone. *Wall Street Journal,* p. B.7.

Pearson, C., & Mitroff, I. (1993). From crisis prone to crisis prepared: A framework for crisis management. *Academy of Management Executive, 7*(1), 48–59.

Pearson, C., & Rondinelli, D. (1998). Crisis management in Central European firms. *Business Horizons, 41*(3), 50–59.

Pennington-Gray, L., Thapa, B., Kaplanidou, K., Cahyanto, I. & McLaughlin, E. (2011). Crisis planning and preparedness in the United States Tourism Industry. *Cornell Hospitality Quarterly, 52*(3), 312–320.

Powell, L., Hickson, III, M., Self, W. R., & Bodon, J. (2001). The role of religion and responses to the Y2K macro-crisis. *North American Journal of Psychology, 3*(2), 295–302.

Preble, J. (1997). Integrating the crisis management perspective into the strategic management process. *Journal of Management Studies, 34*(5), 669–791.

Roberts, D. (2008, June 2). China: Multinationals hear it online. *Business Week Online.* Retrieved June 7, 2012, from http://www.businessweek.com/globalbiz/content/may2008/gb20080530_213248.htm.

Rolston, L., & McNerney, D. (2003). Leading during times of crisis. *Innovative Leader, 12*(5), 1–2.

Schoenberg, A. (2005). Do crisis plans matter? A new perspective on leading during a crisis. *Public Relations Quarterly, 50*(1), 2–6.

Sklarewitz, N. (1991, May). Cruise company handles crisis by the book. *Public Relations Journal,* 34–36.

Solomon, C. (1992, July). The LA riots: An HR diary. *Personnel Journal,* 22–29.

Taylor, P. (1990). *The Hillsborough stadium disaster.* Final Report. London: Home Office.

Technical Series Report 110. (1995). United States Fire Administration, FEMA. J. Gordon Routley, Editor and Scott M. Howell, Investigator.

Walsh, K. (2007, November 19). A film hero up to playing the real role. *U.S. News & World Report,* 50–51.

Weick, K. (1993). The collapse of sensemaking in organizations: The Mann Gulch disaster. *Administrative Science Quarterly, 38,* 628–652.

Wheatley, M. (2006, Summer). Leadership lessons from the real world. *Leader to Leader, 41,* 16–20.

Wilson, J. (2004, June 21–July 11). Now the disaster's happened, what am I supposed to do? *Accounting Today,* 24–25.

Wilson, S. (2003). Develop an effective crisis-management strategy. *Chemical Engineering Progress, 99*(9), 58–61.

Wooten, L., & James, E. (2008). Linking crisis management and leadership competencies: The role of human resource development. *Advances in Developing Human Resources, 10*(3), 352–379.

World Tourism Organisation. (2010). *Handbook on natural disaster reduction in tourist areas.* Madrid: World Tourism Organisation.

Xiao, J., & Li, H. (2012). Online discussion of Sharon Stone's karma comment on China earthquake: The intercultural communication of media events in the age of media convergence. *China Media Research, 8*(1), 25–39.

Xinhua. (2008, May 29). Stone's quake "karma" apology doesn't mollify many Chinese. *China Daily Online.* Retrieved June 7, 2012, from http://www.chinadaily.com.cn/china/2008–05/29/content_6721642.htm.

Zsidisin, G., Melnyk, S., & Ragatz, G. (2005). An institutional theory perspective of business continuity planning for purchasing and supply management. *Internal Journal of Production Research, 43*(16), 3401–3420.

CHAPTER 8

Crisis Communication

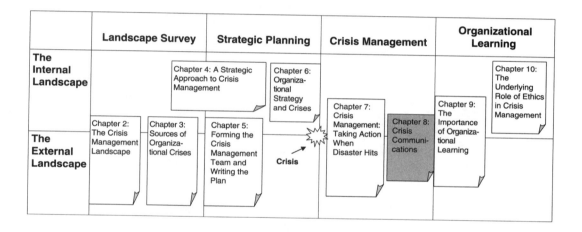

	Landscape Survey		Strategic Planning		Crisis Management		Organizational Learning
The Internal Landscape			Chapter 4: A Strategic Approach to Crisis Management	Chapter 6: Organizational Strategy and Crises			Chapter 10: The Underlying Role of Ethics in Crisis Management
The External Landscape	Chapter 2: The Crisis Management Landscape	Chapter 3: Sources of Organizational Crises	Chapter 5: Forming the Crisis Management Team and Writing the Plan	**Crisis**	Chapter 7: Crisis Management: Taking Action When Disaster Hits	Chapter 8: Crisis Communications	Chapter 9: The Importance of Organizational Learning

Opening Case: The Domino's Boogergate Incident

On Easter Sunday in April 2009, two Domino's Pizza employees posted a video on YouTube showing one of the employees sticking cheese up his nose and then putting it on a sandwich. Because of this and other unsanitary acts in the video, it earned the infamous name "Boogergate" (York & Wheaton, 2009). The now-former employees, Kristy Hammonds and Michael Setzer, were not teenage pranksters but were both in their thirties, which made the event seem even more serious to Domino's top management (Jacques, 2009).

Domino's responded aggressively, but only after an agonizing daylong wait by the general public. Indeed, to understand why the wait was so important; one must look at the sequence of events that occurred:

Easter Sunday: The video is recorded in the store. The two employees are obviously bored because no orders are coming in, a fact that was confirmed by the store's computer system. Hence, despite the comments by Michael Setzer in the video, the sandwich in question was never intended for delivery to a customer (Jacques, 2009).

Monday: The video had been posted and received nearly 1 million views before it was taken off YouTube on Wednesday (York & Wheaton, 2009). Meanwhile, a blog site, *The Consumerist,* posted the video as well. It was not until 11:00 P.M. on Monday night that the store and the two employees had been identified (Jacques, 2009). Ironically, two readers of the *Consumerist* blog identified the store location. Using the Jack-in-the-Box sign visible from the window in the video as a clue, they used a Google satellite images and street views to confirm the Conover, North Carolina, location (York & Wheaton, 2009).

Tuesday: In the morning, Domino's notifies the owner of the store and the local health department and advises the police of the identity of the two employees. As the day progresses, the company works on a response using Twitter, with help from an outside public relations company. The company staffers issue tweets indicating Domino's is aware of the problem. They also refer people to the Domino's website, which has issued a formal statement addressing the crisis (Zerillo, 2009).

Wednesday: Domino's decides to address the crisis by targeting the audience that would be most aware of it: those who spend a lot of time on the Internet, particularly YouTube. By Wednesday afternoon, Patrick Doyle, president of Domino USA, is briefed and prepares to record a video indicating the response of the company, which will be posted on YouTube. Later in the day, the video is recorded and posted on both the company website and YouTube (Jacques, 2009). In the video, Patrick Doyle is both serious and angry.

"We sincerely apologize for this incident. We thank members of the online community who quickly alerted us and allowed us to take immediate action. Although the individuals in question claim it's a hoax, we are taking this incredibly seriously," he said, also adding that the company is revamping its selection processes so that "people like this don't make it into our stores" (York & Wheaton, 2009, p. 24).

Despite its slow response with the YouTube video—almost 48 hours after the incident—Domino's was praised by public relations experts for its tactics in handling the crisis. In fact, several cited this event as a landmark case in crisis management (Beaubien, 2009; Johnson, 2009; York & Wheaton, 2009). The Domino's incident illustrates the merit in the old adage of "learning to fight fire with fire." In this case, Domino's used its own YouTube video to counter a YouTube-induced crisis in order to best respond to concerned consumers (Zerillo, 2009).

Opening Case Discussion Questions

Access the original video from *The Consumerist* at http://consumerist.com/2009/04/dominos-rogue-employees-do-disgusting-things-to-the-food-put-it-on-youtube.html.

1. Why do you think these employees made the video?

2. What information is available online about these two employees?

3. How can Domino's reduce the chances of this type of activity occurring again?

   Now access the response video by Domino's at http://www.youtube.com/watch?feature=endscreen&NR=1&v=dem6eA7-A2I.

4. Why is the company's response effective?

5. Is there anything you would have recommended to Domino's to improve this video?

Opening Case References

Beaubien, G. (2009). Domino's YouTube flap: "A landmark event in crisis management." *Public Relations Tactics, 16*(5), 4.

Jacques, A. (2009). Domino's delivers during crisis: The company's step-by-step response after a vulgar video goes viral. *The Strategist, 15*(3), 6–10.

Johnson, C. (2009). Social media in crisis: Blog and Tweet your way back to success. *Public Relations Strategist, 15*(2), 23–24.

York, E., & Wheaton, K. (2009). What Domino's did right—and wrong—in squelching hubbub over YouTube video. *Advertising Age, 80*(14), 1, 24.

Zerillo, N. (2009). Crisis forces Domino's to revamp social media plan. *PRWeek, 12*(16), 1, 20.

Introduction

Crisis communications has undergone a dramatic shift in the past five years. Social media tools such as YouTube, Twitter, Facebook, and blog pages have changed the entire way we view the communication function. "With social media and the 24-hour news cycle, there will never again be a major disaster that won't involve public participation" (Berinato, 2010, p. 78). Much of what has been taught about crisis communications in the past still holds true. However, with social media, there is a greater need to be ever more cognizant of what is said about the organization in the online environment. Moreover, communications to the public after a crisis need to be made in a matter of minutes, perhaps a few hours at the most. In the "old days" of crisis communications, it was acceptable to wait 24 hours before making a public statement to the media. Today, 24 hours is just too long to wait.

Communication strategies are necessary to successfully manage a crisis. The crisis management team (CMT) needs accurate information in order to communicate quickly to its stakeholders. Issues of fear, hostility, and anger can complicate an already complex situation, and communications can become distorted and inaccurate. These complexities often result in rumors and imprecise information over the Internet that can make the situation worse. Hence, creating a communication structure and flow of information that is objective, truthful, and timely is necessary to inform internal and external stakeholders about the crisis management activities.

The more effective the communication, the better the prospects for resolving the crisis successfully. This chapter discusses crisis management communication practices, how they affect the respective stakeholders, and how the crisis communication function can be managed effectively.

Crisis management and crisis communication are intricately interlinked. As Scanlon (1975) recognized long ago, "Every crisis is also a crisis of information." He goes on to say, "Failure to control the crisis of information can ultimately result in a failure to control the crisis" (p. 431). The study of organizational crisis communication has resulted in a greater understanding of the role communication plays in both defining the origin of a crisis and launching the crisis recovery plan (Spillan, Rowles, & Mino, 2002/2003).

This chapter begins with a discussion on crisis communication basics, which includes communicating with both internal and external stakeholders. This section covers more of the traditional practices used in crisis communications that have been in existence for several decades. We then address a newer form of communication—social media—and how it has influenced the crisis communication function. In this section we offer guidelines on using social media as part of the organization's crisis response. An evaluation of the effectiveness of the crisis communication function is offered next. We conclude the chapter with insights on the training needed for effective crisis communication.

Crisis Communication Basics

Communication strategies for crisis management are needed to explain the pre-crisis and postcrisis plans to all affected stakeholders (Coombs, 2007; Heath, 1997; Pauchant & Mitroff, 1992; Seeger, Sellnow, & Ulmer, 1998; Sturges, 1994). The old adage that "perception is reality" should also be remembered. "Communication provides for the interpretation of the informational environment communally. It sets the stage for how those individuals outside the organization are likely to make sense of the crisis event" (Seeger et al., 1998, p. 235). In the following sections, we overview the basic components of the communication process.

Initiating the Communication Process

When a crisis commences, activating the crisis management team is the first step in managing the event. The CMT will execute the crisis management plan (CMP), which contains communication strategies as part of the crisis response. This part of the plan can be thought of as the organization's crisis communication plan. The purpose of a crisis communication plan is to develop procedures for communicating with internal and external stakeholders during a crisis. The main goal of communications is conveying what has happened and what plans are in place to address the crisis (Nelson, 2004). Communications with stakeholders must be carried out in an expedient manner. It enhances the credibility of the organization and builds trust. The communicated messages should satisfy the unique requirements of each audience and provide the tone, context, and consistency of all additional messages. The point to remember is that the objective and the key messages are consistent, while the detail and delivery methods may vary depending on the audience (Nelson, 2004).

Crisis Communication With Internal Stakeholders

When a crisis strikes the organization, there are two functions that must be addressed concerning communication with internal stakeholders. First, managing the crisis requires a command-and-control function that involves management, the owners, and selected employees. Second, the general employee population needs to be updated on the status of the crisis and how it has affected the organization and what can be expected in the future in terms of its resolution. Each of these issues is examined in more detail.

The Command-and-Control Function

The location of the command center and its accompanying facilities is important to the successful management of the crisis. The command center is the physical area where the company spokesperson and members of the media can communicate. In addition, the physical location should be equipped to disseminate information to stakeholders who are not in the immediate vicinity of the organization. Equipment such as telephones, computer connections, Internet access, appropriate seating facilities, and other infrastructure items are required. It is also feasible to arrange for appropriate video conferencing capabilities (Chandler & Wallace, 2008). Such an arrangement would be useful if the crisis management team is disbursed over a wide geographical area. A mobile system is useful when the crisis involves coordination among multiple locations. Information can be monitored and reported to a central command center where it is assessed, and then it can be determined what strategies to follow to mitigate the crisis (Yuan & Detlor, 2005).

It is common for a large company with a designated corporate headquarters to experience a crisis "in the field," that is, at the unit level. Such would be the case if a restaurant or retail chain experienced a crisis at one of its stores. Under these conditions, the crisis and communication response is typically directed from the home office. The Chi-Chi's hepatitis A illness, the Wendy's finger incident, and the Luby's Cafeteria murders (addressed in previous chapters) were all directed from locations above the unit level. This is not unexpected, since the home office is where the company resources of public relations and crisis expertise are located. Sometimes, however, the home office does not find out about the crisis until an inopportune moment arises. The Domino's YouTube crisis at the beginning of the chapter illustrates this type of situation. This situation occurred with Bowater Incorporated during a weather event involving severe fog.

Bowater Incorporated's Southern Division, a newsprint manufacturer in Calhoun, Tennessee, experienced a horrific crisis on December 11, 1990. At 9:05 A.M. a massive 99-vehicle accident occurred on Interstate 75, about 2 miles from the plant. For years, complaints about industrial fog produced by the mill's aeration ponds had been directed at the company (McLaren, 1994). Ironically, the multi-vehicle accident started when a speeding car collided with one of the company's tractor-trailer trucks on the interstate. The resulting smoke, along with the already present fog, created a whiteout condition that made visibility impossible for drivers near the accident scene. The accident was the worst in Tennessee's history, with 12 motorists perishing in the resulting collisions and fires. Communication within the company was haphazard after the incident. The chairman of the board did not learn of the event until watching the evening news (Maggart, 1994). Internal communications within the company, which consisted of various mills in different locations of the southeastern United States, was haphazard to nonexistent. Some of the other mills received telephone calls shortly after the wreck, unaware that the accident had even taken place.

Communications to the Organization's Employees

Employees are critical to the success of any crisis management communication. They are continuously on the front line of the action and must also communicate with external stakeholders such as customers on a daily basis. In this role, they act as ambassadors for the company and thus should be kept abreast on how management is addressing the crisis (Weiner, 2006). It is also important to communicate with employees who are not directly involved in managing the crisis or responding directly to outside stakeholders. Indeed, employees must also respond to questions from friends, neighbors, and clients (Valentine, 2007). Depending on the crisis, some employees may be apprehensive and fear losing their jobs as a result of the crisis. Keeping them focused on the day-to-day operations can offer reassurance and help maintain morale (Argenti, 2002; Reilly, 2008).

With the growth of the Internet, many organizations have used their company Web pages as a means of communicating with employees and other stakeholders during a crisis (Ulmer, Sellnow, & Seeger, 2007). This form of one-way communication remains a potent weapon in an organization's crisis communications arsenal. When a problem is detected, details of the event and its effects on consumers, employees, and the community can be posted. Utilizing the company intranet (not to be confused with the organization's Internet Web page) can be an excellent way to update employees using more of a two-way form of communication. Setting up a discussion board just for employee access can be therapeutic and enable socialization to continue, especially if employees are geographically separated, say, for example, because of storm damage in the area (Premeaux & Breaux, 2007). Providing a toll-free hotline for employees to call to obtain updates is also useful. During Hurricane Katrina, McDonald's used its toll-free numbers to communicate with employees and also to account for any employees who might be missing as a result of the storm (Marquez, 2005).

One analogy that applies to employee communication during a crisis is the classic "mushroom" problem. Employees often complain that downward communication from management is often infrequent or nonexistent when something goes wrong in the organization. This results in a situation where they feel like a mushroom—"They keep us in the dark and feed us garbage" (Reilly, 2008, p. 335). The remedy, of course, is to keep employees informed, even if the news is not always positive. Otherwise, they may be forced to speculate on what the news actually is; and speculation is dangerous because it can launch a wave of rumors. Employees are generally concerned about their companies and want to be updated with frequent and candid summaries of the status of the crisis (Barton, 2001).

Sometimes rapid communication is required, as in the case of a workplace violence incident. The Virginia Tech massacre illustrates such a scenario. The April 2007 incident, which is discussed in other chapters of this book, consisted of two separate attacks approximately 3 hours apart (Reilly, 2008). What is troublesome in terms of communication is that students were still going to classes several hours after the first shooting (Madhani & Janega, 2007). In response to this crisis, as well as other types of sudden calamities that can hit a university campus, many institutions have installed rapid communication systems that can alert faculty, staff, and students of an impending event such as a tornado or a serious crime in progress. West Virginia University at Parkersburg installed an emergency paging system in all classrooms and key administrative areas. The system consists of paging phones and overhead broadcast speakers that can provide quick messaging, not only on the main campus in Parkersburg but also at its rural Jackson County Center campus, 35 miles away (Gnage, Dziagwa, & White, 2009).

Finally, employees should be reminded not to respond on their own to reporters' questions but should refer all inquires to the organization's designated spokesperson (Coombs, 2007; Wailes, 2003). Using one designated spokesperson helps ensure the organization's message is consistent. Updating employees regularly on the progress and the status of the crisis through internal reports can help maintain a sense of normalcy in day-to-day operations. It also has a major effect on decreasing the flow of rumors and inaccuracies seeping out to the media (Wailes, 2003).

Crisis Communication With External Stakeholders

Communicating with external stakeholders requires designating a spokesperson skilled at interacting with various media outlets and public groups. Communication must also follow a strategy that fits the severity of the situation. Each of these is discussed next.

Designating a Spokesperson

When traditional outlets are used to communicate to the media—that is, through press conferences, interviews, and so on—it is generally best to designate one spokesperson to carry out this function. There is no set rule on who this person should be, except that it should be consistent with the hierarchy and culture of the organization. The appointed person may vary according to the type of crisis encountered. A crisis in the production sector of the company may be headed up by a production or manufacturing member of the CMT. Likewise, a problem with information technology (IT) may be led by a crisis team member from that department in the company.

When should the chief executive officer (CEO) be the spokesperson? In general, the more severe the crisis, the more likely the CEO should be in control and visible to the public. The classic case that supports this adage is the 1989 *Exxon Valdez* oil spill. CEO Lawrence Rawl chose to remain at Exxon headquarters rather than personally visit the oil-drenched Alaskan coast. Instead, he sent other executives to manage the situation, creating the impression that he thought the crisis was trivial (Vernon, 1998). In most cases though, the designated spokesperson will not be the CEO, but a member of the senior staff who is articulate and can speak convincingly and with empathy. In many larger organizations, this person comes from public relations or a similar department.

The spokesperson selected should have the potential to communicate on behalf of the organization in an effective and professional manner, not just because he or she is the most senior person available. Barton (2001) illustrates an example from the 1999 Columbine (Colorado) High School shootings. The initial spokesperson was in that role by virtue of his seniority. Unfortunately, he lacked technical knowledge of the dynamics of the incident and was soon replaced by a more knowledgeable spokesperson. Rank alone should not be the sole consideration when choosing a spokesperson. The traits of the spokesperson are critical because this role is a highly visible one.

Ideal Traits for the Spokesperson

The spokesperson should be able to appear pleasant on camera, answer questions effectively, present crisis information clearly, and have the ability to answer difficult questions (Coombs, 2007). Appearing pleasant on camera means being able to maximize the delivery style element of:

- *Maintaining eye contact.* It is recommended that the speaker look at the audience at least 60 percent of the time.
- *Using hand gestures.* A movement of the hand helps emphasize a verbal point.
- *Varying voice inflection.* Doing so helps avoid a monotone delivery style.
- *Changing facial expressions.* This is necessary to avoid a blank-stare "deer in the headlights" look.
- *Avoiding verbal disfluencies.* These are words like *uhm, uh,* and so on (Coombs, 2007).

Answering questions effectively means that spokesperson addresses each question asked by stakeholders. The spokesperson must not deflect it or answer a different question from the one that was asked. The spokesperson should be able to communicate a sense of compassion and concern for the victims of a crisis. The restaurant chain Chi-Chi's stopped operating in the United States in 2004 due in part to a crisis it faced in September 2003. An outbreak of hepatitis A, stemming from a shipment of green onions used in salsa, resulted in three deaths and more than 600 illnesses (Veil, Liu, Erickson, & Sellnow, 2005). The first official public response by the company was made by a divisional vice president on November 4, 2003. In looking for the compassion and concern of the company's communication response, Veil and colleagues noted:

In this first public comment the spokesperson was not reported as being regretful for the outbreak or compassionate for the hundreds of victims.

In effect, the message failed to characterize the company as caring or willing to serve the public need, and thus lacked the essence of character. (p. 20)

A third trait is the ability to present the crisis information clearly. The spokesperson should avoid using a lot of technical jargon in their explanations. This experience may parallel how many consumers feel when their automobile technicians attempt to explain what is wrong with their car or truck. They simply fail to understand the explanation. Moreover, some listeners may feel it is a way for the organization to avoid telling the truth (Reynolds & Earley, 2010). Hence, the spokesperson needs to be able to explain the details of the crisis in a nontechnical manner that can be understood by a wide audience (Coombs, 2007).

Finally, the spokesperson must be able to handle difficult questions from the audience. These can include one or more of the following five scenarios:

- *Long and complicated questions.* The spokesperson should ask for the question to be repeated or rephrased.
- *Multiple questions.* The spokesperson should reconstruct the question in smaller parts, perhaps numbering each part so the audience is able to follow the explanation better.
- *Tricky or tough questions.* These are often meant to make the spokesperson look incompetent. Some questions may not be answerable, and the spokesperson will need to point this out to the questioner and the audience.
- *Questions that are based on wrong information.* The spokesperson must identify the erroneous assumptions when the question is first asked.
- *Multiple-choice questions based on alternatives that are limited or unacceptable.* The spokesperson must determine whether the response options are fair or not (Coombs, 2007).

Some questions are not really questions at all, but simply a way to make a statement or express a particular viewpoint. Two of the authors were recently at an international meeting on accreditation. During one of the sessions, a prominent speaker was taking questions from the audience, which numbered close to a thousand people. An individual ostensibly wanted to ask a question, but was really venting about a number of problems he had with the speaker's comments. In the end, his question was not a question, but a way of stating his disagreement with the speaker. Although the speaker was friendly and tried to address some of the points, it might have been better to simply say to the audience, "This sounds more like a comment, not a question. Perhaps these are some items that can be discussed in a separate venue outside of this session." Indeed, all crisis spokespersons must be aware of the bully questioners out there and respond to them appropriately.

When handling difficult questions the spokesperson must have the ability to remain calm under pressure. During a crisis, the organization may be criticized, often unfairly, by the media, by elected officials, or by customers. Such was the case for Connective Power Delivery, a distributor of electric power in the mid-Atlantic region, including areas of New Jersey, Maryland, and Delaware. In September 2003, Hurricane Isabel swept through the area and knocked out power to 400,000 customers. Although the company worked hard to restore power quickly, some criticism was received from external stakeholders, yet Connective Power Delivery president Tom Shaw took the "high road" and focused on restoring power instead of worrying about unwarranted criticism (Brown, 2003, p. 32).

With this list of requirements, it is not surprising that many experts recommend media training for the spokespersons.

It is also important that the organization arrange backup spokespersons in case the designated one is not available (Barton, 2001; Coombs, 2007). The organization must still speak with one voice, even if more than one spokesperson is designated. Such could be the case if the primary spokesperson is out of town when a crisis commences. Alternate spokespersons may also be needed if the crisis lingers on for several days. In addition, some advocate designating a team of spokespersons to be available and ready to go on camera. This situation would occur if the organization's audience is particularly diverse or if a certain level of expertise is needed to explain the crisis response in a more detailed manner (Gainey, 2010).

Communicating With the News Media

One of the mistakes many managers make is to assume that members of the media represent the enemy and are out to discredit the organization when a crisis occurs (Sherman, 1989). While some in the media harbor a skeptical view of business organizations, the media can be beneficial in some instances by enabling the company to reach important audiences (Weiner, 2006). Members of the news media are more likely to misrepresent a situation when they lack the facts. The result depends on what the organization does or says in the first few hours following the crisis. The essential rule is to cooperate with the media and understand that journalists are trained to be inquisitive (Barton, 2001; Sherman, 1989; Wailes, 2003). Updating the media periodically enables them to keep the public informed as well. When developing the media message, the organizational spokesperson should be trained to deliver the message in a consistent fashion. In some instances, detractors—and perhaps competitors—will find "experts" who can demonstrate blame against the company. Organizations should be prepared to confront these claims. Crisis communication preparedness includes utilizing third-party experts who are capable of addressing the media to support the organization's position and endorse its response to the crisis (Wailes, 2003).

In order to ensure that the news media obtain a consistent message from a responsible spokesperson, news conferences should be held. News conferences need to be arranged and managed by those experienced in press relations. Table 8.1 offers guidelines for the organization's spokesperson in preparing for a news conference.

One phrase that should be avoided when addressing the media is "No comment." The crisis communication literature is consistent in making this recommendation for several reasons. First, "No comment" implies that the company is hiding something (Vise, 2005). Members of the media, as well as the general public, are skeptical when they hear this statement. There are certainly some situations where certain information cannot be divulged initially to the media. For example,

Table 8.1   Guidelines for News Conferences

1. The spokesperson should continually practice and rehearse, based on potential questions that may be asked by the media.

2. The spokesperson should seek to develop rapport and be candid with members of the media.

3. The spokesperson should avoid canned speeches and instead strive for a presentation that is more conversational and spontaneous.

4. Technical experts should be used if necessary to clarify to the public details about the crisis. This person can also serve to field technical questions from reporters that may be beyond the scope of the regular company spokesperson's knowledge.

5. The spokesperson should maintain a sense of calm and concern, and not resort to anger over questions from reporters.

6. The spokesperson should always report the truth. No attempt should ever be made to mislead the press.

7. The media should be alerted 3 to 4 hours before a news conference is held. Late morning or early afternoon conferences are ideal since they give management time to review its information and also provide ample time for reporters to prepare their story for the evening news.

Source: Barton (2001).

there may be an ongoing criminal investigation and revealing details of the inquiry may damage the case. Also, if there has been an incident where employees or customers have been injured or died, care must be taken always to notify the next of kin first before revealing their identities to the media. Under these circumstances, the spokesperson must inform the media that some information must be withheld until it is authorized for release (Valentine, 2007).

A second reason "No comment" should not be used is that it shows a lack of concern on the part of the organization. Such a terse comment is a sure sign of disrespect to victims and to the media. Third, a "No comment" response forces journalists to obtain their information from some other source (Barton, 2001; Coombs, 2007). When this situation occurs, the company loses control of the information source and its credibility. In many cases, the media will then find sources among stakeholders who may already have an unfavorable view of the organization. For example, disgruntled former employees may be more than willing to talk to a reporter about alleged safety problems at the manufacturing facility where they used to work.

It should go without saying that the organizational spokesperson should always report the truth to the media. Certainly, there will be times some details cannot be revealed at the exact moment a press conference is held or a press release is issued. This could occur when there has been a death on the premises and the victim's next of kin need to be notified before the identity of the victim can be released to the public. However, communicating the truthfulness of an event is important. Communicating the truth may be painful for the organization, but hiding it is not advisable. Barth (2010) notes in his study of crisis management within the Catholic Church that it was the church's hiding of the truth of its pedophile priests that led to much public outcry.

Communicating With Customers

Customers are the lifeblood of any business because they represent the cash flow that every firm needs. They are free to abandon their relationships with the organization because they have their own goals and objectives to achieve. Companies can keep the loyalty of customers by telling them the truth, responding to product or service complaints, and giving them the proper information concerning a crisis. When the facts around a crisis are properly explained, customers tend to understand and may be more likely to continue their relationship with the organization. However, when customers have not been given an appropriate explanation of a crisis problem, particularly if there is a consumer complaint involved, credibility issues arise and they may search for other vendors (Grégoire, Tripp, & Legoux, 2011).

Poor communication with customers can result in unpleasant consequences for any organization whose managers do not appreciate its proper implementation. Utility companies are especially cognizant of the importance of customer concerns because they must communicate to a customer base that is already without power. Customers can be especially irate when they have been without power for an extended period of time. Matt (2004) illustrates this dilemma with the story of customers beating a utility truck with baseball bats when power had not been restored after a hurricane.

The methods of communicating during a crisis should include a mix of different types of media (Gainey, 2010). In the Internet age, the most logical method of communicating is via the company's website. However, as we will see in the next section, social media tools should also be utilized. Details of the crisis and its effects on consumers, employees, and the community should be communicated. Press releases can also be archived on the website for all to view. As an example, school systems use this approach to alert students and parents about class cancellations due to inclement weather and other factors.

Some companies prepare special websites that can be added to the regular website during a crisis. These so-called dark sites contain information that someone could access to obtain the latest information on a crisis (González-Herrero & Smith, 2008; Snellen, 2003). A dark site can contain a prearranged space for questions and answers about the crisis. This section is then updated when a real crisis occurs. Potential questions might include where to return a defective product, what the safety record is for the company, or the latest status on a recall effort. Procter & Gamble used a website successfully when it was suggested that its scent freshener product Febreze could kill pets. To refute these rumors, the Febreze website included an addition that addressed these charges. It also provided a link to an urban legend website that elaborated on the nature of the rumor (Coombs, 2006).

It is easy to assume that all customers will automatically access the organization's website when a crisis occurs, but there is still a segment of the population that is on the other side of the digital divide, and for various reasons does not use the Internet. They might be reached by full-page ads that the company places in newspapers to update the public about a crisis matter. On the other side of this digital divide are customers who may only use certain social media sites to educate themselves about a specific organizational crisis. Because social media is powerful, and relatively new in crisis management history, we address it separately in the next section.

Crisis Communications and Social Media

Social media was once considered a unique communication outlet. Today, it has evolved into a widely used source of news and participation by many stakeholders. As we have seen elsewhere in the book, social media can actually spawn problems for business operations. Social media adds two new dimensions for crisis management practitioners to consider: (1) news travels faster, and (2) news travels farther (Gonzalez-Herrero & Smith, 2010). Some companies have discovered that their products or employees have been the source of a problem by learning about the occurrence from a social media outlet. Blogs can attract negative news (Benjamin, 2008). Along with other forms of social media, they serve as a vehicle for misinformation that can quickly spread into a communication crisis if left unchecked.

Social media includes specific types of websites that promote communication among friends and Web surfers who share a common interest. Such outlets include Facebook, YouTube, and Twitter. In addition, an increasing number of blogging sites are set up like a diary, archiving the thoughts and opinions of experts and non-experts who have an insight or an opinion to share.

One of the outgrowths of social media has been their role in crisis communications. For example, social media tools were used during the October 2007 wildfires in Southern California to communicate news that was not readily available on national or local news outlets. Updates on the progression of the fires, the availability and location of emergency shelters, and the opening or closing of businesses and schools were available in almost real time through social media outlets (Palmer, 2008). As this example illustrates, crisis managers should understand the various ways social media can be used to augment response efforts, particularly as it relates to the communications function. It is also necessary to be aware of how social media can cause or intensify an organizational crisis. Understanding the nature of blogging is an important concept for CMTs.

The Impact of Blogging

Blogging can convey negative news and opinions and should be given special consideration by those in corporate communications (Benjamin, 2008). Bloggers who have significant followings can quickly reach a large audience. These online audiences can then convey their thoughts and opinions on a topic or event to their online friends and colleagues.

Bloggers have achieved the status of "citizen journalists"; anyone can blog about anything. One does not have to have a degree in journalism to circulate an opinion electronically. This situation creates challenges for crisis managers who must be able to distinguish between bloggers who warrant attention and those who do not. The principles of media relations that apply to journalists can also apply to some bloggers. In the past, some public relations professionals created media lists of journalists who were their contact points. Similarly, crisis communicators must now view bloggers as another key stakeholder to establish ongoing two-way communication. Just as traditional media relations strategies revolve around building trust with the media, managers must now earn the trust of bloggers (Ziemnowicz, Harrison, & Crandall, 2011).

Computer maker Dell experienced a blogging crisis in 2005 when a well-known blogger, Jeff Jarvis, wrote about his poor customer service experience with the company. The result was negative publicity damage for the firm (Flynn, 2009). Dell responded slowly at first, but eventually hired a blog specialist to help the company improve its social media strategies. Dell also worked at improving its customer service and communicating these efforts through its newly established blog. Michael Dell even caught up with Jarvis at a social gathering and apologized for the company's poor customer service performance (Conlin, 2007).

In March 2007, Home Depot was the target of an onslaught of negative publicity when MSN money columnist Scott Burns stated that the company was a "consistent abuser" of the customer's time. Within hours, the comment section to MSN was filled with similar stories from customers who were tired of the poor service they were receiving at Home Depot due to cutbacks in store staff. Altogether, there were more than 10,000 angry e-mails and another 4,000 posts criticizing the company for its poor service (Conlin, 2007). CEO Francis Blake responded by going online and apologizing for the poor showing of the company. He promised to improve staffing and even thanked Scott Burns for his critique. There is a point to remember: Negative news concerning poor management on the part of the company can travel exceedingly fast on the Internet even when it originates from a single source. In this event, influential columnist Scott Burns triggered this online media crisis (Ziemnowicz et al., 2011).

Consider the case of Beef Products Inc. (BPI), which was been associated with the term "pink slime" during the first half of 2012. BPI manufactures lean finely textured beef, a common low-fat additive to ground beef products. Food blogger Bettina Elias Siegel noticed the term *pink slime* in a news article referencing lean finely textured beef. She responded by launching an online petition to have it banned from the federal school lunch program (Gruley & Campbell, 2012). Soon *ABC News* covered the story and the blogosphere became active as various stakeholders weighed in on the product.

Lean finely textured beef is made by running scraps of meat through a process that eliminates the fat and is treated with ammonia to kill bacteria such as *E. coli* and salmonella. It is then used as a filler for ground beef, low-fat hot dogs, pepperoni, frozen meat entrees like meatballs, and canned foods. McDonald's, Taco Bell, and Burger King used lean finely textured beef until 2012 (Bloomgarden-Smoke, 2012). There has never been a health-related crisis associated with the product, which has been available for two decades and is considered safe by the U.S. Department of Agriculture (Gleason & Berry, 2012). Nonetheless, this social media related crisis appears to have hurt the lean finely textured beef industry.

Living in a YouTube World

The opening case to this chapter on Domino's illustrates how vulnerable an organization can be in this new world of social media. YouTube offers the viewer a video of almost any negative event that can be recorded. A number of organizational crises have erupted as a result of videos appearing on YouTube. For example, some companies discover a product was defective only when someone aired a YouTube video about it. This was the case for Kryptonite, a maker of heavy-duty locks for bicycles and motorcycles. In September 2004, unexpected publicity resulted when it was revealed, via an online video posting, that using the cap of a Bic ballpoint pen could open the company's locks. In just a few days, the company faced enormous negative Internet-generated hype, resulting in a recall of their locks and an estimated $10 million in lost sales revenue (Kirkpatrick, Roth, & Ryan, 2005; Moore, 2005).

In November 2008, Johnson & Johnson (J&J) placed an online ad featuring a voice-over of a mom saying she carries her baby in a sling because it makes a "fashion statement." The ad contained a short cartoon showing how carrying a baby in a sling can be a bonding experience for the mother and child but can also cause back pain, hence, the need for Motrin pain reliever. However, a small group of online moms complained that the ad was offensive. Some moms vented their outrage by posting their own YouTube videos asking the company to pull the offensive ad. J&J removed the ad shortly after its airing (Johnson, 2009).

The crisis response by J&J to remove the ad was strategic, even though the negative response to it was quite small:

> Mommy bloggers and Twitterers make up a tiny fraction of the U.S. population, 0.15% in the case of Twitter. It just happens that a large number of that 0.15% work in advertising and media. A not-insignificant number of mommy bloggers have worked in advertising or media. In essence, this was a ready-made media firestorm. (Wheaton, 2008, p. 12)

Companies have to accept that mistakes they make are now going to become very public for quite some time. "It's a transparent world—get used to being seen living in it" (Edwards, 2008).

One of the more famous cases involving YouTube concerned an event with United Airlines. In the spring of 2008, Canadian musician Dave Carroll was traveling with his band from Canada to Nebraska when the neck of his guitar was damaged by United personnel. Not only was his guitar damaged by baggage handlers, but he witnessed the event while waiting on the plane during a connection at Chicago's O'Hare airport. Carroll informed three different United employees in Chicago of the event, but none of them took any action or responsibility. After the flight,

Carroll spent nine months trying to get United to pay for the repair, to no avail. Frustrated over this chain of events, Carroll and his band wrote and performed a song, "United Breaks Guitars," and posted it on YouTube on July 6, 2009. The song eventually amassed 8 million hits and created a huge public relations embarrassment for United Airlines. United finally offered compensation for the repair and to change its operations procedures (Grégoire et al., 2011).

The United case is significant for our attention because it shows the attempt of a customer to try to resolve a service mistake with a company. Carroll's attempts to fix the problem over a nine-month period were not taken seriously by the airline. During this time, only a few people knew of the event, which could have been easily remedied by the airline. United's decision to stick with is policies rather than try to remedy an obvious mistake on their part left Carroll no choice but to become a YouTube whistleblower.

> Customers typically engage in online public complaining when a service failure is followed by failed recoveries—that is to say, when firms keep failing to address direct complaints. Such instances are also referred to as "double deviations." That is exactly what happened in Dave Carroll's case. Before he went public, he aimed to solve this problem in direct contact with United Airlines— he even tried for nine months! (Grégoire et al., 2011, p. 28)

The concept of the double deviation, mentioned in the previous quote, makes the United case different from the J&J Motrin ad crisis and the Kryptonite bike lock incident. J&J and Kryptonite both sought to remedy their crises soon after they occurred. On the other hand, United entered a crisis on its own and took several years to resolve it. All three cases illustrate how negative news travels both fast and far.

Impact on Crisis Communications

The impact of social media raises a number of implications for crisis communications policies. These are discussed in the next sections and are based on comments by Ziemnowicz et al. (2011).

Monitor the Internet

An organization should periodically check blog, YouTube, and other Internet activity to determine potential problem areas that may exist with products, services, or company reputation. A new industry is growing with organizations that can help managers track blog and other social networking activity relating to a specific company or crisis event. Various methods such as searching on Google's Whos Talkin or utilizing the services of Technorati can be used to measure the degree of influence of what is being said about a company and who is saying it. Using platforms such as these, managers can find websites and blogs that are discussing their companies. Examining blog activity can yield insights on a crisis and to what magnitude it is being communicated via the Internet (Guo, Vogel, Zhou, Zhang, & Chen, 2009).

Utilize Social Media Outlets as an Ongoing
Component of the Overall Corporate Communications Plan

A look at company websites today reveals that many organizations have Facebook, YouTube, and Twitter links as well as blogs. We expect this trend to continue as companies seek to develop more interactive online communications with their stakeholders. For example, the company blog gives the organization an approachable human element (Kirkpatrick et al., 2005). Whereas blogs are dynamic and aimed at the human side of the Internet audience, corporate Web pages, by contrast, are meant to showcase the company's products, services, and to some degree, its history. Web pages offer only one-way communication and, of course, the opportunity to purchase products where applicable. Social media, though, makes the company more personable by offering two-way communication with its external stakeholders.

Include Social Media Tools as
Part of the Crisis Communications Plan

The CMT should develop a crisis communication plan that specifies how it will use social media tools during a crisis. Larger companies usually have an in-house staff, whereas smaller firms may need to use social media specialists on retainer. Three of the companies discussed previously—Dell, Home Depot, and Domino's—utilized social media to counter the crises they had encountered.

Some experts are calling the incorporation of social networking resources with traditional media "digital crisis communication" (Faulhaber, 2009). Using conventional media outlets remains important, but organizations that do not have Twitter accounts or Facebook pages should probably acquire them and develop fan pages and groups on these sites. Then, in the event of a crisis, these pages can be in place to disseminate messages to stakeholders. In the case of Twitter's message size limits, communicators can use the outlet to link readers to Internet sites providing details of the organization's response (Ziemnowicz et al., 2011).

Communication Response Time
Should Be in Minutes, Several Hours at the Most

Publicly responding to an organizational crisis within 24 hours was once considered the standard by some PR practitioners. Today, however, that standard is now measured in terms of minutes and, perhaps, several hours at most (Flynn, 2009). In this social media world, external stakeholders want information in minutes when a crisis occurs. It took Domino's more than 24 hours to respond with its now-famous YouTube video of Patrick Doyle speaking on the crisis. Tim McIntyre, vice president of communications for Domino's commented:

> So you post a video on YouTube featuring the president of an iconic brand within 48 hours of a hoax video being posted by two idiots. And the [criticism] of this has been amazing to me—because on one hand, we're lauded for doing something unprecedented, something that had never been done before

[posting only a YouTube response]. And yet, we didn't do it fast enough. And yet nobody has been able to answer: How can you do something that's never been done before, but not fast enough? (Jacques, 2009, p. 9)

Clearly, the social media world demands that the company make a response quickly. It is worse when there is no response from the organization's website or social media outlets. Not commenting online can be interpreted as a "No comment" from the company (Taylor & Perry, 2005), a definite taboo that raises suspicion in crisis communications (Gonzalez-Herrero & Smith, 2010).

Prepare the Message for a Wide Audience, Not Just for Journalists

Message development is crucial when using social media outlets. The traditional approach was to design the organization's messages for delivery to various stakeholders via a third party, usually a journalist. However, using social media outlets requires the organization's message sender to function in the role of a journalist. Moreover, a corporate tone such as typically found in an "official" press release posting will not usually be appropriate using social networking media (Ziemnowciz et al., 2011). Twitter may eventually cause a message revolution whereby managers will be forced to become adept at writing clear crisis communications in 140 characters or less (Levinson, 2009).

Use Search Engine Optimization Programs to Move Up Internet Search Results

In the event of a developing organizational crisis, the organization's website might not appear on the first page of a Google or another Internet search. This occurs because news websites and other social networking sites addressing the crisis crowd out the organization's website, pushing it further down the list of search pages. This puts the organization at a disadvantage during the crisis because its side of the story is not getting through to the Internet audience. Furthermore, what the viewers do see may be primarily negative news about the organization.

Utilizing search engine optimization (SEO) programs helps to move the company's Web pages to the first page of an Internet search (González-Herrero & Smith, 2010). Many users only view the first page of a Google search, and few go on to view other pages that follow (Benjamin, 2008). While SEO programs cannot prevent a crisis, they can help mitigate by allowing the organization to reach the Internet audience and tell its side of the story.

Pick Your Battles

When a crisis occurs, some stakeholders will never be satisfied no matter what the organization does to appease them. It is important to be aware of the difference between a *dissatisfied customer* (who can eventually be satisfied) and a *troll* (who will never be satisfied). "Dissatisfied customers can be approached personally and want to change their minds about something. Bigger fights only satisfy trolls.

Bloggers have learned to ignore trolls. . . . PR professionals must develop the same skill—pick your battles" (Johnson, 2009, p. 24).

Dave Carroll, discussed previously in the United Airlines case, was an example of a dissatisfied customer. He was not out to "get" United Airlines but simply wanted fair compensation for his broken guitar. United lost an opportunity to appease a dissatisfied customer. However, there are some websites and blogs that are set up by people who in no way want to have their minds changed concerning a particular company; these are "the trolls" mentioned by Johnson (2009) in the preceding paragraph. Such websites are sometimes referred to as *rogue sites, sucks sites,* or *anti-websites* (González-Herrero & Smith, 2008).

Evaluating the Success of the Crisis Communication Process

Chapter 9 focuses exclusively on the organizational learning that must take place after a crisis. Here, we briefly address the assessment of the organization's crisis communication responses. The evaluation process provides information and facts that build a knowledge base that promotes learning. This process of evaluation is critical because it determines which actions were effective and which were not. Hence, the reality of crisis management (and hence, communications) is that some aspects of implementation may be successful, while others will be unsuccessful (Pearson & Clair, 1998).

In this section, we focus on the successes and failures of the crisis communication process. For example, after the severe hurricane season of 2005, a number of retail chains began reassessing their crisis communications. The successes and failures in this area have led management to implement changes in how communication takes place during a crisis. Some retailers now utilize sophisticated technological applications, including GPS (global positioning systems) and satellite telephones, so they can stay in touch with employees during a crisis (Amato-McCoy, 2007).

Debriefing and Postcrisis Analysis

After a reasonable interval following the crisis, the CMT should meet to evaluate the management of the organization's crisis response. Written notes should be recorded that provide an assessment of internal and external communications. This notes should include an evaluation of how the company communicated to the media as well as how the media portrayed the company. Documenting this process and evaluation is important so the materials can be retrieved for later referral and continuous learning.

The team should make recommendations for improving the crisis communications function. Bovender and Carey (2006) provide a summary of how HCA's (Hospital Corporation of America) Tulane University's hospital assessed its crisis responses and communications after Hurricane Katrina. Key observations made during this hurricane concerning telephone usage included:

- Cell phones may not work after a disaster such as a hurricane.
- Cell phones seeking to call area codes outside of the disaster area might work better than those cell phones calling area codes inside the disaster area.
- Digital phone lines will go down when a building loses power; therefore some analog phones should be kept on hand.
- Amateur radio operators can often fill the void when other types of technical communication systems fail.
- Communication between headquarters (in this case, HCA is based in Nashville) and the field office (Tulane Hospital is in New Orleans) needs to be arranged on a regular schedule. In this case, hourly phone calls were made during the most critical period of the crisis.
- As strange as it may seem, there were not problems with long-distance calls, but making a phone call across town was impossible (Bovender & Carey, 2006).

A case involving the death of a professional wrestler employed by the World Wrestling Entertainment (WWE) illustrates how crisis communications can falter after a tragic event. On Sunday, June 24, 2007, the bodies of WWE wrestler Chris Benoit, his wife, and son were found in their Atlanta home. Benoit was to appear on the WWE's televised *Monday Night Raw* the next day, but due to the tragedy, the event was cancelled. Vince McMahon, CEO of WWE, made the decision to cancel, and instead, a tribute to Chris Benoit was aired, out of courtesy to the employees of the WWE and Benoit's family. During the tribute, McMahon eulogized Benoit as one of the greatest wrestlers of all time (Walton & Williams, 2011). At this point in the crisis, though, the exact circumstances surrounding the death had yet to be determined.

Unbeknownst to McMahon or the WWE, police determined that Benoit had murdered his wife and son by asphyxiation before hanging himself. The timing could not have been worse for airing the tribute to Benoit. The WWE was left with an embarrassing situation; the very person they had honored on Monday was considered a monster on Tuesday, the night of the next WWE broadcast. Furthermore, speculations were now running rampant that Benoit had succumbed to steroid abuse or "roid rage" (Mosconi, Quinn, & Nichols, 2007). This news item had created a second crisis for the WWE, as critics, including Congress, began to question the WWE about its drug policies. In hindsight, an assessment of the WWE's crisis communications concludes that although the tribute showed respect to his family, employees of the WWE, and the fans, it was aired without having full knowledge of the deaths. It was an honest mistake, but a mistake nonetheless (Walton & Williams, 2011).

The evaluation process should lead to revised plans that can be used in future crisis communication preparations and responses. The evaluation can also indicate where crisis communication training may need to be improved. This topic is covered in the next section.

Crisis Communication Training

The CMT is responsible for coordinating the training efforts needed to ensure that relevant organizational members have the necessary knowledge of crisis management procedures. Medium-sized and large organizations with human resource management departments should take advantage of the training expertise these departments can offer. Specifically, the training and development resources are needed to achieve the organization's overall crisis management capabilities (Reilly, 2008; Roemer, 2007).

When it comes to crisis communications training, the burden usually shifts from human resources to the organization's marketing or public relations departments. Staff members in these departments spend their time promoting the company and its products, which makes them a good choice for crisis communications training (Barton, 2008).

Media Training

Media training prepares a spokesperson to communicate effectively with various members of the media, such as newspaper, magazine, and television reporters. The company spokesperson should remember that journalists make a living conducting interviews every day. From this perspective, a company spokesperson is like an amateur taking on a professional (Blyth, 2009). Hence, media training is an absolute must, even for staff with good speaking abilities.

One perspective is to approach training through four basic types of instruction: (1) discussion and staging, (2) instruction, (3) simulation and drama, and (4) evaluation (Caponigro, 2000).

Discussion and Staging

This training involves viewing videos and reading news reports with the intention of comparing effective and ineffective spokespersons. The emphasis here is on the effects their comments have on the audiences. There is a famous crisis training video involving a television interview with former Exxon CEO Lawrence Rawl shortly after the 1989 *Exxon Valdez* oil spill in Alaska. The interview took place on the *Good Morning America* show with anchor Kathleen Sullivan. The interview did not go well for Rawl, who was being pushed to answer questions about Exxon's plan to clean up the oil spill. At one point, Rawl accuses Sullivan of creating a public relations nightmare for Exxon (Lentini, 2009).

Instruction

Modules in this segment instruct the participants about the "behind the scenes" activities in a news organization. These lessons help crisis spokespeople understand media needs and the deadlines that they must meet. As such, the spokesperson can learn to express what the CMT needs to communicate while simultaneously providing the media with the information they need.

Simulation and Drama

This training typically involves responding to potential questions that may be asked by media representatives. The need for continuous rehearsal is emphasized to help the spokesperson become confident with stressful questions (Coombs, 2007). Barton (2008) recommends an approach whereby the CMT develop "the worst 20." These are the 20 most disturbing questions a spokesperson could be asked after a crisis occurs. This part of the training can also take place in a private television studio where participants become accustomed to the basic tools and techniques used in a television interview.

Evaluation

This element of the training focuses on areas that need improvement. Learning from past successes and mistakes is an important part of becoming an effective media spokesperson (Caponigro, 2000).

A key skill spokespersons must learn is how to limit comments to a few well-chosen key messages. Media training instructs the participants to identify those key messages correctly and then to articulate them successfully. It shows the spokesperson how to confront a succession of different questions that might arise in print and broadcast interviews (Wailes, 2003). Generally, it is suggested that this type of training take place every 9–12 months (Caponigro, 2000).

Summary

The crisis management team oversees the function of crisis communications. When a crisis commences, a command-and-control function must be established by the team. Communicating to employees is especially important because they are the ambassadors of the company during the crisis. The organization should not withhold information from employees, as they are the ones who have the most contact with customers and the general public.

Communicating to external stakeholders such as customers, the media, and the general public will need to take place at several levels. For formal press conferences or interviews, a spokesperson will need to be designated well in advance of any crisis. This person should be carefully chosen and must display the appropriate traits for being a high-profile representative of the company. Social media outlets should also be considered in the crisis communications strategy. Using the appropriate outlet—such as the organizational Web page, YouTube, Facebook, or Twitter—will help reach the widest audience, including those who may have firsthand knowledge of the crisis.

The effectiveness of the crisis communications function should always be evaluated during the postcrisis stage, where organizational learning needs to occur.

Finally, care should be taken to insure that the appropriate training is taking place to improve crisis communications.

Questions for Discussion

1. How can effective crisis communication aid in managing the crisis in a more favorable manner?

2. How does communicating to internal stakeholders differ from communicating to external stakeholders?

3. What problems can occur with crisis communications directed to internal stakeholders (i.e., within the organization)?

4. What examples of the "mushroom analogy" of communication have you witnessed in organizations?

5. What traits are needed in a company spokesperson? What examples of poor spokespersons have you seen in the news?

6. What is the impact of a social media on a crisis? What examples can you provide that are not in the chapter?

7. How would you prepare for a news conference if you were the spokesperson and your organization had just been involved in a serious industrial accident?

8. How can the crisis management team evaluate the effectiveness of its communications?

Chapter Exercise

The purpose of this exercise is to become familiar with the various types of crises that are emerging because of the advent of social media. This exercise can be done in groups if the class is large and time is limited. Otherwise, each student in the class finds an organizational crisis that has surfaced on YouTube. Note that for a single crisis, there will likely be a number of videos that address it. For each crisis, address the following questions:

1. Why is this event considered to be a crisis? Remember the book definition of a crisis presented in Chapter 1.

2. If this event has not been recorded on YouTube, would it have still been a crisis?

3. What is the nature of the comments that accompany the YouTube video? Do you feel these comments are justified? Do you see any patterns in the comments?

4. What is the nature of the blame that is being assigned in the videos and comments sections? Is the organization being blamed? If so, is it justified? Is there another party involved that is to blame for the crisis?

Mini-Case: Taco Bell Thanks You for Suing Them

An amazing thing happened during 2011: Taco Bell thanked those who filed a lawsuit against them! Of course, this was not just any thank-you; it was part of a well-orchestrated marketing campaign to tell its side of the story in regard to a lawsuit. In addition, it shows how a company used social media in an effective manner to counter a crisis.

The story began when a disgruntled customer filed a lawsuit against Taco Bell and complained about the beef content in their tacos. The customer claimed that the taco meat was more "filler" than beef. In fact, similar allegations had already been circulating on the Internet (Beaubien, 2011). The impending crisis was now not just a lawsuit, but a potential social media fiasco.

Taco Bell had a preappointed crisis management team, and on January 25, 2011, the day the news of the lawsuit broke, they met to discuss the company's response (Levy, 2011). The response by Taco Bell was a history maker in terms of using social media to address a crisis. Following are the components of the company's crisis communications strategy that were used in what has been labeled "Tacogate":

- A nationwide print campaign featured ads in the *Wall Street Journal,* the *New York Times, USA Today,* the *Boston Globe,* the *Chicago Tribune,* the *Los Angeles Times,* the *San Diego Tribune,* the *San Francisco Chronicle,* and the *Orange County Register* (Beck, 2011).
- The ads contained a headline that read, "Thank you for suing us." Underneath the headline, the company explains in a five-paragraph letter the truth about their seasoned beef. The letter is signed by Taco Bell president Greg Creed. The purpose of the ad, which is bold in that it acknowledges the lawsuit publically, is to get the reader's attention quickly so that Taco Bell can tell its side of the story (Levy, 2011).
- In a YouTube video, Taco Bell president Greg Creed explains the ingredients in the company's taco meat under the title, "Of course we use real beef!" The 1:32 video, verifies that the company's taco meat is 88 percent USDA-inspected beef. The other 12 percent (he grins) is "our secret," which he cheerfully describes as 5 percent water (to keep the meat moist and juicy), 4 percent Mexican spices, and 5 percent oats, caramelized yeast, citric acid, and other ingredients.
- Search engine optimization was used to make sure Taco Bell's point of view appears on the first page of a Google search (Beck, 2011).
- During the crisis, a link on the company's website directed the viewer to a microsite dedicated to addressing the ingredients in the taco meat. It also posted a link to its response on Facebook with a coupon for a free taco (Levy, 2011).
- A Twitter campaign was launched using the hashtag #beef in addition to #Taco Bell in all tweets related to the lawsuit (Daitch, 2011).

The effectiveness of the campaign culminated in the withdrawing of the original lawsuit by the Alabama law firm, Beasley Allen (Becker, 2011).

Mini-Case Questions

1. What other companies besides Taco Bell could be the victim of a similar crisis?

2. What risks did Taco Bell take in running the "Thank you for suing us" ads?

3. The lawsuit did not ask for any monetary compensation. Instead, it asked that Taco Bell change its advertising. Why do you think Taco Bell spent so much money to counter the lawsuit?

Mini-Case References

Beaubien, G. (2011). Taco Bell bites back at beef complaint. *The Strategist, 17*(1), 7.

Beck, K. (2011). Taco Bell's meaty marketing campaign. *Customer Relationship Management, 15*(4), 12–13.

Becker, N. (2011, April 20). Corporate news: Taco Bell's critic drops beef. *Wall Street Journal*, p. B7.

Daitch, C. (2011, February 4). Taco Bell uses humor, social media to dig itself out of beef scandal. *Advertising Age.* Retrieved July 24, 2012, from http://adage.com/article/digitalnext/taco-bell-social-media-emerge-beef-scandal/148675/.

Levy, P. (2011). Crisis control. *Marketing News, 45*(9), 8–9.

References

Amato-McCoy, D. (2007). Ensuring continuity. *Chain Store Age, 83*(6), 50.

Argenti, P. (2002). Crisis communication: Lessons from 9/11. *Harvard Business Review, 80*(12), 103–109.

Barth, T. (2010). Crisis management in the Catholic Church: Lessons for public administrators. *Public Administration Review, 70*(5), 780–791.

Barton, L. (2001). *Crisis in organizations II.* Cincinnati: South-Western.

Barton, L. (2008). *Crisis leadership now: A real-world guide to preparing for threat, disaster, sabotage, and scandal.* New York: McGraw-Hill.

Benjamin, K. (2008, October). Crisis, what crisis . . . *Revolution,* 63–68.

Berinato, S. (2010). You have to lead from everywhere. *Harvard Business Review, 88*(11), 76–79.

Bloomgarden-Smoke, K. (2012, March 27). "Pink Slime": Health crisis or misunderstood meat product? *Christian Science Monitor.* Retrieved September 9, 2012, from http://www.csmonitor.com/USA/2012/0327/Pink-slime-Health-crisis-or-misunderstood-meat-product.

Blyth, A. (2009, February). A word in your ear . . . *Training and Coaching Today,* 10.

Bovender, J., Jr., & Carey, B. (2006). A week we don't want to forget: Lessons learned from Tulane. *Frontiers of Health Services Management, 23*(1), 3–12.

Brown, T. (2003, Winter). Powerful crisis communications lessons: PR lessons learned from Hurricane Isabel. *Public Relations Quarterly,* 31–33.

Caponigro, J. R. (2000). *The crisis counselor: A step-by-step guide to managing a business crisis.* Chicago: Contemporary Books.

Chandler, R., & Wallace, J. (2008). The role of videoconferencing in crisis and emergency management. *Journal of Business Continuity and Emergency Planning, 3*(2), 161–178.

Conlin, M. (2007, April 16). Web attack. *Business Week,* 54–56.

Coombs, W. (2006). *Code red in the boardroom: Crisis management as organizational DNA.* Westport, CT: Praeger.

Coombs, W. (2007). *Ongoing crisis communication: Planning, managing, and responding* (2nd ed.). Thousand Oaks, CA: Sage.

Edwards, J. (2008, November 17). J&J triggers mommy war with Motrin "anti-baby sling" ad. Retrieved June 12, 2012, from http://www.bnet.com/blog/drug-business/j-j-triggers-mommy-war-with-motrin-8216anti-baby-sling-8217-ad/212.

Faulhaber, P. (2009, June 3). Social media and crisis management: Build blogging and tweeting into the CM plan. Retrieved January 13, 2012, from http://www.suite101.com/content/social-media-and-crisis-management-a122449.

Flynn, M. (2009). First response: The importance of acting within minutes, not hours. *Public Relations Tactics, 16*(4), 13.

Gainey, B. (2010). Crisis leadership for the new reality ahead. *Journal of Executive Education, 9*(1), 33–43.

Gnage, M., Dziagwa, C., & White, D. (2009). *Community College Journal of Research and Practice, 33,* 948–950.

González-Herrero, A., Smith, S. (2008). Crisis communications management on the Web: How Internet-based technologies are changing the way public relations professionals handle business crises. *Journal of Contingencies and Crisis Management, 16*(3), 143–153.

González-Herrero, A., Smith, S. (2010). Crisis communications management 2.0: Organizational principles to manage crisis in an online world. *Organization Development Journal, 28*(1), 97–105.

Grégoire, Y., Tripp, T., & Legoux, R. (2011). When your best customers become your worst enemies: Does time really heal all wounds? *New Insights, 3*(1), 27–35.

Gruley, B., & Campbell, E. (2012, April 16). SLIMED: Was a food innovator unfairly targeted? *Bloomberg Businessweek,* 18–20.

Guo, X., Vogel, D., Zhou, Z., Zhang, Z., & Chen, H. (2009). Chaos theory as a lens for interpreting blogging. *Journal of Management Information Systems, 26*(1), 101–127.

Heath, R. L. (1997). *Strategic issues management: Organizations and public policy challenges.* Thousand Oaks, CA: Sage.

Jacques, A. (2009). Domino's delivers during crisis: The company's step-by-step response after a vulgar video goes viral. *The Strategist, 15*(3), 6–10.

Johnson, C. (2009). Social media in crisis: Blog and tweet your way back to success. *Public Relations Strategist, 15*(2), 23–24.

Kirkpatrick, D., Roth, D., & Ryan, O. (2005, January 10). Why there's no escaping the blog. *Fortune,* 43–50.

Lentini Jr., A. (2009). After it hits the fan. *Risk Management, 56*(5), 42–47.

Levinson, P. (2009). *New new media.* Boston: Penguin.

Madhani, A., & Janega, J. (2007, April 17). Slow reaction spurs anger. *Chicago Tribune,* p. A1.

Maggart, L. (1994). Bowater incorporated: A lesson in crisis communication. *Public Relations Quarterly, 39*(3), 29–31.

Marquez, J. (2005, October 10). The best-laid disaster plans are merely works in progress. *Workforce Management Online.* Retrieved June 9, 2012, from http://www.workforce.com/article/20051010/NEWS02/310109992.

Matt, M. (2004). Crisis communication in the eye of the hurricane. *Electric Light and Power, 82*(7), 30, 39.

McLaren, J. (1994). Bowater's Calhoun Mill at center of fog-related highway pileup dispute. *Pulp and Paper, 68*(8), 79–80.

Moore, A. (2005, Autumn). Are you prepared for the power of the blogosphere? *Market Leader, 30,* 38–42.

Mosconi, A., Quinn, T., & Nichols, A. (2007, June 27). Rage roid have him on ropes? Steroids found in house where wrestler, his wife and son died. *New York Daily Times,* p. 17.

Nelson, J. (2004, July). Crisis communication, coordination in the program. *Security, 41*(7), 68.

Palmer, J. (2008, May 3). Emergency 2.0 is coming to a website near you: The web spells a sea change for crisis management. How should emergency services respond? *New Scientist,* 24–25.

Pauchant, T., & Mitroff, I. (1992). *Transforming the crisis-prone organization.* San Francisco: Jossey-Bass.

Pearson, C., & Clair, J. (1998). Reframing crisis management. *Academy of Management Review, 23*(1), 59–76.

Premeaux, S., & Breaux, D. (2007). Crisis management of human resources: Lessons from Hurricanes Katrina and Rita. *Human Resource Planning, 30*(3), 39–47.

Reilly, A. (2008). The role of human resource development competencies in facilitating effective crisis communication. *Advances in Developing Human Resources, 10*(3), 331–351.

Reynolds, B., & Earley, E. (2010). Principles to enable leaders to navigate the harsh realities of crisis and risk communication. *Journal of Business Continuity and Emergency Planning, 4*(3), 262–273.

Roemer, B. (2007). *When the balloon goes up: The communicator's guide to crisis response.* Victoria, British Columbia: Trafford.

Scanlon, J. (1975). *Communication in Canadian society.* Toronto, Ontario: B. D. Singes.

Seeger, M. W., Sellnow, T. L., & Ulmer, R. R. (1998). Communication, organization and crisis. In M. E. Roloff & G. D. Paulson (Eds.), *Communication yearbook* (Vol. 21, pp. 231–275). Beverly Hills, CA: Sage.

Sherman, S. (1989, June 19). Smart ways to handle the press. *Fortune,* 69–75.

Snellen, M. (2003). How to build a "dark site" for crisis management: Using Internet technology to limit damage to reputation. *SCM, 7*(3), 8–21.

Spillan, J. E., Rowles, M. S., & Mino, M. (2002/2003). Responding to organizational crises through effective communication practices. *Journal of the Pennsylvania Communication Association* (Pennsylvania Communication Association Annual), *58/59,* 89–103.

Sturges, D. L. (1994). Communicating through crisis: A strategy for organizational survival. *Management Communication Quarterly, 7*(3), 297–316.

Taylor, M., & Perry, D. (2005). Diffusion of traditional and new media tactics in crisis communication. *Public Relations Review, 31*(2), 209–217.

Ulmer, R. R., Sellnow, T. L., & Seeger, M. W. (2007). *Effective crisis communication: Moving from crisis to opportunity.* Thousand Oaks, CA: Sage.

Valentine, L. (2007). Talk is not cheap. *ABA Banking Journal, 99*(12), 38–41.

Veil, S., Liu, M., Erickson, S., & Sellnow, T. (2005). Too hot to handle: Competency constrains character in Chi-Chi's green onion crisis. *Public Relations Quarterly, 50*(4), 19–22.

Vernon, H. (1998). *Business and society: A managerial approach* (6th ed.). New York: Irwin McGraw-Hill.

Vise, A. (2005). Going beyond "no comment." *Commercial Carrier Journal, 162*(6), 38.

Wailes, C. (2003). Crisis communication 101. *Business and Economics Review, 50*(1), 13–15.

Walton, L., & Williams, K. (2011). World Wrestling Entertainment responds to the Chris Benoit tragedy: A case study. *International Journal of Sports Communication, 4*(1), 99–114.

Weiner, D. (2006, March/April). Crisis communications: Managing corporate reputation in the court of public opinion. *Ivey Business Journal,* 1–6.

Wheaton, K. (2008, December 1). Middle road in Motrin-gate was right choice. *Advertising Age, 79*(44), 12.

Yuan, Y., & Detlor, B. (2005). Intelligent mobile crisis response systems. *Communications of the ACM, 48*(2), 95–98.

Ziemnowicz, C., Harrison, G., & Crandall, W. (2011). The new normal: How social media is changing the way organizations manage a crisis. *Central Business Review, 30*(1–2), 17–24.

CHAPTER 9

The Importance of Organizational Learning

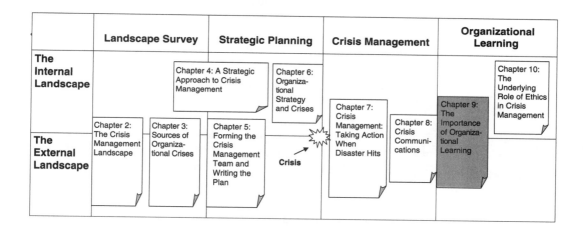

Opening Case: "Passing the Trash" by the Michigan Board of Education

One would expect that a teacher identified as dangerous to his or her students would no longer be allowed to teach. Of particular concern are teachers who have taken indecent liberties with students, many under the age of 18 and some of middle school age. Many cases are not consensual but are examples of sexual assault. Victims are often told not to tell the authorities because nobody would believe them. Unfortunately, in the late 1990s, a number of teachers were caught in sexual relationships with students, only to be quietly terminated from one school district and rehired at another. Some of these "mobile molesters" received glowing recommendations during their departures, a practice labeled "passing the trash" in the education field (Hendrie, 1998; Zemel & Twedt, 1999).

Information asymmetry occurs when one party has information that another party does not. It occurs when the first school district has prior knowledge of a teacher's improper behavior but does not share it with the subsequent district that hires the teacher. Under these conditions, it is virtually impossible for the next hiring school district to make an optimal hiring decision. Hiring school districts have learned, as in any industry, that checking the background of an applicant is important, particularly when the applicant is going to be working among young students. Consider the story of George Crear III, whose case was featured on an October 1999 edition of the television show, *20/20*. In 1987, Crear worked in Flint, Michigan, when two students claimed he had molested them. Because the incidents had occurred a number of years earlier, the statute of limitations had expired and Crear could not be prosecuted. The Michigan Board of Education allowed Crear to resign quietly, and the board purged his personnel file (Zemel & Twedt, 1999). To the next unsuspecting school district, no information would be shared by the Michigan Board of Education on Crear's past behavior because his file no longer existed.

Unfortunately, Crear was later hired as the band director at Miami Palmetto High School, a public school in Dade County, Florida. During his tenure, he molested three female students, one of whom later committed suicide. After hearing about the case in Miami, another student back in Michigan alleged that Crear had sexually assaulted her while she was 13 and in middle school in 1983 and 1984 (Hendrie, 1998). Ironically, Crear was acquitted of charges he faced in Miami but was sentenced to life in prison for the assault on the 13-year-old victim in Michigan.

The "cover-up" by the Michigan Board of Education was not only an embarrassment to that school district but also created an unnecessary crisis for the Dade County School Board, which oversees Miami Palmetto High School. The Dade County School Board would probably not have hired Crear if they had details about the Michigan case. Nonetheless, a jury awarded $720,000 to one of Crear's victims on the grounds that the Dade County School District had created a dangerous climate in which the teacher was able to stalk young girls (Hendrie, 1998). In this case, "passing the trash" had been financially costly to the unsuspecting school district, but even worse, had been a contributing factor in the death of a student.

Opening Case Discussion Questions

1. Victims of sexual assault are often told by their perpetrators that nobody will believe them if they tell the authorities. Unfortunately, this is often true. Why?

2. What could the Michigan Board of Education have done to alert future employers of the threat that Crear posed to students?

3. What could executives in the Dade County Board of Education do to ensure that teachers like Crear do not get in their school system?

Opening Case References

Hendrie, C. (1998). "Passing the trash" by school district frees sexual predators to hunt again. *Education Week, 18*(5), 16.

Zemel, J., & Twedt, S. (1999, October 31). Dirty secrets: Why sexually abusive teachers aren't stopped. *Pittsburgh Post Gazette.com*. Retrieved June 24, 2012, from http://old.post-gazette .com/regionstate/19991031newabuse1.asp.

Introduction

Although it is common to think of a crisis as a negative event, it can also be an opportunity for learning and change in the organization (Brockner & James, 2008; Wang, 2008). Put differently, a crisis should have the capacity to shock an organization out of its complacency (Veil & Sellnow, 2008). New perspectives can be developed that hedge the organization against future crisis attacks. The Chinese concept of a crisis views it as both a dangerous situation and an opportunity (Borodzicz & van Haperen, 2002). Those who do not learn from a crisis bring to mind the adage that those who ignore history are doomed to repeat it and thus are likely to be visited by similar crises in the future (Elliott, Smith, & McGuinness, 2000).

Unfortunately, some organizations do not take even initial steps to prepare adequately for a crisis. Perhaps human nature prevents many of us from addressing a crisis until it has arrived (Nathan, 2000). When an event does occur, learning from a crisis can be haphazard at best. The research that addresses crisis learning is limited but growing (Deverell, 2009; Lalonde, 2007). In this chapter, we examine this growing body of knowledge on learning from a crisis.

What Is Organizational Learning?

Organizational learning is the process of detecting and correcting errors (Argyris & Schön, 1978); it seeks to improve the operation of the organization by reflecting on past experiences (Sullivan & Beach, 2012). In the context of crisis management, learning should occur when the organization experiences a crisis. It should not be assumed that learning always emanates from a crisis, because some organizations do not appear to learn effectively. A distinction between single-loop and double-loop learning is germane. Barriers to organizational learning are presented at the end of this chapter.

Single-Loop Learning

Single-loop learning refers to the detection and correction of an error without changing basic underlying organizational norms (Argyris & Schön, 1978). Suppose you are driving your car in a snow storm and you suddenly loose traction. You sense your car is now veering left into oncoming traffic. To avoid hitting an oncoming vehicle, you steer the car away from the center lane, but in the process you sense that you are now turning too far to the right and running the risk of going off the road. You turn your wheels again, this time to the left so that you are back on the road. You are careful not to turn your wheels too far to the left lest you head into oncoming traffic again. The process of steering to the right and then to the left is an example of single-loop learning. The corrections were made instinctively by responding to the current driving conditions in the best way possible.

Learning From a Structure Fire

Firefighting is an example of a crisis activity that involves a great deal of single-loop learning. (The first author has served as a volunteer firefighter.) For instance, in fighting a structure fire, one must determine how much water to put on the fire. The firefighter will increase or decrease the volume of water and adjust the spray pattern according to the location and size of the blaze. In addition, a minimal amount of water will be used to extinguish the fire so as not to cause excessive damage for the property owner. If possible, firefighters will enter the structure and attempt to "push" the fire out away from the building, meaning they will spray the fire with water in the direction of a window or door. This type of attack extinguishes the fire more quickly and minimizes property damage but also heightens the risk of injury to the firefighter entering a burning building. If a structure is hopelessly consumed by the fire and entry into the building is not feasible, then the fire department will launch a defensive attack, also known as "surround and drown." In this procedure, the firefighters are positioned outside the structure and aim their hoses onto the fire and the structure. There is little attempt to save the property; only to extinguish the fire.

In this example, the principles of firefighting are the same regardless of the type of structure fire encountered. The learning that occurs is based on adjustments that are made along the way. For instance, if the firefighter thinks more water is needed, he or she will increase the volume by adjusting the nozzle of the hose. Alternately, another hose (called a line) may be utilized to supplement the volume of water on the fire. The principles of firefighting do not change in single-loop learning during a fire, only the decisions regarding items such as water volume, pressure, or the type of attack.

Single-loop learning can be illustrated using a simple diagram. Figure 9.1 illustrates this process. In this example, an interior attack is initiated on a fire, which quickly escalates out of control despite the best efforts of the firefighters. They learn from the situation that they must exit the building and use a series of larger lines so that an increased volume of water can be distributed on the fire, thereby extinguishing the blaze. Note that the basic underlying assumptions of fighting the fire have not been changed; hence, it is an example of single-loop learning. In the next section, we employ another example of firefighting to illustrate double-loop learning.

Double-Loop Learning

Double-loop learning involves the detection and correction of an error, but there is also a change in basic underlying organizational norms (Argyris & Schön, 1978). Such learning usually occurs after a process of thoughtful reflection (Kolb,

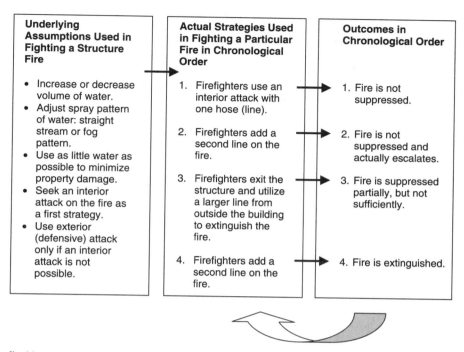

Underlying Assumptions Used in Fighting a Structure Fire	Actual Strategies Used in Fighting a Particular Fire in Chronological Order	Outcomes in Chronological Order
• Increase or decrease volume of water. • Adjust spray pattern of water: straight stream or fog pattern. • Use as little water as possible to minimize property damage. • Seek an interior attack on the fire as a first strategy. • Use exterior (defensive) attack only if an interior attack is not possible.	1. Firefighters use an interior attack with one hose (line). 2. Firefighters add a second line on the fire. 3. Firefighters exit the structure and utilize a larger line from outside the building to extinguish the fire. 4. Firefighters add a second line on the fire.	1. Fire is not suppressed. 2. Fire is not suppressed and actually escalates. 3. Fire is suppressed partially, but not sufficiently. 4. Fire is extinguished.

[In this example, single-loop learning takes place as the firefighters learn and adapt as they battle the blaze. However, no underlying assumptions are changed in the strategies used to fight the fire.]

Figure 9.1 Single-Loop Learning in Fighting a Structure Fire

1984). This type of learning changes the organizational culture and the cognitive arrangement of the company. "Based on an inquiry or some form of crisis, the organization's view of the world will change and, so, stimulate a shift in beliefs and precautionary norms" (Stead & Smallman, 1999, p. 5). Such a change in beliefs can cause organizational leaders to rethink the "It couldn't happen to us" mentality whereby managers feel immune to a crisis (Elliot et al., 2000, p. 17). As Stead and Smallman point out, this evaluation–rethinking process has come to be known by different terms, including "double-loop learning" (Argyris, 1982), "un-learning" (Smith, 1993), and "cultural readjustment" (Turner & Pidgeon, 1997). When these deeper learning processes are applied to crisis learning, the perception that a crisis cannot occur and that the organization is invulnerable usually diminishes.

Learning From the Hagersville Tire Fire

Double-loop learning can also take place as a crisis unfolds and escalates. The 1990 Hagersville tire fire in Ontario, Canada, illustrates how extensive double-loop learning took place not only in extinguishing the fire, but also in how used tires should be managed. Tire fires are difficult to extinguish for several reasons. First, the shape of the tire allows ample air flow that can feed the fire. Second, tires are usually stored in large mounds that may be difficult to reach with conventional fire equipment. Finally, burning tires produce oil, which can ignite as well, adding more heat and flames to the existing fire (Mawhinney, 1990).

Traditional assumptions on firefighting had to be adjusted for the Hagersville fire. Simply adding water to the fire was not a workable option because of the complex nature of the blaze. First, the tires were stacked in large mounds, which made access difficult for firefighters. Initially, the strategy was to attack the fire from the perimeter and gradually advance toward the center of the burning tire pile. This strategy continued for seven days, but because of the intense heat, firefighters were not able to advance to the core of the fire with their hose streams or equipment. It was later determined that the tires would need to be separated and extinguished in smaller batches (Mawhinney; 1990; Simon & Pauchant, 2000). Although this strategy worked, water runoff from the tires was taking oil with it and causing large puddles to form, threatening to contaminate the underground water supply. To address this situation, trenches were dug and sandbag barriers were used to direct the runoff water into ponds. The oil was skimmed off the runoff water and sent to an oil refinery. The runoff water was pumped into tanker trucks to be treated at a local water treatment plant while the oil was sent to the refinery (Mawhinney, 1990).

In addition to the fire, a deeper problem had to be addressed. Should the government regulate the management of used tires? At the time of the fire, the Ministry of Environment in Canada had not taken action except to impose an incineration ban. The local community where the fire occurred was also concerned about the environmental aspects of the fire. Smoke from the fire produces toxic fumes; the resulting water and foam from extinguishing the fire is also dangerous because it could seep into the groundwater supply (Simon & Pauchant, 2000). Attention needed to be focused on preventing another tire fire. Here again, double-loop learning began to take place as traditional assumptions on used tire management were being challenged. Figure 9.2 summarizes the discussion on the Hagersville fire and the role of double-loop learning.

Learning From Failure

Learning from failures is another way organizations have incorporated double-loop learning. In fact, some organizations thrive in environments that should be at high risk for failure and a potential loss of life (Weick & Sutcliffe, 2001). Such organizations have been labeled high-reliability organizations (HROs) and include aircraft carrier flight decks, medical facilities, and firefighting incident command systems (Roberts & Bea, 2001). An extensive literature bases exists on HROs (Bourrier, 2011), and lessons from these organizations have permeated into industries that are not considered as high a risk for catastrophic failure. This move is in the spirit of organizational learning, which seeks to improve critical activities and enhance performance based on an analysis of past events (Sullivan & Beach, 2012).

One of the hallmarks of HROs is their obsession with analyzing past failures so as to prevent future ones. For example, the 1967 accident on the USS *Forrestal* that killed 134 crew members has been studied extensively by the U.S. Navy so that such an accident may never occur again (Brunson, 2008). The event occurred when a rocket from a fighter jet accidently discharged into a group of other aircraft on the

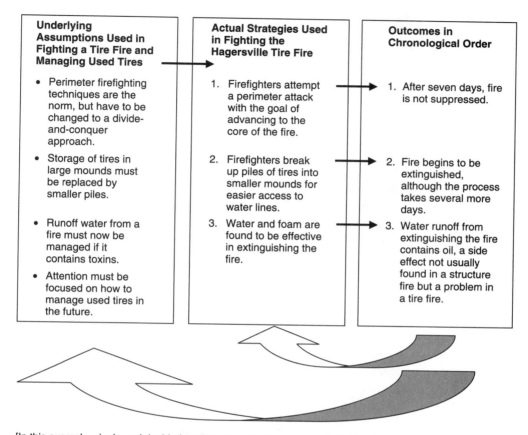

Underlying Assumptions Used in Fighting a Tire Fire and Managing Used Tires	Actual Strategies Used in Fighting the Hagersville Tire Fire	Outcomes in Chronological Order
• Perimeter firefighting techniques are the norm, but have to be changed to a divide-and-conquer approach.	1. Firefighters attempt a perimeter attack with the goal of advancing to the core of the fire.	1. After seven days, fire is not suppressed.
• Storage of tires in large mounds must be replaced by smaller piles.	2. Firefighters break up piles of tires into smaller mounds for easier access to water lines.	2. Fire begins to be extinguished, although the process takes several more days.
• Runoff water from a fire must now be managed if it contains toxins.	3. Water and foam are found to be effective in extinguishing the fire.	3. Water runoff from extinguishing the fire contains oil, a side effect not usually found in a structure fire but a problem in a tire fire.
• Attention must be focused on how to manage used tires in the future.		

[In this example, single-and double-loop learning take place as the firefighters learn and adapt to battling the blaze. Underlying assumptions are challenged and changed in the strategies used to fight the fire and to manage the used tires.]

Figure 9.2 Double-Loop Learning in Fighting the Hagersville Tire Fire

flight deck. The resulting fire was a combination of burning jet fuel and detonating bombs from the remaining aircraft on deck. Much was learned from the mistakes made in the firefighting tactics on board that day. First, because not all sailors were trained for this type of accident, mistakes were made fighting the fire and proper equipment was not utilized effectively. Today, all sailors are also trained as firefighters. Second, foam and water were not used effectively. Foam was used to smother the fire, a typical procedure for a fuel fire, but was subsequently washed off by other firefighters using water. This action caused the fuel and the fire to spread into the bottom compartments of the ship. Moreover, crew members using the foam had to stop and read the directions on how to apply it correctly (Brunson, 2008). As a result of the USS *Forrestal* accident, the U.S. Navy has upgraded its firefighting capabilities and has designated the Farrier Fire Fighting School in Norfolk, Virginia. The school is named after Chief Gerald W. Farrier, who died fighting the fire on the USS *Forrestal* that fateful day.

As this example illustrates, organizations need to adapt a posture whereby they learn from failure and pass these lessons on to future staff and managers. Failures are a byproduct of organizational life and part of operating in a complex and changing world (Cannon & Edmondson, 2005). Confronting failure gives managers the opportunity to reevaluate their assumptions on how a problem should be solved.

Building a Learning Organization

We cannot discuss the topic of organizational learning without acknowledging the work of Peter Senge and how it relates to learning in a crisis management context. Senge (2006) describes the components of the learning organization as systems thinking, personal mastery, mental models, building shared vision, and team learning. Each of these is described next.

Systems Thinking

Everything that occurs in an organization is influenced by something else. Likewise, the events the organization initiates influence other items or systems. This interconnectedness forces managers to think conceptually: How does a decision made at one point in time affect other decisions that are made later?

As we have seen, a crisis is not merely a random event. Instead, it is caused by many other movements of systems that culminate in a trigger event that initiates the crisis. Recognizing that an organization is part of a larger flow of events helps the manager understand how crises emerge. Crisis events do not just occur; they evolve and are influenced by various systems. In the Hagersville tire example, we saw how a number of other systems were influenced by the fire. Smoke from the burning tires affected air quality in the region. Water used to fight the fire contained oil runoff, which could contaminate drinking water if it seeped into the underground water supply. The fire was a system, affecting other systems as well. As the strategies were planned for fighting the fire, those leading the crisis response had to consider what other systems were being affected by their actions.

Personal Mastery

Senge (2006) views personal mastery as a competency that can be developed. It is also an organizational skill set. At its heart is the ability to see reality in an objective manner. Without this ability, learning is not possible. Developing this ability takes time, effort, and a commitment to discovering the truth. For the crisis manager, personal mastery is a must because reality is not always attractive.

The concept of sensemaking occurs during a crisis as managers seek to assign meaning to events. There are times, however, when a crisis is so bizarre that there is a collapse of sensemaking (Weick, 1993). This collapse can be caused by the loss of a frame of reference, because nothing similar has occurred in the past. The human response is one of fear and helplessness, the encountering of the fateful cosmology episode that has been discussed elsewhere in this book. As Weick (1993) describes it, "I have no idea where I am, and I have no idea who can help me" (pp. 634–635). Nonetheless, decision makers in charge of responding to a crisis should acknowledge their need to regroup to see the event as objectively as possible. This mind-set can help the response to the crisis and begin to let the organization learn from the event.

Mental Models

These are the sets of assumptions and viewpoints that we have. Such models are necessary because they help us make sense of the world. Organizations also have mental models that reflect the collective assumptions of their members. Mental models can be useful when they urge us to think creatively about problems being faced. Indeed, some managers thrive on thinking "outside the box," to quote a well-known phrase, because their minds are geared to seeing possibilities behind every problem.

Mental models can also hamper crisis response and, ultimately, organizational learning. When managers insist that a crisis "cannot happen here," they are exhibiting a mental model of denial. Destructive mental models can be seen even when crisis events occur repeatedly in the same organization. For example, scapegoating is a mental model that seeks to shift the blame to some other party. Again, such a model is a form of denial—not a healthy ingredient in an environment for learning.

Building Shared Vision

This ingredient of learning involves a collective agreement by members of the organization on its mission and goals. Inherent is a passion that employees show for the projects they work on and the role their company plays in society. Thus, when a crisis occurs, the whole organization is hurt because the collective vision has been attacked. As a result, efforts at confronting the crisis and getting back to business are embraced enthusiastically. This response can explain why some communities immediately move into action when a disaster strikes. Cleanup crews hit the streets quickly, volunteers abound, and government visibility is heightened as everyone works together to overcome the crisis and return to a sense of normalcy.

In the absence of a shared vision, there is a higher vulnerability to the organization when a crisis does occur. A fragmented organization will not respond cohesively and may even attack itself as the crisis unfolds. Scapegoating may occur among organizational members. Many professional sports teams experience this type of crisis from time to time. The scenario is usually predictable; the team has a bad season, the owners and coaches become confrontational, and the players frequently complain about the owner, the coach, or fellow teammates. Ultimately, some players may demand to be traded. When this type of "venting" occurs, a public relations crisis is born as well.

Team Learning

Senge (2006) describes the familiar situation when an average group of managers can produce an above-average company. The opposite is also true; a group of above-average managers can produce a below-average company. Many crises originate because less-than-ideal dynamics occur among a group of otherwise competent professionals.

According to Senge (2006), the key to better performance, or team learning, is to acknowledge the presence of dialogue. Dialogue is a deeper form of discussion through which new ideas originate from the group. In the end, the team becomes the learning unit for the organization and is capable of reaching new levels of performance that a group of individual managers might not reach on their own. Dialogue is the prerequisite for double-loop learning, because new assumptions may need to be developed as old ones are discarded.

This notion of dialogue is important from a crisis management perspective. Crisis management teams (CMTs) are special units, capable of doing much more than just generating a list of potential threats and crisis plans. The crisis team is the unit that protects the organization, its mission, its values, and its reputation. Thus, the CMT is a strategic unit within the organization. Thinking of the CMT as just a committee or a staff department hampers its ability to promote true learning and long-term benefits for the organization. The status of the CMT must be elevated to a level at which it can attain strategic importance.

Learning From a Crisis

An optimal time to learn from a crisis is shortly after it has occurred. Waiting too long to extract lessons from the crisis could cause the sense of urgency for learning to wane (Kovoor-Misra & Nathan, 2000). In addition, organizational learning cannot occur unless there is feedback (Carley & Harrald, 1997). After a major crisis occurs, managers should reevaluate their crisis management plans based on feedback received during the event. They must be able to determine why specific decisions were made during the crisis. Mechanisms such as debriefings, stakeholder interactions, and technology enable managers to capture and share information with members of the crisis management team. This information can be used in follow-up discussions to learn lessons and develop best practices.

In this book, we place organizational learning as the last stage in the four-stage framework. This placement is not to imply that learning does not take place in early stages. As a formal activity, it is a reflective process that must take place after the crisis has ended. Early crisis management frameworks also posit that learning takes place toward the end of the crisis management process. For example, Pearson & Mitroff (1993) place "learning" as the fifth phase in their five-stage framework. Table 9.1 offers a framework for assessing the learning areas in crisis management. If learning is to be systematic, we must examine the four major areas of the crisis management framework as well as the internal and external landscapes associated with each area.

Table 9.1   After the Crisis: Potential New Learning Areas in Crisis Management

	Landscape Survey	*Strategic Planning*	*Crisis Management*	*Organizational Learning*
The Internal Landscape	Were warning signals missed prior to the crisis occurring? Are there new vulnerabilities in our organization that we need to be aware of? Are there new methods of detection that we can use to sense an impending crisis?	Do we need to change the composition of our crisis management team? Are there aspects of the crisis management plan that need to be changed? Is there enough redundancy in the day-to-day operations of the company? Can the organization take advantage of new types of crisis training?	Were resources deployed effectively during the crisis? Did the organization's departments work together effectively? Are any improvements needed in the crisis communications function? Is there an adequate use of paper and electronic recording during the crisis?	Are we making good use of postcrisis debriefing meetings? Are we building systems that provide feedback?
The External Landscape	Are there new threats in the external environment that can lead to a potential crisis?	Are there additional resources in our industry or government that can help us in our crisis management planning?	How can we better partner with industry and government agencies in managing a crisis?	What can we learn from the best practices of those outside of our organization who have encountered similar types of crises?

Landscape Survey

The landscape survey phase of organizational learning focuses primarily on the crisis threats that existed. The following discussion looks at the questions relating to the internal and external landscapes.

Were There Warning Signals That Were Missed Prior to the Crisis Occurring?

The internal landscape survey looks inside the organization for emerging crisis vulnerabilities. Perhaps an equipment breakdown brought on the initial crisis. Have repairs been overlooked on other equipment? Perhaps the crisis occurred when key personnel left the company and their replacements were not adequately trained, leading to a production accident. In this example, at least two problems should be identified: Why the high exit of employees, and why the poor training of new employees? Problems such as these indicate that human resource issues may need to be addressed.

Are There New Vulnerabilities in Our Organization That We Need to Be Aware of?

Although not explicit in every crisis, every organizational leader should consider one internal vulnerability: the relationship between the organization and its mission. In his analysis of the sexual abuse problem within the Catholic Church, Barth (2010) noted that the protection of the church became more important than its real mission, serving its members. Unfortunately, this self-preservation mentality can hide a multitude of problems. The opening case involving the Michigan Board of Education illustrates how protecting the local school district superseded a more commonsense approach to the problem, which would have been to keep George Crear III out of *any* school system. Instead, the Michigan Board of Education chose to protect its own school system, regardless of what might happen elsewhere.

Of course, George Crear III, not the Michigan Board of Education, is responsible for the crisis that occurred. While we do not overlook this reality, this book is about protecting organizations like the Michigan board from future crises. School boards everywhere have a responsibility to protect their students. As this case illustrates, there are hidden vulnerabilities that must be addressed lest a crisis occur.

Are There New Methods of Detection That We Can Use to Detect an Impending Crisis?

An analysis of the internal landscape may also reveal that new methods of detection should be used to sense an impending crisis. Perhaps new accounting and financial controls are needed to detect potential sources of employee embezzlement and other types of fraud. As mentioned in Chapter 8, monitoring the Internet on a regular basis is a way a company can detect whether it is about to be caught in a viral crisis. Depending on the industry, a firm may identify specific ways it can use technology to help detect an impending crisis.

Are There New Threats in the External Environment That Can Lead to a Potential Crisis?

The external landscape survey can also signal emerging vulnerabilities. A recent crisis might have been weather related; in fact, droughts are common in the area where the authors reside. This situation has created water shortages and low-running wells. In a highly agricultural area like the southeastern United States, such an event is not only a crisis for many organizations but is a data point for a future crisis. To compound this crisis, an influx of new citizens is moving into this region, based on the growth of a nearby military base. Fortunately, learning is also taking place and new plans to satisfy water needs are being developed, even if droughts continue to occur in the future.

Strategic Planning

Organizational learning in regards to the strategic planning process looks at changes that may be needed with the crisis management team, crisis management plan (CMP), and training requirements.

Do We Need to Change the Composition of Our Crisis Management Team?

Organizational learning in the internal landscape may necessitate changes in crisis response plans. The composition of the CMT may require revision. Some current members may not be suitable, while other employees may be excellent replacements. In addition, it may be necessary to alter the size of the team. One of its members should have social media expertise or have access to staff members who do.

Are There Aspects of the Crisis Management Plan That Need to Be Changed?

The CMP can be revised at any time. Perhaps there are new scenarios that need to be added to the plan. The suitability of the command center should also be evaluated. The team should discuss whether the communication functions were readily available and whether the meeting rooms were suitable. Even a minor detail such as cell phone access should be evaluated, because some cell phone users may not have access in certain parts of a building, such as a basement.

Is There Enough Redundancy in the Day-to-Day Operations of the Company?

There is an old saying that "repetition is the mother of learning." The practice of redundancy in an organization's processes helps ensure that everyone understands their jobs and that there are backup systems for computers, files, and mechanical devices. Having a spare tire available for that one time when there is a flat is a common personal example of redundancy. At the organizational level, information technology (IT) professionals learned quickly and early that failure to back up their information systems can lead to disaster. The same is true in any organization. While redundancy is not necessary in every function, it is essential in those areas that are difficult to replicate. The organization that is prepared with backup systems can be resilient.

The same approach is appropriate in crisis management. When a specific process does not function well or at all, managers should have an alternate process that can substitute for the original. Redundancy in crisis management can be seen in the following examples:

- Methods of contacting the CMT in the event of a crisis should include cell phone, regular phone, and e-mail.
- The crisis management plan should be printed in hard copy as well as made available on backup storage sites and posted on the organization's website.

- The primary location of the command center should be backed up by a secondary command center, and perhaps even a third site, lest the first command center become inaccessible during a crisis.
- Selection of alternate crisis team members can be designated, in case one or more of the original members are not available.

Many examples of redundancy already exist in crisis situations. Backup generators may be available when the primary power is offline. Additional counselors may be told to "be ready" after a significant event has taken place on a school campus, such as the death of a student. Battery-powered lights go on in the stairwells when the main power is unavailable. During the Y2K scare, many organizations brought in extra food, water, and sleeping mats, just in case.

Can the Organization Take Advantage of New Types of Crisis Training?

Crisis management training may also need revising. Techniques and assumptions about managing the crisis should be reevaluated during such training. The reevaluation process is based on experience with a previous crisis. The goal is to take what has been experienced from the previous crisis, reflect on and learn from it, and then use it to plan for the next potential crisis. This facet of learning is also referred to as *assessment,* and more specifically, *closing the loop* (Martell, 2007). Striving for this stage is important because it facilitates continuous improvement in the way crisis managers can make the next crisis more manageable.

Are There Additional Resources in Our Industry or Government That Can Help Us in Our Crisis Management Planning?

The external landscape can offer additional training opportunities that can fit the specific needs of the organization. For example, many workshops offered by industry associations and government agencies address the problem of workplace violence, an area that can be a deadly occurrence for the affected organization. In other areas of crisis prevention, various agencies, colleges and universities, and consulting groups are useful because they offer expertise that managers in the company may not possess.

Crisis Management

The crisis management stage addresses the actual response to the acute crisis at hand. Organizational learning that takes place in this stage is intended to improve how the organization manages a crisis once it has commenced.

Were Resources Deployed Effectively During the Crisis?

Additional human and material resources may be needed to enhance the organization's capacity to respond to a crisis. In the 2007 Virginia Tech massacre crisis, communication was a critical factor. If better communications systems had been in place, the number of fatalities might have been reduced (Reilly, 2008). Creating and implementing a communications system on a university campus is an example of a resource application. Indeed, since the Virginia Tech massacre, many colleges and universities have updated their real-time communication networks so that faculty and students can be notified of a crisis in a moment's notice.

In another university-related crisis, the deployment of a certain material resource, pepper spray, was called into question during an Occupy Wall Street Protest at the University of California-Davis in November 2011. Campus police were called in to remove tents occupied by the protesters. During the operation, a group of students sat on a sidewalk and linked arms, refusing to stand. After repeated warnings to disperse by the police, two officers doused them with pepper spray. The event was videotaped and appeared on YouTube, causing worldwide attention and creating a public relations nightmare for Chancellor Linda P. B. Katehi. Almost immediately, calls for her resignation emerged and the campus police department was criticized for using pepper spray on a group of otherwise peaceful students (Stelter, 2011).

The pepper spray incident illustrates an ineffective use of resources, a fact that was later confirmed in a 190-page report by a campus task force. The report described campus leadership as being inadequate in handling the event, and "the pepper spraying incident that took place on November 18, 2011, should and could have been prevented" (Medina, 2012). The incident also highlights the challenges any university president or chancellor faces. Chancellors are influential leaders who must set the strategic direction of their university. They must also reach out to external stakeholders in the area of fund-raising. And yet, the skill set of a chancellor also includes crisis management ability. Some people will always call for a chancellor to resign, even if an event is not directly under his or her sphere of control. In this incident, command and control was handled by campus police department, and yet it was the chancellor who was immediately asked to resign. The extent to which the chancellor should be held responsible for events such as these—including on-the-spot judgments made by university personnel—is debatable.

Did the Organization's Departments Work Together Effectively?

Success managing a crisis is often a function of the degree of cooperation and interdependence that exists among various departments within and across organizations (Carley & Harrald, 1997). Interdependence is important in resolving resource allocation issues and developing teamwork. When a crisis occurs, there should be a unified effort to keep the organization functioning effectively.

A mold outbreak in a university building illustrates the degree of cooperation that must take place. Indeed, the authors have been at universities where this crisis has occurred. This not-too-uncommon scenario requires the redeployment of all personnel and activities from the building affected:

- The physical plant and maintenance department must work to set up the initial cleanup of the facility. The work is often contracted to outsourced firms, but the department must oversee all work and reconstruction.

This department also coordinates any movement of materials, office supplies, and furniture.

- The records office identifies and assigns new classrooms.
- Deans communicate new location information for classes and offices to the affected students and faculty members.
- The university's public information department can disseminate information to students and faculty, but its primary goal is to communicate important news about the crisis to the general public.

Are Any Improvements Needed in the Crisis Communications Function?

Effective communication and cooperation across departments is important if a crisis is to be managed successfully. If there is any consolation, it is that weaknesses in the crisis management practices are exposed and can then be corrected. At that point, learning will be somewhat easier as participants try not to repeat their mistakes.

A classic case involving the need to change communication messages in the midst of a crisis involved the company Source Perrier. This French company bottles Perrier water in the familiar green bottles and faced a significant crisis in February 1990. Ironically, the crisis was discovered by government inspectors in North Carolina who used the bottled water as a diluting agent in its testing of local water samples. As the inspectors were testing the local water supplies, they found traces of benzene in their samples, which had been diluted with Perrier water. Much to their surprise, they eventually discovered that the benzene originated not with the local water being tested, but with the Perrier water.

For Source Perrier, communicating to the general public the origin of the problem was a bit of a challenge. Two days after the initial detection, the company communicated that a careless worker had used cleaner laced with benzene on a bottling line. Upon further investigation, a different reason for the problem emerged: carbon dioxide filters that were used in the bottling process had not been changed properly (Brookes, 1990). Benzene is a natural ingredient in carbon dioxide, thereby requiring filtration. However, upon this revelation, Perrier was forced to reveal that there were actually *two* sources of their "naturally sparkling" water, not one. The water came from one source, while the gas originated from another. The two were combined during the bottling process. Thus, carbon dioxide was used to add an artificial boost of bubbles to a product that was inappropriately labeled "naturally sparkling." This disclosure forced the company to admit that its product was not what it claimed—natural sparkling water. Source Perrier was later required by the U.S. Food and Drug Administration (FDA) to relabel its U.S.-bound bottles "natural mineral water" ("Perrier relabeled," 1990).

Is There an Adequate Use of Paper and Electronic Recording During the Crisis?

Most organizations use technology to supplement their traditional paper-based processes. Word processing, e-mail, and other applications are used to facilitate electronic management of incidents and crises. While these have merit, they do not always lend themselves to effective real-time reporting or easy record keeping during a crisis. In the heat of a crisis, for example, it may be necessary to produce a status report on any aspect of the incident, regardless of whether it concerns people, premises, or press communications. Proper venues for recording information are necessary. The use of crisis management software can be helpful in this regard.

How Can We Better Partner With Industry and Government Agencies in Managing a Crisis?

The external environment can offer learning opportunities through better partnerships with industry and government agencies. At the community level, businesses can partner with their local emergency service providers. Training opportunities often exist through which these providers conduct simulation drills at the business location. After a major disaster, two or more cities may partner and change their emergency response structures to manage their obligations more effectively. Such was the case after the 1997 Red River Flood in Grand Forks, North Dakota. Timothy Sellnow and colleagues discuss how the flood prompted reorganization of emergency services between the adjacent cities of Moorhead, Minnesota, and Fargo, North Dakota (Sellnow, Seeger, & Ulmer, 2002). On the positive side, cooperative structures between the two former rivals emerged after the crisis whereby crisis communication was centralized through Fargo's City Hall.

Crisis learning and subsequent partnerships are taking place in the oil industry after the British Petroleum (BP) Gulf of Mexico oil spill in 2010. Four oil companies—ExxonMobil, Royal Dutch Shell, Chevron, and ConocoPhillips—formed a joint venture to develop a Gulf of Mexico oil spill response and containment system. The four companies have created a $1 billion pool to fund new equipment that will help prevent a future spill like the one that occurred to BP (Pfeifer & McNulty, 2011). In addition, enhancements will be made to the oil spill response and containment systems that are used to collect spilling oil.

Organizational Learning

Within the crisis management framework, organizational learning is the fourth chronological stage in which postcrisis analysis takes place. This phase is when debriefing meetings take place and notes are formally acknowledged on how to improve the organization's crisis management effectiveness.

Are We Making Good Use of Postcrisis Debriefing Meetings?

Within the internal landscape, the organization should learn from the crisis in a constructive manner (Lagadec, 1997). Specifically, how and what is the organization learning from the event, and what changes are being implemented for the prevention and mitigation of future crisis events? Holding debriefings after the crisis has ended is a constructive venue for learning. Outside parties who can help management learn objectively from the crisis should be invited. Depending on the crisis, this could include local fire, police, and emergency personnel, as well as a crisis management consultant.

Are We Building Systems That Provide Feedback?

Within the internal landscape, there is another mechanism that should be utilized: providing adequate feedback to the rest of the organization. Without feedback, learning cannot occur. The reason is that an accumulation of knowledge that "sits" in a compartment of the organization cannot be useful in causing a cultural adjustment; that knowledge must be fed back to other parts of the organization (Smith & Elliott, 2007). Feedback must be channeled back to the landscape survey, strategic planning, and crisis management phases. The feedback loop brings in a separate but related concept in organizational learning: knowledge management.

Knowledge management is the process an organization uses to manage what it has learned (Alavi & Leidner, 2001). Knowledge must be routed, stored, and retrieved when necessary. Generally, there are two types of knowledge: explicit and tacit. Explicit knowledge can be codified and physically stored in databases, whereas tacit knowledge comprises the experiences and mental models of individuals. This type of knowledge is manifested in the form of specific experiences, individual expertise, and intuition. Both forms of knowledge require a feedback process whereby the

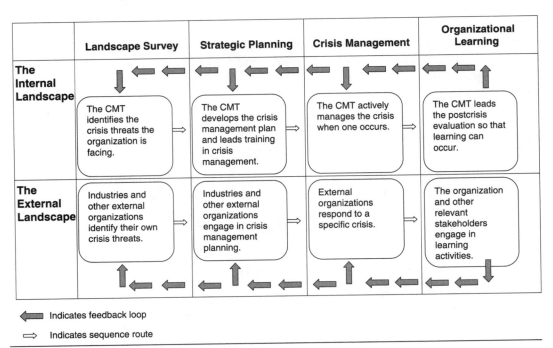

	Landscape Survey	Strategic Planning	Crisis Management	Organizational Learning
The Internal Landscape	The CMT identifies the crisis threats the organization is facing.	The CMT develops the crisis management plan and leads training in crisis management.	The CMT actively manages the crisis when one occurs.	The CMT leads the postcrisis evaluation so that learning can occur.
The External Landscape	Industries and other external organizations identify their own crisis threats.	Industries and other external organizations engage in crisis management planning.	External organizations respond to a specific crisis.	The organization and other relevant stakeholders engage in learning activities.

Indicates feedback loop

Indicates sequence route

Figure 9.3 Feedback in the Crisis Management Framework

appropriate stakeholders can take advantage of its use when needed (Racherla & Hu, 2009). Figure 9.3 illustrates the feedback process as it is incorporated into the crisis management process.

What Can We Learn From the Best Practices of Those Outside of Our Organization Who Have Encountered Similar Types of Crises?

Managers can learn from crisis events by observing the failures and crises of other organizations (Ulmer, Sellnow, & Seeger, 2007). The external landscape can yield numerous resources that can be useful to crisis managers. Books and articles on crisis management comprise one such resource. The book you are reading offers a framework for learning about crisis management, whereas articles tend to be more specialized and often highlight the best practices of specific companies. Many articles focus on lessons learned from a specific crisis. In addition to these outlets, some colleges and universities offer courses in crisis communications and crisis management.

Within the external landscape, crises related to safety problems resulting in fatalities will probably yield learning and changes on the part of government regulators. In other words, there may be collective industry learning that takes place as well. For example, the 2006 Sago Coal Mine accident in Sago, West Virginia, resulted in 12 miner fatalities after methane gas seeping from the mine walls caused an explosion. After the incident was investigated by the Mine Safety Health Administration (MSHA), a new standard was released that increased the required strength of seals used to separate active and inactive sections of coal mines (Madsen, 2009). Unfortunately, one coal mining company, Massey Energy, choose to ignore safety regulations altogether and compromise miner safety. In this example, the company deliberately chose to ignore learning that had occurred in the mining industry. The Massey example is more a violation of business ethics than a lack of organizational learning. We explore the relationship between business ethics and crises in the next chapter.

Degrees of Success in Crisis Learning

The observation that an organization can display degrees of success in crisis management outcomes was first discussed by Pearson and Clair (1998). One of the items they considered was organizational learning from a crisis. Table 9.2 depicts three levels of outcomes: failure, midrange, and success. Each outcome is further distinguished by degree of learning, future impact on the organization, and strategy posture toward crisis management. Companies that experience mostly failure outcomes in the crisis management process have not yet learned from past events. It is not surprising that these organizations continue to repeat their mistakes each time a similar crisis erupts. Such organizations are reactive in nature, and therefore they are unable to learn because they are always in a state of surprise or, perhaps, nonchalance. Table 9.2 conveys the idea that learning success can vary among several ranges of outcomes.

Table 9.2   Levels of Learning Outcomes After a Crisis

	Failure Outcomes	**Midrange Outcomes**	**Success Outcomes**
Degree of learning	No learning occurs.	Learning occurs, but its applications are sporadic.	Learning occurs throughout the organization.
Future impact on the organization	The organization continues to make the same mistakes when similar crises occur.	Some areas of the organization may change for the better while others remain the same.	The organization changes its policies and procedures. Learning is applied to future crisis events.
Strategy posture toward crisis management	The organization is reactive; unwilling or unable to learn.	The organization is reactive; willing to learn yet not ably equipped to learn.	The organization is proactive; willing to learn and take the knowledge to the next step for application.

Source: Adapted from Pearson and Clair (1998), p. 68.

Some companies will experience limited degrees of success in their crisis management practices and thus show some capacity for learning. A degree of learning is possible, but its applications will be sporadic. Therefore, certain areas in the organization will change for the better while others might remain the same. In terms of a strategy posture, the firm is still reactive but shows some willingness and ability to learn.

The ideal, of course, is a total learning organization. Companies that experience success outcomes in this area are willing and able to learn. The result is that policies and procedures are changed as needed. The hope is that in the event of future crisis events, the new learning will enable the organization to respond more effectively.

Barriers to Organizational Learning

Learning is not necessarily a natural outcome of a crisis. In fact, many companies are reluctant to learn and instead choose to return to the status quo as quickly as possible (Cannon & Edmondson, 2005; Roux-Dufort, 2000). There are a number of reasons why this is so. In the next section, we examine the more common reasons organizational members, particularly those in management, may resist learning. Barriers to learning are approached from two perspectives: operational considerations and factors related to the organization's culture.

Operational Considerations

Operational considerations focus on issues related to the day-to-day functioning of the organization. Included in this discussion are an overreliance on programmed decisions, information asymmetry, and the tendency to ignore small failures.

There Is an Overreliance on Programmed Decisions

Programmed decisions—those that are based on some type of decision rule or prearranged logic—can be useful in a number of situations. They tend to work well when management decisions are routine and repetitious, such as the reordering of inventory when levels reach a prespecified number. Programmed decisions have also been factored into certain crisis management procedures. For example, many organizations have a prearranged list of procedures to follow when there is a bomb threat. These are designed to methodically protect assets and people (usually by evacuating the occupants from the building) while seeking as much information as possible about the person making the threat (taking note of background noises, engaging the caller in conversation as long as possible to identify speaking patterns, etc.). Such programmed decisions are useful because they are systematic in their application.

There can be a problem, however, when there is too much reliance on programmed decisions: "The more programmed decisions are utilized by an organization, the more resistant to change it becomes" (Lester & Parnell, 2007, p. 177). This kind of situation can occur in companies where programmed decisions are used to promote efficiency. Because this mode of operation is usually effective, management may become complacent and not seek new approaches to running the operation. This complacency can carry over into the area of crisis management, especially when crisis planning is either not addressed or is left to top management (Nystrom & Starbuck, 1984).

At the employee level, programmed decision making can lead to a work routine in which the worker becomes a "mindless expert," meaning they concentrate on the end result instead of the process of the task (Langer, 1989, p. 20). The end result can be a workplace accident or missing the cue for a crisis altogether.

There Is Information Asymmetry

Information asymmetry can occur when similar incidents involving the same technology transpire over a wide geographic area (Boin, Lagadec, Michel-Kerjan, & Overdijk, 2003). For example, information asymmetry can exist when the manufacturer of a product has information that customers do not possess. Furthermore, different customers may have access to different information as well. The Therac-25 incidents from 1985 to 1987 illustrate this (Leveson & Turner, 1993).

Therac-25 was a computer-controlled radiation machine that administered prespecified doses of radiation to cancerous tumors. The machines were offered by Atomic Energy Canada Limited (AECL) and were introduced in 1982. The machines operated flawlessly until a time period between June 1985 and January 1987. During this period, six incidents occurred when patients received massive overdoses of radiation while undergoing treatment. Several of these patients later died (Leveson & Turner, 1993). What made the crisis especially perplexing was the lack of information transfer that took place among the six medical centers using the Therac-25. Instead, each medical center reported the machine failure directly to the manufacturer, unaware that other medical centers were also experiencing problems. Figure 9.4 illustrates the information asymmetry that existed.

The figure shows four different medical centers that were affected by overdoses of radiation caused by the Therac-25 machines. The incident that started the Therac-25 crisis occurred at Kennestone Regional Oncology Center in June 1985. The second incident occurred at Ontario Cancer Foundation in July 1985. Yakima Valley Memorial Hospital experienced incidents in December 1985 and in January 1987. East Texas Cancer Center experienced incidents in both March and April 1986. The radiation overdoses resulted in three fatalities and three other patients who suffered serious physical injuries (Fauchart, 2006).

As Fauchart reports in his analysis of the case, communication took place between each medical center and the manufacturer, but not among the four medical centers. Thus, the manufacturer, AECL, had complete information but the four medical centers did not. Thus, potential learning opportunities at each of the four medical centers were not possible. Fauchart (2006) maintains that this information asymmetry could have been avoided:

> The manufacturer should have informed all the users that a number of accidents had occurred, but he did not do so. Instead, he told every user who asked for information about other possible incidents that he was not aware of any. He thus used the information asymmetry to pretend that each accident was a one-off fluke. This clearly delayed the instauration of a learning process aimed at fixing the problem and preventing other accidents from occurring. (p. 101)

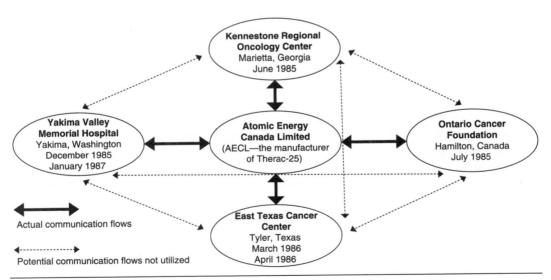

Figure 9.4 The Problem of Information Asymmetry During the Therac-25 Crisis
Source: Fauchert (2006).

Small Failures Are Routinely Ignored

A reoccurring theme in crisis research is that small incidents that are ignored can lead to more substantial incidents or crises (Cannon & Edmondson, 2005; Smith, 1993; Veil, 2011). Such small incidents can be interpreted as warning signals of a larger crisis on the horizon. These early warning signals can be likened to an incubation stage when the crisis is growing, largely unnoticed by organizational members (Seeger, Sellnow, & Ulmer, 2003; Veil, 2011). The term "smoldering crisis" has also been used to describe a situation where management largely ignores a series of smaller events, only to have them erupt into a larger calamity later on down the road (Institute for Crisis Management, 2011). The BP oil disaster in the Gulf of Mexico that resulted in the deaths of 11 workers was an example of a series of smaller problems that were routinely ignored. According to the Institute for Crisis Management:

> Some will argue that the explosion on the BP oil rig Deepwater Horizon was a sudden crisis—an explosion that killed eleven and triggered a major oil spill in the Gulf of Mexico. ICM maintains there is ample evidence there were a series of human errors and ignored problems, that had they dealt with when they first occurred, could have prevented the disaster that cost BP so much money and additional damage to its reputation. (2011, p. 2)

Organizational Cultural Considerations

The belief systems within an organization can stifle progress in attempting to learn from a crisis. As we will see in the discussion below, a track record of success, a culture of scapegoating, a status quo culture, and the painful process of looking at failures are deterrents to the learning process.

There Is a Solid Track Record of "Success" in the Organization

It may seem ironic, but success can ultimately lead to failure (Parnell, Lado, & Wright, 1992). When an organization enjoys success, the result can be an attitude of feeling invincible against crisis events. Success can be defined in a number of ways, such as consistent revenues, accident-free workdays, or a wealth of positive publicity. Sitkin (1996) noted that some level of failure is needed to encourage organizations to learn. After all, where is the incentive to learn if one does not experience a setback from time to time? A track record of success implies that there is nothing new to learn (Veil, 2011).

The organizational culture at NASA has long been recognized as having a culture of success that has overlooked the potential for failure (Barton, 2008; Gilpin & Murphy, 2008; Tompkins, 2005). Despite the fact that the organization has had incredible success in its space program, there have also been setbacks that have proved fatal on three separate occasions.

There Is a Culture of Scapegoating

Scapegoating hinders an organization from learning from a crisis (Elliott et al., 2000). It blames the crisis on another party, thus deflecting attention away from the core source of the problem. There are a number of pitfalls with scapegoating that ultimately prevent learning in the organization. First, the organization is likely to become even more failure prone because key issues and warnings are not raised and addressed (Elliott et al., 2000). This scenario is likely because putting the blame on a scapegoat diverts attention away from the issue that needs attention. For example, manufacturers often blame their suppliers when a product is found defective. While this may be true, it still begs the question of why that supplier was used in the first place. The example mentioned in Chapter 6 of toys manufactured in China that were decorated with lead paint and sold in the United States illustrates this supplier dilemma. The fact that there have been a number of recalls, even as this book was being written, indicates that toymakers are still learning about the pitfalls of outsourcing operations overseas.

Another problem with scapegoating is that it indicates a company's lack of ethics in running the business (Elliott et al., 2000). Scapegoating requires that blame be shifted, even if the company is at fault. Such an ethical stance is a form of denial, which is hardly a healthy atmosphere for organizational learning. The hindrance to learning is that the company's core belief system cannot be changed for the better if managers are in denial as to what went wrong at the outset. Instead of displacing the blame to other parties, the organization needs to develop a culture of learning (Argyris & Schön, 1996). This organizational culture shift to learning enables management to make changes that can prevent future crises (Veil, 2011). However, this shift is difficult if there is a status quo–seeking culture in the organization.

There Is a Status Quo–Seeking Culture

A company's core beliefs are the foundation of its organizational culture. If the culture is entrenched in an unwillingness to change from the status quo, then organizational learning will be virtually impossible (Roux-Dufort, 2000). This type of belief system begins with the attitude that a crisis "cannot happen here" or "it can't happen to us" syndrome. When denial is present, there is a high likelihood that the organization can become crisis prone (Pearson & Mitroff, 1993). When a crisis does occur, the organization must either learn from it and move on, or transfer the blame to another party, thereby entering a state of denial.

Christophe Roux-Dufort studied a 1992 crisis involving a French airliner that crashed into the Saint Odile Mountain while making its final approach for landing. He interviewed a vice president for the airline and was surprised to learn that the executive did not consider the event a crisis. His reasoning was that the day after the accident, reservations for other flights with the airline had not changed (Roux-Dufort, 2000). The problem with this mind-set is that the crisis is written off as just another event—something that happens when you conduct business—and nothing more. Deep learning and attempts to change the organization's culture are difficult to achieve when a company is in such denial; indeed, analyzing failure is painful.

Analyzing Failure Is Painful

Finally, analyzing a crisis that was the result of a failure of some human error is difficult for those involved. Negative emotions usually result when individuals examine their shortcomings, and this can result in a painful loss of self-confidence and self-esteem. Likewise, managers may find it difficult to focus attention on organizational failures because these failures are an extension of their abilities to govern effectively (Cannon & Edmondson, 2005). After all, if anyone is supposed to exert control in the organization, it is the manager. When a crisis occurs due to the failure of the organization, it is ultimately the manager's responsibility.

Research in the area of organizational behavior has revealed how managers may displace the blame for their failures. Attribution error is a concept that has emerged in studies on leadership and attempts to explain how managers attribute blame or success when certain organizational outcomes occur. When a manager achieves success, she may attribute that success to her own personal traits as a leader. However, if that same manager encounters failure, she may attribute that failure to external causes; in other words, it is not her fault. This type of rationale is known as a self-serving bias, or "the tendency to make external attributions (blame the situation) for one's own failures yet make internal attributions (take credit) for one's successes" (Hughes, Ginnett, & Curphy, 2012, p. 51). Hence, managers do not want to experience a crisis based on some fault of their own, and they certainly do not want to talk about it afterward.

Summary

Organizational learning involves the process of detecting problems and then correcting them. There are two types of learning that can take place. Single-loop learning is the detection and correction of an error without changing the basic underlying organizational norms. Double-loop learning is the detection and correction of an error, but with the changing of organizational norms. Such learning usually occurs after a process of thoughtful reflection. Peter Senge (2006) contributed to our understanding of this process through the concepts of systems thinking, personal mastery, mental models, building shared vision, and team learning.

Organizational learning from a crisis should involve evaluating each of the four stages of the crisis management framework. In evaluating the organization's response, management should seek improvements in each stage: landscape survey, strategic planning, crisis management, and organizational learning. Barriers to learning should also be examined both from an operational and a cultural perspective.

Questions for Discussion

1. Define organizational learning within the context of crisis management.

2. What is the difference between single-loop and double-loop learning?

3. How do Peter Senge's concepts of systems thinking, personal mastery, mental models, building shared vision, and team learning apply to crisis management learning?

4. How can learning take place within the four areas of the crisis management framework? Specifically, how does it occur in the landscape survey, strategic planning, crisis management, and organizational learning phases?

5. What examples of organizational learning have you seen where you work? Were any of these examples brought on by a crisis event? If so, explain how the crisis initiated the learning process.

6. What examples of barriers to learning have you seen where you work? How could these barriers be overcome?

Chapter Exercise

You have just been asked to lead the next meeting of the crisis management team of a medium-sized manufacturing facility located in a growing suburb of a large city. In your meeting you are going to discuss an incident that occurred last week in which an armed man entered the production building and threatened to kill his ex-girlfriend. The man in question came in through a back door in the kitchen and entered the employee cafeteria. He was agitated, verbally abusive, and had apparently been drinking. Two security guards restrained the man until police arrived. An unloaded gun was found in his backpack.

The company has a newly formed crisis management team, and it genuinely wants to improve the safety of the workplace. You have been asked to facilitate the next meeting of the CMT. During the meeting, you want to help the new CMT learn from this event as well as position itself to become an effective learning unit. As you plan the meeting, you are thinking of how to address the following questions:

1. What can be learned specifically from this event involving the gunman?

2. How can the CMT address learning within the larger context of the landscape survey, strategic planning, crisis management, and organizational learning phases?

3. What barriers to learning should the CMT be made aware of?

Mini-Case: Stage Collapse at the Indiana State Fair

On August 13, 2011, a thunderstorm with high winds descended on the Indiana State Fair in Indianapolis. In the concert area, a crowd was assembled to watch the country music act, Sugarland, which was scheduled to perform that night. While those attending the concert were probably not surprised to see a summer thunderstorm on the horizon, the calamity that occurred at the stage was another issue. At 8:46 P.M., with high winds and rain signaling the advancement of the storm, the concert stage suddenly collapsed, to the horror of the crowd. The canopy roof and a maze of steel beams fell and crushed people who were either on or near the front of the stage. The accident would eventually claim the lives of seven people and injure another 58 (Young, 2012).

The crisis that ensued was fraught with confusion as to who was in charge of the concert, as well as how temporary staging should be monitored for safety. A review of the events of the evening indicated that confusion existed as to who was in charge of allowing the concert to proceed. In his *Wall Street Journal* article, Jack Nicas (2012b) reviews the sequence of events that transpired:

8:15 P.M.: Officials at the state fair are informed a severe storm is approaching the concert area. The concert is scheduled to begin at 8:45 P.M. If the storm proceeds as forecasted, it will arrive 30 minutes after the concert is scheduled to start.

8:20 P.M.: Officials ask the manager of the band to delay the concert. The manager says Sugarland is not able to delay the start of the concert.

8:30 P.M.: Captain Brad Weaver from the Indiana State Police advises Cynthia Hoye, executive director of the state fair, to either delay or cancel the concert. Meanwhile, up to 12,000 fans are now in the stands awaiting the start of the performance.

8:39 P.M.: The National Weather Service issues a severe storm warning with winds up to 60 miles per hour (mph) possible. Although the warning has been issued, it does not get communicated to the state fair and concert officials.

8:40 P.M.: Cynthia Hoye, unaware that a threatening storm is now close at hand, directs the concert to perform as scheduled.

8:45 P.M.: Captain Weaver intervenes and informs Hoye that the crowd must be evacuated from the stands due to the approaching storm.

8:46 P.M.: The stage collapses.

The collapse was recorded by a number of fans at the concert, and video was soon available on YouTube.

The winds that caused the stage to succumb were in excess of 60–70 mph (Young, 2012). Mid-American Sound, the company that erected the elaborate temporary stage, said it was built to withstand winds of 40 mph. A spokesperson for the company said that over the years it had provided the stage, it informed the State Fair Commission not to use the stage if winds exceeded 25 mph (Nicas, 2012a).

At the heart of the safety issue is the question, Who actually inspects and regulates these temporary structures? The answer, unfortunately, is not consistent across the United States. Industry standards for determining how much wind a structure can withstand are voluntary. That means the enforcement of any standards must occur at the municipal and state government levels (Kilman & Merrick, 2011). In the case of the stage at the Indiana State Fair, it turns out that an official inspection of the structure was not even required. Temporary structures such as scaffolding and entertainment stages do not fall under any governing body in the state of Indiana (Knopper, 2011).

After the accident, officials at the Indiana State Fair hired Thornton Tomasetti, an international engineering firm, to determine the cause of the collapse. The New York–based firm had also been enlisted to investigate the September 11, 2001, collapse of the World Trade Center and the 2007 Interstate 35 bridge collapse in Minnesota that caused 13 fatalities (Merrick, 2011). In regard to the stage at the state fair, the firm concluded that the structure was improperly designed, built, and inspected, leaving it inadequate to withstand winds in excess of 43 mph (Nicas, 2012b).

On February 8, 2012, the Indiana Department of Labor issued fines to the State Fair Commission, a stagehands union, and Mid-American Sound Corporation. The Fair Commission was fined $6,300 for failing to take into account the severe weather conditions and their potential impact on the safety of the concert fans (Young, 2012). Their lack of foresight resulted in the fairgrounds not being evacuated before the arrival of the storm. Local 30 of the International Alliance of Theatrical Stage Employees (IATSE) was fined $11,500 for failing to provide sufficient harnessing and netting for four spotlight operators (one of whom died in the collapse), and for not testing the soil that provides support for the stage structure (Nicas, 2012a). Mid-American Sound Corporation was fined $63,000 and received most of the blame for the accident. According to Labor Commissioner Lori Torres, "The evidence demonstrated that the Mid-American Sound Corporation was aware of appropriate requirements and demonstrated a plain indifference to complying with those requirements" (Young, 2012, p. 44).

Mini-Case Questions

1. In this case, which stakeholder should be in charge of the start of a concert—state fair officials, the band Sugarland, or the state police? Why?

2. Should a temporary stage be built so it can withstand winds of more than 70 mph? Aside from the obvious advantages of such a stage, are there disadvantages as well?

3. How can weather information be communicated so it reaches the officials in charge of an outdoor concert?

Mini-Case References

Kilman, S., & Merrick, A. (2011, August 16). Scrutiny shifts to outdoor stages—Experts cite a lack of uniform inspections for portable structures, concerns about how organizers handled bad weather. *Wall Street Journal*, p. A3.

Knopper, S. (2011, September 15). Who's to blame in deadly stage collapse tragedies? *Rolling Stone*, 13–16.

Merrick, A. (2011). Engineers to probe Indiana fair's stage collapse. *Wall Street Journal*, p. A3.

Nicas, J. (2012a, February 9). Fines set in Indiana collapse. *Wall Street Journal,* p. A2.

Nicas, J. (2012b, April 13). Faulty planning, stage cited in fair collapse. *Wall Street Journal,* p. A2.

Young, C. (2012). Fines fly for Sugarland stage roof collapse. *Pro Sound News, 34*(2), 44, 58.

References

Alavi, M., & Leidner, D. (2001). Review—Knowledge management and knowledge management systems: Conceptual foundation and research issues. *MIS Quarterly, 25*(1), 107–136.

Argyris, C. (1982). *Reasoning, learning, and action: Individual and organizational.* San Francisco: Jossey-Bass.

Argyris, C., & Schön, D. (1978). *Organizational learning: A theory of action perspective.* Reading, MA: Addison-Wesley.

Argyris, C., & Schön, D. (1996). *Organizational learning II: Theory, method and practice.* Reading, MA: Addison Wesley.

Barth, T. (2010). Crisis management in the Catholic Church: Lessons for public administrators. *Public Administration Review, 70*(5), 780–791.

Barton, L. (2008). *Crisis leadership now: A real-world guide to preparing for threat, disaster, sabotage, and scandal.* New York: McGraw-Hill.

Boin, A., Lagadec, P., Michel-Kerjan, E., & Overdijk, W. (2003). Critical infrastructures under threat: Learning from the anthrax scare. *Journal of Contingencies and Crisis Management, 11*(3), 99–104.

Borodzicz, E., & van Haperen, K. (2002). Individual and group learning in crisis simulations. *Journal of Contingencies and Crisis Management, 10*(3), 139–147.

Bourrier, M. (2011). The legacy of the High Reliability Organization project. *Journal of Contingencies and Crisis Management, 19*(1), 9–13.

Brockner, J., & James, E. (2008). Toward an understanding of when executives see opportunity in crisis. *Journal of Applied Behavioral Science, 44*(7), 94–115.

Brookes, W. (1990, April 30). The wasteful pursuit of zero risk. *Forbes,* 160–172.

Brunson, R. (2008, July). Farrier firefighting: A legacy of training. *All Hands,* Issue 1096, 12–17.

Cannon, M., & Edmondson, A. (2005). Failing to learn and learning to fail (intelligently): How great organizations put failure to work to innovate and improve. *Long Range Planning, 38,* 299–319.

Carley, K., & Harrald, J. (1997). Organizational learning under fire: Theory and practice. *American Behavioral Scientist, 40*(3), 310–332.

Deverell, E. (2009). Crises as learning triggers: Exploring a conceptual framework of crisis-induced learning. *Journal of Contingencies and Crisis Management, 17*(3), 179–188.

Elliott, D., Smith, D., & McGuinness, M. (2000, Fall). Exploring the failure to learn: Crises and the barriers to learning. *Review of Business,* 17–24.

Fauchart, E. (2006). Moral hazard and the role of users in learning from accidents. *Journal of Contingencies and Crisis Management, 14*(2), 97–106.

Gilpin, D., & Murphy, P. (2008). *Crisis management in a complex world.* New York: Oxford University Press.

Hughes, R., Ginnett, R. & Curphy, C. (2012). *Leadership: Enhancing the lessons of experience* (7th ed.). New York: McGraw-Hill/Irwin.

Institute for Crisis Management. (2011). *Annual ICM crisis report: News coverage of business crises during 2010.* Retrieved April 8, 2012, from http://crisisconsultant.com/images/2010CrisisReportICM.pdf.

Kolb, D. (1984). *Experiential learning: Experience as the source of learning and development.* Englewood Cliffs, NJ: Prentice Hall.

Kovoor-Misra, S., & Nathan, M. (2000, Fall). Timing is everything: The optimal time to learn from crises. *Review of Business,* 31–36.

Lagadec, P. (1997). Learning processes for crisis management in complex organizations. *Journal of Contingencies and Crisis Management, 5*(1), 24–31.

Lalonde, C. (2007). Crisis management and organizational development: Towards the conception of a learning model in crisis management. *Organizational Development Journal, 25*(1), 17–26.

Langer, E. (1989). *Mindfulness.* Cambridge, MA: Perseus.

Lester, D., & Parnell, J. (2007). *Organizational theory: A strategic perspective.* Cincinnati: Atomic Dog Publishing.

Leveson, N., & Turner, C. (1993). An investigation of the Therac-25 accidents. *IEEE Computer, 26*(7), 18–41.

Madsen, P. (2009). These lives will not be lost in vain: Organizational learning from disaster in U.S. coal mining. *Organization Science, 20*(5), 861–875.

Martell, K. (2007). Assessing student learning: Are business schools making the grade? *Journal of Education for Business, 82*(4), 189–195.

Mawhinney, J. (1990). The Hagersville Tire Fire—February 12 to 28, 1990. *Internal Report No. 593.* National Research Council Canada. Institute for Research in Construction.

Medina, J. (2012, April 12). Campus task force criticizes pepper spraying of protestors. *New York Times,* p. 20.

Nathan, M. (2000, Fall). The paradoxical nature of crisis. *Review of Business,* 12–16.

Nystrom, P., & Starbuck, W. (1984). To avoid organizational crises, unlearn. *Organizational Dynamics, 12*(4), 53–65.

Parnell, J. A., Lado, A., & Wright, P. (1992). Why good things never seem to last: A dialectic perspective of long-term competitive advantage. *Journal of Business Strategies, 9*(1), 62–68.

Pearson, C., & Clair, J. (1998). Reframing crisis management. *Academy of Management Review, 23*(1), 59–76.

Pearson, C., & Mitroff, I. (1993). From crisis prone to crisis prepared: A framework for crisis management. *Academy of Management Executive, 7*(1), 48–59.

Perrier relabeled. (1990). *FDA Consumer, 24*(6), 2.

Pfeifer, S., & McNulty, S. (2011, April 18). Event that changed an industry. *Financial Times,* p. 19.

Racherla, P., & Hu, C. (2009). A framework for knowledge-based crisis management in the hospitality and tourism industry. *Cornell Hospitality Quarterly, 50*(4), 561–577.

Reilly, A. (2008). The role of human resource development competencies in facilitating effective crisis communication. *Advances in Developing Human Resources, 10*(3), 331–351.

Roberts, K., & Bea, R. (2001). Must accidents happen? Lessons from high-reliability organizations. *Academy of Management Executive, 15*(3), 70–78.

Roux-Dufort, C. (2000, Fall). Why organizations don't learn from crises: The perverse power of normalization. *Review of Business,* 25–30.

Seeger, M., Sellnow, T., & Ulmer, R. (2003). *Communication and organizational crisis.* Westport, CT: Praeger.

Sellnow, T., Seeger, M., & Ulmer, R. (2002). Chaos theory, informational needs, and natural disasters. *Journal of Applied Communication Research, 30*(4), 269–292.

Senge, P. (2006). *The fifth discipline handbook: The art and practice of the learning organization.* New York: Currency Doubleday.

Simon, L., & Pauchant, T. (2000, Fall). Developing the three levels of learning in crisis management: A case study of the Hagersville tire fire. *Review of Business,* 6–11.

Sitkin, S. (1996). Learning through failure: The strategy of small losses. In M. D. Cohen & L. S. Sproull (Eds.), *Organizational learning* (pp. 541–578). Thousand Oaks, CA: Sage.

Smith, D. (1993). Crisis management in the public sector: Lessons from the prison service. In J. Wilson & P. Hinton (Eds.), *Public service and the 1990s: Issues in public service finance and management* (pp. 141–170). London: Tudor Press.

Smith, D., & Elliott, D. (2007). Exploring the barriers to learning from crisis: Organizational learning and crisis. *Management Learning, 38*(5), 519–538.

Stead, E., & Smallman, C. (1999). Understanding business failure: Learning and un-learning lessons from industrial crises. *Journal of Contingencies and Crisis Management, 7*(1), 1–18.

Stelter, B. (2011, November 21). California University puts officers who used pepper spray on leave. *New York Times,* p. 13.

Sullivan, J., & Beach, R. (2012). Making organizational learning work: Lessons from a high reliability organization. *International Journal of Business Intelligence Research, 3*(3), 54-61.

Tompkins, P. (2005). *Apollo, Challenger, Columbia: The decline of the space program.* Los Angeles: Roxbury.

Turner, B., & Pidgeon, N. (1997). *Man-made disasters* (2nd ed.). London: Butterworth-Heinemann.

Ulmer, R., Sellnow, T., & Seeger, M. (2007). *Effective crisis communication: Moving from crisis to opportunity.* Thousand Oaks, CA: Sage.

Veil, S. (2011). Mindful learning in crisis management. *Journal of Business Communication, 48*(2), 116–147.

Veil, S., & Sellnow, T. (2008). Organizational learning in a high-risk environment: Responding to the anthrax outbreak. *Journal of Applied Communications, 92,* 75–93.

Wang, J. (2008). Developing organizational learning capacity in crisis management. *Advances in Developing Human Resources, 10*(3), 425–445.

Weick, K. (1993). The collapse of sensemaking in organizations: The Mann Gulch disaster. *Administrative Science Quarterly, 38,* 628–652.

Weick, K., & Sutcliffe, K. (2001). *Managing the unexpected.* San Francisco: Jossey-Bass.

The Underlying Role of Ethics in Crisis Management

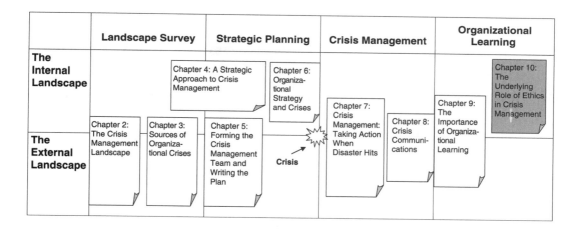

	Landscape Survey	Strategic Planning	Crisis Management	Organizational Learning
The Internal Landscape		Chapter 4: A Strategic Approach to Crisis Management	Chapter 6: Organizational Strategy and Crises		Chapter 10: The Underlying Role of Ethics in Crisis Management
The External Landscape	Chapter 2: The Crisis Management Landscape / Chapter 3: Sources of Organizational Crises	Chapter 5: Forming the Crisis Management Team and Writing the Plan / Crisis	Chapter 7: Crisis Management: Taking Action When Disaster Hits	Chapter 8: Crisis Communications / Chapter 9: The Importance of Organizational Learning	

Opening Case: Hawks Nest

In southern West Virginia, there is an engineering feat that few people know about except for the locals and the tourists who happen to stop by the small roadside park overlooking the project. It is an underground tunnel, about 3 miles long, that carries water from a dam to a small hydroelectric plant perched securely on the side of a mountain. The purpose of the project was to supply electricity to the Union Carbide plant, then located in Alloy, West Virginia, about 6 miles away. The tunnel was built in the 1930s during the Great Depression, mostly by poor workers who migrated to the area seeking employment (Cherniak, 1986).

The project itself was somewhat ingenious because it solved a problem faced by Union Carbide. Additional electricity was needed to power its new plant, but the prospects of supplying it with hydroelectric power appeared bleak because the

New River—one of only a few rivers in the United States that flows north—was (and still is) a slow-moving, narrow band of water that does not have enough force to power a hydroelectric plant in that location. The engineers came up with a clever solution: construct a dam to build up water volume and then pitch it in a downward direction to give it force (Cherniak, 1986). A small hydroelectric building with four turbines was positioned where the water emerged with great force from the tunnel. The result was a facility that makes electricity to this day (Crandall & Crandall, 2002).

But there is a darker side to this project. The tunnel contractor, Virginia engineering firm Rinehart and Dennis, drastically cut corners to save on project time and expenses. Workers were required to enter the dusty tunnel to begin clearing out the debris shortly after explosives had been detonated. Although engineers were supplied with respirators, those doing the manual labor were not. When silica rock was encountered, the resulting fine dust that the explosion had created was inhaled by the workers as they removed debris from the tunnel shaft. As a result, many of these laborers developed silicosis, a debilitating lung disease that eventually causes death. This disease is avoidable if respirators are worn.

Rinehart and Dennis also used another cost-cutting measure: dry drilling. Wet drilling should have been used to minimize dust levels. The downside is that wet drilling slows the extraction process, unlike dry drilling, which is faster but creates more dust (Orr & Dragan, 1981; Rowh, 1981). The additional dust associated with the dry drilling, coupled with the lack of respirators, led to sickness in these workers.

The number of deaths attributed to the Hawks Nest Tunnel can only be estimated because Social Security records did not exist at the time (Cherniak, 1986). The estimates vary depending on the source of information. Rinehart and Dennis submitted a figure of 65 total deaths, whereas Union Carbide, the ultimate user of the Hawks Nest tunnel, counted 109 fatalities. In his account of the Hawks Nest incident, Martin Cherniak estimates a total of 764 deaths. Regardless of the exact number, the figures are high relative to today's standards of industrial safety. As one might expect, the death estimates become more conservative as the source of information moves closer to the tunnel contractor (Crandall & Crandall, 2002).

Although details about the Hawks Nest Tunnel incident are not widely known, a number of management scholars have taken an interest in studying the event because of the apparent disregard for worker safety. It is a case involving excellent productivity (the tunnel was built in only 18 months), a racial element (many of the workers were poor blacks), and a disregard for worker safety (requiring workers to toil in the dusty tunnel without protection for their lungs). Two novels have been written on Hawks Nest. *Hawk's Nest,* by Hubert Skidmore (1941), was banned because of pressure from Union Carbide (Nyden, 2009). Today, the book is back in publication with a new publisher. A more recent novel, *Witness at Hawks Nest,* by Dwight Harshbarger (2009), relies on academic research of the events of the time to create the characters for his story.

Because this event occurred nearly 80 years ago, many might assume that serious safety concerns no longer exist, at least in developed nations like the United States. Unfortunately, a mind-set of promoting profits over worker safety still exists among some organizations, as seen with a recent example in the same state, the unfortunate disaster at the Upper Big Branch mine near Beckley, West Virginia, which resulted in the deaths of 29 miners in 2010. The numerous safety violations and disregard for employee welfare by mine owner Massey Energy illustrate ethical concerns and a disregard for worker safety that have not yet been completely eradicated in the United States. Ironically, the Hawks Nest Tunnel and the Upper Big Branch mine are fewer than 50 miles apart!

Opening Case Discussion Questions

1. Why do you think there is so much discrepancy on the number of reported deaths at Hawks Nest?

2. Why would a once-reputable firm such as Rinehart and Dennis fail to take the measures necessary to protect its workers?

3. Both Hawks Nest and the Upper Big Branch mine were underground work locations. Does this have any significance in the hiding of safety violations? If so, how?

4. Why would a modern organization like Massey Energy repeat the legacy of Hawks Nest by compromising worker safety?

Opening Case References

Cherniak, M. (1986). *The Hawk's Nest incident: America's worst industrial disaster.* New York: Vail-Ballou.
Crandall, W. R., & Crandall, R. E. (2002). Revisiting the Hawks Nest Tunnel incident: Lessons learned from an American tragedy. *Journal of Appalachian Studies, 8*(2), 261–283.
Harshbarger, D. (2009). *Witness at Hawks Nest.* Huntington, WV: Mid-Atlantic Highlands.
Nyden, P. (2009, August 2). Novel offers personal look at Hawks Nest disaster. Republished from the *Charleston Gazette.* Retrieved July 13, 2012, from http://www.witnessathawksnest.com/nyden.html.
Orr, D., & Dragan, J. (1981). A dirty, messy place to work: B. H. Metheney remembers Hawk's Nest tunnel. *Goldenseal, 1*(7), 34–41.
Rowh, M. (1981). The Hawks Nest tragedy: Fifty years later. *Goldenseal, 1*(7), 31–33.
Skidmore, H. (1941). *Hawk's Nest.* New York: Doubleday, Doran and Co.

Introduction

There is an underlying problem in many of the crisis events discussed in this book. This problem does not manifest itself in every crisis, but it is substantial nonetheless. Why do seemingly preventable crises occur again and again? Sometimes the answer can be found with a firm's employees, particularly its managers and top-level business executives and their desire to gain unfairly at the expense of another party. Put simply, an unabated desire for profits without regard to sound moral principles can trigger an organizational crisis. This problem appears in many forms, but the results are usually the same: an organizational crisis of some type, stakeholders who have been hurt, and prevention that would have cost pennies in comparison to the damage done.

The Hawks Nest Tunnel incident was one of the first major industrial crises in the United States. Although the tunnel was a remarkable success, the human resource tragedy was enormous. The deaths of these workers were entirely preventable, but tunnel contractor Rinehart and Dennis decided that breathing protection and other safety measures should be abandoned in order to maximize profits. The contractor did not escape unscathed, however. Within five years of the project, its assets were liquidated—a victim of bad publicity, lawsuits, and loss of revenue.

In an age when Enron, the Catholic Church, Penn State, and Massey Energy are more commonly known scandal-ridden organizations, why focus here on a human tragedy that occurred more than half a century ago? The Hawks Nest Tunnel incident clearly illustrates the fact that some crises have human roots that can be traced back to unethical or irresponsible behavior by key decision makers. In addition, such behaviors are not confined to any specific time period in history. Human-induced crises have always occurred and will continue to occur, an inescapable reality. However, some organizations do a better job than others at avoiding these types of crises because they emphasize ethical behavior among their members. This too, is an inescapable fact, and a cause for hope.

In this chapter we examine human-induced crises more closely, specifically those linked to unethical behavior. The chapter begins with an overview of business ethics. We then examine the four stages of the crisis management framework and their relationship to crises that are caused by ethical breaches. The chapter concludes with a note on the relationship of trust with a crisis.

What Is Business Ethics?

Business ethics examines issues of right and wrong behavior in the business environment (Carroll & Buchholtz, 2012). Some business practices can be legal, but are not necessarily ethical. Put differently, a business may be acting within the law, but not necessarily doing the "right thing." Such behavior from a callous executive might reveal statements such as, "Well, we didn't break any laws," or "Our job is to maximize profits, period." Such behavior can also get a company in trouble.

A related but distinct concept is corporate social responsibility (CSR), which maintains that businesses should seek social benefits for society as well as economic benefits for the business (Post, Lawrence, & Weber, 2002). The concept of CSR is aligned with what has become known as the *stakeholder model,* a viewpoint that seeks to recognize and meet a wide range of groups that have some type of connected interested in the organization. The goal is to balance the needs of the stakeholders in a way that is both beneficial to the organization and to the stakeholders. This thinking is different from the *shareholder model,* which seeks value maximization for the owners of the firm. With the shareholder model, stakeholders are not as highly valued as they are in the stakeholder model unless they have some bearing on wealth maximization (Berman, Wicks, Kotha, & Jones, 1999). A simple example illustrates this difference. When a firm has excess profits, it can choose to distribute those profits in a number of ways. Under the shareholder model, earnings can be funneled back into the company to increase efficiency and productivity (and hence future profits) and/or distributed to the owners in the form of dividends. The shareholder model implies that the owners are to receive the top priority in the distribution of these funds. Under the stakeholder model, excess cash may be given to the local community (sponsoring a youth baseball team or a scholarship at a local university), to the employees in the form of a raise or bonus, or perhaps to upgrading the company's technology so it is more environmentally friendly. The point to remember is that cash that could have gone to the owners went to some other stakeholder instead. In terms of crisis management and long-term viability, it is important for firms to recognize the needs of multiple stakeholders (Alpaslan, Green, & Mitroff, 2009).

A popular framework for looking at the two concepts of business ethics and CSR is shown in Table 10.1. In this framework, proposed by Carroll and Buchholtz (2012), CSR is made up of our four parts: economic, legal, ethical, and philanthropic responsibilities. Above all, businesses must meet their economic responsibility by being profitable while operating within the confines of the law.

Table 10.1   The Components of Corporate Social Responsibility

Component of CSR	Key Thought to Understanding	Manifestations
Economic responsibility	Be profitable.	Maximize sales revenues. Reduce operating expenses. Increase profits. Maximize shareholder wealth.
Legal responsibility	Obey the law.	Abide by all legal regulations. Operate within industry standards. Maintain all contract and warranty obligations.
Ethical responsibility	Avoid questionable practices.	Go beyond just obeying the law; abide by the spirit of the law as well. Avoid practices that may appear to be suspicious, even if they are legal. Do the right thing, and be just and fair to all stakeholders.
Philanthropic responsibility	Be a good corporate citizen.	Make financial contributions to external stakeholders in the community. Seek to be a good neighbor in the community by making it a better place to live. Look for ways to support education, health or human services, and the arts.

Source: Adapted from Carroll and Buchholtz (2012), pp. 37–38.

There is also a realm of business behavior that goes beyond obeying the law. Ethical responsibility seeks to avoid behaviors that are questionable though not necessarily illegal. Practically speaking, it is not possible to develop laws to prohibit every unethical business activity. Consider also that many companies sell products or services that are legal but are considered by many to be unethical in some contexts. Hartley (1993) documents the now-infamous PowerMaster Beer controversy in which malt liquor, a legal product, was heavily marketed to poor urban areas, markets in which crime and youth despair were prevalent. This combination created an unethical situation in the eyes of many community stakeholders, who saw this product contributing to even higher crime problems in urban neighborhoods. More recently, the mortgage crisis of the early 2000s that adversely affected an entire industry could have been avoided if individual lenders had simply refused to issue loans with terms that were likely to create a substantial repayment hardship down the road for borrowers. To their credit, several lenders refused to issue such profitable loans on ethical grounds, a high road not taken by most in the industry (Parnell & Dent, 2009).

Finally, it can be argued that companies have a philanthropic responsibility: the obligation to be good corporate citizens. Some seek to fulfill this responsibility by contributing time and money to the communities in which they operate. Many businesses make financial contributions to school systems as well as colleges and universities. Others encourage their employees to volunteer in their communities and will often compensate these employees for their time invested in civic causes.

Carroll and Buchholtz (2012) maintain that three CSR components—economic, legal, and ethical—are also the most closely tied in with business ethics. Considering organizational crises, it is clear that many are comprised of one or more of these components. In Table 10.2 we provide examples based on the assumption that business ethics crises are motivated by a desire to gain financially at the expense of another stakeholder. For example, at the heart of the economic component is the need to make a profit for the business. Chief executive officers (CEOs) and other top managers are especially cognizant of this need to increase profits because their compensation is usually tied in with how well the firm is performing financially. But doing so without regard to morality can result in breaking the law (the legal component) or taking part in questionable ethical practices (the ethical component), both of which can result in organizational crises.

Business Ethics and the Crisis Management Framework

Many of the crises discussed in this section are examples of what have been labeled "smoldering crises." The Institute for Crisis Management (ICM) notes that these crises start out small and can be fixed early on, but instead they are allowed to fester until they become full-blown crises and known to the public (Institute for Crisis Management, 2011). What makes some smoldering crises ethically induced is that they do not have to occur in the first place. If such a crisis does occur, it can be mitigated through ethical decision making, although not all executives will proceed in this manner. Instead, some escalate the crisis by making additional unethical decisions until the crisis spins out of control.

Table 10.2   Ethical Crises Components

The Basis for an Ethical Crisis	Ethical Crisis Component	Examples of Crises
	Legal: These cases involve behavior on the part of company employees that violates the law.	Company misrepresents its accounting statements by hiding debt, overstating profits, or other forms of fraud. Examples: • Tyco (late 1990s to 2002) • Adelphia Communications Corporation (2002) • Enron (2002) • HealthSouth (2002) • Qwest Communications International (2005) • Bernie Madoff (2009) Company knowingly sells a defective product. Examples: • A. H. Robins Dalkon Shield (1984) • Dow Corning silicone breast implants (1992) Company falsely advertises its product. Example: • Beech-Nut apple juice (1982) Company violates safety standards in the workplace. Examples: • Rinehart and Dennis (1930s) • Warner-Lambert Company (1976) • Film Recovery Services, Inc. (1985) • British Petroleum Texas City explosion (2005) • British Petroleum *Deepwater Horizon* explosion (2010) • Massey Energy (2010).
Economic: The basic motive is a desire to gain financially, often at the expense of another stakeholder.		
	Ethical: These cases involve behavior on the part of company employees that is questionable but does not necessarily violate the law.	Company sells a product that is legal but not necessarily beneficial to society. Examples: • Nestlé Infant Formula (1970s) • PowerMaster Beer (1991) • The tobacco industry (ongoing) • Ashleymadison.com (ongoing) Company outsources production to suppliers that impose harsh conditions on their employees (e.g., sweatshops). Examples: • Discount retail chains (ongoing) • Clothing manufacturing companies (ongoing) • Appliance manufacturing companies (ongoing)

Note: Some of these examples may not be familiar. These will be examined in more detail in the Chapter Exercise.
Sources: Adapted from Carroll and Buchholtz (2012); Coombs (2006, 2007); Hartley (1993); Sethi, and Steidlmeier (1997).

A classic case of unethical decision making concerns the Beech-Nut apple juice case, an example that also illustrates a smoldering crisis that should have been stopped early on. During the late 1970s, Beech-Nut Nutrition Corporation found out that it was the victim of a scam when it discovered the supplier of its apple juice concentrate was selling it fake apple juice. This discovery was especially troublesome because Beech-Nut advertised its apple juice as "100% fruit juice, no sugar added." Because of the bogus apple juice concentrate from its supplier, this advertisement claim was not true. At that point, Beech-Nut could have reported the incident, pleaded ignorance, and most likely escaped any prosecution because it was an innocent victim ("Bad apples," 1989; Hartley, 1993). However, this supplier was providing its product at 25 percent below the market rate, and the cost savings was too attractive for Beech-Nut executives to pass up.

Rather than ceasing to do business with its supplier, Beech-Nut chose to continue buying the counterfeit concentrate from them! From 1977 to 1983, Beech-Nut sold its juice as 100 percent pure when, in fact, it was nothing more than a "100% fraudulent chemical cocktail," according to an investigator close to the case (Welles, 1988, p. 124). What should have been a decision to change suppliers became an ethical misconduct crisis. Beech-Nut president Neils Hoyvald, and John Lavery, vice president for operations, were the main parties who instigated the cover-up. When the crisis was over, both men were found guilty of violating federal food and drug laws. Hartley (1993) estimates the crisis that never should have happened cost Beech-Nut $25 million in fines, legal costs, and lost sales.

Table 10.3 depicts the crisis management framework in relation to business ethics issues. The next sections develop the four areas of the crisis management process.

Landscape Survey: Uncovering the Ethical Boulders

The landscape survey looks for clues in the organization's internal and external environments that may indicate the presence of an unethical event brewing. Potential crisis indicators include the ethical environment of the board of directors, the safety policies of the organization, the economic motives among top executives and management, the degree of industry vulnerability, and the vulnerability of the organization in the global environment. These indicators are discussed next.

The Company Founder, CEO, and the Board of Directors

The ethical environment of the organization is an indicator of the potential for a future crisis. The founder of the company holds a considerable amount of influence in forming this ethical environment. For example, Enron, WorldCom, Adelphia, HealthSouth, and Tyco have all faced ethical scandals. What these firms had in common was their founders, all hardworking entrepreneurs, were at the helm when the crises hit (Colvin, 2003). Furthermore, those in charge of these companies had at least three characteristics in common that led to the scandals. First, these companies had not learned to question the founder or CEO when necessary. Rather, their CEOs were powerful individuals who seemed to answer to no one. Second, an element of greed was apparent at the top levels of these companies. It was as if an entitlement mentality prevailed, with those running the company

Table 10.3   Crisis Management Framework in Relation to Business Ethics

	Landscape Survey	Strategic Planning	Crisis Management	Organizational Learning
The Internal Landscape	■ The company founder, CEO, and the board of directors ■ The safety policies of the organization ■ The economic motives among top executives and management ■ The disconnect between organizational mission and existence	■ The enthusiasm for crisis management planning and training ■ The ethical culture of the organization	■ The management of internal stakeholders o Owners o Employees	■ The evaluation of the ethical management process ■ The commitment to organizational learning
The External Landscape	■ The degree of industry vulnerability ■ The vulnerability of the organization in the global environment	■ The existence of government regulations ■ The existence of industry standards	■ The management of external stakeholders o Customers o Suppliers o Government entities o Local community o The media	■ The benefits of industry renewal ■ The inevitability of new government regulations ■ The anticipation of new stakeholder outlooks

receiving extraordinary amounts of compensation because they felt they deserved it. Finally, all of these companies had leaders who seemed to focus on short-term gains by increasing stock prices without regard to the long-term sustainability of the company. The link between CEO compensation and stock price is an underlying factor in many of the scandals that hit these big corporations (Colvin, 2003). As stock prices increases, CEO compensation typically follows.

This factor presents the corporation with a dilemma. On one hand, CEO compensation should be linked to firm performance; on the other hand, this linkage can be abused in favor of short-term performance versus long-term survival and growth. In response to this quandary, some firms have favored the *balanced scorecard* approach (Kaplan & Norton, 2001), an approach that has pushed the practice of accounting to track long-term as well as short-term performance results. Thousands of companies have now adopted this approach in the United States and abroad (Parnell & Jusoh, 2008).

A major factor that has created this problem is the failure of boards of directors to challenge the CEO (Zweig, 2010). As a result, more scrutiny of corporate boards is starting to occur, with boards facing more accountability and disclosure mandates (Thorne, Ferrell, & Ferrell, 2003). The situation at WorldCom is an example of a board that continually gave in to the desires of then-CEO Bernard Ebbers: "As CEO, Ebbers was allowed nearly imperial reign over the affairs of the company with little influence from the board of directors, even though he did not appear to possess the experience or training to be qualified for his position" (Breeden, 2003, p. 1). Two areas of questionable CEO freedom were requested by Ebbers and approved by the board. The first involved the approval of the collection of $400 million in loans, and the second a rubber-stamping of his request to compensate favored executives to the tune of $238 million. The arrangement was made without standards or supervision and allowed Ebbers to compensate whomever he wanted and in whatever amount he wished (Breeden, 2003). Ultimately, these schemes, along with others, culminated in a crisis that resulted in the largest accounting fraud case in the United States.

Crisis cases like WorldCom illustrate why boards have to be more than just a rubber stamp for the CEO. In response, some boards are taking a more aggressive approach to holding the CEO accountable for ethical behavior. Case in point: Boeing's former CEO, Harry Stonecipher, lost his job after it was revealed he was having an affair with another Boeing executive (Benjamin, Lim, & Streisand, 2005). The relationship violated company policy.

The Safety Policies of the Organization

The organization's safety policies, or the lack of them, have a direct link to the ethical climate of the organization. Ultimately, the adherence to such policies can determine whether or not a major crisis occurs. An ethical stance on the part of management promotes an environment in which all stakeholders (particularly employees) are safe from bodily and emotional harm. However, as every manager and top executive knows, safety costs money and can detract from the bottom line in the short run. In the long run, though, these expenditures can save the company millions and maybe even the company itself.

In looking back at industrial accidents, organizational researchers have never reached a conclusion that indicated that too much money was spent on safety (Crandall & Crandall, 2002). In fact, executives who have experienced a safety issue such as an industrial accident resulting in injuries or deaths probably wish they had spent more. For example, in the 1983 Bhopal, India, gas leak incident, Union Carbide and local government officials in India should have focused more on correcting safety problems that had already been widely documented at the plant prior to the accident (Sethi & Steidlmeier, 1997; Steiner & Steiner, 2000).

Safety measures involve short-term expenses but produce long-term savings by avoiding accidents. Hence, well-crafted remedies need not always be viewed as expensive. Money spent to prevent employee injury and death is not money wasted; it may well save the company millions in lawsuits, as well as the company's reputation, not to mention the saving of human lives. The Hawks Nest Tunnel contractor, Rinehart and Dennis, could have implemented at least three relatively low-cost measures—better ventilation of the tunnel shaft, wet drilling, and providing respirators for workers—to make working conditions safer and thereby prevent workers from developing silicosis. While it is difficult to determine the exact cost of these measures, it is clear that they would have saved many lives. A focus on safety would have also likely prevented the downfall of the company that occurred within 5 years of completing the tunnel.

The Economic Motives Among Top Executives and Management

Economic motives are often linked to unethical and illegal behavior on the part of top management. The reason for this behavior is easy to see. Management competence is measured by key performance indicators such as sales, profits, and market share, all of which can ultimately drive the price of the company's stock. Boards of directors typically reward the CEO when stock valuations increase, because this represents an increase in wealth for the shareholders. At first, this scenario of rewards for stock valuation increases sounds like a win-win situation, but as many recent business crises indicate, abuses can occur that ultimately are not in the best interest of the corporation or its stakeholders. Two such abuses are hiding debt and questionable cost-cutting measures.

Hiding Debt

Hiding debt creates the illusion that the firm is performing better than it actually is, thereby encouraging a false sense of optimism and confidence. The result is that stock prices rise in the short term, and shareholder values increase. The CEO is also rewarded because of the firm's attractive stock price. However, this process is motivated by an attempt at excessive financial gain at the expense of other stakeholders, such as employees or the community in which the company resides. In the short run, this unethical strategy can produce financial benefits for the CEO and the shareholders. In the long run, however, it is a prescription for a major crisis.

Enron remains the poster child for this abuse when the company spiraled downward after its elaborate schemes for hiding debt became known. Enron's debt was hidden through an accounting strategy known as "off-balance sheet" partnerships called special purpose entities (SPEs). These partnerships were allowable under accounting loopholes at the time and were initiated by then-chief financial officer (CFO) Andrew Fastow. The SPEs were actually joint ventures with various groups of investors, but because they were separate entities they were not part of the Enron balance sheet. The sole purpose of these SPEs was to remove unwanted assets and liabilities from Enron's balance statements (Boatright, 2012).

The structures of SPEs have trigger mechanisms that require repayment of the debt under certain circumstances (Henry, Timmons, Rosenbush, & Arndt, 2002). It was these trigger mechanisms that began the "visible" crisis at Enron. That crisis became known with the October 16, 2001, announcement that Enron was taking a

$544 million after-tax charge against its earnings related to transactions involving its SPEs (Powers, 2002). The result was a third-quarter loss of $618 million and a $1 billion reduction in the company's asset value. From that date, the implosion of Enron was rapid and dramatic. Enron's stock price fell from $33 on October 16 to $15 on October 26. On December 2, Enron laid off 4,000 employees and filed for bankruptcy. Only a year earlier, Enron had been touted as a socially responsible firm leading the way in alternative energy, ranking the seventh largest on the *Fortune* 500 list with a stock price of $90 (DesJardins, 2009). The downfall of Enron later paved the way for the Sarbanes-Oxley Act and other regulations.

Questionable Cost-Cutting Measures

Questionable cost cutting is the other abuse that can arise from unethical motives. Such cost cutting is the profit motive at work and will cause some managers to do just about anything. Trimming costs delivers dollars to the bottom line, but doing so without regard for worker safety has resulted in many examples of industrial tragedies. In 1976, when Warner-Lambert was introducing a new line of chewing gum, it took shortcuts in the manufacturing area by allowing high levels of dust near the machinery. The company could have installed a dust collection system, a move that would have reduced dust levels significantly. The cost was seen as prohibitive, however, so the opportunity to buy the system was ignored. The result was a dust explosion that killed six employees and injured 54 others (Sethi & Steidlmeier, 1997).

Although cost cutting is a normal and necessary business activity, it was the major factor in the many deaths that resulted from building the Hawks Nest Tunnel. The use of dry drilling to expedite the project time was discussed earlier. Shortening the project time reduces expenses and increases the bottom line. The decision not to provide tunnel workers with respirators is especially troubling. The only explanation for this seems to be the additional cost that would have been incurred.

The Hawks Nest incident illustrates the connection between ethical decision making—doing what is just and fair for—and protecting worker safety. Perhaps the most famous abuse of worker safety in the United States was the 1911 Triangle Shirtwaist Company fire that occurred on the 10th floor of a factory in New York City. The fire spread rapidly due to the large amounts of linen and other combustible materials close by. One hundred forty-six employees died, most of them immigrant women who were either burned in the blaze or jumped to their deaths. Sadly, the fire escape routes for these employees had been locked by management in order to prevent theft (Greer, 2001; Vernon, 1998). Some may argue that revisiting cases like Hawks Nest and the Triangle Shirtwaist fire is not necessary today. After all, labor unions, labor laws, safety inspectors, and various watchdog groups discourage this kind of behavior (Shanker, 1992). Unfortunately, history has a way of repeating itself.

On September 3, 1991, a fire erupted at the Imperial Food Products poultry plant in Hamlet, North Carolina. A hydraulic line ruptured, spilling a flammable liquid throughout the kitchen. The vapors from the line were ignited by the gas burners from the flying vats, creating a large fire in the 30,000-square-foot plant (Lacayo & Kane, 1991). Before the day was over, 25 employees, most of them single mothers, would perish. "The plant had no sprinkler or fire alarm system, and workers who got to the unmarked fire exits found some of them locked from the outside. Imperial's management was using the same 'loss control' technique as the bosses at Triangle—and with the same results" (Shanker, 1992, p. 27). Many of the victims, unable to open the locked fire exits; died in a cluster by the doorway. Others were found in a freezer where they had sought refuge. The owner claimed that the fire exit doors had been locked to prevent theft of the chickens.

An $800,000 labor code fine was levied against the company. Fourteen months after the fire, a $16 million settlement was reached between the insurers and the claimants. Plant owner Emmet Roe was sentenced to 20 years in prison after pleading guilty to manslaughter (Jefferson, 1993). Eventually, Imperial went bankrupt. As these examples illustrate, unchecked greed comes in various forms and can hurt other stakeholders in the process.

The Disconnect Between Organizational Mission and Existence

At this point in our discussion, a more philosophical question should be raised concerning the organization's mission: Does the organization exist for its mission, or does the mission exist to guide the organization? The mission should clarify the purpose for the organization's existence (Parnell, 2013). Some organizations seem to lose touch with their missions over time, a situation that can lead to ethical breaches.

Schwartz (1990) noted that an organization can exist to do work (its mission), or it can do work in order to exist. This observation is not just a play on words but has tremendous implications in the area of managerial ethics. For example, Barth (2010) notes that the Catholic Church operated in this mode early in its crises concerning priests who were sexually abusing children. The church seemed more interested in protecting its structure than with protecting the children who were victims. Rather than removing the predatory priests altogether, the church chose merely to transfer many of them to other parishes. Whether intended or not, the Catholic Church was communicating that the careers of the priests were more important than the people they were appointed to serve. A disconnect between the organization's mission and the reason for its existence had occurred.

In the business sector, there can be a similar disconnect between a corporation's top management and the firm's shareholders. The result is called the *agency problem* and occurs when managers (i.e., the agents of the shareholders) place their personal goals over those of the owners (Parnell, 2013). For example, Enron's CFO Andrew Fastow benefited greatly from his involvement in the SPE transactions. The Special Investigative Committee of the Board of Directors at Enron noted:

Enron employees involved in the partnerships were enriched, in the aggregate, by tens of millions of dollars they should have never received—Fastow by at least $30 million, Kopper by at least $10 million, two others by $1 million each, and still two more by amounts we believe were at least in the hundreds of thousands of dollars. (Powers, 2002: 3–4)

Andrew Fastow and Michael J. Kopper were identified as active participants in managing the SPEs. Both gained considerably as a result of activities that were ultimately detrimental to Enron. Agency theory illustrates how some in top management view themselves as independent contractors, free to do whatever they wish for their own self-interest.

The Degree of Industry Vulnerability

Some industries seem to be more crisis prone from an ethical perspective. For example, professional wrestling and baseball have had a history of steroid use. Professional cycling, particularly with events like the Tour de France, has faced charges of performance-enhancing drugs among participants. The coal mining industry has a long history of sacrificing miner safety. Indeed, the United Mine Workers of America (UMWA) has a history of being one of the most aggressive unions in existence, due mostly to the abuse of coal miners who have been subject to unsafe working conditions by the mine owners. Certainly, coal mining safety has improved in recent years, but rogue coal companies still seem to exist.

Looking through the lens of "ethical rationality" (Snyder, Hall, Robertson, Jasinski, & Miller, 2006), the challenge is to determine whether an industry is more vulnerable to a crisis because of a higher degree of unethical occurrences. The link between industry-specific factors and unethical behaviors has not been as widely addressed, although some attention has been focused on aircraft manufacturers. Both Lockheed and Northrop were found to have made improper cash payments to overseas sales agents in the 1970s in order to secure contracts to sell aircraft (Securities and Exchange Commission, 1976). More recently, Boeing has been plagued by a number of ethical problems, perpetuated by what has been called a "culture of silence" by Boeing general counsel Douglas Bain. The culture stems from a lack of speaking up on ethical issues, a problem that has plagued the company for a considerable amount of time (Holmes, 2006).

The Vulnerability of the Organization in the Global Environment

As a firm expands its international presence, its vulnerability to an ethical crisis may also increase. Three reasons for potential ethical problems include the temptation to make illegal cash payments, the possibility that a defective product will emerge from a foreign country, and the potential to be linked with sweatshop manufacturing.

The Temptation to Make Illegal Cash Payments

Major scandals often result in new legislation. As a result of the Lockheed bribery scandal, the Foreign Corrupt Practices Act was passed in 1977 (Hartley, 1993). The act prohibits offering cash payments to foreign government officials for the purpose of obtaining business. In addition, foreign companies whose stock is traded in the United States are subject to review by the Department of Justice (Carroll & Buchholtz, 2012). Critics often complain, however, that the act places American firms at a disadvantage when competing for foreign contracts in countries where legal infrastructure requiring that all companies play by the same rules does not exist. In many parts of the world, offering bribes is an accepted way to conduct business. To further complicate the matter, the act does allow some cash payments, called "grease payments"—smaller amounts of cash used to encourage foreign officials to do what they are supposed to do anyway (Carrol & Buchholtz, 2012). A "bribe," on the other hand, is a large cash payment used to entice a foreign official or agent to do something not normally done in the course of business, such as buying from a particular vendor.

As companies expand globally, the temptation to use illegal cash payments increases. Wal-Mart recently found this out in its expansion efforts in Mexico. An April 22, 2012, *New York Times* article broke the case involving bribe payments by Wal-Mart management in Mexico. The trigger point for the crisis was a 2005 e-mail to Wal-Mart headquarters sent by a former Wal-Mart executive who had arranged a number of bribe payments to help facilitate the company's development in the Mexican market. The former executive, Sergio Cicero Zapata, had worked for Wal-Mart until 2004 in the company's real estate development department (Barstow, Xanic, & McKinley, 2012). Two retirement systems, the California State Teachers Retirement System (CalSTRS) and the New York City Pension system, have sued Wal-Mart for mishandling the bribery allegations and covering up the details of the investigations ("NYC pension funds," 2012).

The Possibility That a Defective Product Will Emerge From a Foreign Country

Two problems result when a defective product emerges from another country. First, the product itself can pose a danger. Toymaker Mattel found this out in 2007 when it had to recall more than 22 million toys manufactured in China due to high levels of lead and other toxins (Barton, 2008). What makes this case noteworthy is that Mattel has a long history of safety and social responsiveness. In fact, Mattel owns and operates its factories in China. However, one of its plants either violated a policy by using the lead-laden paint or a supplier provided the paint unknowingly to Mattel (Hartman & DesJardins, 2011).

Second, a foreign-sourced defective product can lead to negative feelings by citizens in the home country. Because many U.S. manufacturing jobs have been lost to foreign sourced companies, a defective product that emerges on the market is a reminder that the product could have been made back in the home country instead of being outsourced, presumably without any quality concerns. The result is a public relations crisis for the home country company because citizens may feel resentment for offshoring in the first place.

The Potential of Being Linked With Sweatshop Manufacturing

Companies that outsource processes to overseas vendors may face potential association with sweatshops—manufacturing facilities that pay low wages, employ child labor, have poor working conditions, require long work hours, and otherwise abuse their workers. Their use has increased as companies seek to lower costs but can also cause companies to be hit with public relations crises. Wal-Mart, Nike, Liz Claiborne, and Disney are large, high-profile companies that have been linked with sweatshops in the past.

Sweatshops are the ultimate "guilt by association" crisis. Although some progress has been made in recent years to improve working conditions in developing countries, the issue will not go away anytime soon. Although a company can "require" its subcontractors to abide by certain working condition standards, the enforcement of these standards can be difficult. Typically, independent monitors are sent to investigate working conditions in plants that are supposed to be compliant with certain standards. However, this system is not foolproof, as inspectors can be deceived by the very companies they are inspecting. One inspector related how pregnant employees were hiding on the roof of a facility in Bangkok during inspection visits. Another company coached employees on how to answer questions posed by an inspector. The strategy was meant to communicate to the inspector that everything was fine at the plant (Frank, 2008).

Despite inspection monitoring, even companies with good ethical reputations can encounter problems. In 2007, some clothing from the retail chain The Gap was traced back to sweatshops in India. In this example, children as young as 10 years of age worked 16 hours a day to produce the garments (Hansen & Harkin, 2008).

Strategic Planning: Confronting the Ethical Boulders

The strategic planning process should generate initiatives to improve the ethical climate of the organization. Improving this climate can reduce the company's vulnerability to an ethics-related crisis. Specific efforts should be directed to generating enthusiasm for crisis management and training, focusing on the prevention of ethical breaches, and abiding by both government regulations and industry standards.

The Enthusiasm for Crisis Management and Training

Neglecting to prepare for a crisis is in itself an ethical problem. Unfortunate events can occur to an organization at any time, and the company's stakeholders expect that it will have a plan to meet these crises. The lack of a crisis management plan (CMP) and the subsequent training that accompanies it will only draw negative perceptions from employees, suppliers, customers, government agencies, and the general public when a crisis does occur. Nobody thinks favorably of an organization that was not prepared.

Simply forming a crisis management team (CMT) and generating a crisis plan is not sufficient. Enthusiasm for the crisis management process and the accompanying training must also be present. For this reason, the organization should seek a crisis management champion from within who will spearhead the process of building an ongoing crisis management program. If the organization is new to crisis planning, an outside consultant should be retained to help the CMT write its first plan. It goes without saying that top management should always support the firm's crisis management efforts.

The Ethical Culture of the Organization

The best approach to dealing with an ethical crisis is to prevent it from happening in the first place. An ethical rationality approach seeks to address events in the life of the organization from a morally driven response perspective (Snyder et al., 2006). However, to a great extent the organizational culture dictates how ethical or unethical decision making will be in the company (Heineman, 2007; Vallario, 2007). For this reason, a cultural change in the organization is also necessary to improve ethical decision making. Changing the culture of an organization requires unseating the deep thought patterns that have prevailed in previous years, particularly if those patterns of behavior are unethical. Even Enron had a code of ethics, but the culture of the company overshadowed the significance of that code. Likewise, the failed accounting firm Arthur Andersen produced an ethics video series once used in U.S. business schools (Fombrun & Foss, 2004).

Changing the culture of an organization is a large undertaking; culture is, after all, the prevailing belief system within the organization. Some cultures simply look the other way when an ethical breach occurs, whereas others are committed to ethical standards in any business decision. All cultures look to upper-level management for cues to right and wrong behavior in the organization (Trevino, Hartman, & Brown, 2000). Table 10.4 overviews the best practices companies take to change their ethical cultures.

The Existence of Government Regulations

Government regulations exist to protect employees, consumers, and the local community. Unfortunately, such regulations can sometimes be sidestepped by businesses, which can lead to catastrophic outcomes in the future. Ignoring regulations is a decision, one that is conscious and deliberate. Many organizations find themselves in trouble with government regulations because of unethical or illegal decisions made by management or other key employees.

In 1997, the Andrew & Williamson Sales Company sold strawberries grown in Mexico to the U.S. Department of Agriculture (USDA). However, there was a major problem with this deal. The USDA distributes food to public school systems, and

Table 10.4 Best Practices Organizations Take to Change Their Ethical Cultures

Measure Taken	Description
Installing a code of ethics	Organization-wide ethical principles and behaviors are outlined in a pamphlet or manual. Managers and employees review the code on a regular basis and sign it, indicating their willingness to abide by the code.
Implementing ethics training	Short classes and workshops that highlight ethical issues and how to respond to them are offered to employees.
Providing an ethics hotline	Employees have a person or department within their organization to whom they can report ethical violations. A hotline can also offer guidance on specific ethical issues an employee may be facing.
Requiring that top management articulate and set the ethical example	Executives in top positions in the company—the CEO, president, and vice presidents—need to realize that lower-level managers get their cues on ethical matters by watching those higher up. Thus, top managers are encouraged to model the right example.
Requiring managers to attain realistic, but not impossible goals	Goals set for managers are well conceived and realistic. Unrealistic goals encourage unethical decision making because managers may feel they must cut corners to attain the goal.
Disciplining for ethical violations	When an ethical violation is discovered, the company works quickly to correct the situation and punish the person responsible.
Scheduling regular ethics audits	As in a financial audit, the company periodically checks itself in a systematic manner to see if it is following proper ethical guidelines in its business processes.
Appointing of chief ethics officers	Ethics officers who serve in top management are being used in some larger companies. Such officers may report directly to the CEO and the board of directors. Their charge is to promote the ethical standards of the organization and to monitor employee concerns.

Sources: Carroll and Buchholtz (2012); Fombrun & Foss, C. (2004), 284–288; Post et al.(2002).

government regulations require that strawberries sold to these school systems be grown in the United States. As part of a cover-up, Andrew & Williamson submitted falsified certificates of origin that indicated the strawberries were grown domestically (Salkin, 1997). Although the company thought its deed would go unnoticed, a major health crisis soon erupted. A number of public school students in Michigan were stricken with hepatitis A, and the ailment was linked to the strawberries sold by Andrew & Williamson. Eventually outbreaks of the hepatitis A strain resulted in 213 cases in Michigan, 29 in Maine, and seven in Wisconsin (Entis, 2007). What started out as an illegal scheme to move excess inventory out of the warehouse resulted in a major crisis across a number of states. When the ordeal ended, Frederick Williamson resigned as president and was sentenced to 5 months in prison, followed by 5 months of home detention. The company was also forced to pay $1.3 million in civil damages, as well as $200,000 in criminal penalties (Entis, 2007).

In the Hawks Nest project, Rinehart and Dennis ignored existing regulations if these slowed down the construction of the tunnel. For example, wet drilling was the required practice because this procedure kept dust levels to a minimum (Cherniak, 1986; Tyler, 1975). Testimony before the U.S. Congress revealed that employees were posted to watch for incoming mine inspectors (Comstock, 1973). When the arriving inspectors were "announced," wet drilling would begin until the inspectors had left the area. Dry drilling would then resume to expedite extraction.

The Existence of Industry Standards

Industry standards are often set by associations for their members to follow. The intent is to set guidelines concerning a particular practice, such as quality control or safety adherence. These guidelines are then adopted by companies in the industry association as the minimally acceptable standard (Vernon, 1998). Such efforts have also been referred to as *self-policing* (Becker, 2006) or *self-regulation* (Hemphill, 2006). Certain professions—including physicians, attorneys, college and university professors, engineers, pharmacists, and accountants—also have standards for their members.

Guidelines for ethical conduct can be proposed by industry associations. In 2001, an industry group of 14 Wall Street firms established ethical conduct standards governing compensation and stock ownership for analysts. This move was prompted by some of the industry leaders, including Goldman Sachs, Merrill Lynch, and Morgan Stanley Dean Witter, to address emerging ethical problems (Carroll & Buchholtz, 2003). In another example, Financial Executives International (FEI) requires all of its members to review and sign a code of ethics. They also recommend that the financial executive deliver the signed copy to the company board of directors. FEI has become a model for companies seeking to comply with Sarbanes-Oxley and New York Stock Exchange mandates (Vallario, 2007).

One caveat should be offered concerning industry standards. Requiring that member companies have a code of ethics is a step in the right direction, but it does not ensure all companies will have leaders who always make ethical decisions. Enron's 62-page code of ethical conduct was not an ingrained part of the Enron culture (Becker, 2006). In a similar vein, many clothing retailers maintain an "ethical sourcing" or "compliance monitoring" link on their company websites, suggesting that they monitor the actions of their foreign suppliers (Frank, 2008). However, compliance can be a game, as one sweatshop inspector noted:

The simplest way to play it (the game) is by placing an order with a cheap supplier and ending the relationship once the goods have been delivered. In the meantime, inspectors get sent to evaluate the factory—perhaps several times, since they keep finding problems—until the client, seeing no improvement in the labor conditions, severs the bond and moves on the next low-priced, equally suspect supplier. (Frank, 2008, p. 36)

According to this sweatshop inspector, some companies can promote ethical sourcing because they use monitors but can continue to purchase from suspect factories, one after another, each time claiming the factory was deficient and severing the tie. With so many substandard factories to choose from, the game need not end.

Crisis Management: Further Considerations During an Ethical Crisis

A crisis should be managed in an ethical manner. "Decision-makers who understand the needs of a wide range of stakeholders as part of their strategic decision-making will make more ethical decisions during a time of crisis" (Snyder et al., 2006, p. 376). Thus, ethical rationality is a habit that must be ingrained in the culture and daily operations of the organization (Fritzsche, 2005). Ethical rationality involves the careful management of the organization's internal and external stakeholders throughout the crisis.

The Management of Internal Stakeholders

Employees and owners are the internal stakeholders who must be managed with integrity when a crisis occurs. Typically, it is the crisis communication function that should be approached in an honest, straightforward manner. Employees are often forgotten in the ordeal. It is important they receive truthful and timely information updates as the crisis progresses.

As for the owners, it should be acknowledged that the crisis may manifest itself in the form of financial loss. If the shareholders are geographically dispersed, the impact of the loss may not be felt until quarterly reports are distributed months after the crisis commences. Likewise, if the company is incorporated with many stockholders, then they, like the employees, may be left in the dark on the details of the crisis at hand. This is not ethical. When the news is bad, the company has an obligation to inform its employees and owners as to what has happened and what is being done to address the crisis.

The organization's website as well as social media tools can be used to communicate with these stakeholders. Updates on the state of the crisis should be made on a regular basis. In addition, the organization should use its managers and supervisors to communicate the details of the crisis to employees. To supplement this type of communication, an organization-wide memo or letter should be circulated to all employees. In addition, face-to-face meetings with employees are always advisable; these provide opportunities for questions and answers, which in turn provide information that can clarify misunderstandings or rumors that may be circulating about the crisis.

The Management of External Stakeholders

External stakeholders include customers, suppliers, government entities, the local community, and the media. As with internal stakeholders, the ethical approach is to make sure that communication to these groups is honest and timely. For example, if the crisis is an untrue rumor, it should be addressed quickly and stated that it is untrue (Coombs, 2007; Gross, 1990). Again, the organization's website can be an excellent vehicle for updated information on the latest developments of the crisis. Setting up a link on the website that directly addresses the crisis is a good practice.

Management should also take advantage of Twitter, a social media tool. With Twitter, the company can send a quick message to its followers on an update to the crisis. The messages can be linked back to the company's website, where more detailed information on the crisis can be accessed. In addition, Twitter hashtags can be created to help readers sort through the previous tweets on a topic related to the crisis (Deveney, 2011).

Organizational Learning: Lessons From the Ethical Crisis

Recovering from an ethical crisis requires a commitment to pursue better behavior in the future. But not all individuals involved will take responsibility for their actions, and some of them will pay for their actions with prison time. Collectively, the organization must also speak with one voice and make it plain that it proposes to remedy the problems that led to the ethical incident to begin with, and to continue with aboveboard behavior in the future.

The Evaluation of the Ethical Management Process

Organizations guilty of moral lapses are usually caught in the process. Unlike a crisis brought on by a natural disaster (e.g., earthquake, torrential weather, or some other act of nature), when the organization is an obvious victim, an ethical crisis generates little public sympathy. Furthermore, sentiments often run against the company, even if it is not to blame for the crisis. For example, if damaging weather hits a company warehouse and knocks out its storage and operations, some critics will still question why the company was not more prepared.

Ethical decision making not only anticipates how to handle the crisis but how to address the organization's critics as well. This observation is why Bertrand and Lajtha (2002) noted that every crisis can be interpreted as a sign of a loss of trust. In this example, stakeholders lose trust in the organization when something unfortunate occurs, whether or not it was caused by the organization. This is not a pretty scenario, but it is real. To witness this phenomenon, simply watch the comments section of any major online news website. Critics frequently emerge to blame just about anyone for a given calamity. When a company is in the midst of a crisis, it will often be perceived by others as blameworthy, even if it did not cause the crisis at hand.

Because some stakeholders respond to with a loss of trust in the organization, management should acknowledge the various viewpoints that exist in the external environment. Certainly, many people in society have a strong distrust for corporate America in general, perceiving that companies will do whatever it takes to increase sales and make a profit. Unfortunately, the actions of some firms appear to justify this perception. Not surprisingly, many will be critical of a company when it is faced with a crisis regardless of whether or not the firm is at fault. Other stakeholders will be more rational and will see the crisis from a more realistic perspective. In their minds, the organization may not have experienced an unfortunate negative event. Either way, company management needs to communicate that it is doing everything it can to learn from each crisis and to improve at making ethical decisions in the marketplace. Of course, management should not only communicate this message—the message should be sincere. Again, the external stakeholders are trying to rationalize this question in their minds: "Can we trust the company?"

The Commitment to Organizational Learning

Chapter 9 focused on the process of organizational learning after a crisis. Crises involving ethical breaches should not be repeated. Once an ethical crisis has been resolved, the organization must commit itself to a learning process that seeks to avoid repeating the mistake. Unfortunately, crisis management history teaches us that some companies resort to a "defense-and-attack" mode (Nathan, 2000, p. 3), a tactic that in itself is unethical. The A. H. Robins company used this tactic to discredit the victims who used the Dalkon Shield, a contraceptive device that was surgically inserted into the uterus. When recipients of the Shield became sick, the company resorted to attacking the victims and questioning their sexual practices and partners (Barton, 2001; Hartley, 1993). This is no way to fight a crisis, and A. H. Robins paid dearly in the end by enduring an endless onslaught of consumer lawsuits.

It is also not appropriate for a company to attack its suppliers publically as the cause of the problem. While the problem may be traced to a supplier, positioning the company in a way that appears to avoid responsibility only displaces the blame. Some critics will always respond by saying, "Well, then why did you use that supplier to begin with?" Again, if crisis are an issue of trust, then the public is asking, "Can we trust you as a company to tell us the truth?"

What is expected by both internal and external stakeholders is a commitment by the company to "get it right" by abiding by the law and staying within ethical guidelines. This learning process may involve a number of measures, including getting rid of the executives and managers who caused the problem in the first place. New controls may need to be implemented as well.

The Benefits of Industry Renewal

Some industries seem to have more problems with ethical matters than others. This statement may sound odd, given that people, not industries, commit unethical acts. But some industries have had more "experience" in this area than others. The tobacco industry certainly falls in this category. Many question the ethics of selling a product that causes serious health problems. The tobacco industry maintained for years that cigarettes were not harmful, even though illnesses from tobacco represented a heavy burden on the health care system. In 1998, however, 46 state attorneys general reached an agreement with the five largest tobacco manufacturers in the United States. The settlement required the companies to pay billions of dollars to the state governments each year, ostensibly to alleviate the burden on the state health care systems (Thorne et al., 2003).

In terms of industry renewal, there has been a decline in tobacco advertising aimed at youth and teenagers, a problem that existed during the Joe Camel advertising days in the late 1980s and 1990s. Joe Camel was a recognizable character that appeared in advertisements for Camel cigarettes, a product manufactured by R. J. Reynolds (RJR). Unfortunately, the character was recognized by minors as well. One study found that among children between the ages of 3 and 6, more than half could associate the Joe Camel character with a cigarette (Shapiro, 1993). The Joe Camel campaign lasted from 1987 to 1997, a time during which underage smoking increased. In 1997, the Federal Trade Commission (FTC) asked RJR to remove the character from any venue where it might be seen by a child (Carroll & Buchholtz, 2012). RJR complied, thus beginning a period of industrial renewal in the tobacco industry.

The catalyst for industry renewal in the tobacco industry was ultimately a push from state governments. However, some industries have attempted to change their ethical problems before the government has had a chance to intervene. Marketing practices within the pharmaceutical industry represent one example of an industry establishing its own reforms. Prior to these reforms, gifts and other incentives were frequently lavished on physicians by representatives advocating the use of their company's drugs (Hemphill, 2006). The intent was to influence the prescription process, which in itself was not unethical, but the means to achieve this goal was of growing concern. In response, the American Medical Association (AMA) adopted ethical guidelines in 1990 on gift-giving practices. The initial responses were positive, but, as Hemphill (2006) noted, a reappraisal of pharmaceutical marketing codes of conduct needs to be performed.

The Inevitability of New Government Regulations

After a major crisis, the government may impose new regulations. This is especially true if the company is large and efforts at self-policing have not been effective. The intent of self-policing is to generate positive change without government mandates (Becker, 2006). Hartley (1993) has noted a general progression from public apathy, to media attention, to public outcry, and finally to government regulation. Table 10.5 overviews this progression.

Table 10.5 The Progression From Public Apathy to Government Regulation

	Public Apathy →	Media Attention →	Public Resentment and Outcry →	Imposition of Government Regulations →
General Description	The general public is not too concerned about potential crises. Likewise, the company is not proactive in diffusing any potential crises.	The media focuses on a crisis event and brings it to the attention of the general public.	The general public reacts to the crisis by asserting that "something must be done" to correct the situation and keep it from reoccurring.	The government will wait for an appropriate period of time in hope that the company or industry will self-regulate. Government regulations will follow if self-regulation does not occur.
Example: **The Hawks Nest Crisis**	The Great Depression is at its height and most people just want to work.	In the late 1930s, media attention highlights the abuses of workers who are now dying of silicosis.	Public sympathy is slow at first, but eventually builds momentum to the point that lawsuits and government investigations ensue.	Silicosis legislation is passed in 46 states.[1]
Example: **September 11, 2001, Terrorist Attacks**	Although terrorist threats at airline targets were recognized by the government, passengers, and airlines, few anticipated that a jet airliner would be used as a terrorist weapon.	The attacks on the World Trade Center and the Pentagon are known immediately throughout the world. Facilitated by the Internet, news unfolds in real time and with an abundance of visual images.	Airline ticket sales drop dramatically after the attacks. All airlines experience financial shocks, and some eventually go into bankruptcy.	The government responds with the creation of the U.S. Department of Homeland Security and the Transportation Safety Administration (TSA).
Enron Scandal	Few people had heard of Enron since its founding in 1985, and those who had were not familiar with its business model.	Enron becomes a household name when officials announce a restatement of earnings in October 2001. A month later, the company goes bankrupt.	Thousands of Enron employees lose their jobs and their retirement savings. Public outrage occurs over a number of practices, including the reporting of off-balance sheet entities.	The Sarbanes–Oxley Act (2002) is passed.

Source: Adapted from Hartley (1993), p. 26.

Today, we see numerous examples of how the government seeks to protect society through regulation. The Environmental Protection Act resulted from public outcry against the pollution crises. The Occupational Safety and Health Administration was a government response to safety inadequacies in the workplace. Although the effectiveness of such government interventions can be debated, their links to previous crises is clear.

The Anticipation of New Stakeholder Outlooks

There is a sad irony in the realm of organizational crises events: a significant loss of human life often launches a company into immortality. Unfortunately, this is a stakeholder memory that is hard to erase. For many people from the Baby Boomer generation, just mentioning the company Union Carbide immediately brings to mind the Bhopal, India, gas leak disaster that killed thousands in 1983. Indeed, a Google search using "Union Carbide" produces many references to this disaster. The name and incident association is strong. Likewise, the Hawks Nest Tunnel contractor Rinehart and Dennis will not be remembered for its previous successful engineering projects; instead, its name will forever be associated with the needless loss of hundreds of workers who died from silicosis while building the tunnel.

There is another irony to the Hawks Nest crisis. The company receiving the electricity that was produced by the tunnel project was Union Carbide. There has been some speculation as to how active Union Carbide was in the tunnel crisis. Some critics have assumed the firm was guilty by association, while others claim the company was not involved in promoting unsafe working conditions for the tunnel workers (Deitz, 1990; Jennings, 1997). Nonetheless, name recognition has a strong emotional component; it is associated with good products and services, but it can also be associated with death.

There are other stakeholder outlooks that can result from crisis events. Consider the following crisis events and how they changed the viewpoints of many people:

- The September 11 terrorist attacks forced air travelers to accept new security measures. They have also created the mind-set that the ethical thing for companies to pursue is the safety and welfare of their customers. This viewpoint was implied in the past but today is expected from companies in safeguarding their people.
- As the manufacturing of goods is outsourced to overseas vendors, firms can lose direct contact with the means of production (Bertrand & Lajtha, 2002). This anxiety rises when products shipped to the domestic country are flawed in some way, such as toys with lead paint. The question of ethics arises when those who have lost their jobs to outsourcing end up purchasing products—some of them defective—from other countries. In light of the global outsourcing problems mentioned —and a weakening U.S. dollar—a number of companies are considering the use of reshoring, bringing manufacturing back to the home country.

- Recent weather patterns suggest that global warming is occurring. Some scientists link global temperatures to human activity, namely the production of carbon emissions. The ethical viewpoint held by many is that firms should reduce emissions because this may be an issue of long-term survival.
- Hurricane Katrina and the ineffective government response prompted wide criticism. Many cite the poor communication and coordination among government agencies that should have been prepared to manage these types of problems. The ego and turf wars that existed among city, state, and federal branches of the government were also obvious and invited the scorn of many who felt let down when elected officials did not work in the best public interest.

The Problem of Loss of Trust

Bertrand and Lajtha (2002) have concluded that all crises can be interpreted as signs of a loss of trust. If this statement is true, then the ethical repercussions are enormous. What this means is that no matter the crisis, some stakeholders will feel a loss of trust in the organization.

Consider these examples when the party obviously at fault is not included in the blame equation, and yet blame is deflected back onto the organization. The countering questions that follow each event are often raised by the media or can be seen on blogs when similar events occur.

- A recently fired employee walks into his former place of work and kills his supervisor along with several other employees: Why was the employee allowed back on the premises? What did the company do to make this employee so agitated?
- An employee is killed on his factory job because he did not follow standard procedures in performing a work task, thus leading to the fatal accident: Why did the company hire this person in the first place? How many similar accidents have occurred at this workplace? Why did the company not enforce its own procedures?

Responses like these are common when a crisis occurs. In an attempt to make sense out of what has happened, many people will cognitively distort the situation and assign an ethical cause to the crisis; in their minds, the cause is often the organization. Bertrand and Lajtha's comment about the loss of trust is based on a perception. Nonetheless, perceptions can influence behavior more than reality. Hence, ethical decision making must be at the forefront of all management actions.

Summary

Business ethics examines the morality of behavior in the business world. Unethical behavior can be legal, yet damaging to the organization. In practice, all businesses should consider four responsibilities to their stakeholders: (1) making a profit, (2) operating within the law, (3) behaving ethically, and (4) supporting social and community activities that relate to the mission of the firm. The basic motive that triggers an ethical crisis is often the desire to gain financially, often at the expense of another stakeholder.

The four stages of the crisis management framework reveal the underlying role of ethics in crisis management. The landscape survey uncovers the ethical weak points that may exist within the organization and its industry. The strategic planning stage promotes what can be done to improve the ethical climate of the business and its industry in general. The crisis management stage examines the ethical behaviors involved when addressing a specific crisis. Finally, the organizational learning stage promotes improving an organization's ethical performance by learning from a specific crisis event.

Questions for Discussion

1. Provide an example of an ethical problem that has occurred either where you currently work or have worked in the past.

2. Using the crisis management framework (Table 10.3), conduct a landscape survey and determine the current status of potential ethical issues in your present organization and in the industry in which your company operates.

3. Identify a well-known crisis event that involved an organization that violated an ethical standard but did not actually break the law. What defense did the organization provide for its behavior? What could the organization have done differently?

3. How can the ethical culture of an organization be improved?

4. Why is the example provided by top management so important in promoting the ethical culture of the organization?

5. What examples of major crises illustrate how government intervention can help prevent a similar crisis in the future? Consider Table 10.5 as a starting point in your discussion.

6. Why is a crisis also a symbol of a loss of trust in the organization?

Chapter Exercise

Table 10.2 lists a number of crisis events that the class may not be familiar with. Select several unfamiliar cases. Outside of class, research each case and write a one-page summary of what happened and the outcome of the case. Discuss these in class. Be sure to address the following topics:

- What crisis did the organization face?
- How did mismanagement contribute to the crisis?
- How was the crisis finally resolved and what legal implications were present (the settlement of lawsuits, etc.)?

Mini-Case: The Melamine Milk Crisis in China

Melamine is a product that is used in the making of plastics and laminates. Unfortunately, it has also been illegally added to milk to boost its protein rating. The product is extremely dangerous once consumed and can cause kidney stones and renal failure (Pickert, 2008). In China, a scandal erupted in which dairy middlemen were spiking milk with melamine after they had watered down the milk to extend the product usage. The higher protein content enabled these middlemen to command higher prices on the market (Long, Crandall, & Parnell, 2010).

One Chinese company, the Sanlu Group, was purchasing melamine-laced milk for use in its baby formula. Initially, Sanlu management was unaware of the melamine presence in the product. However, some Sanlu staff eventually discovered the melamine but continued to produce and distribute their baby milk formula, even months afterward (DeLaurentis, 2009). The case is reminiscent of Beech-Nut's 1979 discovery, discussed earlier in the chapter, of fake apple juice concentrate that it had unknowingly purchased from one of its suppliers (Hartley, 1993). Rather than abandoning the supplier, Beech-Nut executives continued to use the supplier covertly and eventually found itself in the midst of a major crisis.

The fallout from the Beech-Nut apple juice scandal did not include health problems for the babies that consumed its apple juice. Unfortunately, the same outcome would not be true for the Sanlu Group. On June 28, 2008, an infant with kidney stones was admitted to a hospital in Gansu's provincial capital of Lanzhou. The parents told doctors they had been feeding their baby milk produced by the Sanlu Group. Within two months, 14 infants with similar problems had been admitted to the hospital. Other cases were reported in provinces of the Ningxia Hui Autonomous region, Shandong, Jiangxi, Hubei, Shanxi, Jiangsu, Shandong, Anhui, and Hunan. All of the affected infants had been fed the milk formula produced by the Sanlu Group (Long et al., 2010).

By September 2008, the cases of melamine-induced sickness escalated over a much wider geographic area. The World Health Organization (WHO) reported more than 54,000 children in China had sought medical treatment, with four fatalities reported (Schlein, 2010). In other countries, reports of the melamine scandal began to surface. Bans on the Chinese-made milk products were reported in Japan, Malaysia, Bangladesh, Tanzania, and Gabon. The 27-nation European Union also put a ban on all baby food containing Chinese milk (Long et al., 2010).

The Sanlu Group moved slowly in its response to the crisis. In fact, even before the hospitalization of children in June, the company had received complaints about its baby formula milk in March 2008. At that time, the Sanlu Group claimed its products had repeatedly passed quality tests, met national quality standards, and that sick babies must have been fed counterfeit milk powder that used the Sanlu brand name. However, the company later learned that melamine had indeed been introduced into its milk supply. The discovery occurred in early August when its co-owner, New Zealand-based Fonterra, used melamine-testing equipment to verify the presence of the substance. At that time, Fonterra owned 43 percent of the Sanlu Group ("Sanlu Dairy," 2009). Although Sanlu confirmed the melamine contamination in August, it did not report the problem to the Chinese government, nor did it reveal the information to the public until September 11. So why the delay? It appears there was concern about social stability during the August 8–24, 2008, Summer Olympic Games, because a food scare would be damaging given the events that were about to take place in Beijing (Liu, 2008).

For Fonterra, the situation was especially delicate, as it was now faced with a crisis of life and death, literally. It was also concerned about saving the face of its Chinese partner. Nonetheless, Fonterra executives, realizing they had a major problem on their hands, contacted the New Zealand embassy, which began the process of alerting the Chinese central government of the food contamination problem.

Once the matter became public on September 11, the Sanlu Group received much criticism from Chinese parents and the public. Zhang Zhenling, Sanlu's vice president, delivered an apology letter on behalf of the company at a news briefing on September 15. The apology expressed regret and included a declaration to recall all the infant milk powder produced prior to August 6, as well as an optional recall for milk produced after that date if consumers had concerns about sick infants. The late apology and the dismissal of Sanlu president Tian Wenhua did did not satisfy the public sufficiently, and many citizens lost confidence in the Sanlu brand ("Four officials sacked," 2008). Within four months of the scandal going public, the Sanlu Group declared bankruptcy.

Mini-Case Questions

1. The Sanlu case illustrates how a supplier can be the cause of a crisis for the affected organization. However, blaming the supplier instead of taking responsibility is not an acceptable strategy in the eyes of the general public. Why do you think this is the case?

2. This case also illustrates the problem a company like Fonterra can face when it partners with companies in other countries. Identify other examples of a partner company being drawn into a crisis as a result of the actions of another company.

3. From a cultural perspective, it is important for students to know what happened to some of the executives involved in the scandal, because penalties for the Sanlu Group crisis were rather extreme by American standards. Conduct an Internet search and find out what happened to the executives and managers involved in this scandal.

Mini-Case References

DeLaurentis, T. (2009). Ethical supply chain management. *China Business Review, 36*(3), 38–41.
Four officials sacked following baby milk scandal. (2008, September 17). *China Daily Online.* Retrieved July 25, 2012, from http://www.chinadaily.com.cn/china/2008–09/17/content_7034236.htm.
Hartley, R. (1993). *Business ethics: Violations of the public trust.* New York: Wiley.
Liu, M. (2008, October 6). Saving face goes sour. *Newsweek,* 7.

Long, Z., Crandall, W., & Parnell, J. (2010). A trilogy of unfortunate events in China: Reflecting on the management of crises. *International Journal of Asian Business and Information Management, 1*(4), 21–30.

Pickert, K. (2008, September 17). Brief history of melamine. *Time Online.* Retrieved July 25, 2012, from http://www.time.com/time/health/article/0,8599,1841757,00.html.

Sanlu Dairy assets to be sold off. (2009, March). *Dairy Industries International,* 11.

Schlein, L. (2008). China's melamine milk crisis creates crisis of confidence. *Voice of America News Online.* Retrieved July 25, 2012, from http://www.voanews.com/english/archive/2008–09/2008–09–26–voa45.cfm?CFID=64268891&CFTOKEN=95716309.

References

Alpaslan, C. M., Green, S. E., & Mitroff, I. I. (2009). Corporate governance in the context of crises: Towards a stakeholder theory of crisis management. *Journal of Contingencies and Crisis Management, 17*(1), 38–49.

Bad apples: In the executive suite. (1989, May). *Consumer Reports,* 294.

Barth, T. (2010). Crisis management in the Catholic Church: Lessons for public administrators. *Public Administration Review, 70*(5), 780–791.

Barstow, D., Xanic, A., & McKinley, J. (2012, April 12). Vast Mexico bribery case hushed up by Wal-Mart after top-level struggle. *New York Times,* p. 1.

Barton, L. (2001). *Crisis in organizations II.* Cincinnati: South-Western.

Barton, L. (2008). *Crisis leadership now: A real-world guide to preparing for threat, disaster, sabotage, and scandal.* New York: McGraw-Hill.

Becker, C. (2006). Police thyself. *Modern Healthcare, 36*(41), 28–30.

Benjamin, M., Lim, P., & Streisand, B. (2005, March 28). Giving the boot. *U.S. News & World Report,* 48–50.

Berman, S., Wicks, A., Kotha, S., & Jones, T. (1999). Does stakeholder orientation matter? The relationship between stakeholder management models and firm financial performance. *Academy of Management Journal, 42*(5), 488–506.

Bertrand, R., & Lajtha, C. (2002). A new approach to crisis management. *Journal of Contingencies and Crisis Management, 10*(4), 181–191.

Boatright, J. (2012). *Ethics and the conduct of business* (7th ed.). Upper Saddle River, NJ: Pearson.

Breeden, R. (2003, November/December). WorldCom: The governance lessons. *Corporate Board,* 1–6.

Carroll, A., & Buchholtz, A. (2012). *Business and society: Ethics sustainability, and stakeholder management* (8th ed.). Mason, OH: South-Western Cengage Learning.

Cherniak, M. (1986). *The Hawk's Nest incident: America's worst industrial disaster.* New York: Vail-Ballou.

Colvin, G. (2003, May 12). History repeats itself at HealthSouth. *Fortune,* 40.

Comstock, J. (1973). 476 graves. *West Virginia Heritage* [Yearbook], *7,* 1–194.

Coombs, W. (2006). *Code red in the boardroom: Crisis management as organizational DNA.* Westport, CT: Praeger.

Coombs, W. (2007). *Ongoing crisis communication: Planning, managing, and responding* (2nd ed.). Thousand Oaks, CA: Sage.

Crandall, W. R., & Crandall, R. E. (2002). Revisiting the Hawks Nest Tunnel incident: Lessons learned from an American tragedy. *Journal of Appalachian Studies, 8*(2), 261–283.

Deitz, D. (1990, Fall). "I think we've struck a gold mine": A chemist's view of Hawks Nest. *Goldenseal,* 42–47.

DesJardins, J. (2009). *An introduction to business ethics* (4th ed.). New York: McGraw-Hill.

Deveney, J. (2011). Being creative in the face of crisis: How innovation plays a role in communication. *Public Relations Tactics, 18*(8), 14.

Entis, P. (2007). *Food safety: Old habits, new perspectives.* Malden, MA: Blackwell.

Fombrun, C., & Foss, C. (2004). Business ethics: Corporate responses to scandal. *Corporation Reputation Review, 7*(3), 284–288.

Frank, T. (2008, April). Confessions of a sweatshop inspector. *Washington Monthly,* 34–37.

Fritzsche, D. (2005). *Business ethics: A global and managerial perspective* (2nd ed.). New York: McGraw-Hill.

Greer, M. (2001). 90 years of progress in safety. *Professional Safety, 46*(10), 20–25.

Gross, A. (1990, October 11). How Popeye's and Reebok confronted product rumors. *Adweek's Marketing Week, 31,* 27, 30.

Hansen, M., & Harkin, T. (2008, June 12). Gap's message on child labor. *Women's Wear Daily,* 18.

Hartley, R. (1993). *Business ethics: Violations of the public trust.* New York: Wiley.

Hartman, L., & DesJardins, J. (2011). *Business ethics: Decision making for personal integrity and social responsibility.* New York: McGraw-Hill/Irwin.

Heineman, B., Jr. (2007). Avoiding integrity land mines. *Harvard Business Review, 85*(4), 100–108.

Hemphill, T. (2006). Physicians and the pharmaceutical industry: A reappraisal of marketing codes of conduct. *Business and Society Review, 111*(3), 323–336.

Henry, D., Timmons, H., Rosenbush, S., & Arndt, M. (2002, January 28). Who else is hiding debt. *Business Week,* 36–37.

Holmes, S. (2006, March 13). Cleaning up Boeing. *Business Week,* 63–68.

Institute for Crisis Management. (2011). *Annual ICM crisis report: News coverage of business crises during 2010.* Retrieved April 8, 2012, from http://crisisconsultant.com/images/2010CrisisReportICM.pdf.

Jefferson, J. (1993). Dying for work. *ABA Journal, 79*(1), 46–51.

Jennings, C. (1997, Spring). Was Witt Jennings involved? The Hawks Nest tragedy. *Goldenseal,* 44–47.

Kaplan, R., & Norton, D. (2001). *The strategy focused organization.* Boston: Harvard Business School Press.

Lacayo, R., & Kane, J. (1991, September 16). Death on the shop floor. *Time,* 28–29.

Nathan, M. (2000, Fall). From the editor: Crisis learning—Lessons from Sisyphus and others. *Review of Business,* 3–5.

NYC pension funds sue Wal-Mart over claims of bribery in Mexico. (2012, June 25). *Pensions and Investments, 40*(13), 25.

Parnell, J. A. (2013). *Strategic management: Theory and practice* (4th ed.). Thousand Oaks, CA: Sage.

Parnell, J. A., & Dent, E. L. (2009). Philosophy, ethics and capitalism: An interview with BB&T CEO John Allison. *Academy of Management Learning and Education, 8*(4), 587–596.

Parnell, J. A., & Jusoh, R. (2008). Competitive strategy and performance in the Malaysian context: An exploratory study. *Management Decision, 46*(1), 5–31.

Post, J., Lawrence, A., & Weber, J. (2002). *Business and society: Corporate strategy, public policy, ethics.* New York: McGraw-Hill.

Powers, W. (2002). *Report of Investigation by the Special Investigative Committee of the Board of Directors of Enron Corp.* Retrieved July 8, 2012, from http://f11.findlaw.com/news .findlaw.com/wp/docs/enron/specinv020102rpt1.pdf.

Salkin, S. (1997). Attn: School foodservice directors and other commodity purchasers. *Foodservice Director, 10*(7), 82.

Schwartz, H. (1990). *Narcissistic process and corporate decay: The theory of organizational ideal.* New York: New York University Press.

Securities and Exchange Commission. (1976, May 12). *Report on questionable and illegal corporate payments and practices.* Exhibits A and B, submitted to U.S. Congress, Senate, Committee on Banking, Housing, and Urban Affairs.

Sethi, S., & Steidlmeier, P. (1997). *Up against the corporate wall: Cases in business and society* (6th ed.). Upper Saddle River, NJ: Prentice Hall.

Shanker, A. (1992, February 17). The Hamlet, N.C., fire: A postmortem. *New Republic,* 27.

Shapiro, E. (1993, August 11). FTC staff recommends ban of Joe Camel campaign. *Wall Street Journal,* p. B1.

Snyder, P., Hall, M., Robertson, J., Jasinski, T., & Miller, J. (2006). Ethical rationality: A strategic approach to organizational crisis. *Journal of Business Ethics, 63,* 371–383.

Steiner, G., & Steiner, J. (2000). *Business, government, and society: A managerial perspective* (9th ed.). New York: McGraw-Hill.

Thorne, D., Ferrell, O., & Ferrell, L. (2003). *Business and society: A strategic approach to corporate citizenship.* New York: Houghton Mifflin.

Trevino, L., Hartman, L., & Brown, M. (2000). Moral person and moral manager: How executives develop a reputation for ethical leadership. *California Management Review, 42*(4), 128–142.

Tyler, A. (1975, January). Dust to dust. *Washington Monthly,* 49–58.

Vallario, C. (2007). Is your ethics program working? *Financial Executive, 23*(4), 26–28.

Vernon, H. (1998). *Business and society: A managerial approach* (6th ed.). New York: McGraw-Hill.

Welles, C. (1988, February 22). What led Beech-Nut down the road to disgrace? *Business Week,* 124–128.

Zweig, D. (2010). The board that couldn't think straight. *Conference Board Review, 47*(2), 40-47.

CHAPTER 11

Emerging Trends in Crisis Management

Opening Case: The Problem of Hanging Out With the Crowd

Most people would think that meeting with friends at a concert or sporting event would be a pleasant experience, and it should be. Yet, under certain conditions, it could also get you killed. Such a scenario can occur when a group of people is packed tightly in a small space. The result is what crowd behavior scholars call a "crush" or "stampede." People become so tightly entwined that they cannot breathe, or if they happen to fall, are trampled to death.

The Crowd Crush

An example of a well-documented crowd crush occurred in Cincinnati, Ohio, at a December 3, 1979, concert by the rock band, the Who. Approximately 8,000 fans had assembled outside the Riverfront Coliseum to gain entry when pushing started from those in the back of the line. Because the doors had not been opened, those in the front responded by pushing back, creating shock waves throughout the line. As people began to fall, others fell on top of them and were trampled. Eleven people died as a result of the crush (Seabrook, 2011).

At similar event 20 years later, eight people died and dozens were injured during a Pearl Jam concert in Roskilde, Denmark. The open-air concert did not have assigned seating and was part of a larger four-day festival that attracted 90,000 people (Ali, 2000). During this crush, thousands of fans were pushing forward toward the stage. A barrier broke between the stage and the crowd, and a number of fans lost their footing and were trampled.

Research indicates that in developing countries, religious festivals are the most likely events to develop into crowd crushes. However, in developed countries, rock concerts and soccer matches are potential breeding grounds for crushes as well

(Seabrook, 2011). In Chapter 7, we discussed one such event, the 1989 Hillsborough crush at a soccer match in Sheffield, England, that resulted in the deaths of 95 soccer fans (Elliott & Smith, 1993). However, potential crowd crushes are common occurrences after sporting events when fans rush a basketball court or football field to celebrate. Anyone who falls risks being trampled to death. At football games, fans risk being hurt when the goal post is brought down. Planning for these events and establishing crowd control policies in advance are required to keep fans safe.

Paul Wertheimer is one of a limited number of researchers who studies the impact of crowd behavior on human safety. After the 1979 Who concert, Wertheimer was appointed to investigate the event and make recommendations on how to prevent future occurrences. At the time, he was working as a public information officer for the city of Cincinnati. Wertheimer traveled all over the country and learned how crowds were managed at other public venues, including concerts. This learning process developed into a lifelong passion and career as a crowd management consultant. Wertheimer even conducted field research by venturing into mosh pits at rock concerts to learn more about crowd behavior, an effort that earned him the nickname, "the old man in the pit" (Seabrook, 2011). His expertise on crowds culminated into a big event in his own career in July 2010, as he testified in a trial involving Wal-Mart. Circumstances surrounding this case are described next.

Black Friday at Wal-Mart

The day was November 29, 2008, also referred to as "Black Friday," the biggest retail day of the year in the United States. Typically, retailers offer deep discounts on certain items to entice shoppers to begin a month-long surge of retail activity that ends with the Christmas holidays. At a Valley Stream, New York, Wal-Mart near New York City, 2,000 customers were waiting impatiently to enter the store at 5:00 A.M. for the advertised Blitz Day. When the doors were finally opened, a stampede commenced that knocked down the security employee at the entrance, Jdimytai Damour. Damour, 34, was a large individual at 6 feet 5 inches and 270 pounds, but his large frame did not save him from being trampled to death. The Nassau County medical examiner ruled that he died of asphyxiation. Eleven other people were also injured in the incident (Lynch, 2009).

A major problem with the event at Wal-Mart was the heavy media attention that had advertised bargains, but only limited quantities of merchandise were available. According to Nassau County Police Commissioner, Lawrence Mulvey, "When you advertise products, and you market it heavily, and it garners public interest, and it's great bargains with limited quantities of merchandise, and you have a crowd that can grow beyond the quantity available, it is a recipe for disaster" (Neff, 2008, p. 23).

Another problem with the event is simply the dynamics of a long queue (i.e., line of people). Individuals at the back of the queue are not aware of what is going on at the front. Typically, those in the back often push forward, not realizing that at that very moment, someone may be trampled underneath others who are being carried along with the flow of the crowd. Author John Seabrook described it this way in a recent article in the *New Yorker*:

The transition from fraternal smooshing to suffocating pressure—a "crowd crush"—often occurs almost imperceptibly; one doesn't realize what's happening until it's too late to escape. Something interrupts the flow of pedestrians—a blocked exit, say, while an escalator continues to feed people into a closed–off space. . . . At a certain point, you feel pressure on all sides of your body, and realize that you can't raise your arms. You are pulled off your feet, and welded into a block of people. The crowd forces squeeze the air out of your lungs and you struggle to take another breath. (Seabrook, 2011, p. 33)

While some have written off such crowd behavior as a sort of bizarre mob psychology, in reality, individuals in the crowd lose control at a certain point when the crowd resembles a single fluid entity. Crowd researcher John Fruin noted that an occupancy rate of seven persons per square meter causes the crowd to act more like a fluid mass. Under these circumstances, a person no longer has control over physical movement and may not even be able to breathe. That is why many people who die in crowd crushes experience compressive asphyxia (Fruin, 1993). However, blaming "the crowd" for trampling a person is not always valid, because crowd movement is based on the shock waves that are sent through it. Such shock waves can be initiated by someone pushing from the back of the queue. Under these circumstances, a dense crowd can only move forward, trampling anything that happens to be in its way.

The Aftermath

Rather than face a criminal prosecution, Wal-Mart opted to pay $1.5 million to Nassau County Social Services. In addition, the retailer set up a $400,000 fund for the victims and agreed to develop a crowd management plan for all of its New York stores (Lynch, 2009). The Occupational Safety and Health Administration (OSHA) also cited the company for inadequate crowd management during the Black Friday event. Advertising has also changed since 2008. Wal-Mart no longer calls Black Friday "Blitz Day" but rebranded it as "The Event" (Seabrook, 2011).

Opening Case Discussion Questions

1. What is the best way to manage a Black Friday event? As you discuss your answer, consider the following alternatives:

   - Increase security?
   - Advertise unlimited quantities on sale items as long as they are purchased by a certain day?
   - Decrease advertising?
     Consider the revenue and expense implications of each alternative.

2. Do you think Wal-Mart was unfairly implicated in the death of its employee? Should "the crowd" be considered at fault as well? How can individual responsibility be assigned when someone is injured because of a crowd?

3. Some outdoor concerts have no assigned seating, enabling concert promoters to sell more seats and encouraging patrons to arrive early and rush to the best ones. What guidelines should be provided for issuing tickets for events such as these?

Opening Case References

Ali, L. (2000, July 20). A horrible nightmare. *Newsweek*, 32.

Elliott, D., & Smith, D. (1993). Football stadia disasters in the United Kingdom: Learning from tragedy? *Industrial and Environmental Crisis Quarterly, 7*(3), 205–229.

Fruin, J. (1993). The causes and prevention of crowd disasters. Paper presented at the First International Conference on Engineering for Crowd Safety, London, England.

Lynch, M. (2009, May 7). Wal-Mart to pay $1.9 million in stampede death. *Women's Wear Daily*, 14.

Neff, J. (2008). Marketing blamed in Wal-Mart death. *Advertising Age, 79*(45), 23.

Seabrook, J. (2011, February 7). Crush point. *New Yorker*, 32–38.

Introduction

The opening case illustrates a problem that many may not consider when discussing crisis management, the potential of dying in a crowd. As the case illustrates, there are two ways this might occur: being trampled to death or being suffocated while standing. This is nothing new; such crowd crushes have occurred many times in history. With the world's growing population, the potential will continue to exist. Since more is known about crowd crushes today than was 30 years ago (when the Who concert tragedy took place), more is expected of organizations in making sure such accidents do not occur. The burden is on the business, not the crowd, to ensure that the environment is reasonably conducive to safety.

In this final chapter, we examine other trends emerging in the area of crisis management by examining each of the four phases of the crisis management framework. Table 11.1 presents an overview of these trends. As you study each of these phases, consider how they can affect your career.

The Landscape Survey

Throughout the book, the landscape survey has examined the organization's environment and identified the trends therein. Now we consider trends that may appear on the horizon.

The Internal Landscape

The internal landscape considers the state of the organization and its ability to withstand—or even cause—a crisis. What follows is an identification of emerging internal landscape trends and how you may be affected.

Table 11.1   Emerging Trends in Crisis Management

	Landscape Survey	*Strategic Planning*	*Crisis Management*	*Organizational Learning*
The Internal Landscape	■ The SWOT analysis will become an important tool in assessing crisis vulnerability. ■ The link between crisis and moral failure will strengthen.	■ Virtual crisis management plans will become the norm. ■ Crisis management planning will be integrated into the organization's strategic planning process.	■ Contingency responses to specific crisis events will become more common. ■ The organization's website and social media networks will become chief communications tool during a crisis.	■ Organizational learning will provide an important feedback loop necessary for the strategic planning process. ■ Learning after a crisis will lead to the abolishment of the status quo.
The External Landscape	■ Victims of crises will become more visible and powerful as stakeholders. ■ A crisis will be viewed as a reason to mistrust an organization.	■ Crisis management teams will engage in more planning with crisis teams from outside their organization. ■ The focus efforts of crisis management will expand to include a wider range of stakeholders. ■ Sustainable development will become more of an expectation.	■ Social media will play a greater role in determining the outcome of a crisis. ■ Time will be a key measure that will be used to evaluate an organization's response to a crisis	■ Crisis management frameworks and models will become more complex and sophisticated. ■ Crisis research will continue to use cases but will incorporate more statistical analysis as well. ■ Crisis research will take on a long-range perspective.

The SWOT Analysis Will Become an Important Tool in Assessing Crisis Vulnerability

In Chapter 4 we discussed the importance of using the SWOT analysis (strengths, weaknesses, opportunities, and threats) to detect crisis vulnerabilities. We discovered that organizational strengths can precede certain crises. A charismatic chief executive officer (CEO) or an athletic coach with a loyal following can be a wonderful asset to the organization. It can also hide a "smoldering crisis" that can lead to a major crisis. Likewise, opportunities, those options external to the organization that can signal new growth, can also lead to crises. Many companies have enthusiastically expanded production and markets to overseas locations only to encounter crises along the way.

The SWOT analysis not only reveals vulnerabilities but also helps identify the organization's strategic options. By conducting a thorough assessment of its strengths, weaknesses, opportunities, and threats, a business can build a matrix of options that are better aligned with its capabilities and limitations (Parnell, 2013). The SWOT analysis should always include input from internal and external stakeholders. Long-term decisions that rely on internal assessments can be shortsighted. Stakeholders such as employees, suppliers, and business advisory boards see the organization differently from top management, and thus their insights can be invaluable.

The Link Between Organizational Crises and Moral Failure Will Strengthen

Some have taken the viewpoint that crisis events can be likened to moral failures on the part of the organization. This thinking is understandable, given the number of ethically related organizational crises that have occurred over the past three decades. The Institute for Crisis Management has noted that the majority of organizational crises are human induced, with management initiating more than 50 percent of all crises, while employees account for 32 percent (Institute for Crisis Management, 2011). The institute further classifies 61 percent of all crises to the category of "smoldering." Such crises start out small, internal, and manageable but escalate into crises that are visible to the public. A greater emphasis needs to be placed on addressing these smoldering crises before they become full blown.

In this book we have discussed a number of smoldering crises that were not properly addressed by management. Many of these were due to ethical breaches in the organization. Adequate attention was not focused on remedying the core problem, and the situation escalated to a crisis. Based on the nature of human behavior and the record of ethical breaches leading to crisis, such breaches will likely continue despite the best efforts of business schools, religious leaders, and management writers. What does appear to make a difference in reducing such moral shortcomings in a given organization is the example set by upper management (Carroll & Buchholtz, 2012). It is encouraging that many organizations are able to achieve a high level of ethical integrity in the way they conduct business.

The implication for management is to set the ethical tone of the organization at the top levels of the company. In the absence of knowing what to do, employees will look one level higher for cues on how to respond in a certain situation. Promoting good business ethics can go a long way in preventing an organizational crisis caused by unethical behavior.

The External Landscape

Within the external landscape, emerging issues are focusing in two areas: the growing power of victims of a crisis and the eroding trust stakeholders experience when an organization is either the cause of a crisis or it is negligent in carrying out its duties during a crisis.

Victims of Crises Will Become More Visible and Powerful as Stakeholders

In the past, victims of crisis events have been acknowledged to some degree but were eventually forgotten. Indeed, certain victims, particularly those of natural disasters, are often poor and are considered outcasts in society. As a result, they are not long remembered. Patrick Lagadec (2004) made this observation in examining the fatalities from the killer heat waves in France (2003) and Chicago (1995). In both events, those who died were often the poor, the elderly, and those who were isolated to some degree from society. After Hurricane Katrina in 2005, victims of the storm began to receive much media attention. One of the reasons these victims were heard was because of the ineptness of government agencies when responding to this disaster.

Today, victim visibility has been enhanced by the presence of social media. An Internet search of a crisis event also includes YouTube videos that are available depicting the event. Videos can be played and replayed, perpetuating the memory of the crisis and its victims. Hence, victims are less likely to be forgotten if they can be viewed on a laptop on a moment's notice.

A Crisis Will Be Viewed as a Reason to Mistrust an Organization

A crisis can be an issue of trust (Bertrand & Lajtha, 2002). This viewpoint maintains that the organization shares some of the blame for the crisis, either in causing the crisis or in how it managed the crisis response. Even in the event of a natural disaster, the organization can be blamed if it was not adequately prepared. Hence, stakeholders perceive that organizations get the blame they deserve, and in proportion to their degree of unpreparedness. While such an attitude does not always seem fair, the onslaught of media attention that accompanies crisis events certainly seeks a party to blame (Boin, 't Hart, McConnell, & Preston, 2010). Valid or not, this scapegoat mentality does help add meaning to an otherwise meaningless situation. Even if an organization is not to be directly blamed for the results of a crisis, a loss of public confidence is still a likely outcome (Bertrand & Lajtha, 2002).

Management is a symbol of trust that the organization has with its stakeholders. Within the organization, leaders must be trusted to manage the crisis as effectively as possible. Employees also expect that management will not induce a crisis. Such a crisis would create a trust issue if management made ill-advised cuts in safety training or equipment. Should an employee be injured due to a cutback of this sort, then employee trust in the organization would be compromised.

External stakeholders also trust the organization to prevent crises when possible and mitigate them when they do occur. As we have discussed previously, the media, the community, and the customers are often critical of the organization when it does not manage a crisis effectively. Simply stated, the issue of trust is becoming more important. If stakeholders lose confidence in the organization, its ultimate survival may be in jeopardy. All stakeholders want to be able to say, "We trust you as an organization to do the right thing."

Strategic Planning

Strategic planning is the proactive stage when management has a chance to plan for future crisis events. The trends and implications in this important area are discussed next.

The Internal Landscape

Virtual Crisis Management Plans Will Become the Norm

Prior to the availability of the Internet, crisis management plans (CMPs) were kept in bound guidebooks. Such notebooks were similar to other standard operating procedure (SOP) materials that organizations kept on their bookshelves. Today, increasing numbers of organizations are posting these plans on their websites. This approach makes the plan readily available to all stakeholders with Internet access, and its general distribution ensures the plan can be accessed in a wider geographic context. It also enables crisis planners to evaluate other published plans when formulating or revising their own. Finally, because these plans are electronic documents, they can be easily edited and redistributed, unlike bound documents in notebooks, which take more effort to change.

One implication of this trend is that the organization's information technology (IT) department must be actively involved in the distribution of the crisis management plan. This relationship is a welcome one, since IT is an integral part of crisis recovery.

Crisis Management Planning Will Be Integrated Into the Organization's Strategic Planning Process

The planning process for a crisis has traditionally been implemented by designated crisis management teams (CMTs). In the early days of crisis management, companies with such teams typically had them operate outside of the strategic management process (Preble, 1997). An emerging trend is to incorporate crisis management and strategic planning (Chong & Park, 2010; Coombs, 2006; Parnell, 2013; Preble, 1997), a theme consistent with this book. The advantage of this approach is that it makes crisis awareness an ongoing process that is reviewed in conjunction with the organization's long-range plans. Crisis vulnerability planning is incorporated into the SWOT analysis component of planning. The implication for management is that it must ensure that the entire crisis management process does not take place in a far corner of the organization, away from the main players who need to be included. Crisis management should be part of an ongoing strategic planning process, not a separate activity that occurs only occasionally.

The External Landscape

In the strategic planning area, the crisis management team is also interacting with teams outside of the organization.

Crisis Management Teams Will Engage in More Planning With Other Crisis Teams From Outside Their Organizations

Traditionally, one crisis team is organized for each organizational unit. For example, a large company with several plants may have one crisis team for each manufacturing facility. In addition, there may also be an overall team for the entire organization. This type of arrangement works well when the crisis event is localized.

In crises that are more complicated and geographically diverse, organizational crisis management units must interact with similar teams from other organizations. In addition, a host of government agencies may also be involved in this network of crisis teams. These interlinking crisis teams that form during an event such as a natural disaster have been called "hastily formed networks" (Denning, 2006). Hurricane Katrina led to the formation of a number of hastily formed networks among aid agencies, crisis management teams, military units, emergency response teams, and local governments.

With a crisis like Hurricane Katrina, it is important to note that a unified chain of command may not exist within a local geographic area. What results is a modified chain of command that considers both the various stakeholders who are part of the disaster and the disaster relief efforts. Typically, a hurricane response is coordinated by local governmental agencies, but in the case of Katrina, the city of New Orleans lacked some key resources and did not manage others effectively (Berinato, 2010). The result was a hastily formed network that was coordinated by a number of agencies.

The implication of this trend is important. Crisis management team leaders must begin to network with their counterparts in other organizations. There are opportunities for knowledge transfer as well as the planning of disaster drills. The time to interact with these groups is before the crisis occurs. In this way, crisis team members are familiar with their counterparts and have already developed working relationships.

The Focus Efforts of Crisis Management Will Expand to Include a Wider Range of Stakeholders

The traditional focus of crisis management originally focused primarily on media relations ('t Hart, Heyse, & Boin, 2001; Marra, 1998). The thinking was that a good relationship with the media would help ensure that the public perceives the company in a positive manner.

Today, the scope of crisis management outreach is beginning to adopt a broader stakeholder approach. This approach advocates meeting the needs of the multiple groups that have distinct vested interests in the organization (Carroll & Buchholtz, 2012). Certainly, employees represent one such stakeholder group (Lockwood, 2005).

This sometimes forgotten group needs to know both the good and the bad news that occurs during a crisis. Employees are a key resource and can help pull the firm through a perilous time.

Other stakeholders who may be affected by a crisis include customers and the local communities in which they reside. The response by several large private-sector companies to Hurricane Katrina in New Orleans and the surrounding areas provides an example. Wal-Mart, Home Depot, and FedEx tracked the hurricane and moved aggressively to meet community needs after the storm hit (Olasky, 2006). While they certainly desired to increase business as well, these firms were poised to fill a humanitarian role in the aftermath of the storm.

The implication for crisis managers is to expand the scope of organizational response to include aiding local stakeholders when possible. Such a strategy is especially welcomed when a local geographical area has been affected by a natural disaster. This response will vary according to the type of services offered by the organization. Several applications become apparent:

- Food service establishments may offer certain products during times when these items may be scarce in the community. Offering products for free or at a reduced cost may be feasible. However, raising prices to reflect scarcity will be viewed by many as a form of inappropriate opportunism and will create community ill will that can last long after the crisis subsides. The community will perceive that the business took advantage of the victims.

- Retailers can ensure that adequate supplies of staple items such as flashlights, batteries, and portable stoves will be available. Managers who place orders for these items must be able to anticipate the kind of emergency products that will be needed and order accordingly. Again, opportunistic price increases will create bad feelings in the community. Organizations with access to automotive or van fleets may be able to offer transportation for the elderly or needy. This service could be accomplished by offering pickup and delivery for needy citizens to local stores, similar to what a bus service would offer in a city. Although offering this type of service may sound preposterous to some managers, doing so on a temporary emergency basis will be appreciated and well received by the community.

To summarize, planning for a crisis means considering the interests of both the company and the stakeholders in the community.

Sustainable Development Will Become More of an Expectation

Sustainable development has been emerging as a trend in recent years, and many organizations are now embracing sustainability as part of the strategic mission. Executives and others must learn more about sustainability issues associated with the use of nonrenewable resources. Of course, the government will play a role as well. Sustainable development should not be confused with protecting the environment from pollution and avoiding calamities like oil spills, although these incidents certainly waste resources. The former is associated with accidents, while the latter concerns everyday business practice. Hence, sustainable development implies that organizations use resources in a manner that conserves resources for future generations as well (Stead & Stead, 2004). In other words, resources that are utilized, such as trees, should be renewable. Nonrenewable resources should be used sparingly and with an eye for the future. An outgrowth from this movement is that companies must not only practice sustainability, but those practices should also exist through their supply chains.

The relationship between crisis management and sustainable development must also be acknowledged (Crandall & Mensah, 2008). These two areas are closely related because an environmental crisis triggered by an organizational mistake can quickly consume sustainable resources. Oil spills are at the forefront of the news when they occur. Consumers become angry when the environment is damaged and nonrenewable resources are squandered, and public disdain mounts daily for the affected oil companies. But other less obvious examples exist in the crosshairs of crisis and sustainable development. Sustainable development efforts are costly in terms of both time and money. A company that ignores sustainable development will soon find itself lagging behind its rivals. This in itself can result in a crisis, because no company needs to be playing catch-up. Such a scenario can create a public relations problem when the company must explain to its public stakeholders why it has not been embracing sustainability when other companies have been doing so for years.

Consider one company that has been an industry leader in sustainable development. Atlanta-based Interface manufactures modular carpet and has been innovating in the area of sustainability since 1994. Modular carpet requires considerable energy resources and space to manufacture and requires considerable landfill space when disposed. In its quest to be a leader in sustainable development, Interface created a model that describes the closed-loop process it seeks in its manufacturing and disposal processes (Nelson, 2009). The model at Interface builds on a foundation of seven principles:

1. *Eliminate waste.* Not just reduce it, but eliminate it altogether in the production process.

2. *Produce only benign emissions.* Eliminate all harmful emissions in the manufacturing of its products and in the products themselves.

3. *Use renewable energy.* Reduce the use of nonsustainable energy sources (oil) and increase the usage of renewable ones, such as wind, solar, and landfill gas. By 2020, the goal is to operate all facilities with only renewable sources of energy.

4. *Close the loop.* Design the manufacturing process so that waste byproducts are recycled into some aspect of the manufacturing process.

5. *Use resource-efficient transportation.* Transport the company's people and products in a way that reduces pollution, greenhouse emissions, and oil consumption.

6. *Sensitize stakeholders.* Educate the company's stakeholders (employees, partners, customers, communities, suppliers, and owners) on the need to promote a culture of sustainability in the community.

7. *Redesign commerce.* Become a role model to other business, supply chains, and industries on how sustainability can be incorporated in business practices (Nelson, 2009).

Interface's strategy is aggressive, to be sure. However, it does give other companies a benchmark to begin their own sustainable development initiatives.

Crisis Management

Crisis management is the reactive phase of the four-stage model outlined in this book. Specifically, it is the stage at which the organization responds to a given crisis. Emerging trends within the internal landscape are discussed next.

The Internal Landscape

Contingency Responses to Specific Crisis Events Will Become More Common

Conventional crisis planning has typically followed a standardized procedure in addressing incidents. As a result, most crisis plans contain specific procedures to follow in a particular event. For example, bomb threats are common crisis events that are addressed, and plans for these usually contain a step-by-step procedure for responding. Another example is the evacuation of a building, a procedure that should be carried out in an organized, methodical fashion. Responding to complex crises, however, will also involve contingency approaches. This line of thinking maintains that there may not be one best approach to addressing every crisis.

Shrivastava (1993) noted the beginning of a shift from procedures to broader-based crisis skills in the early 1990s. Included in this skill set are "decentralized decision making" and "managerial autonomy and flexibility" (p. 28). This way of thinking recognizes that flexible contingencies may be required along the way. Bertrand and Lajtha (2002) refer to this ability as the "breaking of inflexible mindsets" or "training oneself to deal with the unexpected" (p. 186).

While becoming more adaptive in its response, the organization may develop greater resilience, the ability to recover from an unfortunate event such as a crisis (Horne & Orr, 1998; Sutcliffe & Vogus, 2003). Resilience is not a step-by-step methodology in terms of crisis response, but is more of an inherent trait of the organization that takes advantage of its ability to adapt and improvise when a crisis unfolds (Somers, 2009).

The implications for management are twofold. On one hand, crisis planners need to anticipate specific vulnerabilities and how they should be managed in a step-by-step process if the threat can be addressed in this manner. On the other hand, the crisis response should maintain flexibility in more complex situations. Making adjustments along the way is part of contingency thinking, and this in itself is both an art and a science. Crisis response, then, requires a set of plans that become the backbone for managing the event. It also requires a degree of improvisation, an ability to create new responses in light of new information that the crisis may reveal.

The Organization's Website and Social Media Networks Will Become Chief Communications Tools During a Crisis

The organization's website will become the main communication vehicle to its stakeholders during a crisis. Unfortunately, some crises have caused websites to "go down," rendering them useless. Union University, a small private college in western Tennessee, experienced this in February 2008 when a tornado hit the campus, damaging buildings and causing the website to become unavailable for several hours. Yet Virginia Tech was able to remain online by loading a simplified "light version" of its website after the April 2007 shooting rampage by student Seung-Hui Cho (Joly, 2008). The website became the key communication device with the public during the ordeal. Following the shootings, the website received up to 150,000 visits per hour. It normally transfers 15 gigabytes a day, but on the day of the shooting the Web server transferred 432 gigabytes (Carlson, 2007).

One of the more interesting outgrowths of the Internet is the use of social media tools in crisis communication. Social media enable firms to disseminate information even if the organization's website becomes inoperable. Such was the case after the aforementioned Union University tornado. The university's website was not operating after the storm, so a blog was set up at blogspot.com to provide updates on the damage and recovery. In addition, the university was able to use its Facebook page to share updates, photos, and videos (Joly, 2008).

Crisis managers must educate themselves about the various social networking tools available. Unlike websites, which often require individuals with specialized skills to operate, social networking tools are relatively easy to use and manage. However, social media also include the added burden of communicating in a two-way environment, sometimes referred to as Web 2.0. Managers should become proficient with Facebook and Twitter if they have not done so already, because both can be useful for crisis management situations (Crowe, 2010).

The External Landscape

Social media will become more powerful due to its ability to transfer news quickly about a crisis. Two implications of this trend are discussed next.

Social Media Will Play a Greater Role in Determining the Outcome of a Crisis

Social media will become more powerful in their ability to influence the outcome of a crisis. To understand this power, one must go back to the early 1990s when their use was becoming popular. One of the first companies directly affected by an Internet-related crisis was Intel, when its flawed Pentium chip surfaced in 1994. The crisis began rather innocently when math professor Thomas Nicely at Lynchburg College in Virginia found a computer error when he was working on a math problem. He e-mailed a colleague about the matter, and soon his spreadsheet problem demonstrating an Intel calculation error was all over the Internet (Weiss, 1998). Intel had become one of the first victims of substantial negative Internet publicity, a phenomenon known as "flaming."

In terms of crisis management, the power of the Internet can be seen in its ability to transmit information—usually negative—about a company to a large audience. Social media tools add the ability to communicate in real time using media other than the printed word, through computers and even cell phones. Because of this power, social media will also become more pivotal in influencing the outcome of a crisis. We reviewed several cases that were influenced by social media in Chapter 8.

Time Will Be a Key Measure That Will Be Used to Evaluate an Organization's Response to a Crisis

In a social media reality, organizations are under greater pressure to respond to crises more rapidly. The longer a company waits to respond, the more likely stakeholders will perceive it as either indecisive or has something to hide. Waiting more than 24 hours to issue any kind of a statement is no longer acceptable. Statements need to appear on the organization's website within a few hours (or less) of the crisis. The company's Facebook page should be used to convey information and encourage dialogue with external stakeholders when necessary. Those stakeholders who follow their news using Twitter will expect updates at least twice a day (González-Herrero & Smith, 2010).

Organizational Learning

Organizational learning after a crisis is necessary so that the company's crisis response will be more effective when the next incident arrives. Learning also helps to prevent certain types of crises from reappearing in the future. The discussion following outlines the importance of establishing a feedback loop in the strategic planning process and abolishing the status quo when necessary.

The Internal Landscape

Organizational Learning Will Provide an Important Feedback Loop Necessary for The Strategic Planning Process

Many in the crisis management field have called for a renewed focus on the postcrisis stage, when learning and evaluation need to take place (Deverell, 2009; Racherla & Hu, 2009; Veil, 2011). What is significant about organizational learning is that it initiates the feedback loop (see Chapter 9, Figure 9.3) that is necessary in the strategic management framework (Racherla & Hu, 2009).

The implication of this emerging trend is significant and remains a central theme of this book. Indeed, the crisis management process, from landscape survey to organizational learning, needs to be an integral part of the organization's strategic planning process. The days when crisis management consisted of a small, select group of managers who wrote the crisis plan and met occasionally are gone. Crisis events affect strategy in the long run; therefore, planning, managing, and learning from these events must be carried out within the strategic management framework.

Learning After a Crisis Will Lead to the Abolishment of the Status Quo

Returning to "business as usual" after a crisis has been the traditional goal of many organizations. However, a crisis offers an opportunity to change or even abolish the status quo. "Crises are, by their very nature, an invitation to abandon standard ways of doing things. They offer an opportunity to think and work laterally and to de-compartmentalize/break down encrusted silos in the company" (Bertrand & Lajtha, 2002, p. 186). Inherent in this mind-set is the notion that a crisis can trigger the forces of renewal in an organization (Dynes, 2003; Olshansky, 2006). Some liken the changes after a crisis to a process called "self-organization." This metamorphosis occurs when an organization works through a crisis and transforms into a more adaptable organization (Murphy, 1996). For example, the Red River Valley flood of 1997 and the subsequent organizational renewal that took place were analyzed through the lens of chaos theory. The local government of Fargo, North Dakota, emerged as a new leader in that geographic area, taking over the lead in emergency response management from the county, which had formerly carried out this function. In other words, the status quo of how emergencies had been managed in the past was now broken and replaced with a better system (Sellnow, Seeger, & Ulmer, 2002). In a similar vein, crisis planning at movie theaters changed forever when James Holmes entered a packed theater in Aurora, Colorado, and shot 70 people on July 20, 2012 (Berzon, Banjo, & Audi, 2012).

The implication for crisis managers and strategic planners is one of hope. Although crises are negative events, they can engender positive change. However, for this positive change to occur, the learning process must be tied back to the strategic planning process. Managers need to be cognizant of their role as potential change agents in their organizations.

The External Landscape

Outside of the organization, an abundance of learning on crisis management is continually taking place. This area includes the work of crisis scholars who conduct research at colleges and universities. Generally, this type of research falls into three categories: conceptual, empirical, and industry application studies (Tavitiyaman, Leong, Dunn, Njite, & Neal, 2008). The following are emerging trends in the field of crisis management research.

Crisis Management Frameworks and Models Will Become More Complex and Sophisticated

Frameworks of crisis management have traditionally been simple, with most depicting a sequential format for understanding the evolution and resolution of a crisis. The most basic framework consists of a precrisis, crisis, and postcrisis sequence as overviewed in Chapter 1. Smith (1990) and Richardson (1994) utilized this approach in their studies. Four- and five-stage frameworks have also been proposed (see Fink, 1996; Hosie & Smith, 2004; Myers, 1993; Pearson & Mitroff, 1993); this book also employs a four-stage approach. Crisis frameworks have also been offered for types of crisis categories as well as crisis management communication strategies. Such strategies were examined in Chapter 8.

Although frameworks offer a general approach to understanding the components of crisis phenomena, models are designed to examine the different variables that interact with each other before and during a crisis. Some progress has been made in the area of organizational crisis model building. Shrivastava, Mitroff, Miller, and Miglani (1988) offered one of the first industrial crisis models. Sheaffer, Richardson, and Rosenblatt (1998) studied the 1995 collapse of Barings, a conservative and once solid British bank, and proposed two models, a crisis–causal antecedents model and an early warning signals model. Pearson and Clair (1998) examined the crisis management process and proposed a success–failure outcomes model. Elsubbaugh, Fildes, and Rose (2004) developed a crisis preparedness model using data from the Egyptian textile industry. More recently, Jin and Liu (2010) developed a blog-mediated crisis communication model to help public relations professionals adopt strategies when responding to blogs.

Crisis Research Will Continue to Use Cases but Will Incorporate More Statistical Analysis as Well

Crisis management research has been dominated by the case study approach (Carmeli & Schaubroeck, 2008). Indeed, much can be gleaned from examining a past crisis in detail. In the 1980s, Union Carbide's Bhopal disaster, Johnson & Johnson's Tylenol cyanide sabotage, and the *Exxon Valdez* oil spill were well documented. A number of high-profile events made valuable case studies in the 1990s, including the bombing of the Murrah Federal Building in Oklahoma City, the crash of ValuJet Flight 592 in Florida's Everglades, and the Luby's Cafeteria massacre in Killeen, Texas. Since the beginning of the millennium, the September 11, 2001, toppling of the World Trade Center Towers, Hurricane Katrina in August 2005, the Asian tsunami of December 2004, and the 2008 China earthquake (also known as the Great Sichuan Earthquake) have been subjects for case studies. The late 2000s and early 2010s brought three more events that will no doubt be studied intensely as case studies: the BP *Deepwater* oil spill, the Toyota recall, and the Colorado movie theater crisis.

Although crisis management case studies will continue to be popular, research incorporating multivariate statistical analysis will likely expand. Such empirical research is necessary as researchers seek to construct models that help managers assess their organizations and prepare for crises in a systematic manner.

In an early empirical study, Marcus and Goodman (1991) examined corporate announcements pertaining to crises and firm stock values. Greening and Johnson (1996) used regression analysis to discover how management teams and strategies correspond to catastrophic events. Sheaffer and Mano-Negrin (2003) used factor analysis to examine executive orientations to crisis management policies and practices. More recently, Choi, Sung, and Kim (2010) employed hierarchical regression analysis to examine the dynamics of group behavior in crisis management teams. The intricacies of these methods are beyond the scope of this book, but the use of such tools demonstrates the growing sophistication of crisis management research.

Research combining case studies and empirical analysis are not common but have significant potential. The Transboundary Crisis Management (TCM) data are housed in the Moynihan Institute of Global Affairs at Syracuse University in New York. Case studies have been analyzed, and various nominal and ordinal variables have been extracted from each case for statistical analysis. The data set was developed by social scientists and graduate students using a rigorous case writing methodology and a coding scheme. More than 100 cases have been analyzed, including terrorist incidents, pandemics, and economic crises (Hermann & Dayton, 2009). All of the cases have expanded over wide geographic borders; hence the name *transboundary crises*. In the past, case studies and empirical research have often emerged separately.

Crisis Research Will Take on a Long-Range Perspective

The traditional approach in crisis management research has been to analyze short-term events, typically single-event crises. The study of these events includes an analysis of the various phases of the crisis from the precrisis stage to the learning stage. However, the long-term effects of these crises have not been widely evaluated. Revisiting the sites and stakeholders involved in a crisis to determine what learning and policy changes have been implemented is often appropriate ('t Hart et al., 2001). A long-term view of crisis also looks at the precursors of these events. Analyzing variables such as the organizational culture and other mini-steps that led to the crisis can yield useful information to both researchers and managers.

Although the area of crisis research may appear to have little significance for students, or for practicing managers, for that matter, nothing could be farther from the truth. Research data are drawn from the activities and experiences of practicing managers whose organizations are engaged in crisis management. In the future you may be called on to answer a questionnaire for a research study that is being conducted to learn more about organizational crises and their management. If you have an opportunity to participate in such a survey, do so enthusiastically, because ultimately, it will assist the researchers, who are attempting to learn how organizations can respond more effectively to a crisis. In some cases, you may even be asked for an interview. Perhaps your organization experienced a crisis and the researchers want to learn more about how your crisis management team responded. Referring the researcher to your official company spokesperson will help that person gain insights that are not possible through a survey.

Summary

This chapter examined the emerging trends in the field of crisis management. One of the key trends mentioned is also a central theme of this book: that crisis management should be seen as an integral part of the strategic management process. In the past, much of what we call crisis management planning existed in a vacuum, away from the strategic planners who guided the future of their organizations. In the future, a change in this approach to crisis planning will be required.

Questions for Discussion

1. Why do you think crisis management has not always been heavily emphasized in the strategic management process?

2. Hastily formed networks are an emerging trend in crisis management, particularly in the area of disaster management. If a major storm were to hit your local area, what groups do you think should be part of the network to coordinate crisis and disaster relief?

3. Sustainable development is a trend in many organizations. What efforts at sustainability do you see at your college or university? What is being done where you work to implement sustainable development? What changes do you recommend?

4. Searching for the positive side of a crisis might seem contradictory, but it is an emerging trend. What positive outcomes can you see that resulted from a crisis in an organization in your area or perhaps where you have worked? How did the organization improve itself? Were any laws or regulations changed?

5. Much has been written on the importance of business ethics, and yet it continues to cause many crises in businesses. Why do you think ethical violations continue to be a source of crises in organizations today?

6. Crisis management research is a developing field. What areas do you think need to be researched more in the future?

Chapter Exercise

Many organizational crisis management plans are now available online. In this exercise, the class will examine different plans posted on company websites. Begin by locating your college or university's CMP online. As an alternative, you may wish to locate plans that exist where the students work or at a prominent organization in your community. Once the organizations have been identified, evaluate each as a class and consider the following:

- How long is the CMP? Do you think it is too short, or perhaps too long?
- What items are left out of the plan that should have been included?
- Which organizations did not have a plan posted that should have had one publically available? Why do you think the plans were not posted?
- Do the plans post potential crisis vulnerabilities that the organization may face?
- Do the plans acknowledge the presence of potential environmental crises that may occur?
- Do the plans include provisions for postcrisis debriefing? In other words, are their opportunities for organizational learning to occur?

Closing Book Case: The Great Boston Molasses Flood

It may seem odd to end a chapter on the future of crisis management with a classic industrial crisis in the United States. But a close look at this unusual incident reveals a number of themes that have been addressed in this book, plus some items that provide an eye for the future.

The Flood

The scene was Boston, Massachusetts, on a warmer than average winter day, January 15, 1919. In an industrial area of town, the United States Industrial Alcohol (USIA) Company was the location for a huge storage tank of molasses that measured 58 feet tall (almost as tall as a six-story building) and 90 feet in diameter. On that fateful day the tank was filled with 2.3 million gallons of the dark sugary liquid (Park, 1983). At around 12:30 P.M., the tank split open and spewed its contents onto the local firehouse, an elevated train, numerous houses and buildings, and a number of innocent bystanders. The tidal wave of molasses took out the supports of a nearby train, causing the track to sag to street level. The liquid wave literally knocked over the fire station and pushed it toward the sea. In the adjacent Public Works Department, five men eating lunch were killed immediately when the hot bubbling molasses poured over them (Mason, 1965).

Visualizing the disaster is almost unfathomable. Imagine a heavy sludge, 15 feet high in places, moving at around 35 miles per hour, sucking up people and knocking over structures along its way. When the casualties had been tallied several days later, 21 people were dead, 150 had been injured, and 20 horses owned by the city had been killed (Potter, 2011). Some of the victims had been crushed to death in the fallen buildings, while others literally drowned in the molasses.

The Tank

The industrial need for molasses at the time may surprise some. Today, we think of it as an ingredient used in baking cookies and other sweets. During World War I, molasses was used as a standard sweetener for cooking, but also in fermentation to make ethanol that could be transformed into a special type of liquor used in military munitions (Lyons, 2009). Of course, molasses could also be used in making alcohol for consumption, an especially noteworthy topic given the state of Prohibition talks at that time.

At the center of the disaster was failure of the molasses storage tank, built only three years earlier in 1915. Why it had failed was unclear. During the subsequent trial, USIA blamed Italian anarchists for bombing the tank. Indeed, the explanation was plausible, because anarchists were known to be active in Boston at the time (Lyons, 2009; Mason, 1965). However, the real problem was later deemed to be a structural flaw in the tank that likely occurred when it had been originally constructed, what safety experts call "inadequate design" (Thyer, Jagger, Atherton, & Ash, 2009).

The tank had been built using large curved steel plates fastened together with rivets. The structure was housed on a concrete slab only 200 feet from the adjacent harbor. Ships from Cuba brought the molasses to the port, where it was stored temporarily in the large holding tank before being shipped by train to its next destination (Lyons, 2009). When the tank had been completed in December 1915, it should have been tested with water. However, the full capacity test never occurred because a shipment of molasses was soon to arrive. In fact, the only test conducted was with only 6 inches of water, at which time the company pronounced it safe for use. The tank was never inspected by an architect or engineer, neither of which was required by law (Puleo, 2001).

From the beginning of its use, the tank sprung numerous leaks. Stephen Puleo (2003) described in his book on the disaster, *Dark Tide*, how the company responded to existing leaks in the tank by painting the tank brown so that molasses seepage would not be detected—an example of a cover-up, literally. Even the locals knew about the leaks:

> From the beginning leaks had appeared. Streaks of molasses ran down the sides of the tank, and people living nearby filled up cans for home use. Children would scrape the leaks onto sticks to make molasses suckers. Neighbors and workmen had also reported ominous rumbling noises inside the structure. (Lyons, 2009, p. 41)

When the tank finally ruptured, the rivets holding the metal plates together shot out quickly, and according to the local patrolman in the area, resembled the sound of a machine gun (Puleo, 2001).

The day of the accident was warm for a January winter in Boston. It is speculated that the warmer temperatures might have been a factor in the eventual demise of the tank. Moreover, that same morning, a half a million gallons of warmer molasses had been pumped into the tank and mixed with the cooler molasses that was already there. The resulting mixture can initiate fermentation process that produces gas (Potter, 2011). This chemical reaction exerted greater pressure on the walls of a tank that had already been poorly built.

The Legal Process

The resulting litigation turned out to be a marathon affair lasting six years. A total of 119 lawsuits were filed against USIA. The company continued to allege sabotage. Indeed, 40 other explosions had taken place in the Boston area between January 1, 1918, and July 1, 1919, and police had discovered placards nearby that advocated the annihilation of U.S. leaders, including Woodrow Wilson, and signed by "The American Anarchists" (Puleo, 2001). The company also noted that the tank had been filled to full capacity previously and had not suffered an incident.

Plaintiffs demonstrated that the construction of the tank was inadequate from the beginning, however. A Massachusetts Institute of Technology professor, C. M. Spofford, testified that the metal plates of the tank were too thin and did not contain enough rivets. Spofford calculated that the actual stress on the sides of the tank before it failed was double what it should have been. He concluded, "The tank was improperly designed and its failure was due entirely to structural weakness" (Puleo, 2001, p. 63).

Six years after the flood, and after 45,000 pages of testimony and some 3,000 witnesses, Judge Colonel Ogden wrote a 51-page report fixing blame on USIA. He rejected the anarchist theory as well (Puleo, 2001). Settlements included $25,000 to the city of Boston, $42,000 to the Boston Elevated Railway Company, and $6,000 to the family of each victim (Lyons, 2009).

Government Regulations

Regulations often follow crises such as this one, particularly when the public's safety is at risk. The building of the molasses tank was wrought with failures in safety testing and engineering. Overseeing the project for USIA was its treasurer, A. P. Jell, who enlisted the Hammond Iron Works Company to build the tank. For Hammond, it was to be the largest tank it had constructed. For Jell, it was a project he had no experience in overseeing. He had no engineering background and did not consult with other experts on appropriate safety requirements for such an undertaking. He even rushed construction because of an upcoming shipment of molasses due in a matter of days (Puleo, 2001). This time constraint also explains the inadequate 6-inch water capacity test described earlier.

After the accident, things changed dramatically. New Boston city regulations required plans for construction projects to be approved by an engineer or architect. The plans then had to be filed with the city's building department. This practice soon spread across the country (Lyons, 2009).

And to This Day . . .

Today, a youth baseball field and recreational park has been built where the tank once sat. A small plaque at the park describes the events that occurred that fateful day. Today, locals claim that on a hot summer day, the faint smell of molasses can still be detected (Lyons, 2009).

Closing Book Case Discussion Questions

1. What examples of cost cutting do you see in this case?

2. Why do you think it was so easy to build the tank with so little oversight from inspectors?

3. A large number of people were put at risk because of the location of the tank. What practices exist today that would protect large groups from similar types of storage tanks? To answer this question, think of the location of buildings, production equipment, and so on.

Closing Book Case Sources

Lyons, C. (2009). A sticky tragedy. *History Today, 59*(1), 40–42.

Mason, J. (1965, January). The molasses disaster of January 15, 1919. *Yankee,* 52–53, 109–111.

Park, E. (1983). Without warning, molasses in January surged over Boston. *Smithsonian, 14*(8), 213–230.

Potter, S. (2011). January 15, 1919: Boston Molasses Flood. *Weatherwise, 64*(1), 10–11.

Puleo, S. (2001). Death by molasses. *American History, 35*(6), 60–66.

Puleo, S. (2003). *Dark tide: The great Boston molasses flood of 1919.* Boston: Beacon.

Thyer, A., Jagger, S., Atherton, W., & Ash, J. (2009). A review of catastrophic failures of bulk liquid storage tanks. *Loss Prevention Bulletin,* Issue 205, 3–11.

References

Berinato, S. (2010). You have to lead from everywhere. *Harvard Business Review, 88*(11), 76–79.

Bertrand, R., & Lajtha, C. (2002). A new approach to crisis management. *Journal of Contingencies and Crisis Management, 10*(4), 181–191.

Berzon, A., Banjo, S., & Audi, T. (2012, July 23). Suspect's rapid descent. *Wall Street Journal,* pp. A1, A4.

Boin, A., 't Hart, P., McConnell, A., & Preston, T. (2010). Leadership style, crisis response and blame management: The case of Hurricane Katrina. *Public Administration, 88*(3), 706–723.

Carlson, S. (2007, August 3). Emergency at Virginia Tech shows the power of the Web, says campus official. *Chronicle of Higher Education, 53*(48), 28.

Carmeli, A., & Schaubroeck, J. (2008). Organisational crisis preparedness: The importance of learning from failures. *Long Range Planning, 4,* 177–196.

Carroll, A., & Buchholtz, A. (2012). *Business and society: Ethics sustainability, and stakeholder management* (8th ed.). Mason, OH: South-Western Cengage Learning.

Choi, J. N., Sung, S. Y., & Kim, M. U. (2010). How do groups react to unexpected threats? Crisis management in organizational teams. *Social Behavior and Personality, 38*(6), 805–828.

Chong, J., & Park, J. (2010). A conceptual framework and research propositions for integrating TQM into crisis planning. *Review of Business Research, 10*(2), 69–74.

Coombs, W. (2006). *Code red in the boardroom: Crisis management as organizational DNA.* Westport, CT: Praeger.

Crandall, W. R., & Mensah, E. C. (2008). Crisis management and sustainable development: A framework and proposed research agenda. *International Journal of Sustainable Strategic Management, 1*(1), 16–34.

Crowe, A. (2010). The social media manifesto: A comprehensive review of the impact of social media on emergency management. *Journal of Business Continuity and Emergency Planning, 5*(1), 409–420.

Denning, P. (2006). Hastily formed networks: Collaboration in the absence of authority. *Communications of ACM, 49*(4), 15–20.

Deverell, E. (2009). Crises as learning triggers: Exploring a conceptual framework of crisis-induced learning. *Journal of Contingencies and Crisis Management, 17*(3), 179–188.

Dynes, R. (2003). Noah and disaster planning: The cultural significance of the flood story. *Journal of Contingencies and Crisis Management, 11*(4), 170–177.

Elsubbaugh, S., Fildes, R., & Rose, M. (2004). Preparation for crisis management: A proposed model and empirical evidence. *Journal of Contingencies and Crisis Management, 12*(3), 112–127.

Fink, S. (1996). *Crisis management: Planning for the inevitable.* New York: American Management Association.

González-Herrero, A., Smith, S. (2010). Crisis communications management 2.0: Organizational principles to manage crisis in an online world. *Organization Development Journal, 28*(1), 97–105.

Greening, D., & Johnson, R. (1996). Do managers and strategies matter? A study in crisis. *Journal of Management Studies, 33*(1), 25–51.

Hart, P., Heyse, L., & Boin, A. (2001). New trends in crisis management practice and crisis management research: Setting the agenda. *Journal of Contingencies and Crisis Management, 9*(4), 181–188.

Hermann, M., & Dayton, B. (2009). Transboundary crises through the eyes of policymakers: Sense making and crisis management. *Journal of Contingencies and Crisis Management, 17*(4), 233–241.

Horne III, J., & Orr, J. (1998). Assessing behaviors that create resilient organizations. *Employment Relations Today, 24*(4), 29–39.

Hosie, P., & Smith, C. (2004). Preparing for crisis: Online security management education. *Research and Practice in Human Resource Management, 12*(2), 90–127.

Institute for Crisis Management. (2011). *Annual ICM crisis report: News coverage of business crises during 2010.* Retrieved April 8, 2012, from http://crisisconsultant.com/images/2010CrisisReportICM.pdf.

Jin, Y., & Liu, B. (2010). The blog-mediated crisis communication model: Recommendations for responding to influential external blogs. *Journal of Public Relations, 22*(4), 429–455.

Joly, K. (2008, April). It's 2008: Is your 911 website ready? *universitybusiness.com.* Retrieved July 18, 2012, from http://www.universitybusiness.com/article/its-2008-your-911-website-ready.

Lagadec, P. (2004). Understanding the French 2003 heat wave experience: Beyond the heat, a multi-layered challenge. *Journal of Contingencies and Crisis Management, 12*(4), 160–169.

Lockwood, N. (2005). Crisis management in today's business environment: HR's strategic role. *HRMagazine 50*(12), 1–10.

Marcus, A., & Goodman, R. (1991). Victims and shareholders: The dilemmas of presenting corporate policy during a crisis. *Academy of Management Journal, 34*(2), 281–305.

Marra, F. (1998). Crisis communication plans: Poor predictors of excellent public relations. *Public Relations Review, 24*(4), 461–474.

Myers, K. (1993). *Total contingency planning for disasters: Managing risk . . . minimizing loss . . . ensuring business continuity.* New York: Wiley.

Murphy, P. (1996). Chaos theory as a model for managing issues and crises. *Public Relations Review, 22*(2), 95–113.

Nelson, E. (2009). How Interface innovates with suppliers to create sustainable solutions. *Global Business and Organizational Excellence, 28*(6), 22–30.

Olasky, M. (2006). *The politics of disaster: Katrina, big government, and a new strategy for future crisis.* Nashville: W Publishing Group.

Olshansky, R. (2006). Planning after Hurricane Katrina. *Journal of the American Planning Association, 72*(2), 147–153.

Parnell, J. A. (2013). *Strategic management: Theory and practice* (4th ed.). Thousand Oaks, CA: Sage.

Pearson, C., & Clair, J. (1998). Reframing crisis management. *Academy of Management Review, 23*(1), 59–76.

Pearson, C., & Mitroff, I. (1993). From crisis prone to crisis prepared: A framework for crisis management. *Academy of Management Executive, 7*(1), 48–59.

Preble, J. (1997). Integrating the crisis management perspective into the strategic management process. *Journal of Management Studies, 34*(5), 769–791.

Racherla, P., & Hu, C. (2009). A framework for knowledge-based crisis management in the hospitality and tourism industry. *Cornell Hospitality Quarterly, 50*(4), 561–577.

Richardson, B. (1994). Socio-technical disasters: Profile and prevalence. *Disaster Prevention and Management, 3*(4), 41–69.

Sellnow, T., Seeger, M., & Ulmer, R. (2002). Chaos theory, informational needs, and natural disasters. *Journal of Applied Communication Research, 30*(4), 269–292.

Sheaffer, Z., & Mano-Negrin, R. (2003). Executives' orientations as indicators of crisis management policies and practices. *Journal of Management Studies, 40*(2), 573–606.

Sheaffer, Z., Richardson, B., & Rosenblatt, Z. (1998). Early-warning-signals management: A lesson from the Barings crisis. *Journal of Contingencies and Crisis Management, 6*(1), 1–22.

Shrivastava, P. (1993). Crisis theory/practice: Towards a sustainable future. *Industrial and Environmental Crisis Quarterly, 7*(1), 23–42.

Shrivastava, P., Mitroff, I. I., Miller, D., & Miglani, A. (1988). Understanding industrial crises. *Journal of Management Studies, 25*(4), 285–304.

Smith, D. (1990). Beyond contingency planning: Towards a model of crisis management. *Industrial Crisis Quarterly, 4*(4), 263–275.

Somers, S. (2009). Measuring resilience potential: An adaptive strategy for organizational crisis planning. *Journal of Contingencies and Crisis Management, 17*(1), 12–23.

Stead, W., & Stead, J. (2004). *Sustainable strategic management.* Armonk, NY: ME Sharpe.

Sutcliffe, K. & Vogus, T. (2003). Organizing for resilience. In K. Cameron, (Ed.), *Positive Organizational Scholarship.* San Francisco: Berrett-Koehler.

Tavitiyaman, P., Leong, J., Dunn, G., Njite D., & Neal, D. (2008). The effectiveness of lodging crisis management plans. *Journal of Quality Assurance in Hospitality and Tourism, 8*(4), 24–60.

Veil, S. (2011). Mindful learning in crisis management. *Journal of Business Communication, 48*(2), 116–147.

Weiss, J. (1998). *Business ethics: A stakeholder and issues management approach.* Fort Worth, TX: Dryden.

Appendix

Crisis Management Plan Template

Name of Company Goes Here

Company Logo Goes Here (Optional)

Crisis Management Plan

Last Revision Date

Contents

Purpose of the Crisis Management Team (CMT)   313

Definition of a Crisis   314

Activating the CMT   315

Command Center Location   316

CMT Members and Contact Information   317

CMT Role Responsibilities   318

Responses to Specific Types of Crises   319

Worksheet 1 – SWOT Analysis   320

Worksheet 2 – PEST Analysis   321

Important Phone Numbers and Contact Information   322

Purpose of the Crisis Management Team (CMT)

1. The CMT identifies the crisis threats the organization may encounter.

2. The CMT develops the crisis management plan.

3. The CMT leads training in the area of crisis management.

4. The CMT actively manages the crisis should one occur.

5. The CMT leads the postcrisis evaluation so that learning can occur.

Definition of a Crisis

A *crisis* is an event that has a low probability of occurring, but should it occur, can have a vastly negative impact on our organization.

The causes of the crisis, as well as the means to resolve it, may not be readily clear; nonetheless, its resolution should be approached as quickly as possible.

Finally, the crisis impact may not be initially obvious to all of the relevant stakeholders of our organization.

Activating the CMT

1. In the event of an emergency or crisis, any member of the CMT can activate the team by notifying one or more of its members.

2. Upon activation of the CMT, the remaining team members will be notified of the crisis in the most expedient manner possible.

3. The CMT will meet at the primary command center. If this location is not operational, the secondary location will be utilized.

4. The CMT will meet to discuss strategies for managing the specific crisis at hand. Other meetings will be called as necessary until the crisis is resolved.

Command Center Location

1. Primary Command Center Location

This location is where the CMT meets when a crisis is present and a meeting needs to be held. Our primary command center location is:

Building   _____

Room   _____

2. Secondary Command Center Location

In the event that the primary command center is not available, perhaps due to fire or a weather event, the secondary command center location will be used. Our secondary command center location is:

Building   _____

Room   _____

CMT Members and Contact Information

Name	Cell Phone	Work Phone	E-mail	Home Phone

Extend this list as necessary.

CMT Role Responsibilities

Two key roles need to be determined within the CMT:

1. The leader of the team, and

2. The person who is designated to talk to the media

In our organization: The CMT leader is:

_____

The CMT member who talks to the media is:

_____

In larger organizations, the members of the CMT are usually selected from the major departmental areas. In smaller organizations, the CMT often consists of the owner, the managers, and other designated employees.

Regardless of the size of the organization, the two key roles above must be designated before a crisis ever occurs.

Responses to Specific Types of Crises

The types of crises our organization may encounter are listed in this section. For each potential crisis, there is a short summary of how we will respond and begin to address that crisis.

Use Worksheets 1 and 2 to assist in compiling a list of potential crises.

Worksheet 1: SWOT Analysis

Our Company Strengths Include:	The Potential Crises That Could Result From Those Strengths Include:
Our Company Weaknesses Include:	**The Potential Crises That Could Result From Those Weaknesses Include:**
Our Company Opportunities Include:	**The Potential Crises That Could Result From Those Opportunities Include:**
Our Company Threats Include:	**The Potential Crises That Could Result From Those Threats Include:**

Worksheet 2: PEST Analysis

Potential Crises That Could Result From the Political–Legal Environment Include:

Potential Crises That Could Result From the Economic Environment Include:

Potential Crises That Could Result From the Social Environment Include:

Potential Crises That Could Result From the Technological Environment Include:

Important Phone Numbers and Contact Information

The contact information below should be included in your cell phone as well.

Emergency Management Providers

Name	Phone	Other Contact Information
Emergency Services	911	
Fire Department		
Police Department		
Ambulance Service		
Power Company		
Telephone Company		

Employee Phone Numbers

Name	Phone	Other Contact Information

Suppliers and Key Industry Contacts

Name	Phone	Other Contact Information

Stakeholders: List other contact information for parties who have some type of vested interest in the organization.		
Name	**Phone**	**Other Contact Information**
Radio Station		
Television Station		

Index

ABC News, 208
Abingdon, Virginia, 144
Accenture, 144
Accounting and finance representation, 112
Action strategies
　decision-making strategies, 177 (table)
　emergency preparedness plans, 170–171
　Gulf of Mexico oil spill case study,
　　167–169, 188–190
　initial response actions, 171–179
　mid-crisis action strategies, 179–184
　post-crisis action strategies, 184–186
　summary discussion, 186–187
Active shooter exercises, 123–124
Adamson, J., 148, 164
Adams, R., 143, 164
Adelman, M., 172, 191
Adelphia Communications Corporation,
　261 (table), 262
Adizes, I., 70, 76
Adler, J., 72, 77
Aeppel, T., 40, 47
Aetna, 148
AFA Foods, Inc., 179
African Americans, 61, 148
Agency theory, 267–268
Aggressive behaviors, 117
A. H. Robins Company, 91, 144, 145 (table),
　261 (table), 276
Air plane crashes, 246
AirTran, 144, 145 (table)
Air travel industry, 66, 72–73, 86, 143–144,
　150, 152–154, 278 (table), 279

Alaskan oil pipeline leaks, 168
Alavi, M., 240, 251
Alcohol-related deaths, 121 (table)
Alexander, D., 122, 133
Alfred P. Murrah Federal Building, 32
Ali, A., 32, 33, 47, 183, 191
Ali, L., 287, 290
Ali, S., 32, 33, 47, 183, 191
Allen, Thad, 172
All-Nippon Airways, 55, 56 (table)
Alloy, West Virginia, 255
Alpaslan, C., 8, 22, 259, 284
Alpha Natural Resources, 144, 145 (table)
Alternate spokespersons, 204
Altria, 144
Amato-McCoy, D., 213, 219
Amazon.com, 146
Ambiguity of cause, 3–4
Ambiguity tolerance, 111
American Home Products, 91
American Medical Association (AMA), 277
Amish population, 64
Amoco, 168
Anacortes, Washington, 131–132
Anagnos, G., 180, 192
Anatomy of a catastrophe (*Fortune*), 52, 53
Anderson Consulting, 144
Anderson, S., 164
Andrew & Williamson Sales Company,
　271–273
Anheuser-Busch, 62
Annapolis, Maryland, 61, 148
Anonymous, 76

Ansberry, C., 40, 47
Ansell, C., 30, 31, 47
Anti-female policy, 94
Anti-hail cannons, 89
Antisocial behavior, 35
Anti-websites, 213
Apache Corporation, 190
Appalachian Heating Company, 26, 46
Apple, 75
Applebome, P., 72, 76
Apple Computer, 146
Apple juice crisis, 261 (table), 261–262, 282
Appliance manufacturing companies, 261 (table)
Archstone Consulting, 44
ARCO Chemical plant, 126
ARCO service stations, 174
Argenti, P., 200, 219
Argyris, C., 225, 226, 227, 246, 251
Arndt, M., 265, 285
Arnfield, R., 125, 133
Arthur Andersen, 271
Ash, J., 306, 308
Ashleymadison.com, 261 (table)
Asphyxiation, 288–289
Assessment, 236
Atherton, W., 306, 308
Athletics scandals, 18–21, 120 (table), 268
Atomic Energy Canada Limited (AECL), 243–244, 244 (figure)
Attribution error theory, 247
Audi, T., 301, 308
Aurora, Colorado, movie theater massacre, 301, 302
Automobile industry, 58–59, 146, 151
Aviation and Transportation Security Act (2001), 56 (table)
Ayala, Ann, 71

Bachman, R., 21
Background checks, 103, 224
Backup spokespersons, 204
Bacterial contamination, 151, 154, 208
Bad apples: In the executive suite, 262, 284
Bahamas, 72–73, 86, 154
Bain, Douglas, 268
Baker, A., 123, 134
Balanced scorecard indicators, 158, 158 (table), 263
Baldanza, Ben, 153

Baldauf, S., 143, 164
Balkin, D., 117, 134
Bangladesh, 40
Banjo, S., 301, 308
Bankruptcy crises, 186
Banks, 125
Baran, B., 172, 191
Bargains, 60–61
Barnard, B., 191
Barr, Aaron, 75–76
Barrett, P., 60, 76, 91, 92, 104, 138, 141, 144, 164, 188, 190
Barstow, D., 269, 284
Barth, T., 206, 219, 234, 251, 267, 284
Bartlett, N., 185, 191
Bartlett, T., 82, 83, 102, 103
Barton, L., 37, 47, 91, 104, 110, 112, 115, 118, 133, 181, 183, 191, 201, 202, 204, 205, 205 (table), 215, 216, 219, 245, 251, 269, 276, 284
Basken, P., 82, 83, 103
    see also Bartlett, T.
Baton Rouge, Louisiana, 178
Batteries, 64
Bazerman, M., 90, 106
Beach, R., 225, 228, 252
Bea, R., 89, 105, 228, 252
Beasley Allen law firm, 219
Beaubien, G., 1, 22, 196, 197, 218, 219
Beaver Valley Mall, 154
Beaver, West Virginia, 47
Becker, C., 273, 277, 284
Becker, N., 219
Beck, K., 218, 219
Beckley, West Virginia, 25, 60, 257
Beech-Nut apple juice, 261 (table), 261–262, 282
Beech-Nut Nutrition Corporation, 261
Beef processing industry, 179–180
Beef Products, Inc. (BPI), 179–180, 208
Beer industry, 62–63
Behavioral Sciences of Terrorism and Political Aggression, 33
Beirne, M., 144, 164
Belief systems, 245–247
Bell, J., 123, 124, 133
Bellman, E., 43, 47
Benchmarks, 156–160
Benjamin, K., 207, 212, 219
Benjamin, M., 264, 284

Benner, K., 52, 53

Bennett, J., 59, 76

Benoit, Chris, 72, 214

Benzene, 238

Berinato, S., 172, 191, 197, 219, 295, 308

Berman, S., 259, 284

Bernstein, J., 34, 47

Berry, I., 179, 180, 192, 209

Berry, W., 64, 76

Bertrand, R.
    see Robert, B.

Berzon, A., 301, 308

Beucke, D., 89, 105

Bhopal, India, 5, 40–41, 83, 143, 159,
    264, 279, 302

Biden, Joe, 154

Bienvenu, S., 76
    see also Chin, T.

Big box retailers, 60–61, 150

Biggest Loser, The, 62

Birchall, J., 34, 48

Bishop, Amy, 81–82, 101–103, 120 (table)

Bishop, Seth, 102

Black Friday, 288

Black-hat hackers, 75

Blake, Francis, 208

Blankenship, Don, 60, 91

Blitz Day, 288

Blogs, 33–34, 197, 207–209, 211

Bloomgarden-Smoke, K., 208, 219

Blowout preventers (BOPs), 139, 163, 189

Blyth, A., 215, 219

Board of directors, 263 (table), 264

Boatright, J., 265, 284

Bodon, J., 175, 192

Boeing, 268

Boin, A., 29, 30, 47, 48, 243, 251, 293,
    295, 308, 309
    see also Ansell, C.; 't Hart, P.

Boneless lean beef trimmings, 179–180,
    208–209

Boogergate, 195–196

Borodzicz, E., 170, 191, 225, 251

Boston Elevated Railway Company, 307

Boston Globe, 218

Boston, Massachusetts, 305–307

Boston, R., 175, 191

Boundary spanning, 90

Bourrier, M., 89, 104, 228, 251

Bovender, J., Jr., 214, 219

Bovens, M., 115, 133

Bowater Incorporated, 199–200

Boycotts, 98 (table)

Bradley, Thomas, 174

Braintree (Massachusetts) Police
    Department, 102

Brand Keys, 152

Brathwaite, S., 148, 164

Brautigam, T., 129, 133

Breaux, D., 200, 221

Breeden, R., 264, 284

Brent Spar oil platform, 90

Bresland, John, 132

Brewster, P., 152, 164

Bribery, 55, 269

Bridgeport, West Virginia, 124

Briggs, R., 115, 134
    see also Nunamaker, J., Jr.

British Petroleum (BP), 30, 38, 39, 137–140,
    162–164, 167–169, 188–190, 245,
    261 (table)

Brockner, J., 225, 251

Brookes, W., 238, 251

Brooks, Garth, 154

Brown, E., 21

Browne, John, 168, 190

Brown, K., 43, 48

Brown, M., 271, 286

Brown, T., 204, 219

Brundtland Commission, 63, 76

Brunson, R., 228, 229, 251

Bryan-Low, C., 66, 76

Buchholtz, A., 35, 48, 55, 76, 159, 165,
    258, 259, 259 (table), 260, 261 (table),
    269, 272 (table), 273, 277, 284, 292,
    295, 308

Buckman, R., 40, 48

Buehlmann, U., 150, 164

Buffering strategies, 89

Building evacuation drills, 123

Building mold, 121 (table)

Bullock's Bar-B-Q, 154

Bumgardner, M., 150, 164

Burdett, P., 123, 126, 135

Burger King, 208

Burke, D., 138, 141, 168, 169, 190
    see also Elkind, P.

Burkholderia cepacia, 151

Burns, Scott, 208

Burrows, P., 147, 164

Bush, George W., 58
Busick, J., 25, 26, 27, 46, 47
Business continuity, 184–185
Business ethics
    background information, 257–258
    basic concepts and components,
        258–260, 259 (table)
    board of directors, 263 (table), 264
    chief executive officer (CEO), 262–264,
        263 (table)
    company founder, 262–264, 263 (table)
    crisis management framework, 260–262,
        263 (table)
    defective products, 269–270
    economic motives, 263 (table), 265–267
    emerging trends, 292
    ethical commitment, 276
    ethical culture, 263 (table), 271,
        272 (table), 274
    external stakeholders, 263 (table), 275
    global vulnerability, 263 (table),
        268–270
    government regulations, 263 (table),
        271–273, 277, 278 (table), 279
    Hawks Nest Tunnel case study, 255–257,
        258, 265, 266, 273, 278 (table), 279
    illegal cash payments, 269
    industrial vulnerability, 263 (table), 268
    industry renewal benefits,
        263 (table), 277
    industry standards, 263 (table), 273–274
    internal stakeholders, 263 (table),
        274–275
    landscape survey, 262–270, 263 (table)
    loss of trust, 275–276, 280
    melamine-laced milk case study,
        282–283
    new stakeholder outlooks, 263 (table),
        279–280
    organizational learning, 263 (table),
        275–280
    organizational learning commitment,
        263 (table)
    organizational mission-existence discon-
        nect, 263 (table), 267–268
    response evaluations, 263 (table),
        275–276
    safety policies, 263 (table), 264–265
    strategic planning, 263 (table),
        270–274
    summary discussion, 280–281
    support and enthusiasm, 263 (table),
        270–271
    sweatshop manufacturing, 270, 273–274
Business-level strategies
    combination low-cost and differentia-
        tion strategies, 155
    differentiation strategies, 151–152, 155
    focus-differentiation strategies, 153–155
    focus–low-cost strategies, 152–153
    formulation guidelines, 149
    low-cost strategies, 149–151, 155

Cabbage Patch Dolls, 60
Cable, J., 44, 48
Cadrain, D., 103
Cafaro Company, 124
Cahyanto, I., 92, 105, 117, 134, 185, 192
Calhoun, Tennessee, 199
California State Teachers Retirement System
    (CalSTRS), 269
Cameron International, 139, 189
Cameron, K., 69, 70, 71, 78
Campbell, E., 208, 220
Campbell, H., 168, 169
Campbell-Hunt, C., 149, 165
Caniato, F., 42, 49
Cannes Film Festival, 181
Cannon, M., 230, 242, 245, 247, 251
CAN SPAM Act (2003), 56 (table)
Canton, Massachusetts, 102
Canton, Mississippi, 89
Caponigro, J., 178, 184, 191, 215, 216, 219
Carbendazim, 2
Carbon dioxide, 63, 67
Careless, J., 122, 133
Carey, B., 214, 219
Carey, S., 150, 165
Carley, K., 232, 237, 251
Carlson, S., 299, 308
Carmeli, A., 14, 22, 99, 104, 302, 308
Carnival Corporation, 67
Carnival Cruises, 67
Carpenter, M. A., 85, 104
Carraher, S., 69, 77
Carroll, A., 35, 48, 55, 76, 159, 165, 258, 259,
        259 (table), 260, 261 (table), 269, 272
        (table), 273, 277, 284, 292, 295, 308
Carroll, Dave, 31, 209–210, 213
Carrows restaurant, 149

Case studies
    Concord College, 107–108
    crisis management framework, 18–21
    crowd crushes, 287–289
    Domino's Pizza, 195–196
    great Boston molasses flood, 305–307
    Gulf of Mexico oil spill, 137–140,
        162–164, 167–169, 188–190
    Hawks Nest Tunnel, 255–257, 258, 265,
        266, 273, 278 (table), 279
    Indiana State Fair stage collapse,
        248–250
    Kleen Energy power generation plant,
        51–53
    Little General Store explosion, 25–27,
        46–47
    melamine-laced milk, 282–283
    "passing the trash"/Michigan Board of
        Education, 223–224, 234
    Penn State University scandal, 18–21
    Sony Corporation, 75–76
    Taco Bell, 218–219
    Tesoro Corporation refinery accident,
        131–132
    university faculty member incident,
        81–82, 101–103
Casey, N., 146, 150, 165
Castle, N., 123, 133
Catholic Church, 206, 234, 267
Cato, F., 60, 76
Cavanaugh, J., 171, 172, 191
CBS Evening News, 61
Cell phone service, 214
Cement slurry stability, 189
Ceniceros, R., 60, 76
Center for Science in the Public Interest, 62
CEO compensation-stock price
    relationship, 263
Chalk, A. B. (Pappy), 72–73
Chalk's Flying Service, 73
Chalk's Ocean Airways, 72, 86, 153–154
Chancellors, university, 237
Chandler, R., 111, 115, 116, 117, 133, 199, 220
Chappell, L., 89, 104
Chapter organization and development, 15
    (figure), 15–17
Chazan, G., 190
Chemical spills, 127
Chen, C., 41, 48
Chen, H., 210, 220

Chermack, T., 121, 134
Cherniak, M., 255, 256, 257, 273, 284
Cheung, C., 30, 48, 93, 104
Chevron, 239
Chevy Volt, 2, 64, 151
Chicago Tribune, 218
Chi-Chi's restaurants, 68, 154–155, 202–203
Chief executive officer (CEO), 112,
    201–202, 262–264, 263 (table)
Children's Hospital Boston, 102
Children's Tylenol products, 151–152
Child sexual abuse, 18–21
China
    earthquakes, 181–182, 302
    environmental pollution, 39
    global outsourcing, 40, 44, 150, 269
    melamine-laced milk case study,
        282–283
    strategic alliances, 146
Chin, T., 61, 76
Cho, C., 117, 133
Choi, J. N., 303, 308
Chon, G., 190
Chong, J., 84, 92, 104, 294, 308
Choo, C., 36, 37, 38, 48
Cho, Seung-Hui, 8, 299
Chrysalis Capital Partners, 186
Chrysler Motor Company, 146, 148
Churchill, N., 69, 70, 76
Chu, W., 146, 165
Cincinnati, Ohio, 34, 287, 288
Cisco, 42
Citizen journalists, 208
Civil Rights Act (1964), 55 (table)
Clair, J., 3, 4, 14, 22, 33, 48, 172, 213, 221,
    241, 242 (table), 252, 302, 309
Clark, D., 186, 191
Clark, J., 109, 110, 111, 134
Clean Air Act (1963), 168
Climate change, 63, 280
Closing the loop philosophy, 236, 297
Clothing manufacturing companies, 261
    (table), 273–274
Coal mining industry, 27, 60, 91–92, 144,
    178–179, 241, 257, 268
Coalson, Roy, 27
Coca-Cola Company, 2, 62, 68
Cockburn, I. M., 142, 165
Coco's restaurant, 149
Codes of ethics, 271, 272 (table), 273

Cognitive maps, 122
Cold sites, 185
Collective vision, 231
College and university crises potential, 120–121 (table)
Collegiality, 81–82
Colorado movie theater crisis, 301, 302
Columbine school shooting, 124, 202
Colvin, G., 262, 263, 284
Command centers, 119, 125, 199, 235
Commercial air travel, 66
Communication skills
    crisis communication, 197–217
    crisis management teams, 111, 197–199
    initial response action strategies, 177–178
    internal and external stakeholders, 181–182
    Internet usage, 125, 178, 199, 206–207
    mid-crisis action strategies, 181–182
    organizational learning, 236–237
Communication systems, 125
Community involvement, 128
Company blogs, 211
Competitive strategy, 142
Complex environments, 87–88
Comstock, J., 273, 284
Concord College, 107–108, 125, 129
Condia, J., 114, 115, 135
Confalone, James, 73
Conlin, M., 34, 48, 208, 220
Connective Power Delivery, 203–204
Connor, J., 38, 49
ConocoPhillips, 239
Conover, North Carolina, 196
Consumer-credit relationship, 57–58
Consumerist, 196
Consumer lawsuits, 98 (table)
Contagious diseases, 121 (table)
Containment stage, 11, 180
Contingency responses, 298–299
Contractors slam "self-serving" BP spill report; Dudley takes charge, 189, 190
Controlling the Assault of Non-Solicited Pornography and Marketing Act (2003), 56 (table)
Cook, N., 138, 139, 140, 141, 162, 164, 189, 190
Coombs, W. T., 4, 8, 13, 22, 39, 48, 67, 71, 76, 92, 100, 104, 109, 110, 111, 112,
    118, 123, 134, 159, 160, 173, 178, 181, 183, 191, 198, 201, 202, 203, 204, 205, 206, 216, 220, 261 (table), 275, 284, 294, 308
Cooperative efforts, 237–238
Copeland, M., 62, 77
Copycat websites, 34
Corporate America, 60
Corporate average fuel economy (CAFE) standards, 58
Corporate headquarters, 199
Corporate-level strategies
    growth dimension, 145–149
    industry dimension, 142–145, 145 (table)
Corporate social responsibility (CSR), 258–260, 259 (table)
Corrective action strategies, 160
Corvair automobile, 4
Cosmology episodes, 88, 172
Costa Concordia, 67
Costa Cruises, 67
Cost containment strategies, 149–151
Cost-cutting measures, 266–267
Cover page, 118
Cowan, D. E., 176, 191
Cracker Barrel, 61, 71
Crandall, R., 41, 48, 95, 104, 256, 257, 264, 284
Crandall, W. R., 3, 5, 7, 9 (table), 22, 23, 34, 39, 41, 48, 50, 95, 104, 125, 128, 129, 134, 181, 191, 192, 208, 221, 256, 257, 264, 282, 284, 297, 308
    see also Ziemnowicz, C.
Crawford, M., 61, 77
Crear, George, III, 224, 234
Credit extensions, 57–58
Creed, Greg, 218
Crichton, M., 171, 173, 191
Crisis
    classifications, 7–8
    definition and characteristics, 3–5
    life cycle, 5–6
    occurrences, 1–2
    stages, 8–11, 9 (table)
    strategic challenges, 6–7
Crisis communication
    basic principles, 198–207
    business ethics, 274–275
    command centers, 119, 125, 199, 235

customers, 206–207
Domino's Pizza case study, 195–196
emerging trends, 291 (table)
employee communication, 200–201
external stakeholders, 201–204, 275
initiation response, 198–199
internal stakeholders, 199–201,
    274–275
Internet usage and monitoring,
    210–213
media training programs, 215–216
news media, 204–206, 205 (table)
postcrisis debriefing meetings, 213–214
response evaluations, 213–214, 238
social media impacts, 197–198, 207–213,
    274–275, 291 (table), 299
summary discussion, 216–217
Taco Bell case study, 218–219
Crisis management, definition of, 13–14
Crisis management frameworks
business ethics, 260–262, 263 (table)
contingency responses, 298–299
crisis management, 12 (figure), 13–14,
    15 (figure), 180 (figure)
developmental process, 3–7
emerging trends, 291 (table), 298–300,
    302
feedback process, 240 (figure)
general characteristics, 11–12
landscape survey, 12 (figure), 12–13, 15
    (figure), 180 (figure)
lessons learned, 232 (table), 236–239
organizational learning, 12 (figure),
    14–15, 15 (figure), 180 (figure)
Penn State University case study, 18–21
strategic challenges, 6–7
strategic planning, 12 (figure), 13, 15
    (figure), 180 (figure)
Crisis management landscape
business ethics, 262–270
emerging trends, 290–294, 291 (table)
environmental damage, 38–40
feedback process, 240 (figure)
globalization, 40–44
human-induced crises, 34–38
lessons learned, 232 (table), 233–234
Little General Store explosion case
    study, 25–27, 46–47
proactive and reactive perspectives, 180
    (figure)

resource sustainability, 38–40
social media and the Internet, 33–34
terrorism threats, 32–33
transboundary crises, 29–32
trends, 28–44, 29 (figure)
typologies, 28
Crisis management plan
basic components, 118–120
command centers, 119, 125, 199, 235
communication strategies, 198–199
distribution, 121
emerging trends, 291 (table)
flexibility, 118, 122
importance, 117–118
initial response action strategies, 171
organizational learning, 235
prospective crisis events, 119–120,
    120–121 (table)
summary discussion, 129–130
support and enthusiasm, 270–271
team member information, 118–119
Crisis management research, 302–303
Crisis management team
activation procedures, 119, 171
command centers, 119, 125, 199, 235
communication strategies, 111,
    197–199
Concord College case study, 107–108
crisis management plan, 117–121
crisis management training, 121–129
designated spokesperson, 201–205,
    205 (table)
emerging trends, 291 (table)
external landscapes, 295–298
goals, 109 (figure), 109–110
importance, 108
internal landscapes, 294
leadership skills and effectiveness,
    171–172
organizational learning, 235
potential problems, 115–117
response evaluations, 213–214
strategic importance, 232
strategic planning, 294
stressors, 172
summary discussion, 129–130
support and enthusiasm, 270–271
team composition, 112–113, 118
team member characteristics, 110–111
team member responsibilities, 118–119

Tesoro Corporation refinery accident case study, 131–132
virtual crisis management teams, 113–115, 114 (table)
Crisis management training
disaster drills, 123–124
functional role, 121
mock disasters, 124–129
organizational learning, 236
regular meetings, 122
Crisis planning, 99–100
Crisis-prepared organizational cultures, 99–100
Crisis stages
five-stage frameworks, 9 (table), 10–11
four-stage frameworks, 9 (table), 10, 180 (figure)
three-stage frameworks, 9 (table), 10
Critical Studies on Terrorism, 33
Critical thinking skills, 111
Crooks, E., 38, 48, 139, 141, 169
Crowd crush case studies, 287–289, 290
Crowe, A., 299, 308
Cruise ship industry, 67, 176–177
Crystal Cruises, 176–177
Crystal Harmony, 176
Culture of silence, 268
Culture of success, 245
Cummins, C., 55, 77
Curley, Timothy M., 19, 20
Curphy, C., 247, 251
Customer communication, 206–207
Cyanide poisoning, 6, 70, 302
Cybercrime, 65–66, 75, 96, 97 (table)

Dade County School Board, 224
Daitch, C., 218, 219
Dalkon Shield, 91, 144, 261 (table), 276
Dallas, Texas, 43
Damage containment, 180, 180 (figure)
Damage limitation stage, 11, 180
Damon B. Bankston (ship), 163
Damour, Jdimytai, 288
Darby, Greg, 47
Dark sites, 206
Dark Tide (Puleo), 306
Das, T. K., 85, 104
David, F., 90, 105
Davis, A., 184, 192
Davis, S., 115, 134

Dawson, B., 159, 165
Dayton, B., 303, 309
Deal, T. E., 100, 104
Dean, J., 40, 48
Debriefing meetings, 129, 213–214, 239–240
December 11, 1995: Fire destroys Malden Mills, 186, 191
Decentralized decision-making, 298
Decision-making skills, 116–117, 177 (table), 243, 275–276
Deepwater Horizon drilling rig, 138, 139
Deepwater Horizon oil disaster, 137–140, 162–164, 167–169, 188–190, 245, 261 (table)
Deep-water versus offshore drilling, 138
Defective products, 269–270
Degree of learning, 241–242, 242 (table)
de Havilland Comet, 66
Deitz, D., 279, 284
DeLaurentis, T., 282, 283
Delaware State University, 120 (table)
Delhi, India, 43
Dell Computers, 147, 208
Dell, Michael, 208
de Mayoro, C. A., 30, 49
Denial-of-service attacks, 34, 71, 85, 96, 97 (table)
Denning, P., 295, 308
Denny's restaurants, 61, 147–148
Dent, E. L., 260, 285
Departmental cooperation, 237–238
Department of Homeland Security, 33
Designated spokespersons, 119, 177–178, 183, 199, 201–205, 205 (table)
DeSilva, J., 76
   see also Chin, T.
DesJardins, J., 266, 269, 284, 285
Dess, G. G., 155, 166
Destination tourism, 32, 92–93
Detlor, B., 199, 221
Deveney, J., 275, 284
Deverell, E., 225, 251, 300, 308
Deviant behaviors, 35
Dewan, S., 82, 83, 102, 104, 123, 134
Dialogue, 232
Diamond, M., 8, 22
Diefendorff, J., 35, 48
Differentiation strategies, 151–152, 155
Digital crisis communication, 211

Dillard's, 69

Dior, 182

Dior China, 182

Disaster drills, 123–124

Disaster recovery, 184–185

Discount retail industry, 60–61, 149–151, 261 (table)

Discrimination, 61, 148

Disney Company, 270

Dissatisfied customers, 212–213

Divestment strategies, 147, 148–149

Dobbs, L., 43, 48

Dobbs, Lou, 43

Dodd-Frank Wall Street Reform and Consumer Protection Act (2010), 56 (table)

Domino's Pizza, 1, 195–196, 211

Domino USA, 196

Donahue, B., 176, 191

Dooley, L., 121, 134

Double deviation, 210

Double-loop learning, 225–226, 229 (figure)

Dow Chemical, 143, 145 (table)

Dow Corning silicone breast implants, 261 (table)

Downsizing, 148

Doyle, Patrick, 196, 211

Dragan, J., 256, 257

Drillships, 138

Drucker, J., 43, 48

Dry drilling, 256, 273

Dry Max Pampers, 33–34

Dube, Arindrajit, 42

Dudley, Robert, 190

Duhe, S., 178, 191

Duke University, 120 (table)

Duncan, R. B., 88, 104

Duncan, W. W., 99, 105

Dunn, G., 301, 310

Durham County Health Department, 154

Durham, North Carolina, 154

Dust explosions, 159, 266

Du, W., 182, 191

Dynes, R., 301, 308

Dziagwa, C., 201, 220

D'Zurilla, W., 144, 165

Earley, E., 203, 221

Earthquakes, 30, 92–93, 181–182, 302

East Texas Cancer Center, 244, 244 (figure)

Ebbers, Bernard, 264

E. coli outbreaks, 70, 127, 154

Economic forces
    characteristics, 54 (figure)
    oil price surge, 58–59
    overexpansion of credit, 57–58

Economic motives, 263 (table), 265–267

Economic responsibilities, 259 (table), 260, 261 (table)

Edid, M., 42, 48

Edmondson, A., 230, 242, 245, 247, 251

Edwards, J., 209, 220

Ehrenreich, B., 58, 60, 77, 95, 105

Electric vehicles, 2, 64, 151

Elkind, P., 138, 139, 140, 141, 168, 169, 189, 190

Elliott, D., 6, 22, 99, 106, 173, 192, 225, 227, 240, 246, 251, 252, 288, 290

Ellison, S., 62, 63, 77

e-Loan, 43

El Salvador, 40

Elsubbaugh, S., 302, 309

Emergency messaging, 123

Emergency paging systems, 201

Emerging trends
    case study versus statistical research approach, 302–303
    contingency responses, 298–299
    crisis management, 291 (table), 298–300, 302
    crowd crush case studies, 287–289
    external landscapes, 291 (table), 292–300
    great Boston molasses flood, 305–307
    internal landscapes, 290–292, 291 (table), 294, 298–299
    landscape survey, 290–294, 291 (table)
    loss of trust, 291 (table), 293–294
    modeling approaches, 302
    moral failures, 291 (table), 292
    organizational learning, 291 (table), 300–303
    response times, 300
    stakeholders, 295–296
    strategic planning, 291 (table), 294–298
    summary discussion, 304
    sustainable development, 296–298
    SWOT (strengths, weaknesses, opportunities, and threats) analysis, 291 (table), 291–292

Emerging vulnerabilities, 234
Employee communication, 200–201
Employee error, 36–37
Employee needs, 185–186
Endsley, M., 173, 192
Englehardt, K., 143, 144, 165
Enron
 codes of ethics, 271, 273
 ethical crises, 261 (table), 262
 government regulation, 56 (table)
 government regulations, 278 (table)
 industry dimension, 145, 145 (table)
 off-balance sheet arrangements, 265–266, 267–268
 retrenchment strategies, 147
 warning signs, 37
Entis, P., 273, 284
Environmental damage, 38–40
Environmental Defense Fund (EDF), 39
Environmental Protection Act, 279
Environmental Protection Agency (EPA), 68
Environmental scanning, 90–92
Environmental sustainability, 63
Environmental uncertainty, 87–90, 156
Epistemic blind spots, 37
Erben, Ralph, 183
Erickson, Rodney, 20–21
Erickson, S., 68, 79, 155, 166, 202, 221
Ericsson, 42
Ethical crises components, 261 (table)
Ethical responsibilities, 259 (table), 260, 261 (table)
Etter, L., 42, 48
Eubank, W., 32, 49
Evacuation drills, 123
Everly, G., 192
 see also Leskin, G. A.
Explicit knowledge, 240
External landscapes
 business ethics, 263 (table)
 characteristics, 11–13, 12 (figure), 15 (figure)
 crisis management, 299–300
 economic forces, 54 (figure), 57–59
 emerging trends, 291 (table), 292–303
 feedback process, 240 (figure), 240–241
 organizational learning, 14, 232 (table), 234, 236, 239, 241, 301–303

 organizational sources, 54 (figure), 54–66
 political–legal forces, 54 (figure), 54–57
 proactive and reactive perspectives, 180 (figure)
 social forces, 54 (figure), 59–63
 strategic management process, 85–101
 strategic planning, 295–298
 technological forces, 54 (figure), 63–66
External stakeholders, 14, 181–182, 201–204, 263 (table), 275
Extortion threats, 71, 98 (table)
Extra-strength Tylenol, 6
Exxon, 38, 126–127, 178, 215
ExxonMobil, 239
Exxon Valdez oil spill, 38, 39, 56 (table), 126–127, 202, 215

Facebook, 34, 85, 197, 211, 218, 300
Failure, learning from, 228–230, 241, 245–247
Failure outcomes, 241–242, 242 (table)
Fannie Mae, 58
Fargo, North Dakota, 239, 301
Farmington Savings Bank (FSB), 125
Farrell, F., 62, 77
Farrell, G., 62, 77
Farrier Fire Fighting School, 229
Farrier, Gerald W., 229
Fast-food industry, 62
Fastow, Andrew, 265, 267–268
Fatal air crashes, 66, 72–73, 86, 143–144, 150, 246, 302
Fatigue, 116
Fauchart, E., 244, 244 (figure), 251
Faulhaber, P., 211, 220
Febreze, 206
Federal Aviation Administration (FAA), 143–144
Federal Bureau of Investigation (FBI), 124
Federal Mine Safety and Health Act (1977), 55 (table)
Federal-Mogul, 148
Federal Reserve, 57–58
Federal Trade Commission (FTC), 277
FedEx, 296
Feedback process, 240 (figure), 240–241, 300–301

Feigley, C., 135
   see also Richter, J.
Ferrellgas Company, 26, 46
Ferrell, L., 264, 285
   see also Thorne, D.
Ferrell, O., 264, 285
   see also Thorne, D.
Feuerstein, Aaron, 186
Fildes, R., 302, 309
Film Recovery Services, Inc., 261 (table)
Film Recovery Systems, Inc., 70
Financial crisis, 56 (table)
Financial Executives International
   (FEI), 273
Fink, S., 9 (table), 10, 22, 302, 309
Fire departments, 125–126, 127
Firefighting principles and strategies,
   226–229, 227 (figure), 229 (figure)
Fires, 1, 120 (table), 127, 207, 226–228,
   266–267
Firm strategy, 142
Fischman, J., 82, 83, 103
   see also Bartlett, T.
Fiscor, S., 92, 105
Fisher, C., 186, 192
Fishman, B., 42
Fishman, C., 48, 61, 77, 95, 105, 143, 150, 165
Fisk, M., 91, 105
Fitzpatrick, F., 20, 21
Five-stage frameworks, 9 (table), 10–11
Flaming, 300
Flexibility, 298–299
Flight 592 (ValuJet), 143–144, 302
Flin, R., 171, 191
   see also Crichton, M.
Flint, Michigan, 224
Floods, 120 (table)
FlyersRights, 153
Flynn, M., 208, 211, 220
Focus-differentiation strategies, 153–155
Focus–low-cost strategies, 152–153
Fogarty, K., 71, 77
Fombrun, C., 271, 272 (table), 284
Fonterra, 282, 283
Food Allergen Labeling and Consumer
   Protection Act (2004), 56 (table)
Food and Drug Administration (FDA),
   151–152

Food manufacturing industry, 85–86
Food traceability, 86
Ford Motor Company, 59, 146, 151
Foreign Corrupt Practices Act (1977), 55,
   56 (table), 269
Forrestal (Navy ship), 228–229
Fortier, J., 57, 77
Foss, C., 271, 272 (table), 284
Four officials sacked following baby milk
   scandal, 283
Four-stage frameworks, 9 (table), 10,
   180 (figure)
Foust, D., 89, 105
Fragile supply chains, 41–42
Frank, T., 270, 273–274, 284
Freddie Mac, 58
Freeh, L., 19, 20, 21
Freeh, Louis, 21
Freeh Report, 21
Freifeld, K., 91, 105
Friedman, H., 137, 141
Friedman, L., 137, 141
Friend, J., 120 (table), 134
Friesen, P. H., 69, 70, 71, 78
Fritzsche, D., 274, 285
Fruin, J., 289, 290
Fruin, John, 289
Frye, M., 150, 164
Fuel economy standards, 58–59
Fuller, K., 61, 77
Furman, Jason, 42

Gagne, M., 19, 21, 22
Gainey, B., 204, 206, 220
Gandolfi, F., 148, 165
Ganguly, K., 89, 105
Gap Inc., 270
Gardner, D., 182, 192
Garland, D., 173, 192
Gasoline prices, 58–59, 151
Gates, Daryl, 174
GE Capital Services (GECIS), 42
Gegax, T., 72, 77
General Electric (GE), 42
General Motors (GM), 2, 4, 59, 64, 146, 151
Ghent Volunteer Fire Department, 26
Ghent, West Virginia, 25–27
Gilpin, D., 110, 111, 134, 245, 251

Ginnett, R., 247, 251

Glaesser, D., 32, 48

Gleason, S., 179, 180, 192, 209

Glenn, D., 82, 83, 103
    see also Bartlett, T.

Glew, D., 35, 49

Global outsourcing
    basic concepts, 40
    cost containment strategies, 150–151
    defective products, 269–270
    fragile supply chains, 41–42
    operational control problems, 40–41
    organizational crises, 40–44
    potential crises, 12–13, 279
    reputational crises, 42–43
    reshoring movement, 43–44

Global warming, 63, 280

Gnage, M., 201, 220

Goldman Sachs, 273

Gomez-Mejia, L., 117, 134

Gonzalez, G., 119, 134

González-Herrero, A., 33, 34, 48, 206, 207,
    212, 213, 220, 300, 309

Goodell, J., 60, 77

Goodman, R., 7, 22, 303, 309

Good Morning America, 215

Goodnough, A., 73, 77

Google, 71, 210, 212

Government regulations, 85–86,
    263 (table), 271–273, 277, 278 (table),
    279, 307

Grand Forks, North Dakota, 239, 301

Gray-hat hackers, 75

Gray, S., 62, 77

Grease payments, 269

Great Boston molasses flood, 305–307

Great Sichuan Earthquake, 302

Greenberg, A., 75, 76

Greenberg, D., 33, 48

Greenberg, J., 33, 48

Greenhouse gases, 63, 280

Greening, D., 303, 309

Greenpeace, 90

Green, S. E., 259, 284

Greenwald, Robert, 42

Green, W., III, 30, 31, 48

Greer, M., 266, 285

Grégoire, Y., 31, 48, 206, 210, 220

Griffin, Merv, 73

Griffin, R., 35, 48, 49

Griffith, M., 89, 105

Griggs, J. W., 138, 141

Groom, J. R., 90, 105

Gross, A., 275, 285

Gross domestic product (GDP), 57

Grossman, R., 94, 105

Groupthink, 37, 116–117

Growth dimension
    growth strategies, 145–146
    retrenchment strategies, 147–149
    stability strategies, 146–147

Gruley, B., 208, 220

Grumman Turbo Mallard (G-73T), 72, 73

Guiner, T., 160, 165

Guin, K., 89, 105

Gulf of Mexico oil spill case study, 137–140,
    162–164, 167–169, 188–190

Guo, X., 210, 220

Hacking attacks, 34, 64, 75–76, 97 (table), 127

Hacktivists, 75–76

Hagersville tire fire (1990), 227–228, 229
    (figure)

Hail damage, 89

Hall, Arsenio, 147

Halliburton, 188, 189

Hall, M., 268, 285
    see also Snyder, P.

Hamlet, North Carolina, 266–267

Hammond Iron Works Company, 307

Hammonds, Kristy, 195

Hanni, Kate, 153

Hansen, M., 270, 285

Happy Meals, 62

Hardee's, 62

Hargreaves, James, 64

Harkin, T., 270, 285

Harman, M., 109, 110, 111, 134

Harmon, Thomas, 19

Harrald, J., 232, 237, 251

Harrington, K., 42, 48

Harrison, G., 34, 50, 208, 221
    see also Ziemnowicz, C.

Harshbarger, D., 256, 257

Harshbarger, Dwight, 256

Hartley, R., 5, 22, 35, 38, 41, 48, 55, 77, 83,
    91, 105, 127, 134, 260, 261 (table),
    262, 269, 276, 277, 278 (table), 282,
    283, 285

Hartman, L., 269, 271, 285, 286
Hart, Owen, 72
Hawk's Nest (Skidmore), 256
Hawks Nest Tunnel case study, 255–257, 258, 265, 266, 273, 278 (table), 279
Hayes, C., 124, 134
Hayhurst, L., 67, 77
Hayward, Tony, 168, 189, 190
HB Gary Federal, 75–76
Health and fitness trends, 62–63
HealthSouth, 261 (table), 262
Heath, R. L., 198, 220
Heineman, B., Jr., 271, 285
Hellier, K., 63, 77
Hemphill, T., 273, 277, 285
Henderson, J., 12, 22
Henderson, R. M., 142, 165
Hendrie, C., 225
Henry, D., 265, 285
Hepatitis A outbreak, 68, 154–155, 202–203, 273
Herbane, B., 3, 22, 184, 192
Herman, M., 181, 192
Hermann, M., 303, 309
Herring, C., 90, 103, 104
Herring, J., 105
Herron, J., 168, 170, 190
Heyman, D., 26, 27
Heyse, L., 295, 309
    see also 't Hart, P.
Hickson, M., III, 175, 192
Hidden debt, 265–266
Higgins, A., 57, 77
High-reliability organizations (HROs), 89, 228–230
Highway accidents, 199–200
Hillsborough soccer tragedy (1989), 173, 288
Hirai, Kazuo, 75
Hofer, C., 66, 77
Holladay, S., 109, 134
Holly, C., 189, 190
Holmes, James, 301
Holmes, S., 268, 285
Home Depot, 208, 296
Home office/corporate headquarters, 199
Honduras, 40
Hood-Phillips, Ray, 148
Hopkins, A., 36, 37, 48
Horne, J., III, 298, 309

Horyn, C., 182, 192
Hosie, P., 302, 309
Hosmer, L., 145, 165
Hospital Corporation of America, 213–214
Hot sites, 185
Hoye, Cynthia, 249
Hoyos, C., 139, 141
Hoyvald, Neils, 262
Hu, C., 241, 252, 300, 309
Hughes, R., 247, 251
Human error, 36–37
Human-induced crises
    human error, 36–37
    management-induced crises, 34–35
    normal accident theory, 36–37
    sloppy management, 37–38
    workplace violence, 35
Human resource management (HRM), 94, 112, 121
Hurricane Ike, 30
Hurricane Isabel, 203
Hurricane Katrina
    building evacuation drills, 123
    crisis communication, 200, 213–214, 280
    crisis management case studies, 302
    emergency preparedness plans, 178, 179
    ineffective government response, 280, 293
    media coverage, 179, 293
    strategic planning, 295, 296
    transboundary crises, 30, 31
    weather-related crises, 121 (table)
Hurricanes, 30, 127
Hussein, Saddam, 55
Hyatt, Michael, 175
Hybrid vehicles, 151
Hydrocodone, 72
Hydroelectric dams, 255–256
Hydrogen attacks, 132

IBM, 146
Identity theft, 64
Illegal cash payments, 269
Imitation strategies, 89–90
Imperial Food Products poultry plant fire (1991), 266–267
India, 40, 42–43
Indiana Department of Labor, 250
Indiana State Fair stage collapse case study, 248–250

Individual safety, 168–169
Indoor shopping malls, 69, 123–124
Indoor tanning industry, 96–98
Indoor tanning: Unexpected dangers,
    97, 105
Industrial fog incident, 199–200
Industrial Revolution, 64
Industrial safety, 86, 91, 256–257, 258,
    264–266, 278 (table)
Industrial vulnerability, 263 (table), 268
Industry dimensions
    involvement and risk factors, 145 (table)
    multiple related industry profile,
        143–144, 145 (table)
    multiple unrelated industry profile,
        144–145, 145 (table)
    single industry profile, 142–143,
        145 (table)
Industry life cycle
    decline stage, 68–69
    growth stage, 67
    introduction stage, 66
    maturity stage, 68
    shakeout stage, 68
Industry renewal, 263 (table), 277
Industry standards, 263 (table), 273–274
Infant formula crisis, 282–283
Information asymmetry, 224, 243–244,
    244 (figure)
Information quality, 87–88
Information technology, 64
Information timeliness and accuracy,
    178–179
Initial response action strategies
    crisis management plan, 171
    crisis management team leadership,
        171–172
    decision-making strategies, 177 (table)
    information needs, 178–179
    initial communications, 177–178
    mitigation strategies, 176–177
    situational assessment, 173–176
Institute for Crisis Management, 34–35, 48,
    84, 95, 105, 170, 192, 245, 251, 260,
    285, 292, 309
Intel, 300
Interface manufacturing company, 297–298
Internal landscapes
    business ethics, 263 (table)
    characteristics, 11, 12 (figure), 15 (figure)

contingency responses, 298–299
crisis management, 298–299
emerging trends, 290–301, 291 (table)
feedback process, 240 (figure), 240–241,
    300–301
organizational learning, 14, 232 (table),
    233–234, 235, 300–301
proactive and reactive perspectives,
    180 (figure)
strategic management process, 85–101, 86
strategic planning, 13, 294
Internal stakeholders, 14, 181–182,
    199–201, 263 (table), 274–275
International Alliance of Theatrical Stage
    Employees (IATSE), 250
International House of Pancakes, 103
Internet usage
    communication strategies, 125, 178, 199,
        206–207
    crisis communication, 207–213, 299
    cybercrime, 65–66, 96, 97 (table)
    mock disasters, 125
    organizational crises, 33–34, 299–300
Intranets, 200
Intrauterine contraceptive device (IUD), 91,
    144, 261 (table), 276
Iraq War, 55
Irvine, L., 129, 134
iTunes, 75

Jack, A., 152, 165
Jackson, J., 168, 170, 189, 191
Jackson, Tennessee, 121 (table)
Jacobson, L., 124, 134
Jacques, A., 85, 105, 195, 196, 197, 212, 220
Jagger, S., 306, 308
James, E., 171, 193, 225, 251
Janega, J., 201, 220
Janis, I., 37, 49, 116, 134
Jarvis, Jeff, 208
Jasinski, T., 268, 285
    see also Snyder, P.
J.C. Penney, 69
Jefferson, J., 267, 285
Jell, A. P., 307
Jennings, C., 279, 285
Jensen, T., 144, 164
JetBlue Airways, 150, 155
Jin, Y., 302, 309
Joe Camel advertising campaign, 277

Johnson & Johnson (J&J), 2, 6, 151–152, 209, 210, 302
Johnson, Adriel D., Sr., 102
Johnson, C., 196, 197, 209, 213, 220
Johnson, D., 97, 105
Johnson, R., 303, 309
Johnston, J., 47
Joly, K., 299, 309
Jones, T., 259, 284
Jonsson, P., 103, 104
Journal of Homeland Security and Emergency Management, 33
Jusoh, R., 263, 285
Just-in-time (JIT) work system, 36

Kaiser, A., 182, 192
Kane, J., 267, 285
Kane, L., 123, 135
Kaplanidou, K., 92, 105, 117, 134, 185, 192
Kaplan, R., 158, 165, 263, 285
Karma comment, 181–182
Kass, J., 124, 134
Katehi, Linda P. B., 237
Kay, John, 64
Keane, T., 192
    see also Leskin, G. A.
Keating, C., 144, 165
Keller, A., 30, 47
    see also Ansell, C.
Kennedy, A. A., 100, 104
Kennedy, James, 175
Kennestone Regional Oncology Center, 244, 244 (figure)
Kiernan, P., 2, 22
Kilborn, P., 69, 77
Killeen, Texas, 183
Kilman, S., 249, 250
Kimble, C., 115, 134
Kim, M. U., 303, 308
King, N., Jr., 55, 77
King, Rodney, 173–174
Kinston, North Carolina, 159
Kirkpatrick, D., 209, 211, 220
Kleen Energy power generation plant case study, 51–53
Kline, S., 57, 77
Knopper, S., 250
Knowledge management, 240
Kolb, D., 226–227, 251
Kondraschow, R., 183, 192

Koppel, N., 43, 47
Kopper, Michael J., 268
Kotha, S., 259, 284
Kovoor-Misra, S., 6, 14, 22, 34, 49, 110, 134, 232, 251
Kozlowski, Dennis, 159–160
Kranhold, K., 43, 49
Krauss, C., 144, 166
Kristofferson, Kris, 154
Kroll, M., 64, 79
Kruger, D., 149, 165
Kruse, C., 96, 105
Kryptonite, 209, 210
Kumar, K., 90, 105

Labor costs, 44
Lacayo, R., 267, 285
Lado, A., 245, 252
Lagadec, P., 29, 49, 115, 134, 239, 243, 251, 293, 309
Lajtha, C., 90, 104, 115, 116, 118, 133, 275, 279, 280, 284, 293, 298, 301, 308
Lalonde, C., 225, 252
Landscape surveys
    business ethics, 262–270
    crisis management framework, 12 (figure), 12–13, 15 (figure)
    emerging trends, 290–294, 291 (table)
    environmental damage, 38–40
    feedback process, 240 (figure)
    globalization, 40–44
    human-induced crises, 34–38
    lessons learned, 232 (table), 233–234
    Little General Store explosion case study, 25–27, 46–47
    proactive and reactive perspectives, 180 (figure)
    resource sustainability, 38–40
    social media and the Internet, 33–34
    terrorism threats, 32–33
    transboundary crises, 29–32
    trends, 28–44, 29 (figure)
    typologies, 28
Langer, E., 243, 252
Langfitt, F., 179, 192
Langley, M., 168, 170, 190
Langston, R., 146, 165
Lannom, A., 47
Lauche, K., 171, 191
    see also Crichton, M.

Lavery, John, 262
Law, R., 30, 48, 93, 104
Lawrence, A., 70, 77, 258, 285
Lawrence, Massachusetts, 185–186
Layoffs, 148
Lead paint, 150, 246, 269
Learning from failure, 228–230, 241,
    245–247
Lebanon, Tennessee, 61, 71
Lee, G., 30, 49
Legal counsel, 113
Legal responsibilities, 259 (table),
    261 (table)
Legoux, R., 31, 48, 206, 220
    see also Grégoire, Y.
Lehren, A., 73, 77
Leidner, D., 240, 251
Leno, Jay, 148
Lentini, A., Jr., 215, 220
Leong, J., 301, 310
Leskin, G. A., 180, 192
Lessons learned, 11, 14–15, 232 (table),
    232–241, 275–280
Lester, D., 39, 49, 69, 77, 243, 252
Leung, S., 62, 77
Leveson, N., 243, 244, 252
Levick, R., 154, 165
Levinson, P., 212, 220
Levitz, J., 103, 104
Levy, P., 218, 219
Lewis, V., 69, 70, 76
Libraries, 123
Li, H., 182, 193
Lihra, T., 150, 164
Lim, P., 264, 284
Lintonen, R., 116, 134
Lipka, S., 15, 22
Liquidations, 147, 149
Listening skills, 111
Little General Store explosion case study,
    25–27, 46–47
Litz, B., 192
    see also Leskin, G. A.
Liu, B., 302, 309
Liu, M., 68, 79, 155, 166, 202, 221, 283
Livet, M., 135
    see also Richter, J.
Liz Claiborne, 270
Lockdown drills, 124
Lockheed, 55, 56 (table), 268, 269

Lockheed Electra, 66
Lockwood, N., 94, 105, 112, 134, 295, 309
Lockyer, S., 71, 77, 154, 155, 165
Logos, 118
Loh, A., 98, 105
Long, Z., 181, 192, 282, 284
Lopez, Y., 35, 48
Los Angeles Police Department (LAPD),
    173–174
Los Angeles riots (1992), 173–174
Los Angeles Times, 218
Loss of trust, 275–276, 280, 291 (table),
    293–294
Low-cost business strategies, 149–151, 155
Lublin, J. S., 148, 165
Luby's Cafeteria, Inc., 183, 302
Luddites, 64
Luhnow, D., 40, 49
LulzSec, 75–76
Lundegaard, K., 58, 78
Lynchburg College, 300
Lynch, M., 288, 289, 290
Lyons, C., 306, 307, 308

Machiavellian personalities, 117
Macky, K., 148, 165
Maclean, T., 33, 48
Macondo oil well, 138, 139
Macroenvironment
    see External landscapes
Mad Cow disease, 57
Madhani, A., 201, 220
Madoff, Bernie, 261 (table)
Madsen, P., 27, 28, 241, 252
Maggart, L., 200, 220
Magnuson, E., 66, 77
Maher, K., 21, 40, 49
Maki, A., 69, 77
Malcolm, T., 64, 77
Malden Mills fire (1995), 185–186
Mallaby, S., 42, 49
Mall of Memphis, 69
Management information systems (MIS),
    184–185
Management support and involvement,
    116, 127
Manchin, Joe, III, 27
Mangalindan, M., 146, 165
Mann Gulch, Montana, forest fire, 88
Manning, William, 27

Mano-Negrin, R., 4, 22, 91, 106, 303, 310
Manufacturing industries, 60–61
Marcus, A., 7, 22, 303, 309
Marek, A., 124, 134
Markham, D., 44, 49
Marler, Bill, 154
Marquez, J., 200, 220
Marra, F., 100, 105, 295, 309
Martell, K., 236, 252
Martinez, A., 67, 77
Mason, J., 305, 306, 308
Massey Energy, 60, 91–92, 144, 145 (table),
    241, 257, 261 (table)
Mattel, 150–151, 269
Matt, M., 206, 220
Mawhinney, J., 228, 252
McAteer, David, 91–92
McBroom, W., 60, 78
McCartney, M., 7, 22
McConnell, A., 293, 308
McCurry, J., 186, 192
McDonald's, 38–39, 62, 142–143, 145
    (table), 155, 200, 208
McGuinness, M., 225, 251
    see also Elliott, D.
McIntyre, Tim, 211–212
McKay, B., 2, 22, 62, 77
McKinley, J., 269, 284
McLaren, J., 200, 220
McLaughlin, E., 92, 105, 117, 134, 185, 192
McLaughlin, K., 182, 192
McMahon, Vince, 214
McMinn, L., 175, 192
McMullen, K., 123, 135
McNerney, D., 172, 193
McNulty, S., 38, 48, 139, 141, 169, 239, 252
McQueary, Mike, 20
Meadowbrook Mall, 124
Meckler, L., 58, 78
Media coverage, 128
Media training programs, 215–216
Medina, J., 237, 252
Meekins, Jerry, 152–153
Mehta, K., 35, 48
Meichtry, S., 182, 192
Melamine-laced milk case study, 282–283
Melnyk, S., 36, 41, 50, 184, 193
Memphis, Tennessee, 69
Menefee, M., 181, 191
Mensah, E., 39, 48, 297, 308

Mental models, 231
Merrick, A., 249, 250
Merrill Lynch, 273
Merv Griffin television program, 60
Message development, 212
Methyl isocyanate (MIC), 5, 41, 83, 159
Mexico
    global outsourcing, 40
    Wal-Mart bribery payments, 269
Miami, Florida, 72, 86
Miami Palmetto High School, 224
Michaels, D., 58, 78
Michaels, David, 53
Michel-Kerjan, E., 243, 251
Michigan Board of Education, 223–224, 234
Michigan State University, 120 (table)
Microsoft, 71
Mid-American Sound Corporation,
    249, 250
Mid-crisis action strategies
    communication strategies, 181–182
    crisis assessment, 179–180
    damage containment, 180
    response evaluation, 182–184
Middletown, Connecticut, 51
Midrange outcomes, 241–242, 242 (table)
Miglani, A., 302, 310
Miles, G., 66, 78
Millar, M., 112, 134
Miller, A., 174, 192
Miller, D., 69, 70, 71, 78, 302, 310
Miller, J., 21, 153, 165, 268, 285
    see also Snyder, P.
Miller, Robert (Steve), 148
Millman, J., 40, 49
Mine Safety and Health Administration
    (MSHA), 60, 241
Mino, M., 198, 221
Minton-Eversole, T., 103
Mintzberg, H., 72, 78
Minute Maid, 2
Miramar, Florida, 152
Misra, M., 34, 49
Missing cruise ship passengers, 67
Mitroff, I., 7, 8, 9 (table), 10, 12, 22, 84, 99,
    100, 105, 109, 134, 141, 166, 180, 183,
    192, 198, 221, 232, 246, 252, 259, 284,
    302, 309, 310
Moats, J., 121, 134
Mobile communication systems, 125, 199

Mobile molesters, 223–224
Mock disasters
    debriefing meetings, 129
    definition, 124–125
    in-progress guidelines, 128–129
    objectives, 126–127
    post-disaster guidelines, 129
    purpose, 125–126
    recording arrangements, 129
    setting-up guidelines, 126–128
    training programs, 129
Mock reporters, 127–128
Mock victims, 128
Modular carpet, 297
Molasses flood, 305–307
Mold conditions, 121 (table)
Monast, Ben, 26–27
Monday Night Raw, 214
Monster Thickburger, 62
Moore, A., 209, 220
Moorhead, Minnesota, 239
Moral failures, 291 (table), 292
Moreno, K., 186, 192
Morgan Stanley Dean Witter, 273
Morland, L., 192
    see also Leskin, G. A.
Morrison, M., 143, 165
Morse, D., 40, 49
Mortgage crisis, 56 (table), 57–58, 260
Morton, J., 126, 134
Mosconi, A., 214, 220
Moser, H., 44, 49
Moser, Harry, 44
Motivational speakers, 58
Motrin, 2, 152, 209, 210
Mouawad, J., 67, 78, 169
Moynihan Institute of Global Affairs,
    Syracuse University, 303
Multinational corporations, 113–115
Multiple related industry profile, 143–144,
    145 (table)
Multiple sourcing, 42
Multiple unrelated industry profile,
    144–145, 145 (table)
Multi-vehicle highway accidents, 199–200
Mulvey, Lawrence, 288
Munneke, G., 184, 192
Murphy, P., 110, 111, 134, 245, 251,
    301, 309
Murray, M., 148, 165

Murrells Inlet Cracker Barrel, 61
Mushroom communication, 200–201
Myers, K., 7, 9 (table), 10, 22, 302, 309
Myrtle Beach, South Carolina, 61

Nader, R., 4, 22
Naidu, S., 76
    see also Chin, T.
Nassau County, New York, 288–289
Nathan, M., 6, 14, 22, 84, 99, 105, 110, 134,
    225, 232, 251, 252, 276, 285
National Collegiate Athletic Association
    (NCAA), 19, 21
National Highway Traffic Safety
    Administration (NHTSA), 64
National Transportation Safety Board
    (NTSB), 72, 73, 78, 86, 143–144
Natural disasters, 29–30, 96, 98 (table),
    120–121 (table), 127, 183
Navarro, P., 39, 49
Neal, D., 301, 310
Neff, J., 288, 290
Negative pressure tests, 140, 169
Negative publicity, 207–209
Nelson, E., 297, 298, 309
Nelson, J., 198, 199, 220
Nestlé, 68, 261 (table)
Newman, Steven, 188
New Orleans, Louisiana, 121 (table)
News conferences, 204, 205 (table)
News media, 204–206, 205 (table)
New York City Office of Emergency
    Management, 115
New York City Pension system, 269
New Yorker, 288–289
New York Times, 218, 269
Ng See-Yuen, 182
Nicas, J., 152, 153, 165, 249, 250, 251
Nicely, Thomas, 300
Nichols, A., 214, 220
Nickerson, R., 33, 49
Nike, 42, 270
9/11 Commission, 37, 49
9/11 terrorist attacks, 28, 32, 33, 115,
    278 (table), 279, 302
Nissan, 89
Njite, D., 301, 310
"No comment" guidelines, 204–205
Norfolk, Virginia, 229
Normal accident theory, 36–37

North Carolina Department of Agriculture
    and Consumer Services, 154
Northrop, 268
North Sea, 90
Norton, D., 158, 165, 263, 285
Nunamaker, J., Jr., 114 (table), 115, 134
NYC pension funds sue Wal-Mart over
    claims of bribery in Mexico,
    269, 285
Nyden, P., 256, 257
Nystrom, P, 243, 252

O&G Industries, 52, 53
Obama, Barack, 58, 189–190
Occupational Safety and Health Act (1970),
    55 (table)
Occupational Safety and Health
    Administration (OSHA), 26, 52–53,
    279, 288–289
Occupy Wall Street movement, 60, 237
Ocean Isle, North Carolina, 120 (table)
O'Connor, J., 42, 48
Odwalla, Inc., 70, 154
Off-balance sheet arrangements, 265
Officials: Eggs, not employees caused
    illnesses at Durham restaurant,
    154, 165
Official spokespersons, 113, 126, 201–204,
    215–216, 303
Offshore outsourcing, 43–44
Offshore versus deep-water drilling, 138
Ogden, Hugh, 307
Oil Pollution Act (1990), 56 (table)
Oil price surge, 58–59
Oil spill disasters
    Deepwater Horizon oil disaster,
        137–140, 162–164, 167–169,
        188–190, 245, 261 (table)
    Exxon Valdez oil spill, 38, 39, 56 (table),
        126–127, 202, 215
    industrial partnerships, 239
Oklahoma City terrorist bombing, 32, 302
Olasky, M., 178, 179, 192, 296, 309
O'Leary-Kelly, A., 35, 49
Olshansky, R., 301, 309
Online extortion, 71
Online oversight, 34
Online public complaints, 31, 209–210
Online services, 96, 97 (table)
Ontario, Canada, 227–228

Ontario Cancer Foundation, 244,
    244 (figure)
Operations department, 113
Opportunistic price increases, 296
Orange County Register, 218
Organizational crises
    characteristics, 3–5
    economic forces, 54 (figure), 57–59
    emerging trends, 290–307, 291 (table)
    external environment, 54 (figure), 54–66
    industry life cycle, 66–69
    Kleen Energy power generation plant
        case study, 51–53
    organizational life cycle, 69–73,
        73 (figure)
    political–legal forces, 54 (figure), 54–57
    social forces, 54 (figure), 59–63
    Sony Corporation case study, 76–77
    sources, 51–74
    summary discussion, 73–74
    technological forces, 54 (figure), 63–66
Organizational culture, 99–100, 245–247
Organizational learning
    barriers, 242–247, 244 (figure)
    business ethics, 263 (table), 275–280
    communication strategies, 236–237
    components, 230–232
    crisis management framework,
        12 (figure), 14–15, 15 (figure),
        180 (figure)
    definition, 225
    degrees of success, 241–242, 242 (table)
    departmental cooperation, 237–238
    double-loop learning, 226–230,
        229 (figure)
    emerging trends, 291 (table), 300–303
    ethical commitment, 263 (table), 276
    feedback process, 240 (figure), 240–241,
        300–301
    government regulations, 263 (table),
        277, 278 (table), 279
    Indiana State Fair stage collapse case
        study, 248–250
    industrial and governmental
        partnerships, 239
    industry renewal benefits, 263 (table), 277
    learning from failure, 228–230, 241,
        245–247
    lessons learned, 232 (table), 232–241,
        275–280

mental models, 231
new stakeholder outlooks, 263 (table),
    279–280
operational considerations, 243–245,
    244 (figure)
organizational cultural considerations,
    245–247
"passing the trash"/Michigan Board of
    Education case study, 223–224, 234
personal mastery, 230–231
postcrisis debriefing meetings, 239–240
potential opportunities, 225
proactive and reactive perspectives,
    180 (figure)
record-keeping methods, 238–239
redundancy, 235–236
resource deployment, 236–237
shared vision, 231
single-loop learning, 225–226,
    227 (figure)
summary discussion, 247
systems thinking, 230
team learning, 232
Organizational life cycle
    decline stage, 72–73, 73 (figure)
    existence/entrepreneurial stage, 69–70,
        73 (figure)
    renewal stage, 71–72, 73 (figure)
    success stage, 71, 73 (figure)
    survival/growth stage, 70, 73 (figure)
Organizational metamorphosis, 301
Organizational mission-existence
    disconnect, 263 (table), 267–268
Organizational strategies
    basic concepts, 141–142
    business-level strategies, 149–155
    corporate-level strategies, 142–149
    corrective action strategies, 160
    Gulf of Mexico oil spill case study,
        137–140, 162–164
    strategic control, 155–160, 158 (table)
    summary discussion, 160–161
O'Rourke, M., 85, 105
Orr, D., 256, 257
Orr, J., 298, 309
Orwall, B., 168, 170, 190
Outside consultants, 113
Outsourcing, 40–44, 150–151
    see also Global outsourcing
Overdijk, W., 243, 251

Overexpansion of credit, 57–58
Oversight, online, 34

Pacelle, M., 186, 192
Pacific Area Travel Association (PATA), 92
Package of disasters, 30–31
Pain killer use, 72
Palmer, J., 207, 220
Pan Am Air Bridge, 73
Papalini, Darlene, 176–177
Paradigm blindness, 170
Park, E., 305, 308
Park, J., 84, 104, 294, 308
Parnell, J., 9 (table), 30, 39, 49, 64, 66, 67,
    68, 69, 77, 78, 79, 85, 92, 94, 95, 105,
    141, 142, 146, 147, 149, 151, 152, 155,
    156, 165, 181, 192, 243, 245, 252, 260,
    263, 267, 282, 284, 285, 292, 294, 309
Partnerships, 36, 145–146, 239, 265
Parton, Dolly, 154
Passariello, C., 182, 192
"Passing the trash"/Michigan Board of
    Education case study, 223–224, 234
Pasztor, A., 146, 150, 165
    see also Casey, N.
Paterno, Joseph V., 18, 19, 20
Patient Protection and Affordable Care
    Act (2010), 56 (table)
Pauchant, T., 141, 166, 198, 221, 228, 252
Peabody, Massachusetts, 103
Pearl Jam concert, 287
Pearson, C., 3, 4, 7, 9 (table), 10, 12, 14,
    22, 84, 99, 100, 105, 109, 134, 172,
    180, 183, 192, 213, 221, 232, 241, 242
    (table), 246, 252, 302, 309
Pedahzur, A., 32, 49
    see also Perliger, A.
Pennington-Gray, L., 92, 105, 117, 134,
    185, 192
Penn State University scandal
    background information, 18–19, 120 (table)
    board of trustees response, 20–21
    NCAA response, 21
    scandal description, 19–20
Pennsylvania State University, 120 (table)
Penny, J., 121 (table), 134
Pentagon terrorist attacks, 28, 278 (table)
Pentium chips, 300
People's Republic of China
    see China

Pepper spray incident, 237
PepsiCo, 62, 68
Performance improvement, 232
Perliger, A., 32, 49
Perrier relabeled, 238, 252
Perrier water, 238
Perrigo, 152
Perrow, C., 36, 37, 49
Perry, D., 212, 221
Perry, R., 125, 134
Personal mastery, 230–231
Pfeifer, S., 38, 48, 139, 141, 169, 239, 252
Phantom recalls, 152
Pharmaceutical industry, 151–152, 277
Philanthropic responsibilities,
    259 (table), 260
Philip Morris, 144
Philips Electronics, 42
Pianigiani, G., 67, 78
Picken, J. C., 155, 166
Pickert, K., 282, 284
Pickup trucks, 59
Pidgeon, N., 227, 253
Pines, W., 112, 134
Pink slime, 179–180, 208–209
Pipken, W., 132, 133
Piracy, 64
Pittsburgh, Pennsylvania, 154
Plane crashes, 66, 72–73, 86, 143–144,
    150, 302
PlayStation Network, 75–76
Podila, Gopi K., 102
Podolak, A., 112, 134
Polartec, 186
Polczer, S., 189, 190
Poley, Sam, 154
Police departments, 125–126, 127
Political–legal forces
    characteristics, 54 (figure)
    laws and regulations, 55–56 (table), 55–57
    politically motivated events, 54–55
Porter, M. E., 149, 155, 166
Port Said, Egypt, 67
Positive thinking movement, 58
Post-crisis action strategies
    business continuity, 184–185
    debriefing meetings, 239–240
    emerging trends, 300–301
    employee needs, 185–186
    response evaluations, 184

Postcrisis periods, 6
Post, J., 258, 285
Potential crises analysis, 127
Potter, S., 305, 306, 308
Powell, L., 175, 192
PowerMaster Beer, 260, 261 (table)
Powers, W., 266, 268, 285
Preble, J., 84, 105, 141, 166, 170, 192,
    294, 309
Precondition events, 5
Premeaux, S., 200, 221
Presidents, company, 112
Presidents, university, 237
Press releases, 206
Preston, T., 293, 308
Primary stakeholders, 14
Princess Cruises, 67
Probst, G., 93, 105, 142, 147, 166
Process safety, 169
Process technology, 66
Procter & Gamble (P&G), 33–34, 60, 206
Product tampering, 71
Product technology, 66
Professional sports, 268
Professional wrestling, 71–72, 214
Programmed decisions, 243
Propane tank explosion, 25–27, 46–47
Prospective crisis events, 119–120,
    120–121 (table)
Prudhoe Bay, Alaska, 168
Psychological preparation, 116
Public relations department, 113
Puleo, S., 306, 307, 308

Questionable cost-cutting measures,
    266–267
Question-answering skills, 203
Quinn, B., 42, 49
Quinn, R., 69, 70, 71, 78
Quinn, T., 214, 220
Qwest Communications International,
    261 (table)

Racherla, P., 241, 252, 300, 309
Racial discrimination, 61, 147–148
Radiation overdose incident, 243–244,
    244 (figure)
Rados, C., 97, 105
Ragatz, G., 36, 41, 50, 184, 193
Ragland, Maria, 102

Raisch, S., 93, 105, 142, 147, 166
Rapid communications systems, 201
Rashid, F., 75, 76
Rawl, Lawrence, 202, 215
Recession, 57–58
Record-keeping methods, 238–239
Recovery stage, 11
Red, C., 72, 78
Red River Flood (1997), 239, 301
Redundancy, 235–236
Refineries and chemical plants explosions, 132, 178
Regional shopping mall industry, 69
Regression analysis, 303
Regulatory flaws, repeated violations put oil refinery workers at risk, 132, 133
Reilly, A., 200, 201, 215, 221, 237, 252
Reinig, B., 115, 134
    see also Nunamaker, J., Jr.
Related diversification strategy, 143–144, 145 (table)
Religious extremists, 32
Religious festivals, 287
Renewable resources, 39
Rent-A-Center, 94
Rentschler, C., 123, 126, 135
Repenning, N., 99, 105
Reputational crises, 42–43
Reshoring movement, 40, 43–44, 279
Resilience, 298
Resource deployment, 236–237
Resource sustainability, 38–40
Response times, 300
Retrenchment strategies, 147–149
Reuer, J. J., 146, 166
Reynolds, B., 203, 221
Rheingold, H., 64, 78
Rice, J., 42, 49
Richardson, B., 9 (table), 10, 22, 302, 309, 310
Richter, D., 135
Richter, J., 122, 135
Rickman, J., 189, 190
Rielage, R., 78
Rinehart and Dennis engineering firm, 256, 258, 261 (table), 265, 273
Ringel, J., 76
    see also Chin, T.
Risk denial, 37
Rite Aid, 191

R. J. Reynolds (RJR), 277
Robb, D., 85, 105
Robbery, 69
Robert, B., 90, 104, 115, 116, 118, 133, 275, 279, 280, 284, 293, 298, 301, 308
Roberts, D., 182, 192
Roberts, K., 89, 105, 228, 252
Robertson, J., 268, 285
    see also Snyder, P.
Robinson, S., 35, 49
Robots, 125
Rock, Chris, 61
Rock concerts, 287, 288
Rockoff, J., 151, 152, 166
Rock, Rose, 61
Roe, Emmet, 267
Roemer, B., 215, 221
Rogue sites, 213
Rolling Stone, 60
Rolston, L., 172, 193
Rondinelli, D., 180, 192
Rose, M., 302, 309
Rosenberg, Paul, 102–103
Rosenblatt, Z., 302, 310
Rosenbush, S., 265, 285
Rosenker, Mark, 86
Roseville Galleria, 123
Roskilde, Denmark, 287
Roth, D., 209, 220
    see also Kirkpatrick, D.
Roux-Dufort, C., 5, 22, 111, 135, 242, 246, 252
Rowh, M., 256, 257
Rowles, M. S., 198, 221
Royal Caribbean, 67
Royal Dutch Shell, 90, 239
Royal Princess, 67
Russell, P., 189, 190
Ryan, O., 209, 220
    see also Kirkpatrick, D.
Ryan, T., 69, 78

SabreTech, 143–144
Sadri, G., 114, 115, 135
Safety considerations, 120 (table)
Safety policies, 263 (table), 264–265
Sago Mine disaster, West Virginia, 27, 178–179, 241
Salkin, S., 272, 285
Sallot, L., 143, 165
    see also Englehardt, K.

Salmonella outbreaks, 154, 176
San Diego Tribune, 218
Sandusky, Jerry, 18, 19–20
San Francisco Chronicle, 218
San Jose, California, 71
Sanlu Dairy assets to be sold off, 282, 284
Sanlu Group, 282–283
Saporito, B., 75, 76
Sarbanes–Oxley (SOX) Act (2002),
    56 (table), 266, 273, 278 (table)
Saul, S., 82, 83, 104
    see also Dewan, S.
Sawayda, J., 168, 170, 189, 191
Scammell, H., 86, 105
Scanlon, J., 198, 221
Scanning, environmental, 90–92
Scapegoating, 231, 246
Schaefer, N. A., 32, 49
Schaubroeck, J., 14, 22, 99, 104, 302, 308
Schein, E. H., 100, 106
Schettino, Francesco, 67
Schlein, L., 284
Schneider, R., 138, 141, 163, 164
Schoenberg, A., 172, 193
Schoenfeldt, L., 186, 192
Schön, D., 225, 226, 246, 251
School violence, 127
Schrader, R., 86, 106
Schreiber, J., 169, 170
Schultze, Q., 64, 78
Schultz, Gary C., 19, 20
Schwartz, H., 267, 285
Schwarzenegger, Arnold, 181
Scott, G., 135
    see also Richter, J.
Seabrook, J., 287, 288, 289, 290
Seabrook, John, 288–289
Search-and-rescue drills, 128–129
Search engine optimization (SEO)
    programs, 212, 218
Secondary stakeholders, 14
Second Mile, The, 18, 20
Securities and Exchange Commission
    (SEC), 268, 285
Security department, 112–113
Seeger, M. W., 198, 200, 221, 239, 241, 245,
    252, 253, 301, 310
Seitel, Fraser, 153
Self-organization, 301
Self-policing, 27, 273, 277, 278 (table)

Self-regulation, 273
Self, W. R., 175, 192
Sellnow, T., 68, 79, 155, 166, 198, 200,
    202, 221, 225, 239, 241, 245, 252,
    253, 301, 310
    see also Seeger, M. W.
Semi-submersible drilling rigs, 138
Senge, P., 230, 232, 247, 252
Senge, Peter, 230
Sensemaking, 230–231
September 11, 2001 terrorist attacks, 28, 32,
    33, 115, 278 (table), 279, 302
Sethi, S., 39, 41, 49, 70, 78, 143, 166, 261
    (table), 264, 266, 285
Seton Hall University, 120 (table)
Setzer, Michael, 195–196
Sevastopulo, D., 78
Sexual victimization, 223–224
    see also Penn State University scandal
Shanker, A., 266, 267, 285
Shapiro, E., 277, 285
Shappell, B., 29, 49
Shared vision, 231
Shareholder model, 258–259
Sharfman, M., 66, 78
Sharfstein, Joshua, 152
Sharpton, Al, 61
Shaw, J., 186, 192
Shaw, Tom, 204
Sheaffer, Z., 4, 22, 91, 106, 302, 303, 310
Sheetz convenience store chain, 176
Sheetz, Stan, 176
Sheetz, Steve, 176
Sheetz, Travis, 176
Sheffield, England, 173, 288
Shell, E., 43, 44, 49, 60, 61, 78
Sheltering-in-place drills, 124
Shenhav, Y., 99, 106
Sherman, S., 204, 221
Ship fires, 67
Shopping malls, 69, 123–124
Shower drills, 124
Shrivastava, P., 83, 106, 298, 302, 310
Siegel, Bettina Elias, 208
Siegler, B., 62, 78
Signal detection, 11
Silicosis, 256, 278 (table)
Sillanpää, M., 14, 23
Simbo, A., 99, 106
Simola, S., 113, 117, 135

Simon, L., 228, 252

Simple environments, 87–88

Simply Orange, 2

Singh, H., 146, 166

Single industry profile, 142–143, 145 (table)

Single-loop learning, 225–226, 227 (figure)

Single sourcing, 41–42

Sitkin, S., 245, 252

Situational assessments, 173–176

$16.6 million in fines for fatal Connecticut
    explosion, 53

Six workers die in Washington refinery fire,
    132, 133

Skidmore, H., 256, 257

Skidmore, Hubert, 256

Skinner, Jim, 62

Sklarewitz, N., 176, 177, 193

Slack, C., 154, 165

Sloppy management, 37–38

Small incidents, 245

Smallman, C., 12, 23, 99, 106, 227, 252

Smith, C., 302, 309

Smith, D., 5, 6, 9 (table), 10, 22, 83, 99, 106,
    141, 166, 173, 192, 225, 227, 240, 245,
    251, 252, 288, 290, 302, 310
    see also Elliott, D.

Smith, George, 67

Smith, R., 51, 52, 53

Smith, S., 33, 34, 48, 60, 78, 206, 207, 212,
    213, 220, 300, 309

Smoldering crises, 245, 260, 291–292

Snapper, 143

Snellen, M., 206, 221

Snipes, W., 76
    see also Chin, T.

Snook, S., 38, 49

Snow, C., 66, 78

Snyder, P., 268, 271, 274, 285

Soccer matches, 173, 287–288

Social forces
    characteristics, 54 (figure), 59–60
    corporate America, 60
    discount retail industry, 60–61
    environmental sustainability, 63
    health and fitness trend, 62–63
    social equality, 61
    trustworthiness, 60

Social media
    crisis communication, 197–198,
        207–213, 274–275, 291 (table), 299

mock disasters, 125
    organizational crises, 33–34, 299–300
    organizational opportunities, 85

Social values, 59

Solomon, C., 174, 193

Solomon, J., 43, 49

Somers, S., 84, 106, 298, 310

Sony Corporation, 75–76

Source Perrier, 238

South Charleston, West Virginia, 126

Southern Sun Company, 46

Southwest Airlines, 144, 149

Spanier, Graham B., 19, 20

Speaking skills, 111

Special purpose entities (SPEs), 265–266,
    267–268

Spillan, J., 3, 9 (table), 23, 30, 39, 49,
    198, 221

Spirit Airlines, 152–153

Spofford, C. M., 307

Spokesperson traits, 202–204

Sporkin, S., 19, 21
    see also Freeh, L.

Sport utility vehicles (SUVs), 59, 151

Springston, J., 143, 165
    see also Englehardt, K.

Sprovieri, J., 44, 49

Stability strategies, 146–147

Stable environments, 87–88

Stakeholder model versus shareholder
    model, 258–259

Stakeholders, 5, 13–14, 115, 181–182,
    199–204, 263 (table), 274–276,
    279–280, 290–300
    see also External stakeholders; Internal
    stakeholders

Stallard, M., 31, 50

Stampedes, 287–288

Stampfer, Meir, 62–63

Starbucks, 68

Starbuck, W. H., 70, 78, 87, 106, 243, 252

Star Princess, 67

State Fair Commission (Indiana), 249, 250

Status quo–seeking culture, 246, 301

Stead, E., 12, 23, 227, 252

Stead, J., 38, 50, 297, 310

Stead, W., 38, 50, 297, 310

Steele, T., 60, 78

Steidlmeier, P., 39, 41, 49, 70, 78, 143, 166,
    261 (table), 264, 266, 285

Steinberg, B., 55, 62, 77, 78

Steiner, G., 264, 285

Steiner, J., 264, 285

Stelter, B., 237, 252

Sterman, J., 99, 105

Stern, S., 142, 165

Steroid use, 72, 214

Stetson University Law Library, 123, 126

Stewart, J., 135

    see also Richter, J.

Stewart, J. B., 59, 78, 151, 166

Stieghorst, T., 72, 73, 78

Stonecipher, Harry, 264

Stone, Sharon, 181–182

Strandholm, K., 90, 105

Strategic alliances, 36, 145–146

Strategic challenges, 6–7

Strategic control

    balanced scorecard indicators, 158,
        158 (table), 263

    basic concepts, 155–156

    process guidelines, 156–160

    strategic management process, 85, 86,
        87 (figure)

Strategic management process

    basic principles, 84–86, 87 (figure),
        141–142

    crisis planning, 99–100

    environmental scanning, 90–92

    environmental uncertainty, 87–90

    organizational culture, 99–100

    organizational strategies, 141–161

    summary discussion, 100–101

    SWOT (strengths, weaknesses,
        opportunities, and threats)
        analysis, 92–99, 93–94 (table),
        95–96 (table), 97 (table), 98–99
        (table), 291 (table), 291–292

    university faculty member case study,
        81–82, 101–103

Strategic planning

    business ethics, 263 (table), 270–274

    characteristics, 12 (figure), 13

    crisis management framework, 15 (figure)

    crisis management teams, 294

    emerging trends, 291 (table), 294–298

    feedback process, 240 (figure)

    lessons learned, 232 (table), 235–236

    proactive and reactive perspectives,
        180 (figure)

    response evaluations, 86

    stakeholders, 295–296

Strategy execution, 85, 86, 87 (figure)

Strategy formulation, 85, 86, 87 (figure)

Strawberry contamination incident,
    271–273

Streisand, B., 264, 284

Strengths, weaknesses, opportunities, and
    threats (SWOT) analysis

    see SWOT (strengths, weaknesses,
        opportunities, and threats)
        analysis

Stressful environments, 111, 172

Stringer, Howard, 75

Structural impediments, 37–38

Structure fires, 226, 227 (figure)

Strupp, J., 128, 135

Student protests, 237

Student safety, 120 (table)

Sturges, D. L., 198, 221

Subprime mortgage industry, 57–58

Subramanian, R., 90, 105

Success outcomes, 241–242, 242 (table), 245

Sucks sites, 213

Suffocation, 288–289

Sugarland, 248

Suicide bombings, 32

Sullivan, B., 91, 105

Sullivan, E., 19, 21

    see also Freeh, L.

Sullivan, J., 225, 228, 252

Sullivan, Kathleen, 215

Sung, S. Y., 303, 308

Supply chains, 41–42

Sustainable development, 63

Sutcliffe, K., 99, 106, 228, 253, 298, 310

Sweatshop manufacturing, 270, 273–274

Swift, K., 126, 135

SWOT (strengths, weaknesses,
    opportunities, and threats) analysis

    basic principles, 92

    emerging trends, 291 (table), 291–292

    external opportunities and potential
        crises, 96, 97 (table)

    external threats and potential crises,
        96–98, 98–99 (table)

    internal strengths and potential crises,
        92–93, 93–94 (table)

    internal weaknesses and potential crises,
        94–95, 95–96 (table)

Symbolic impacts, 115
Synergy, 143
Syracuse University, 128, 303
Systems thinking, 230

Table of contents, 118
Tabletop exercises, 122
Tacit knowledge, 240
Taco Bell, 208, 218–219
Tacogate, 218–219
Talley, J. Ernest, 94
Tankersley, J., 138, 141
Tavernise, S., 144, 166
Tavitiyaman, P., 301, 310
Taylor, E., 59, 78, 151, 166
Taylor, M., 212, 221
Taylor, P., 173, 193
Team learning, 232
Teamwork, 111
Technical Series Report 110, 193
Technological forces
    characteristics, 54 (figure), 63
    resistance movements, 64–66
    technology challenges, 63–64
Technorati, 210
Telephone systems, 125, 214
Temporary chief executive officers, 148
Teng, B., 85, 104
Tennant, M., 59, 78
Terlep, S., 2, 23, 64, 78, 151, 166
Terrorism threats
    mock disasters, 127
    organizational crises, 32–33, 99 (table)
Tesoro Corporation refinery accident case
    study, 131–132
Texas City, Texas, 168, 261 (table)
Thapa, B., 92, 105, 117, 134, 185, 192
't Hart, P., 115, 133, 293, 303, 308, 309
The Biggest Loser, 62
Therac-25 incident, 243–244, 244 (figure)
The Second Mile, 18, 20
Thompson, J. D., 89, 106
Thorne, D., 264, 277, 285
Thornton Tomasetti, 250
Three Mile Island nuclear accident, 36–37
Three-stage frameworks, 9 (table), 10
Thrifty Corporation, 174, 191
Thurman, E., 30, 49
Thyer, A., 306, 308
Tian Wenhua, 283

Tibet, 181–182
Tight coupling theory, 36–37
Time zone factors, 117
Timmons, H., 50, 265, 285
Tire fires, 227–228, 229 (figure)
Tobacco industry, 69, 261 (table), 277
Toccoa Falls College, 120 (table)
Toll-free hotlines, 200
Tompkins, P., 245, 253
Tornadoes, 1, 121 (table), 299
Torres, Lori, 250
Tour de France, 268
Tourism industry, 183
Toyota Camry, 84
Toy recalls, 150, 246, 269
Toys "R" Us, 146
Trachtenberg, J., 55, 78
Track record of success, 245
Trampling, 287–289
Transboundary crises
    case study versus statistical research
        approach, 303
    functional boundaries, 30–31
    geographical boundaries, 29–30
    interlinking critical infrastructures,
        31–32
    time boundaries, 31
Transboundary Crisis Management (TCM)
    data, 303
Transocean, 138, 139, 162, 188–189
Transocean Investigation Report, 162–163, 164
Transportation Safety Administration
    (TSA), 278 (table)
Trevino, L., 271, 286
Triangle Shirtwaist Company fire (1911), 266
Trigger events, 5, 83, 265–266
Tripp, T., 31, 48, 206, 220
    see also Grégoire, Y.
Trolls, 212–213
Trottman, M., 58, 78
Trust, 60, 115, 275–276, 280, 291 (table),
    293–294
Tsikoudakis, M., 20, 22
Tsunamis, 1, 29, 30, 92–93, 302
Tucson, Arizona, 123
Tulane University hospital, 213–214
Turnaround strategies, 147–148
Turner, B., 37, 50, 227, 253
Turner, C., 243, 244, 252
Twedt, S., 225

20/20, 224

Twitter, 196, 197, 209, 211, 212, 218, 275, 300

2Checkout, 71

Tyco, 145, 145 (table), 159–160, 261 (table), 262

Tylenol scare, 6, 302

Tyler, A., 273, 286

Ulmer, R. R., 198, 200, 221, 239, 241, 245, 252, 253, 301, 310
  see also Seeger, M. W.

UME Cineplex chain, 182

Uncertainty
  crisis management teams, 111
  environmental uncertainty, 87–90, 156

Underage smoking, 277

Union Carbide, 5, 40–41, 68, 83, 143, 145 (table), 159, 255–256, 264, 279, 302

Union University, 121 (table), 299

United Airlines, 31, 150, 209–210, 213

United Breaks Guitars video, 31, 209–210

United Mine Workers of America (UMWA), 268

United States Industrial Alcohol (USIA) Company, 305–307

University chancellors/presidents, 237

University faculty member case study, 81–82, 101–103

University of Alabama at Huntsville (UAH), 81–82, 101–103, 120 (table)

University of California-Davis, 237

University of Colorado, 120 (table)

University of Georgia, College of Veterinary Medicine, 120 (table)

Unpasteurized juice products, 70, 154

Unrelated diversification strategy, 144–145, 145 (table)

Unstable environments, 87–88

Upper Big Branch coal mine accident, 144, 257

Urbina, I., 27, 28

USA Today, 218

U.S. Chemical Safety and Hazard Investigation Report, 26, 46

U.S. Chemical Safety Board (CSB), 26, 27, 46, 47, 52, 53, 132

U.S. Coast Guard, 189

U.S. Department of Agriculture (USDA), 209, 271

U.S. Department of Homeland Security, 278 (table)

User error, 36–37

U.S. Food and Drug Administration (FDA), 85, 238

U.S. Navy, 228–229

U.S. oil refiner fined before deadly blaze, 132, 133

USS *Forrestal*, 228–229

Valentine, L., 199, 205, 221

Vallario, C., 271, 273, 286

Valley City State University, North Dakota, 120 (table)

Valley Stream, New York, 288

ValuJet, 143–144, 145 (table), 302

van Haperen, K., 170, 191, 225, 251

Variant Creuztfeldt-Jakob disease (vCJD), 57

Veil, S., 68, 79, 92, 106, 155, 166, 202, 221, 225, 245, 246, 253, 300, 310

Verbal aggression, 117

Verbal skills, 111

Vernon, H., 202, 221, 266, 273, 286

Victims of crisis events, 291 (table), 293

Videoconferences, 115, 199

Vines, M., 86, 106

Vintage seaplanes, 72–73, 86, 153–154

Violent crimes, 69

Violent weather, 1

Virginia Tech massacre incident, 8, 120 (table), 124, 201, 236–237, 299

Virtual crisis management teams/plans, 113–115, 114 (table), 291 (table), 294

Vise, A., 204, 221

Vogel, D., 210, 220

Vogus, T., 298, 310

Volcanic eruptions, 127

Vulnerabilities, 86, 234, 263 (table), 268–270, 291–292

Wachtendorf, T., 31, 50

Wailes, C., 201, 204, 221

Wakabayashi, D., 75, 76

Wald, M., 73, 77

Wallace, A., 82, 83, 102, 103, 104

Wallace, J., 115, 116, 133, 199, 220

Wall Street Journal, 91, 153, 218, 249

Wal-Mart
  Black Friday stampede, 288–289
  Hurricane Katrina, 178, 296
  illegal cash payments, 269
  life cycle stage, 68
  low-cost strategies, 61, 95, 143, 149, 150
  negative press, 42
  single industry dimension, 142–143, 145 (table)
  sweatshop manufacturing, 270
WAL-MART: The High Cost of Low Price (film), 42
Walsh, K., 181, 193
Walton, L., 72, 79, 214, 221
Wang, J., 225, 253
Ward, K., 92, 106
Warm sites, 185
Warner-Lambert Company, 261 (table), 266
Warning signs, 37–38, 83–84, 233–234, 245
Washington Department of Labor and Industries, 132
Washington state fines Tesoro more than $2 million after refinery explosion that killed seven workers, 132, 133
Waste Management, 148
Watkins, M., 90, 106
Watson Island, 73
Watson, S., 153, 166
Weather-related crises, 1, 121 (table), 183, 248–250, 280, 299
Weaver, Brad, 249
Weber, J., 258, 285
Websites, 206–207, 210–213, 274–275, 299
  see also Internet usage; Social media
Weick, K., 88, 99, 106, 172, 193, 228, 230, 231, 253
Weinberg, L., 32, 49
Weiner, D., 200, 204, 221
Weir, D., 99, 106
Weiss, J., 300, 310
Weitz, E., 99, 106
Weitzman, H., 62, 77
Welch, Jack, 42
Weldon, Bill, 152
Well-drilling process
  blowout preventers (BOPs), 139, 163, 189
  casing cementing process, 139–140, 189
  negative pressure tests, 140, 169
Welles, C., 262, 286

Wendy's, 71, 145
Wertheimer, Paul, 288
West Pharmaceuticals, 159
West Virginia Fire Commission, 26
West Virginia State Police, 124
West Virginia University at Parkersburg, 201
Wet drilling, 256, 273
Whealin, J., 192
  see also Leskin, G. A.
Wheatley, M., 170, 193
Wheaton, K., 2, 23, 195, 196, 197, 209, 221
Wheeler, D., 14, 23
White, D., 201, 220
White-hat hackers, 75
Whitford, D., 138, 141, 168, 169, 190
  see also Elkind, P.
Who rock concert, 287, 288
Whos Talkin (Google), 210
Wicks, A., 259, 284
Wildfires, 127, 207
Williams, K., 72, 79, 214, 221
Williamson, Frederick, 273
Wilson, J., 173, 193
Wilson, R., 82, 83, 103
  see also Bartlett, T.
Wilson, S., 177 (table), 193
Wilson, Woodrow, 307
Winchester, J., 66, 79
Winterplace Ski Resort, 25
Wipro Ltd., 42
Wise, J., 154, 166
Witness at Hawks Nest (Harshbarger), 256
Wolff, A., 19, 21, 22
Wooten, L., 171, 193
Worker safety, 60, 256–257, 258, 264–266, 266, 278 (table)
Workforce reductions, 148
Workplace aggression, 35
Workplace deviance, 35
Workplace safety, 168–169
Workplace violence, 35, 124, 201
WorldCom, 262, 264
World Health Organization (WHO), 282
World Tourism Organisation, 183, 193
World Trade Center terrorist attacks, 28, 32, 33, 115, 278 (table), 279, 302
World Wrestling Entertainment (WWE), 72, 214
Wren, D., 64, 79
Wrestling, professional, 71–72, 214

Wright, P., 64, 79, 245, 252
Wrongful death suits, 67
WV Governor's report places blame for
    Upper Big Branch explosion on
    Massey, agencies, 60, 79
Wyeth, 144

Xanic, A., 269, 284
Xiao, J., 182, 193
Xinhua, 182, 193

Y2K computer bug crisis, 31–32, 175–176
Yakima Valley Memorial Hospital, 244,
    244 (figure)
Yeh, F., 123, 135
York, B., 42, 50
York, E., 195, 196, 197
Young, C., 249, 250, 251
Young organizations, 69–70
Youngstown, Ohio, 124
YouTube, 1, 31, 33, 196, 197, 209–210,
    211, 218, 293
Yuan, Y., 199, 221

Zalmanovitch, Y., 32, 49
    see also Perliger, A.
Zamiska, N., 146, 165
    see also Casey, N.
Zapata, Sergio Cicero, 269
Zemel, J., 225
Zerillo, N., 196, 197
Zezima, K., 82, 83, 104
    see also Dewan, S.
Zhang, J., 85, 106
Zhang, Z., 210, 220
Zhang Zhenling, 283
Zhou, Z., 210, 220
Ziemnowicz, C., 7, 22, 34, 50, 208,
    210, 211, 212, 221
Zoch, L., 178, 191
Zollo, M., 146, 166
Zsidisin, G., 36, 41, 50, 184, 193
Zweig, D., 93, 106, 264, 286
Zyglidopoulos, S., 90, 106

About the Authors

William "Rick" Crandall, Ph.D., University of Memphis, is professor of management in the School of Business at the University of North Carolina at Pembroke. Previously, Dr. Crandall taught for eleven years at Concord College in Athens, West Virginia. During his tenure, he developed an interest in crisis management and served on the college's crisis management team. Dr. Crandall's articles on crisis management have appeared in *SAM Advanced Management Journal, Central Business Review, Internal Auditing, Business Horizons, International Journal of Sustainable Strategic Management, Security Management,* and *Southern Business Review.* Dr. Crandall has addressed various audiences on crisis management in the United States, Austria, China, Poland, and the United Kingdom. Dr. Crandall is also coauthor of the book, *New Methods of Competing in the Global Marketplace: Critical Success Factors from Service and Manufacturing,* and *Principles of Supply Chain Management,* both with CRC Press. Prior to entering higher education, Dr. Crandall worked in management for ARA Services (now ARAMARK), a service management firm based in Philadelphia.

John A. Parnell, Ed.D., Campbell University, Ph.D., University of Memphis, is the William Henry Belk Chair of Management at the University of North Carolina at Pembroke. Dr. Parnell's recent work on crisis management, strategic management, and related topics have appeared in the *Academy of Management Learning and Education, British Journal of Management, European Management Journal, Journal of Business Ethics, Journal of Business Strategies, Journal of Contingencies and Crisis Management, Journal of Management Studies,* and *Management Decision.* Dr. Parnell is a Fulbright Scholar (Egypt) and lectures in a number of countries, including Mexico, China, and Peru. He is also the author of the textbook, *Strategic Management: Theory and Practice,* now in its fourth edition with SAGE. Prior to entering higher education, Dr. Parnell owned and operated a direct-mail firm.

John E. Spillan, Ph.D., Warsaw School of Economics, serves as professor of business administration at the University of North Carolina at Pembroke. His research interests center on crisis management, international marketing, entrepreneurship and international business with specific interest in Latin America and Eastern Europe. He has traveled extensively with extended visits to Europe, Latin America, Africa, and Asia. His articles have appeared in the *International Journal of Marketing and*

Marketing Research, Journal of Business in Developing Nations, Journal of East West Business, European Management Journal, Journal of Teaching in International Business, Journal of Small Business Strategy, International Small Business Journal, Journal of Crisis and Contingency Management, Journal of Small Business Management, Journal of Marketing Theory and Practice, Journal of World Business, Latin American Business Review, International Journal of Sustainable Strategic Management, Journal of Business Logistics, among others. Prior to entering higher education, Dr. Spillan worked in New York State as a rate-setting analyst.